The Book of
INCREDIBLE
INFORMATION

A WORLD OF NOT-SO-COMMON KNOWLEDGE

WEST
SIDE
PUBLISHING

J. K. Kelley has a BA in history from the University of Washington in Seattle. Thus far he has contributed to three Armchair Reader™ books. He resides in the sagebrush of eastern Washington with his wife, Deb, his parrot, Alex, and Fabius, the Labrador Retriever.

Additional contributions by: Donna Beech, Wim Coleman, Jacque E. Day, Phaedra de Vere, James Duplacey, Mary Fons, Aron Johnson, Erika Cornstuble Koff, Tamra B. Orr, Pat Perrin, Eric Peterson, Carol Parenzan Smalley, Stephen Theunissen, Jodi M. Webb, Robert Wolff, Ph.D., Anna Zaigraeva

Factual verification by: Lawrence Greenberg, Jennifer J. McCune, Ph.D., Marci McGrath, Regina J. Montgomery, Christy M. Nadalin, Helen Erwin Schinske, Chris Smith

Cover Illustrator: Adrian Chesterman

Interior Illustrators: Robert Schoolcraft, Nicole H. Lee, Shavan R. Spears

CONTENTS

✳ ✳ ✳ ✳

✳ ✳ ✳ ✳

READ AND LEARN

✳ ✳ ✳ ✳

It is my great pleasure to introduce you to the newest member of the Armchair Reader™ family—*The Book of Incredible Information*. This volume is the culmination of hundreds of hours of work on the part of our outstanding team of writers, editors, and researchers, all of whom deserve a big round of applause (and several resounding *huzzahs!*) for their efforts.

You might ask, "What is *The Book of Incredible Information*?" Well, that's a tough one to answer. Once upon a time, Albert Einstein was asked if he had a simple explanation for his Theory of Relativity. I love his response: "When a man sits with a pretty girl for an hour, it seems like a minute. But let him sit on a hot stove for a minute, and it's longer than any hour. That's relativity."

So in response to your theoretical question, I'd have to say that at the very least, this book is a treasure trove full of anecdotes, stories, tantalizing bits of trivia, and unusual facts collected from hundreds, if not thousands, of sources and pulled together in one volume that will fascinate, entertain, amuse, and—most important—inform you. You can drop in anywhere in the book and learn about something that's little known, unusual, or unexpected; it was created for folks of all ages and interests. Just take a look at a few examples, and I think you'll see what I mean:

- Peek into the scandalous love lives of queens, kings, and royal mistresses. *Edward III's mistress, Alice Perrers, stole the rings off his fingers as he lay dying.*

- Ponder some interesting—and strange—foods enjoyed around the world. *In some parts of Italy, people savor a worm-filled cheese called casu marzu.*

- Witness the most entertaining on-court tantrums in pro tennis. *John McEnroe did a lot more than yell, "You cannot be serious!"*

- Uncover the stories behind unusual and long-honored college-sports mascots. *Students at the University of California–Santa Cruz cheer on their teams with the help of a giant banana slug.*

- Gain insight into the peculiarities of U.S. presidents. *George Washington never shook hands with people. Instead, he bowed.*

- Get the dirt on environmentally friendly architecture. *You can beautify your home with nonpolluting paints and recycled-glass windows.*

- Revel in the unusual ways people ring in the New Year. *In Cuba and Mexico, some celebrants eat 12 grapes at midnight to ensure 12 months of good luck.*

- Enjoy interviews with a professional golf ball diver and a snake milker. *Retrieving golf balls from lakes can be lucrative, but you have to watch out for alligators! No, snakes don't have udders. It's their fangs that get milked.*

- Recoil at the number of germs you're exposed to every day. *In a 24-hour period, you'll breathe in more than 100,000 bacteria.*

We all hope you enjoy our newest book as much as we enjoyed creating it for you. Please make yourself comfortable and feel free to sit, sprawl, slouch, or recline as you discover *Armchair Reader™: The Book of Incredible Information.*

Yours until next time,

Allen Orso
Publisher

P.S. If you have questions, concerns, or thoughts pertaining to this book or would like more information about other titles from the West Side Publishing family of books, please contact us at **www.armchairreader.com.**

ARE YOU GOING TO *EAT* THAT?

✳ ✳ ✳ ✳

In recent years, Hollywood has learned that people like watching others chow down on calf pancreas and camel spiders. Even so, one person's offal is another person's delicacy. Here are interesting foods enjoyed around the world.

Poi (Hawaii): Taro root is boiled to remove the calcium oxalate poison, then mashed to a muddy purple paste. To most non-Hawaiians, it also tastes like muddy purple paste.

Muktuk (Alaska, Canada): Enjoy a hunk of whale blubber, which looks and feels in the mouth like densely packed cotton soaked in oil. It's attached to a thick piece of whale skin with the look and feel of worn tire tread. You cut off chunks of blubber and chew them—for a long time.

Black pudding (Britain, Ireland): Try some congealed pig blood that's been cooked with oatmeal and formed into a small disk. It doesn't taste like blood; more like a thick, rich, beef pound cake.

Chorizo (Iberia, Latin America): This is what remains after all the respectable pig offal has been made into normal sausage. By now we're down to the lips, lymph nodes, and salivary glands. It's spicy and tasty, provided you don't mind dining on an immune system.

Menudo (Mexico): Basically, it's cow-stomach soup. If you can tolerate the slimy, rubbery tripe chunks, the soup itself tastes fine. It's often served for breakfast to cure a hangover.

Scrapple (Pennsylvania): The Amish and Mennonites don't waste much, and pig butchers chop up leftover guts, cook them with cornmeal, then pour it all into bricklike molds to solidify.

Casu marzu (Sardinia): It's illegal in Italy to sell wormy cheese, so pragmatic citizens make their own by sticking a perfectly good round in the cupboard for a couple of months so flies can lay eggs on it. The larvae produce enzymes that break down the cheese into a tangy goo, which Sardinians dive into and enjoy, larvae and all.

Balut (Philippines): Ever get a hankering for soft-boiled duck or chicken embryos? Some Filipinos think there's nothing finer, even though one must sometimes pick miniature feathers out of the teeth.

Surströmming (Sweden): Primarily a seasonal dish in northern Sweden, this rotten fermented herring could knock out a wolverine. Even the Swedes rarely open a can of it indoors, except for playful children who swipe some and hide it in their school's air vents.

Fugu (Japan): Despite precise preparation by specially qualified chefs, this toxic puffer fish delicacy kills about 300 people per year. The emperor of Japan isn't allowed to eat fugu lest it be his last meal. For all that work and risk, it still tastes like fish, but you have to respect the chefs: To prove their skills, they must cook and eat their own fugu.

Jellied eels (England): If you find yourself hungry as you hustle through London, grab a jellied eel from a street vendor. It tastes like pickled herring with a note of vinegar, salt, and pimiento, all packed in gelatin. Next time you're asked to bring something congealed to a potluck, interpret the request loosely and watch the fun.

Haggis (Scotland): Drink enough Scotch, and you'll eventually get so hungry you'll eat sheep innards mixed with oatmeal and boiled in the sheep's stomach. Safety-minded haggis chefs suggest poking holes in the stomach so it doesn't explode when the oatmeal expands.

Pombe (East/Central Africa): History shows that people will make alcohol from any ingredients available. That includes bananas, mashed with one's bare feet and buried in a cask. The result is pombe, an east African form of beer.

Durian (Southeast Asia): This football-size fruit with spines poses one of the weirdest contrasts in the culinary world. It smells like unwashed socks but tastes sweet. Imagine eating vanilla pudding while trying not to inhale.

Vegemite (Australia): "Yeast extract" is a brewery by-product that looks like chocolate spread, smells like B vitamins, and tastes overwhelmingly salty. Australians love it on sandwiches or baked in meatloaf, and it goes well with cheese.

Lutefisk (Sweden): It's simply fish boiled in lye. The lye gelatinizes the fish, but if it's soaked too long, the mixture starts turning into soap. The taste is actually fairly mild; the smell depends on the fish used (reportedly, cod isn't the best choice).

Kimchee (Korea): A cultural staple, this spicy dish of cabbage fermented with salt and pepper smells like garbage to many. Most people have less trouble with the taste than the aroma, but we do taste partly with our noses.

Stinkheads (Alaska): If you travel to Alaska's Bering Sea coast someday, stop at a Yup'ik village and ask the natives about their culture. They have great fun introducing visitors to salmon heads that have spent the summer buried in the ground.

Sago beetle grubs (Papua New Guinea): Some tribespeople consider these bugs delicious. Then again, many of the same folks eat a lot of sago pulp (the inside of a palm tree). After months of eating tree innards, perhaps one would relish a roasted bug.

Gulyás (Hungary): Pronounced "guh-yawsh" in Hungarian, this isn't a strange food, but most people would like the real thing better than so-called "goulash," which doesn't do justice to Hungary's national dish. There are probably as many gulyás recipes as there are cooks. The genuine article is a spicy beef-and-potato stew with vast amounts of paprika.

Qat (Horn of Africa): From Yemen to East Africa, people chew this leaf to get a little buzz. One doesn't so much chew it as pack it between one's cheek and gum to get the full qat pleasure. Bear in mind that it is illegal in the United States.

Ayrag (Mongolia): When you're a nomad of the Gobi and there are no taverns, you're happy to settle for fermented mare's milk. It takes only a couple of days to ferment and turns out lightly carbonated.

Kava (Polynesia): It's the social lubricant of many island nations. Take a pepper shrub root (*piper methysticum*), and get someone to chew or grind it into a pulp. Mix with water and enjoy.

STATE CAPITALS

✳ ✳ ✳ ✳

The capitals of more than half of the 50 United States were once somewhere else. Some states moved their capitals for convenience or political gain. Others used to have co-capitals or rotating capitals. Match each state to its former capital.

State	Capital
Alabama	Bowling Green
Arkansas	Cahawba
California	Charleston
Connecticut	Chillicothe
Delaware	Corydon
Georgia	Detroit
Illinois	Donaldsonville
Indiana	Exeter
Iowa	Guthrie
Kentucky	Iowa City
Louisiana	Kaskaskia
Maine	Kingston
Michigan	Lancaster
Mississippi	Milledgeville
Missouri	Murfreesboro
New Hampshire	Natchez
New York	Neosho
North Carolina	New Bern
Ohio	New Castle
Oklahoma	New Haven
Pennsylvania	Newport
Rhode Island	Portland
South Carolina	Vallejo
Tennessee	Washington
Vermont	Wheeling
West Virginia	Windsor

Some Current States and Their Early Names

- *Delaware—Lower Counties on Delaware*

- *Connecticut—Connecticut Colony*

- *Rhode Island—Colony of Rhode Island and Providence Plantations*

- *Vermont—Province of New York and New Hampshire Grants*

- *Kentucky—Virginia (Kentucky County)*

- *Tennessee—Province of North Carolina, Southwest Territory*

- *Ohio—Northwest Territory*

- *Maine—Massachusetts*

- *Texas—Republic of Texas*

- *California—California Republic*

- *Oregon—Oregon Territory*

- *Hawaii—Kingdom of Hawaii, Republic of Hawaii*

Alabama—Cahawba; Arkansas—Washington; California—Vallejo; Connecticut—New Haven; Delaware—New Castle; Georgia—Milledgeville; Illinois—Kaskaskia; Indiana—Corydon; Iowa—Iowa City; Kentucky—Bowling Green; Louisiana—Donaldsonville; Maine—Portland; Michigan—Detroit; Mississippi—Natchez; Missouri—Neosho; New Hampshire—Exeter; New York—Kingston; North Carolina—New Bern; Ohio—Chillicothe; Oklahoma—Guthrie; Pennsylvania—Lancaster; Rhode Island—Newport; South Carolina—Charleston; Tennessee—Murfreesboro; Vermont—Windsor; West Virginia—Wheeling

INFLUENTIAL FIRST LADIES OF THE UNITED STATES

✳ ✳ ✳

First ladies have had a lot of things in common. Nearly all have ambitiously boosted their husbands' careers and had input into public affairs. Nearly all have entertained, set trends, and promoted social causes. Here are some of the women who helped strengthen and expand the platform on which their successors would stand.

Martha Washington (First Lady 1789–1797): No one elects a president's spouse, nor has she ever received a salary for hosting dinners, tolerating fools, and supporting her husband—but that's tradition, not law. This ethic originated with down-to-earth Martha, who established patterns of duty and dignity in the new republic's executive residence.

Abigail Adams (1797–1801): It's not clear if Martha Washington was involved in public policy, but Abigail Adams certainly was. As John Adams's key political advisor, she wrote letters to newspapers (the era's genteel approach to public discourse), listened to congressional debates, and tried in vain to get her husband to write women's rights into the Constitution. In fact, she threatened him with a women's rebellion.

Dolley Madison (White House Hostess 1801–1809; First Lady 1809–1817): Dolley was widely considered the most influential woman in the United States in the 1800s. As widower Thomas Jefferson's official White House hostess (a role filled by someone other than the president's wife) and then James Madison's first lady, Dolley was always graceful, valiant, and patriotic. She rescued national treasures from the White House in 1814 as the British army approached and the militia fled.

Dolley stayed relevant to the roles of hostess and first lady for half a century. She mentored White House hostesses Angelica Van Buren and Priscilla Tyler, then first ladies Julia Tyler and Sarah Polk. When Dolley died in 1849, Congress adjourned immediately to mourn a beloved heroine.

Louisa Adams (1825–1829): The only foreign-born first lady (she was born in London), Louisa was the first to be directly involved in her husband's election campaign (she actually managed it). Without her political savvy, John Quincy Adams likely would have lost the presidency.

Julia Tyler (1844–1845): Julia married widower and president John Tyler, taking over for his daughter Letitia and daughter-in-law Priscilla, who had held the fort as White House hostesses. Julia was the first presidential wife to use a press secretary to manage the media. She was also the first to have the marine band play "Hail to the Chief" for her husband.

Sarah Polk (1845–1849): The wife of James K. Polk was arguably the first co-president—a full political partner in her husband's administration. She was a speechwriter, press secretary, political tactician, hostess, and confidante, integrating the varying roles laid out by her predecessors into a dominant political force.

Harriet Lane (White House Hostess 1857–1861): Niece of James Buchanan (the only president who remained a bachelor), Harriet was best known for championing her personal causes. She worked hard on behalf of Native Americans and supported the movement to establish a national art gallery. Harriet Lane blazed the trail of social activism among first ladies and White House hostesses.

Eliza Johnson (1865–1869): What can one say about a first lady with enough political pull to influence her husband's stay in office? When the sharks circled Andrew Johnson, Eliza overcame fragile health to lead the anti-impeachment effort. Since this process also determined future interpretation of the Constitution, Eliza helped establish the rights of the presidency itself.

Lucy Hayes (1877–1881): When a president is elected, favor-seekers swarm, looking for jobs and perks. When they tried to approach President Rutherford B. Hayes, his wife, Lucy, handily dismissed them, creating a policy that dovetailed with her husband's merit-based reform of civil service. She also picked up a torch long fallen from Abigail Adams's hands: women's rights. Her quiet activism inspired and fueled the growing political voice of women.

Edith Wilson (1915–1921): Edith was the first full presidential gatekeeper. A stroke (or possibly encephalitis) felled Woodrow Wilson in September 1919; he never fully recovered and was incapacitated until early 1920. Edith (not Vice President Thomas Marshall) determined what and whom her husband would see, delegating anything she considered unimportant.

Florence Harding (1921–1923): Not all groundbreaking is admirable. Many know that Warren G. Harding's administration was full of monkey business; few realize how well Florence manipulated the media to maintain the administration's popularity. Other first ladies had guided the media expertly, but no one had yet managed so well to hide corruption. Florence must take credit (or perhaps blame) for her strong effort to shield herself and her husband from retribution.

Lou Hoover (1929–1933): Lou was the first presidential spouse to broadcast by radio, to appear in public while pregnant, and to invite an African-American woman for tea. (Just ten years earlier, Woodrow Wilson had supported the Ku Klux Klan.) Lou valued White House history, turning much old "junk" into treasured heritage. More practically, she got Herbert to issue an executive order that reduced civil service barriers for women.

Eleanor Roosevelt (1933–1945): Far more a political partner than other presidents' spouses had been, Eleanor connected the presidency with the people as no first lady ever had. It's doubtful FDR could have pressed his full domestic agenda without Eleanor, even considering his advanced political skills.

Jacqueline Kennedy (1961–1963): Like most first ladies, Jackie had been a tremendous help during her husband's rise. Once established in the White House, her multilingualism proved a foreign relations asset. The widest furrow Jackie plowed, though, was in the realm of sheer popularity—she was the most glamorously visible first lady in history. Not even Eleanor publicized the presidency as well as Jackie did. When she led a nation in mourning after her husband's assassination, she sealed her place in history.

Claudia "Lady Bird" Johnson (1963–1969): Lady Bird was all that most first ladies were, with one more thing: She changed the very look of the nation. By the 1960s, highways in the United States were a clutter of billboards overlooking ditches full of trash. Lady Bird declared war on ugly. Down came most of the billboards, and people adopted a national ethic against litter.

Elizabeth Ford (1974–1977): Betty Ford started to shatter Puritanical taboos when doctors diagnosed her breast cancer. Betty spoke publicly about her mastectomy, hoping to encourage more women to get checked. She admitted suffering from depression and seeing therapists, though she kept her substance abuse private until Gerald Ford left office. Even then, she turned her battle into a way to help others by establishing the Betty Ford Center.

Hillary Clinton (1993–2001): Like most politically active and visible first ladies, Hillary was controversial in the role. She was the first to use it as a ramp to build her own independent political base, becoming the first former first lady to be elected to the U.S. Senate in her own right and the first to run for the office of president.

- *Abigail Adams was the first first lady to live in the White House.*
- *Lucy Hayes was once the only female student at Ohio Wesleyan University.*
- *Dolley Madison initiated the inaugural ball.*
- *Lou Hoover spoke fluent Chinese.*
- *Sarah Polk hosted the first annual Thanksgiving dinner at the White House.*
- *Hillary Clinton was twice honored as one of the top 100 lawyers in the United States.*
- *Eleanor Roosevelt was known to serve scrambled eggs on unmatched dishes at White House lunches.*

SLITHERING DANGER

✳ ✳ ✳ ✳

The fear of snakes, ophidiophobia, *is one of the most widespread phobias in the world. There are many types of harmless snakes, but the venom from some poisonous varieties can kill a person. The following snakes have the most potent venom.*

Hook-nosed Sea Snake

The worst of the worst is this four-foot-long waterborne menace that lives along the coastlines of South Asia. The hook-nosed sea snake doesn't attack humans often, but when it does, just 1.5 milligrams of its venom can cause death. Its preferred prey are fish, which the snake paralyzes with its venom.

Russell's Viper

This three- to five-foot yellowish-brown snake is frequently found in Pakistan, India, Southeast Asia, and China. The Russell's viper preys primarily on rodents but will also kill cats, squirrels, crabs, and even scorpions. Its bite causes pain, swelling, and bleeding, as well as decreased blood pressure and heart rate.

Inland Taipan

Averaging nearly six feet in length, this snake lives in dry regions of Australia. An average bite from an inland taipan is estimated to have at least 50 lethal human doses. Fortunately, it shies away from people and dines on rodents, which it subdues by striking quickly and hanging on until they die. In contrast, it releases larger prey after biting them to avoid getting hurt in a struggle—but it tracks them down after the venom kicks in.

Dubois's Sea Snake

This treacherous swimming snake is found from the coasts of western and northern Australia to the islands of New Guinea and New Caledonia. Although the Dubois's sea snake has one of the deadliest venoms known, its bite delivers less than one-tenth of a milligram—more than enough to kill a mouse but generally not enough to kill a person.

Eastern Brown Snake

Another species native to Australia, the Eastern brown snake averages three to four feet in length but can grow longer than six feet. This aggressive land snake injects very little venom when it bites, but it's still enough to cause rapid death in its victims. It eats mostly small mammals, such as rats, mice, and reptiles, but will also eat eggs, birds, and frogs.

Black Mamba

This nasty serpent from southern and central Africa is actually a greenish-yellow or gray; its name comes from the color of its mouth. One of the quickest and largest deadly snakes, it averages 8 feet long but can grow to more than 14 feet. The black mamba preys on small mammals and birds, delivering small, fast bites. If it attacks a person, as little as two drops of its venom can cause dizziness, rapid heart rate, and shallow breathing. Some of its human victims have fallen into a coma and died.

Boomslang

Africa's savannah grasslands are home to the deadly five-foot boomslang, which eats chameleons and other lizards, as well as birds and their eggs. Even small amounts of its venom can kill a person; the victim experiences nausea, dizziness, and a deceptive recovery before sudden death from internal hemorrhaging.

Common Indian Krait

This deadly snake is found across India, Pakistan, and other parts of southern Asia. It is not aggressive, but if alarmed it will bite and inject its venom, which can cause sleepiness and respiratory failure, killing most human bite victims who don't receive antivenin. Kraits, which average around four feet long, eat not only small lizards but also snakes—including other kraits.

Talk to the Expert
SNAKE MILKER

* * * *

Q: So where are the udders on a snake?

A: Funny! But I admit that the process does look a lot like milking. I extract venom from some of the most dangerous reptiles in the world. Snakes here in Australia are much worse than most North American vipers, including the copperhead. In any event, there's a constant need for snake venom, so I don't expect to be out of work anytime soon.

Q: What use is the venom?

A: The primary value is in creating antivenin to help a victim recover from a snakebite. These work the same way vaccines work—if you inject a living being with something harmful, its body will generally produce the antigens to fight the invasion. Sheep are most commonly used to produce antivenin. An antivenin can't put right what has already been damaged by a toxin, but it can help the victim's body halt further damage. Time is of the essence.

Q: How do you milk the snakes?

A: Much of it lies in being good at wrangling snakes. Here at the Australian Reptile Park, we have quite a few captive snakes and spiders. They don't produce a lot of venom, so we have to get every drop; we usually let them go a couple of weeks between milkings. Please don't try this at home: First I stretch some latex rubber over a glass beaker. I hold the snake carefully, as close behind the head as possible so it can't backlash. The snake doesn't care for this, and I let it strike at the beaker. If I do it right, the snake's fangs go through the latex and inject venom into the beaker.

Q: How many times have you been bitten?

A: Just two nicks. You see, most snakes husband their venom with care. They don't like to waste it. If the snake can't get its fangs out of its victim, it annoys and scares the snake; it knows that while its fangs are stuck in something, it's utterly vulnerable. In that case the snake pumps in more poison. The nicks were unpleasant but not severe—nothing like what I'd have received had I stepped on the creature in the bush.

Q: What are the most dangerous snakes you milk?

A: The coastal taipan, inland taipan, and Australian brown snake are all bad news. But other regions in the world have some very dangerous snakes as well. I'd avoid a bite from an Indian king cobra if I were you, and the same goes for Central America's bushmaster.

Q: On to the commercial side of snake milking: Are there companies that deal in snake venom?

A: There are in Australia, with careful government oversight. Some snake species are threatened—we can't afford to lose a single broad-headed snake, for example, so we take great care not to damage the population.

Q: How much is the venom worth?

A: Some of it sells for a few hundred U.S. dollars per gram. If you want a gram of death adder venom, expect to pay $4,000. It all depends on supply and demand; some venom can be used to produce broad-spectrum antivenin, while others are useful against only one kind of bite. Some reptiles are harder to milk, or produce less venom, and that affects the price as well.

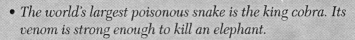

- *The world's largest poisonous snake is the king cobra. Its venom is strong enough to kill an elephant.*

- *There is no visible physical difference between male and female snakes.*

- *Snakes have no eyelids, and their eyes turn a milky white just before they shed their skin.*

MUSH-RUMINATIONS

✳ ✳ ✳ ✳

- France was the first country to cultivate mushrooms, in the mid-17th century. From there, the practice spread to England and made its way to the United States in the 19th century.

- In 1891, New Yorker William Falconer published *Mushrooms: How to Grow Them—A Practical Treatise on Mushroom Culture for Profit and Pleasure*, the first book on the subject.

- In North America alone, there are an estimated 10,000 species of mushrooms, only 250 of which are known to be edible.

- A mushroom is a fungus (from the Greek word *sphongos,* meaning "sponge"). A fungus differs from a plant in that it has no chlorophyll, produces spores instead of seeds, and survives by feeding off other organic matter.

- Mushrooms are related to yeast, mold, and mildew, which are also members of the "fungus" class. There are approximately 1.5 million species of fungi, compared with 250,000 species of flowering plants.

- An expert in mushrooms and other fungi is called a mycologist—from the Greek word *mykes,* meaning "fungus." A mycophile is someone whose hobby is to hunt edible wild mushrooms.

- Ancient Egyptians believed mushrooms were the plant of immortality. Pharaohs decreed them a royal food and forbade commoners to even touch them.

- White agaricus (aka "button") mushrooms are by far the most popular, accounting for more than 90 percent of mushrooms bought in the United States each year.

- Brown agaricus mushrooms include cremini and portobellos, though they're really the same thing: Portobellos are just mature cremini.

- Cultivated mushrooms are agaricus mushrooms grown on farms. Exotics are any farmed mushroom other than agaricus (think shiitake, maitake, oyster). Wild mushrooms are harvested wherever they grow naturally—in forests, near riverbanks, even in your backyard.

- Many edible mushrooms have poisonous look-alikes in the wild. For example, the dangerous "yellow stainer" closely resembles the popular white agaricus mushroom.

- *Toadstool* is the term often used to refer to poisonous fungi.

- In the wild, mushroom spores are spread by wind. On mushroom farms, spores are collected in a laboratory and then used to inoculate grains to create "spawn," a mushroom farmer's equivalent of seeds.

- A mature mushroom will drop as many as 16 billion spores.

- Mushroom spores are so tiny that 2,500 arranged end-to-end would measure only an inch in length.

- Mushroom farmers plant the spawn in trays of pasteurized compost, a growing medium consisting of straw, corncobs, nitrogen supplements, and other organic matter.

- The process of cultivating mushrooms—from preparing the compost in which they grow to shipping the crop to markets—takes about four months.

- The small town of Kennett Square, Pennsylvania, calls itself the Mushroom Capital of the World—producing more than 51 percent of the nation's supply.

- September is National Mushroom Month.

- One serving of button mushrooms (about 5) has only 20 calories and no fat. Mushrooms provide such key nutrients as B vitamins, copper, selenium, and potassium.

- Some experts say the taste of mushrooms belongs to a "fifth flavor"—beyond sweet, sour, salty, and bitter—known as *umami,* from the Japanese word meaning "delicious."

REALLY SUPER HEROES

✳ ✳ ✳ ✳

The most recognizable superheroes aren't just preternatural crime fighters. Born in the pages of comic books decades ago, these powerful and popular icons are as beloved as ever.

Superman: The definitive superhero debuted in *Action Comics* #1, published in 1938. Kal-El, the only survivor of the planet Krypton, escapes its explosion after his father, Jor-El, puts him in a spaceship that crash-lands near Smallville, U.S.A. Kal-El, named Clark Kent by his adoptive parents, has superpowers of all kinds on Earth. Co-creator Jerry Siegel said he came up with Superman on a sleepless night in the early 1930s, but it took him several years to actually sell the pitch.

Batman: The alter ego of millionaire socialite Bruce Wayne first appeared in *Detective Comics* #27 in 1939. In response to his parents' murder at the hands of a thief, Wayne pushes his body and mind to their limits and becomes a mysterious vigilante. Batman was actually born in 1938, after Bob Kane created a birdlike prototype for a superhero of the night. Comic-book writer Bill Finger collaborated with Kane and decided that a "Bat-Man" would be more sinister.

Spider-Man: Premiering in *Amazing Fantasy* #15 in 1962, Spider-Man was teenager Peter Parker, who'd been bitten by a radioactive spider at a demonstration of a particle accelerator. The incident gave Parker spiderlike characteristics, such as the ability to cling to walls, as well as superhuman agility and speed. Marvel Comics' Stan Lee and Steve Ditko created Spider-Man as the first superhero with real problems, such as dating and paying rent.

Wonder Woman: The first major superheroine, Wonder Woman made her comic-book debut in 1941 in *All-Star Comics* #8. One of a race of warrior women called Amazons, Wonder Woman was given mega-strength and otherworldly powers by a cadre of Greek goddesses and gods. She was created by psychologist William Marston, who criticized comics for their "bloodcurdling masculinity." Marston used Wonder Woman's golden manacles (a symbol of female subjugation in a patriarchal society) to convey the idea that war could be eliminated if women took control.

The Hulk: In *The Incredible Hulk* #1 (1962), Dr. Bruce Banner saves teenager Rick Jones from rays emanating from a gamma-bomb test, but in the process, he gets irradiated. After that, whenever Banner becomes angry, he transforms into the green-skinned, seven-foot, 1,000-pound Hulk. Drawing on the Atomic Age for the Hulk's origin, co-creator Jack Kirby said he was also inspired by a news account of a woman lifting a car to save her child. He combined the disparate concepts of emotion-fueled adrenaline and radiation into this uncontrollable antihero.

Wolverine: The first appearance of Canadian mutant antihero Wolverine was in *The Incredible Hulk* #180, published in 1974. The source of Wolverine's supernatural healing rate and heightened senses are his mutant genetics, but secret experiments gave him a skeleton reinforced with superstrong adamantium and retractable adamantium claws. Creator Len Wein originally saw him as an actual four-legged mammal mutated to near-mortal form, a concept that changed when Wolverine joined the X-Men in 1975 and became more human.

Invisible Girl: Along with teammates Mr. Fantastic, the Human Torch, and the Thing, the Invisible Girl (aka Susan Storm) was introduced in *Fantastic Four* #1 (1961). After the superhero team was exposed to cosmic radiation while on an unapproved space-flight, Marvel's superheroine could turn invisible at will, as well as make others invisible and generate invisible force fields. The team's creators, Stan Lee and Jack Kirby, were inspired by genres outside the traditional superhero comic, cobbling together elements from romance, monster, science fiction, and Western titles. When artist and writer John Byrne took over the series in 1981, he felt that the Invisible Girl was too passive, often portrayed as a damsel in distress who had to be rescued by her superhero teammates. As Byrne expanded the Invisible Girl's powers, she became more assertive and eventually assumed the name the Invisible Woman.

Folklore: Myth or Truth?
MOLLY PITCHER:
REBEL MILITIAWOMAN

✳ ✳ ✳ ✳

*Historians disagree about Molly; not over whether she lived,
but over her true identity. Did a cannon-cocker's wife truly step up
and serve a gun under fire in the American Revolution?*

Was Molly Pitcher real? A couple of Revolutionary women's stories
sound a lot like Molly's. Because women have "pitched in" during
battle in just about every war, that's neither surprising nor a revelation. It wasn't rare in that era for wives to accompany their husbands
on military duty, to say nothing of those daring few women who
masqueraded as men. So who was Molly? Many historians say she
was an Irish immigrant named Mary Hays (later McCauly). Some
believe that Molly was Margaret Corbin, a Pennsylvania native. The
most likely case is that both were real women who did pretty much
as history credits them, and that the legend of Molly Pitcher com-
mingles the two.

What did Mary Hays do? The story, likely accurate, credits her first
with bringing water (the "pitcher" part explained) to the artillery
gunners at the Battle of Monmouth (1778). Not just to drink; a
soldier had to wet-sponge a cannon after a shot in order to douse any
residual embers. If he or she didn't, the person pushing in the next
powder charge would suffer the consequences. Accounts describe
Mary as a woman who was always ready with a choice profanity and
was as brave as any man, and she is widely credited with evacuating
wounded men. After her husband fell wounded, she stepped forward to help crew his gun. Mary died around 1832.

And Margaret Corbin? Her tale enters focus at the Battle of Fort
Washington (1776) and has her first helping her husband crew a cannon, then firing it unassisted after his death in action. (That would
be possible, but very slow.) Taken out of action by grapeshot—a

cannon firing musket balls as a super shotgun—she was evacuated and given a military pension by the Continental government. Considering said government's notorious poverty and lousy credit, there's doubt whether poor Margaret ever collected any money in time to help her. She died in 1789, a partly disabled veteran.

How did the stories get so muddled together? One must consider the times. No one videotaped Mary or Margaret; eyewitnesses spoke or wrote of their deeds. Others retold the tales, perhaps inflating or deemphasizing them. As the war lingered on, people who had heard both stories probably assumed they were variants of the same story, and they retold it in their own words. Regardless, dozens of American women besides Mary and Margaret fought for independence; many thousands more helped the cause with all their strength. Molly Pitcher is an emblem, a Rosie the Riveter of her era.

- *Another woman of folklore was Joan of Arc, who proclaimed that she heard voices from God telling her to recover France from English domination late in the Hundred Years' War. The uncrowned King Charles VII sent her to the siege at Orléans, where she persevered and ultimately lifted the siege in only nine days. She was burned at the stake for heresy when she was 19 years old, but the Pope overruled the judgment. Joan was declared a martyr 24 years later.*

- *Hua Mulan is the Chinese folklore heroine of a fable that depicts her as a young woman who disguised herself as a man to take her elderly father's place in the army. After her service ended, she was offered a government post by the emperor, which she turned down to attend to her family.*

- *According to folklore, Chief Earth Woman was an Ojibwa in the 19th century who claimed to have been granted supernatural powers in a dream and therefore was allowed to accompany Ojibwa men on the warpath.*

THE SIN BIN:
HOCKEY'S HOUSE OF HUMILITY

✴ ✴ ✴ ✴

This is the time-out seat of professional sports, where hotheaded hockey players go "to feel shame." It is the penalty box, an off-ice office of purgatory for on-ice transgressors.

For the first 50 years of the National Hockey League's existence, every league arena had only one penalty box, which meant that players who engaged in a lively tussle on the ice served their penance together, with only an obviously nervous league official sitting between them to act as a buffer. Quite often, the combatants would continue their fisted arguments inside their temporary, cramped quarters.

On one occasion, this led to the infamous "pickling" of New York Rangers' forward Bob Dill. On December 17, 1944, Bob Dill and Montreal Canadiens fireball Maurice "The Rocket" Richard engaged in a raucous set-to that banished them both to the shower stall of shame. Inside the box, the obviously dazed and confused Dill attacked the Rocket again and received another sound thumping for his lack of common sense.

It wasn't until midway through the 1963–1964 season that the league introduced a rule requiring every rink to have separate penalty benches. A particularly vicious confrontation between Toronto Maple Leaf Bob Pulford and Montreal Canadien Terry Harper on October 30, 1963, precipitated by Harper's questioning of Pulford's sexual preference, spearheaded the NHL's decision to arrive at a sensible solution.

The undisputed king of the sin bin was Dave "Tiger" Williams, who logged nearly 4,000 minutes sitting on his punitive throne during his 15-year career in the NHL. Having spent his formative years with the Toronto Maple Leafs, Williams had a personal affinity for the Maple Leaf Gardens' penalty box, which he described as "a gross place to go. The guys in there are bleeding…and no one's cleaned the place since 1938."

Williams may hold the career mark for sin bin occupancy, but the rap sheet for a single-season sentence belongs to Dave "The

Hammer" Schultz. During the 1974–1975 campaign, the Philadelphia Flyers enforcer cooled his carcass in the hotel of humility for 472 minutes, nearly 9 full games. He was so at home in the house, he actually recorded a single titled "The Penalty Box," which became something of a cult hit in and around the City of Brotherly Love.

Philadelphia's post of punition was also the scene of one of hockey's most hilarious highlights. During a game between the Flyers and Maple Leafs in 2001, Toronto tough guy Tie Domi was sent to the box. Upon his arrival in the cage, he was verbally accosted by a leather-lunged Philly fan named Chris Falcone, who wisely used the glass partition to shield himself from Domi. Known as "The Albanian Assassin," Domi responded to the goading by spraying his heckler with water. The broad-shouldered Falcone lunged toward Domi, fell over the glass, and landed in a heap at Domi's feet, which resulted in a comic wrestling match between lug head and lunatic.

- *Before the invention of the hockey puck, players swatted at rubber balls, which were difficult to control because they bounced all over the ice. For a time, wooden blocks replaced the balls.*

- *Early hockey games allowed each team as many as 30 players on the ice at a time, and the goals were two stones frozen into either end of the ice.*

- *Dave Ritchie scored the first goal for the National Hockey League on December 19, 1917.*

- *The first goaltender to regularly wear a facemask during games was the Montreal Canadiens' Jacques Plante. A shot broke his nose in 1959, and he wore a mask from then on. Apparently, his teammates teased him mercilessly about it.*

- *The NHL passed a rule in 1979 requiring all players who came into the league from that point on to wear a helmet.*

I'm No Expert, But...
BIRDS NO LONGER WATCHED

✳ ✳ ✳ ✳

What became of some of the world's most interesting birds? In short, people either slaughtered them or slaughtered their habitats. Sadly, you will never see one, unless DNA can someday provide a miracle.

Q: What were passenger pigeons?

A: They were about the size and shape of a mourning dove, but mostly blue-gray with orange on the neck. They once represented 25 to 40 percent of all birds in North America. Their flocks darkened the skies for hours or days in passing—which sounds like exaggeration but is not. Passenger pigeons were all but wiped out in the wild by 1900, and the last known bird died in a zoo in 1914. The passenger pigeon is one of history's most incredible examples of transforming plenty to zero by sheer ignorance.

Q: Were dodos actually stupid?

A: It's fairer to call them naïve. The dodo lived only on Mauritius in the Indian Ocean and had no natural predators before European arrival. Had the Dutch hunters not slaughtered them, the settlers' dogs and pigs would have. The last one died by 1681. Dodos were great big flightless things weighing about 50 pounds, mostly gray with nine-inch bills.

Q: What in the world was a Great Auk?

A: It was a distant relative of the penguin that lived in the North Atlantic, mostly in modern Canada, Greenland, and Iceland. This ungainly looking creature stood nearly a yard tall and weighed ten pounds at most; though flightless like a penguin, it swam as fluidly as most birds fly. It was black-backed, black-beaked, and white-fronted, and the last live sighting was off Newfoundland in the mid-1800s. Humans hunted the Great Auk to extinction for food, eggs, and its soft, downy feathering.

Q: Did the United States really once have a native parrot species?

A: Yes. The Carolina parakeet, or Carolina conure, was a lovely small parrot with shading that ranged from spring green to aqua to yellow to orange, going from tail to head. A combination of hunting (for the feathers), disappearing forest habitat, and disease wiped them out by about 1918. Mexico's thick-billed parrot used to range into the extreme southwestern United States; it isn't extinct, but it now stays south of the border in its core habitats.

Q: Are there any ivory-billed woodpeckers left?

A: We hope so, and for many years we didn't dare hope. Also called the "Good God Bird" because that's what people exclaimed when they saw one, the ivory-bill is (or was) one of the largest woodpeckers north of Mexico. Twenty inches tall with a wingspan of nearly a yard, this blue-black, white, and red bird looks so much like the more common pileated woodpecker that it's hard to confirm sightings. Timber companies cut down most of its habitat—the swamps and forests of the lower Mississippi in Arkansas and Louisiana. Since 2000, some intriguing sightings, nest discoveries, and distinctive tapping sounds have led scientists to believe that a few survive.

- *In the Middle Ages, peacocks and swans were sometimes served at Christmas dinners.*

- *It's estimated that in the United States alone, more than 100 million birds die each year after they crash into windows.*

- *The oldest bird on record is Cocky, a cockatoo, who died in the London Zoo at the age of 82.*

- *The bird with the highest recorded flight was a Ruppell's vulture that reached 37,000 feet and collided with a plane.*

- *Approximately 3,000 birds collide with U.S. Air Force planes every year, causing an estimated $60 million in damages.*

FUNCTIONAL ART: THE AMERICAN QUILT

✳ ✳ ✳ ✳

Whether you curl up for a nap under your grandmother's quilt or do a little quilting yourself, rest assured, your interest in this beloved bedding is steeped in tradition.

The First Few Stitches

Quilting is the process of sewing together layers of fabric and filler. The bottom layer is called the "backing," the middle layer is the filling or "batting," and the top layer is called, well, the "top." The layers are sewn together to create cozy bedding or clothing.

People have been quilting—but not necessarily making quilted blankets—for a long time. An ivory carving from around 3600 B.C. depicts a king in a quilted cloak. Excavation of a Mongolian cave revealed a quilted linen carpet, and a pair of quilted slippers found near the Russia/China border was probably from the eighth or ninth century.

Patchwork, the process of piecing together scraps of fabric to make a larger whole, was widely practiced in Europe through the 1600s because it was economical. Old clothes and blankets were often recycled into something entirely new.

Early Amish Influence

The roots of the traditional quilt began to take hold in Europe and the United States in the 18th century. The oldest existing piece is the Saltonstall quilt. It was made in Massachusetts in 1704 and, though tattered, provides a window to the quilt-making styles of the era.

Amish settlers arrived in Pennsylvania in the early 1700s, and their quilts, known for jewel-toned fabrics and striking geometric patterns, surfaced in the 1800s. Our concept of patchwork quilts, patterns, and blocks has been greatly influenced by Amish quilters.

An Industrial Revolution

By the end of the 18th century, the textile industry in England had been fully mechanized, and the French were coming up with better, faster, and cleaner ways to dye fabric. Large quantities of colorfast, printed cottons became readily available, much to the delight of people everywhere.

By the time the War of Independence rolled around, the vast English textile industry was exporting thousands of tons of cotton to America. These fabrics made up the majority of the clothes and quilts of the era.

Social Hour

It's a misconception that people made quilts just for practical purposes. In fact, most quilters engaged in the hobby because they loved the craft—not because they needed a blanket. By 1820, sewing groups were widespread, allowing people to work together to sew quilts that were pulled across large frames. Many of the close-knit community sewing bees (or "sewing circles") of yesterday still function as quilting guilds and clubs today.

Patterns and Designs

Though some quilters specialize in whole-cloth quilts, most of the quilts made today are of the patchwork variety. Pieces of fabric are sewn together to make a single block; multiple blocks are then stitched to each other, creating the quilt top.

One of the most admired quilt styles comes from Hawaii. These quilts incorporate just two colors—usually red and white—and one large cutout design sewn directly onto the quilt top. The striking geometric shapes and intricate stitching have made Hawaiian quilts popular among quilters and quilt admirers for two centuries.

Modern-Day Quilts

Quilting in the United States experienced a revival in the 1970s, largely due to the country's 200th birthday. As part of the celebration, women and men alike took a renewed interest in quilting and in folk art and crafts in general.

The surge in the popularity of quilting turned this humble pastime into the $3.3-billion-a-year industry it is today. The current movement toward more simple, eco-friendly lifestyles will likely keep quilting alive for years to come.

LANDMARK MOVIE LOCATIONS

✶ ✶ ✶ ✶

Lots of people plan trips to visit the sites where their favorite movies were shot. But sometimes the "location" is computer generated, or it's just a movie set that's on two different continents

The Godfather (1972) The Corleone mansion where Connie's wedding is held isn't on plush Long Island, New York, but rather on blue-collar Staten Island.

Jaws (1975) The beach on fictitious Amity Island where sunbathers and waders get a scare is actually Joseph A. Sylvia State Beach on Martha's Vineyard in Massachusetts.

Star Wars (1977) Several desert locales on Luke Skywalker's home planet of Tattoine are in Death Valley National Park, California. Several other Tattoine locations—including Luke's home—are in Tunisia.

Pulp Fiction (1994) The spot where Vince and Jules eat Big Kahuna burgers before their morning hit is on Van Ness Avenue, north of Hollywood Boulevard, in Los Angeles.

Fargo (1996) As depicted in the movie, the Coen brothers shot mainly in and around Brainerd, Minnesota, but a particularly mild winter there forced them to film a number of scenes in Grand Forks, North Dakota.

North by Northwest (1959) One of Alfred Hitchcock's crowning directorial achievements, *North by Northwest* was shot largely on locations scattered across the United States. At the beginning of the film, Cary Grant's character is abducted from the Plaza Hotel in New York City. Later, he is attacked by a crop duster in a field in Wasco, California.

Thelma and Louise (1991) The climactic car-over-the-cliff scene in this Ridley Scott film was shot at the dramatic Shafer Overlook at Gooseneck State Park in southeastern Utah. The movie's plot begins in Arkansas, but Southern California fills in for the authentic South in the film.

Dead Poets Society (1989) Welton Academy is actually St. Andrew's School in Middletown, Delaware. The Dead Poets Society meets in Wolf Cave, also in Delaware, though the cave scenes were shot in a faux cavern in a nearby warehouse.

Taxi Driver (1976) Martin Scorsese's misanthropic classic was shot on location in New York City. Unhinged cabbie Travis Bickle works for a taxi company at 57th Street and 11th Avenue in Manhattan.

Planet of the Apes (1968) Although most locations on the ape-controlled planet are near the Grand Canyon in northern Arizona, the seashore where Charlton Heston's character realizes he's been on Earth all along is Westward Beach in Malibu, California.

Raiders of the Lost Ark (1981) The story for Steven Spielberg's re-invention of the pulp serial opens in a South American jungle, but its scenes were shot in and around the Huleia River in Kauai, Hawaii.

The Shining (1980) Though author Stephen King's Overlook Hotel was inspired by the Stanley Park Hotel in Estes Park, Colorado, Stanley Kubrick's film adaptation opens with exterior images of the Timberline Lodge atop Mount Hood in Oregon. Interiors were shot in a studio in England but drew upon the Ahwanee Hotel in Yosemite National Park, California.

Forrest Gump (1994) The bus-stop bench where Forrest tells commuters his stories was in Chippewa Square in Savannah, Georgia. However, it was installed for the movie's production and removed afterward.

Frankenstein (1931) The classic monster movie was shot almost entirely on the Universal Studios lot in Hollywood. A notable exception is the scene in which Frankenstein throws the woman into the lake: That's Sherwood Lake in Sherwood Forest, northwest of Los Angeles.

Do the Right Thing (1989) In Spike Lee's groundbreaking film, Sal's Famous Pizzeria is on Stuyvesant Street between Quincy and Lexington in Brooklyn, New York.

Butch Cassidy and the Sundance Kid (1969) The scene in which Butch and Sundance escape their pursuers by jumping off a cliff into the rapids far below was shot at Trimble Bridge over the Animas River, near Durango, Colorado. However, the leap was not as death-defying as depicted: Robert Redford and Paul Newman's fall was cut short by a platform a mere six feet below the bridge itself.

Apocalypse Now (1979) Francis Ford Coppola shot his war epic in the Philippines instead of Vietnam. The Philippine government allowed him to use its military helicopters, only to divert them to fight insurgents several times during the shoot.

The Matrix (1999) The Wachowski brothers, the minds behind *The Matrix*, set this science-fiction classic in their hometown of Chicago, but the futuristic metropolis was actually filmed halfway across the world in Sydney, Australia.

Gladiator (2000) Russell Crowe's character is sold into slavery in a scene shot in Aït Ben Haddou, a village in Morocco. Before *Gladiator*, the town had starring roles in other Hollywood movies, including *Lawrence of Arabia* and *Jewel of the Nile*.

Good Will Hunting (1997) In the film that won Matt Damon and Ben Affleck Oscars for Best Original Screenplay, Toronto replaced Boston for much of the shoot. Damon's character, Will Hunting, works as a janitor at MIT, but most of the classroom interiors were shot on the campus of the University of Toronto.

THE BITING WIT OF WINSTON CHURCHILL

✳ ✳ ✳ ✳

*Winston was witty, but he could also coat the literary
dagger with 15-molar nitric acid. Here are some colorful
quotes you may never have read.*

- In 1916, after a social meeting with Admiral John de
  Robeck, whom Churchill held responsible for the
  Gallipoli fiasco:
  "Get me a stiff whisky and soda, and get it quick.
  I have just done something I hoped I would never
  have to do. I have shaken hands with de Robeck."

- A memo to Admiralty in 1939:
  "Kindly explain the reasons which debar individuals
  in certain branches from rising by merit to commissioned rank.
  If a telegraphist may rise, why not a painter? Apparently there is
  no difficulty about painters rising in Germany!"

- Lady Astor's caustic comment at a dinner party:
  "Winston, if I were your wife I'd poison your coffee."
  Churchill's reply: "Nancy, if I were your husband, I'd drink it."

- Churchill didn't spare himself. Young Winston preparing for an
  important dinner party:
  "I must be upon my best behavior: punctual, subdued, reserved—
  in short display all the qualities with which I am least endowed."

- In 1940, when the German and Soviet foreign ministers met in
  Berlin, Churchill sent them scrambling for shelters with a bombing raid. Asked about it, he said:
  "We had heard of the conference beforehand, and though not
  invited to join in the discussion did not wish to be entirely left out
  of the proceedings."

- In 1941, on embracing Stalin as a new ally:
  "I have only one purpose, the destruction of Hitler, and my life is
  much simplified thereby. If Hitler invaded Hell I would make at

least a favourable reference to the Devil in the House of Commons."

- In an Admiralty memo:
  "Is it really necessary to describe the Tirpitz as the Admiral von Tirpitz in every signal? This must cause a considerable waste of time for signalmen, cipher staff, and typists. Surely Tirpitz is good enough for the beast."

- In the North African desert, referring to the famously ascetic politician Sir Stafford Cripps:
  "Here we are, marooned in all these miles of sand—not one blade of grass or drop of water or a flower. How Cripps would love it."

- Another jab at poor Cripps, who had just given up stogies:
  "Those cigars were his last contact with humanity."

- At the White House, Franklin D. Roosevelt wheeled in one day and caught Churchill buck naked. Winston smiled and said:
  "The prime minister of Great Britain has nothing to hide from the president of the United States."

- Describing U.S. Secretary of State John Foster Dulles:
  "The only bull who brings his own china shop with him."

- In 1944, refuting complaints on issuing captured German arms to the Free French forces:
  "It is almost like saying, 'Don't shoot that German with a German-made pistol now. Far better be shot yourself by him and have a thoroughly harmonious type of armament developed on a scientific scale a few years after your funeral.'"

- In a cabinet meeting, ranting about needlessly long reports:
  "This paper, by its very length, defends itself against the risk of being read."

- Apparently Winston's style was catching. During World War I, he was first lord of a hardworking Admiralty. Said a subordinate:
  "We have made a new commandment. The seventh day is the Sabbath of the First Lord, and on it thou shalt do all manner of work."

Fast Facts

- The Very Large Array is a not-so-creatively named radio astronomy telescope group in New Mexico. There are 27 antennas that work together to make images of space visible only within radio wavelengths.

- The largest planet yet discovered is TrES-4. It's 1,400 light years from Earth and nearly twice the size of Jupiter. It is a planetary oddball, though, because of its low density—which is about the same as balsa wood.

- The smallest will in history was written on the back of a postage stamp—complete with witness signatures.

- An adult human body contains approximately five quarts of blood.

- The average person forgets 80 percent of what he or she learns in a day.

- The Statue of Liberty's face was modeled after designer Frédéric-Auguste Bartholdi's mother.

- Stretching your joints, such as your knuckles, releases oxygen and other gases from the fluid that lubricates the joints. This is what makes the cracking sound.

- Vatican City in Rome isn't just the headquarters of the Catholic Church, it's also the smallest sovereign country in the world, with an area approximately a quarter of a square mile. Fortunately, it's not crowded living—fewer than 1,000 people live there permanently.

- The Greeks were professionals when it came to deific micromanagement. They had specific deities for such things as pain relief (Achelois), forgetfulness (Lethe), and the color scarlet (Erythia). There was also a goddess of dramatic dance (Terpsichore).

HENRY VIII

* * * *

- Henry was the third child and second son of Henry VII and Elizabeth of York. Two brothers and two sisters predeceased their father, while Henry and two sisters survived. When his older brother, Arthur, died at the age of 15, Henry became heir to the throne. Henry's sister Margaret became the queen of Scotland, and his sister Mary was briefly the queen of France.

- Henry was crowned king just before he turned 18, and he died at age 55, one of England's most beloved, and feared, monarchs.

- One of Henry's first acts as king was to execute his father's two most successful (and therefore hated) tax collectors, Edmund Dudley and Sir Richard Empson.

- Henry was at least six-foot-three, one of the tallest kings in English history. His suits of armor, some of which are still on display in the Tower of London, give a good idea of his formidable size.

- Although famous for having had six wives, Henry was married to his first, Catherine of Aragon, for more than 20 years.

- Queen Catherine was the widow of Henry's brother, Arthur (they were married only six months). This caused considerable speculation over whether her marriage to Henry was ever legal.

- Henry's great passion for his second wife, Anne Boleyn, led to the Protestant Reformation in England. The Pope refused to dissolve Henry's marriage to his first wife, so Henry split from the Catholic Church, declared himself head of the Church of England, and ordered his own annulment.

- Jane Seymour was said to have been Henry's favorite wife, as she was the only one to give birth to a son, Edward. Henry was buried with Jane, and she is featured in all of the dynastic portraits.

- King Henry had ten children by his first three wives, but only three—Mary, Elizabeth, and Edward—survived infancy. All three eventually ruled England, but none had children of their own.

- One of Henry's favorite sports was tennis. The athletic king popularized the game in England, and in 1529 he built a tennis court on the grounds of his Hampton Court palace. It was rebuilt in 1625 and is now the oldest tennis court in existence.

- Though his break with Rome fueled the Protestant Reformation, Henry considered Protestants to be heretics. His reforms were more legal than religious—the religion was still basically Catholic, but the king took the role of the Pope. The real disagreement between Catholicism and Protestantism was fueled by Henry's children—Mary was a strict Catholic, and Edward and Elizabeth strongly supported Protestantism.

- Henry was the first king to authorize an English translation of the Bible.

- For all his claims of chivalry and honor, Henry seemed to have no problem making up charges in order to arrest and execute people he considered an irritation or a threat.

- Henry spent the equivalent of approximately 2 million pounds on clothing each year.

- After his brother Arthur's death, Henry's childhood became stifling. He was kept under strict supervision and forbidden any activities that could possibly jeopardize his safety. Henry's friends had to get his father's permission before they were allowed to visit.

- Legend has it that when Jane Seymour was in labor with Prince Edward, she was having such difficulty that the doctors asked the king which they should save—his wife or his child. Although he loved her, the callous king is said to have replied, "Save the child, by all means, for other wives may be easily found."

- Henry was well known as a talented musician who frequently composed his own music. Contrary to popular lore, however, he did not write "Greensleeves."

CANADA'S MUSICAL GREATS

✳ ✳ ✳ ✳

Anne Murray, Gordon Lightfoot, Avril Lavigne, Rush, and Celine Dion are Canadian. So is New Brunswick, and that also isn't news. In fact, a number of popular acts over the years have either come from Canada or have a Canadian connection.

Individual Artists

Paul Anka, born in Ottawa, Ontario. When he got started in music (1955), Canada was still flying the Red Ensign. You've heard this renowned songwriter's music in dozens of movies, and he wrote "My Way" for Frank Sinatra.

Maynard Ferguson, born in Verdun, Quebec. Ferguson was one of the most incredible trumpet players ever, performing with a charisma that made jazz fun even for non–jazz buffs. That's his horn you hear in "Gonna Fly Now" (from the movie *Rocky*, 1976).

Terry Jacks, born in Winnipeg, Manitoba. For a few years in the early 1970s, you heard this pop singer on the radio day and night, usually singing "Seasons in the Sun." He has since become a record producer in Vancouver.

Guy Lombardo, born in London, Ontario. This bandleader's rendition of "Auld Lang Syne" emblemizes New Year's Eve. If you take the word of Louis Armstrong, you know this: "The man gets the melody right."

Sarah McLachlan, from Halifax, Nova Scotia. The winner of three Grammys and eight Junos might be most famous for starting Lilith Fair, a popular all-female tour that featured both aspiring artists and established stars and ran from 1997 through 1999.

Joni Mitchell, born in Ft. MacLeod, Alberta. She started singing while laid up with polio as a child and became a big name in folk music during the 1960s. She's also an accomplished photographer and painter who designed many of her album covers.

Alanis Morissette, born in Ottawa. This rock artist was first popular in her native land before breaking into the U.S. market in 1995. She won an impressive number of awards in 1996 for her breakthrough album, *Jagged Little Pill.*

Neil Young, born in Toronto, Ontario, but considers himself a Manitoban. With his wife, Pegi, he founded the Bridge School, which assists emotionally and physically handicapped children.

Groups

April Wine, formed in Halifax in 1969. Despite a few hiatuses, they're still rocking, touring often in Canada and enjoying a devoted following.

Bachman-Turner Overdrive, formed in Winnipeg in 1970. These rockers owned mid-1970s airplay but never glorified wild living— Randy Bachman was an observant member of the Church of Latter-day Saints.

Barenaked Ladies, formed in 1988 in Scarborough, Ontario. This major force in alternative rock has never had a woman in the band. They enjoyed years of success in Canada before achieving global fame.

Crash Test Dummies, formed in Winnipeg in 1989. This folk-rock band won wide acclaim through the 1990s. Their second album, *God Shuffled His Feet* (1993), earned them international praise.

Irish Rovers, an Irish-Canadian group, has been a heavy hitter in the Irish folk genre since 1963. A bantery stage style takes their performances from the realm of music into pure entertainment.

Propagandhi is another Winnipeg act (1986), this one in progressive punk. Their unabashed activism—including long onstage sociopolitical rants—hasn't hurt their popularity. Their album *Less Talk, More Rock* (1996) reflects their sense of humor about reactions to the rants.

EXPOSING THE VIRUS

✳ ✳ ✳ ✳

- A virus that infects and destroys bacteria is called a "bacterio-phage," ("phage," for short). Phages exist in some preserved foods, including pickles and pastrami.

- The deadliest disease in history was the Influenza Pandemic of 1918, also known as Spanish Flu. In just two years, the strain took more than 50 million victims worldwide—nearly twice as many as were killed in World War I.

- Unlike most flu outbreaks, Spanish Flu did not pose a greater danger to very young children, people in poor health, or the elderly. The virus invaded the body's immune system and caused it to attack its victims' lungs, so it killed more people with strong immune systems than those with weak ones.

- The word *vaccination* comes from the Latin word *vacca*, meaning "cow." The first European vaccinations infected people with cowpox, a disease similar to but less severe than smallpox. After the cowpox infection cleared, people were then immune to smallpox, as well.

- Antibiotics treat only bacterial infections (e.g., strep throat), but people often take them for viral illnesses, such as common colds or the flu. This misuse contributes to the development of antibiotic-resistant bacteria.

- In the United States in 1989, a new strain of Ebola killed a large number of monkeys in a primate facility in Reston, Virginia. The source of Ebola Reston was infected monkeys imported from the Philippines, and it is the only Ebola strain known to be spread by air.

- Because each virus targets a specific type of cell, certain strains can be used to treat, or even cure, diseases. Scientists are currently using "virotherapy" to genetically engineer a virus that attacks only cancer cells, and the use of virotherapy to treat the human immunodeficiency virus (HIV) is being investigated.

CONTRARY TO POPULAR BELIEF...

✳ ✳ ✳

*Just because something is common knowledge doesn't
mean it's based on fact. Here are some popular
perceptions that are just plain wrong.*

A Lead Pencil Hath No Lead

The Romans were crazy about lead. They drank from lead cups,
painted their faces with lead makeup, and used lead rods as
writing utensils. As most people know, all that lead went to their
heads and caused no end of health problems. Fortunately, lead
hasn't been used in pencils for hundreds of years, thanks to the
discovery of graphite, which is mixed with clay and formed into
small rods that are wrapped in wood.

You Say Tomato, I Say Fruit

If you ask a scientist, you'll likely be told a tomato is a fruit. After all,
fruits are classified as such because they develop from the ovary of
flowers and contain the seeds of the plant from which they sprouted.
A tomato is a perfect example of this process. But in 1893, the Supreme Court ruled that the tomato is legally a vegetable. The case
reached the high court because of a tax and tariff problem—people
paid more taxes for imported vegetables than fruits. The Supreme
Court ruled that even though a tomato is a "fruit of the vine," in the
"common language of the people" it's a bona-fide vegetable.

Food Fantasies

Ever wonder why your fast-food hamburger looks smashed and
dried-out when you unwrap it, while the same type of burger un-
wrapped on TV looks thick and juicy? The difference can be attributed to food stylists who spend hours making sure that their products are picture perfect. Stylists cook burgers just enough to brown
them, which also keeps them plump and moist. And the glistening
tomato and crispy lettuce covered in drops of dew? The effect is
created with spray-on gelatin, which makes food shine under hot
studio lights. Unblemished buns are hand-chosen, and sesame seeds

are individually glued into place. Buns are lined with waxed paper to prevent that soggy look.

India Ink Is Homesick

It was the Chinese, not the people of India, who perfected what we understand today to be India ink. Originally, the ink was made by mixing soot from pine smoke with lamp oil, then adding gelatin derived from donkeys. These days, India ink is made from a blend of natural and synthetic materials and is produced in plants around the world.

The Identity Crisis of the Horny Toad

The *Phrynosoma*, or horned lizard, is usually referred to as the horny toad or horny frog. The reptile isn't even related to frogs, but its short, wide body and froglike visage have wrongly convinced people of its identity. Call a horned lizard a toad at your own risk—when these critters get angry, they shoot blood out of their eyes.

Quantum Leaps: Not that Big of a Deal

At the start of the 20th century, quantum mechanics officially set the scientific world on fire and spawned a whole new lexicon for researchers and the general public. Advertisers jumped on terms such as "light years ahead" and "a quantum leap." Relatively speaking, an electron that makes a quantum leap is a pretty big deal, but in reality, a quantum leap is only .00000000001 centimeter. The next time you hear about a beauty product or oil change service that claims to be making a "quantum leap" in technology, just yawn.

The Panda: Barely a Bear?

It's official: The panda may or may not be an actual bear. Opinions vary on the matter. Scientifically speaking, the panda is a member of the *Carnivora* order, the family that comprises dogs, bears, raccoons, weasels, mongooses, hyenas, and cats. The panda's ancestors were bears, but there is disagreement about whether certain types of pandas (e.g., the red panda) should belong in the bear, or *Ursidae*, category. Some suggest they be grouped with the raccoon family, the *Procyonidae*, or in an entirely new all-panda family, the *Ailuridae*.

PRETZEL FACTS

* * * *

In the 1,400 years since the pretzel was invented, bakers have come up with a wide variety of shapes and flavors. The history of this adaptable snack shows its versatility.

- The world can thank a frustrated teacher with leftover bread dough for the invention of the soft pretzel. In A.D. 610, while baking bread, an Italian monk decided to create a treat to motivate his distracted catechism students. He rolled out ropes of dough, twisted them to resemble hands crossed on the chest in prayer, and baked them. The monk christened his snacks *pretiola*, Latin for "little reward." Parents who tasted their children's classroom treats referred to them as *brachiola*, or "little arms." When *pretiola* arrived in Germany, they were called *bretzels*.

- Perhaps because of its religious roots, the pretzel has long been considered a good-luck symbol. German children wear pretzels around their necks on New Year's Day. In Austria in the 16th century, pretzels adorned Christmas trees, and they were hidden along with hard-boiled eggs on Easter morning.

- The phrase "tying the knot" came from the Swiss, who still incorporate the lucky pretzel in wedding ceremonies. Newlyweds traditionally make a wish and break a pretzel, in the same way people in other cultures break a wishbone or a glass.

- In Austria, signs outside many bakeries depict a lion holding a pretzel-shaped shield. According to a legend that dates to 1510, pretzel bakers working before dawn heard Ottoman Turks tunneling under Vienna's city walls and then sounded an alarm. The city was saved, and the bakers were awarded their unique coat of arms by the Viennese king.

- Hard pretzels were "invented" in the late 1600s, when a snoozing apprentice in a Pennsylvania bakery accidentally overbaked his pretzels, creating crunchy, seemingly inedible, knots. His job was spared when the master baker, attempting admonishment, took an angry bite out of one—and loved it.

- Julius Sturgis opened the first commercial pretzel bakery in Lititz, Pennsylvania, in 1861. He received his original pretzel recipe as a thank you from a down-on-his-luck job seeker after Sturgis gave the man dinner.

- Until the 1930s, pretzels were handmade, and the average worker could twist 40 a minute. In 1935, the Reading Pretzel Machinery Company introduced the first automated pretzel machine, which enabled large bakeries to make 245 pretzels per minute, or five tons in a day.

- More than $550 million worth of pretzels are sold in the United States annually; 80 percent are made in Pennsylvania, where hard pretzels originated.

- The average U.S. citizen consumes up to two pounds of pretzels per year, but Philadelphians snack on about 12 pounds of pretzels per person every year.

- And then there's Joey "Jaws" Chestnut, the 2007 World Pretzel-Eating Champion, who ate 21 soft pretzels in ten minutes.

- President George W. Bush was munching on a pretzel in the White House when he choked and lost consciousness while watching the 2002 Baltimore–Miami NFL playoff.

- Pretzel bakers may have been the first to advertise "We deliver!" Medieval street vendors carried pretzels on a stick and sold them to the locals. Today, soft pretzels remain a popular pushcart item in Philadelphia and New York City.

- Joe Nacchio, of Federal Baking in Philadelphia, holds the record for baking the largest pretzel: It's 5 feet across and weighs 40 pounds.

- National Pretzel Day is April 26. Eat a bunch of pretzels with someone you love!

THE EIFFEL TOWER

✳ ✳ ✳ ✳

- Gustave Eiffel designed his monument to the French Revolution in 1887 as a grand entranceway to the 1889 International Exposition in Paris. Today, the tower attracts more than 6 million visitors per year.

- Eiffel and his crew of 300 workers assembled the tower's 18,000 pieces of iron in 2 years, 2 months, and 5 days. They came in under budget and on time for the start of the fair.

- Every 7 years, at least 25 workers use approximately 60 tons of paint to rustproof the tower.

- On a clear Parisian day, a person at the top of the Eiffel Tower can see about 42 miles in every direction.

- In just one year, the tower recouped nearly the entire cost of its construction—thanks to elevator ticket sales. The tower was one of the first tall structures in the world to utilize passenger elevators.

- The Eiffel Tower is 989 feet tall and weighs approximately 10,000 tons.

- On the four sides of the tower, the names of 72 famous French scientists and engineers are engraved to honor their national contributions.

- There are 2.5 million rivets (short metal pins) in the Eiffel Tower.

- There are 1,665 steps to the top of the tower, though it's widely thought there are 1,792, representing the year of the First French Republic.

- Heat from the sun can cause the tower to expand up to three-fourths of an inch. During the cold winter months, the tower shrinks approximately six inches.

- The French landmark was nearly demolished in 1909, when its original 20-year permit expired. But because its antennae were used for telecommunications, the tower was spared.

GOING ON ABOUT GOLF

* * * *

- King James II of Scotland banned golf in 1457 because golfers spent too much time on the game instead of improving their archery skills.

- The first golf course in England was the Royal Blackheath Golf Club, founded in 1608.

- The first golf course constructed in the United States was Oakhurst Links Golf Club in White Sulfur Springs, West Virginia, in 1884. It no longer exists.

- The oldest golf club in the United States still in existence is St. Andrews Golf Club in New York. It was formed by the Apple Tree Gang in 1888.

- The first golf balls were made of wood. Next were leather balls filled with goose feathers, followed by rubber balls, gutta-percha balls (made of a leathery substance from tropical trees), and then modern wound balls.

- The first sudden-death playoff in a major championship was in 1979, when Fuzzy Zoeller beat Tom Watson and Ed Sneed in the Masters.

- The longest sudden-death playoff in PGA Tour history was an 11-hole playoff between Cary Middlecoff and Lloyd Mangrum in the 1949 Motor City Open. They were declared co-winners.

- Beth Daniel is the oldest winner of the LPGA Tour. She was 46 years, 8 months, and 29 days old when she won the 2003 BMO Financial Group Canadian Women's Open.

- Most golf courses in Japan have two putting greens on every hole—one for summer and another for winter.

- Tiger Woods has won nine PGA Player of the Year Awards as of the 2007 season, the most won by any PGA Tour player. Tom Watson is second, with six awards.

- The youngest player to win a major championship was Tom Morris, Jr., (known as "Young" Tom), who was 17 years old when he won the 1868 British Open.

- The PGA Tour ranks Sam Snead as the best golfer in its history. Snead has 82 victories, followed by Jack Nicklaus with 73 wins, Ben Hogan with 64, Arnold Palmer with 62, and Tiger Woods with 61 wins through the 2007 season.

- The LPGA Hall of Fame is a tough one to make. Among other qualifications, players must be active on the tour for ten years, have won an LPGA major championship, and secured a significant number of trophies. It is considered one of the the most difficult accomplishment in golf.

- The shortest hole played in a major championship is the 106-yard, par-3 7th hole at Pebble Beach.

- The longest hole in the United States is the 841-yard, par-6 12th hole at Meadows Farms Golf Club Course in Locust Grove, Virginia.

- The first wooden tee was created in 1920 by Dr. William Lowell, a New Jersey dentist. Before tees were invented, golfers elevated balls on a tiny wet-sand mound.

- The oldest player to win a major championship was 48-year-old Julius Boros at the 1968 PGA Championship.

- The youngest golfer to shoot a hole-in-one was five-year-old Coby Orr. It happened in Littleton, Colorado, in 1975.

- The chances of making two holes-in-one in a single round of golf are 1 in 67 million.

- There are more than 11,000 golf courses in North America.

- Playing on a downhill hole and with the help of a tailwind, Bob Mitera sank a 444-yard hole-in-one on the Miracle Hill Country Club course in Omaha, Nebraska.

I'm No Expert, But...

THE EXECUTIVE OFFICE

✳ ✳ ✳ ✳

One would assume there were precise rules about who might be president and vice president, and who should succeed them. We asked around and learned it's not at all clear-cut.

Q: Who's in line to be president?

A: The vice president, of course, followed by the Speaker of the House of Representatives and the president pro tempore of the Senate. After that it goes to the Cabinet: secretary of state, secretary of the treasury, secretary of defense, attorney general, and on through the rest of the cabinet posts. The secretary of homeland security is last.

Q: Can an immigrant become president?

A: No. "No Person except a natural born Citizen, or a Citizen of the United States, at the time of the Adoption of this Constitution, shall be eligible to the Office of President." That's out of Article II of the Constitution. Because no one is still alive from 1788 (the year the Constitution was ratified), most legal scholars interpret this to say that one must be born to United States citizenship to be eligible for the presidency.

Q: How about vice president?

A: The 12th Amendment says that no one ineligible to be president can be elected vice president. However, that amendment mainly governs the meeting of the electoral college—an important distinction. If the president appoints you vice president, you aren't elected.

Q: Can a two-term president run for vice president?

A: There's debate about it. The 12th Amendment seems to rule it out. The 22nd Amendment says you can't be elected more than twice; it doesn't say you can't run, just that the electoral college electors cannot elect you. However, if the elected vice president died or resigned, the president could presumably appoint a former two-term president as vice president. Some argue that this means the former two-term president isn't constitutionally ineligible at all, and thus could actually be elected vice president. The Supreme Court prays it will never have to rule on the subject.

Q: What does it really mean when we "impeach" a president?

A: This caused a lot of confusion when it almost happened to president Richard Nixon. Everyone assumed "impeach" meant "remove." It doesn't. If you impeach someone, you have damaged that person's honesty or credibility. When Congress passes articles of impeachment against a president—which more or less translates to "The president has wronged"—it can then choose to vote to remove him or her. Andrew Johnson and Bill Clinton are the only U.S. presidents who have actually been impeached.

- *Thomas Jefferson's pet mockingbird flew freely inside the White House unless the president had guests.*

- *John Q. Adams was the first president to be photographed.*

- *Millard Fillmore established the White House library. Before this, there was no permanent collection of books in the White House.*

- *Chester A. Arthur thought the White House was out-of-date and gloomy, so he replaced 24 wagon-loads of old furniture with new items.*

- *Dwight D. Eisenhower was the first president to utilize a helicopter that took off and landed on the White House lawn.*

- *Nine presidents never attended college: Washington, Jackson, Van Buren, Taylor, Fillmore, Lincoln, A. Johnson, Cleveland, and Truman.*

THE MYSTERY OF THE MISSING COMMA

✳ ✳ ✳ ✳

Legend implies that a punctuation error sparked one of history's greatest unsolved mysteries: Did Queen Isabella give the order for her husband's death, or was it a misunderstanding?

King Edward II of England is primarily remembered for his weakness for certain men and the way he died. He spent most of his life in submission to his alleged lovers, Piers Gaveston and, later, Hugh le Despenser, granting their every wish. When Edward married 12-year-old Princess Isabella of France in 1308, he politely greeted her upon her arrival in England—and then gave her wedding jewelry to Gaveston.

Isabella grew up as a queen accustomed to being pushed aside in favor of her husband's preferred companions. Even after Gaveston was murdered for being a bad influence on the king, Edward did not change, turning his affections to the greedy Despenser, whom the queen loathed and feared. When the opportunity arose for her to negotiate a treaty with her brother, the King of France, she took it, traveling to Paris and refusing to return.

The Queen's Revenge
After nearly 20 years in an unhappy marriage, Isabella had had enough. Along with her lover, Roger Mortimer, she raised an army and led it into England in order to depose her husband. Once the king was in custody, the queen forced him to abdicate the throne to their 14-year-old son, Edward III, and proceeded to send a letter giving orders on how the deposed Edward should be treated in captivity.

Conspiracy or Miscommunication?
Something very important was missing from Isabella's orders. In the letter, she wrote, "Edwardum occidere nolite timere bonum est." Many historians think she intended this to mean, "Do not kill Edward, it is good to fear." However, she neglected to write in a

necessary comma. If the comma is inserted in a different place, the letter means "Do not be afraid to kill Edward; it is good." It's clear how Edward's jailers construed the message: Shortly after it was received, several men allegedly murdered Edward in his jail cell. Who knew that forgetting something as small as a comma could result in the murder of a king?

- *Three of Isabella's brothers became kings of France: Louis X, Philip V, and Charles IV. Charles IV was the brother whom Isabella visited before returning to England with her army.*

- *She was depicted in the movie* Braveheart *by Sophie Marceau. Contrary to what was depicted on film, Isabella never met William Wallace (Mel Gibson's character). She didn't even marry Prince Edward until three years after Wallace was executed.*

- *Isabella and Mortimer ruled England as regents for the teenage King Edward III. The young king wasn't happy with that arrangement, however, and three-and-a-half years after taking the throne in name, he took the throne in fact, deposing his mother and her lover. Mortimer was executed for treason about a month later. Edward could not order the same for his mother, and she was sent to live at Castle Rising in Norfolk, away from the capital in London.*

- *Although Edward II is alleged to have given power to his various male lovers, there is little speculation that Edward III and his siblings, John of Eltham, Eleanor of Woodstock, and Joan of the Tower, were not the natural offspring of Edward and Isabella.*

- *Isabella lived until 1358, seeing her children and grandchildren frequently.*

SUPREME BUNGLING:
BAD GENERALSHIP
IN THE CIVIL WAR

* * * *

Oh, how they bungled. Suicidal attacks, failures of military intelligence, lack of human intelligence, even cowardice. Some of the generals were admirable leaders who just had bad days; others should never have worn the bars or the stars.

Nathaniel Banks, U.S.A. Banks's many losses included Shenandoah Valley and Cedar Mountain (Virginia, 1862), plus Port Hudson (Louisiana, 1863). He didn't get the nickname "Commissary" for his superior logistical skill; rebel troops gave him that nickname in appreciation for the supplies they captured from him. His crowning blunder was the Red River Expedition (Louisiana, 1864), in which his troops floundered toward Shreveport without achieving anything.

Braxton Bragg, C.S.A. You would want discipline-stickler Bragg running a basic training center, but not your army. The Bragg cycle would start when he'd botch in some way: mishandle a battle, or pick the wrong terrain, or fail to exploit a win. His subordinates would either defy him or write home to Richmond begging reprieve. Bragg would learn of this, then punish them for insubordination before committing a new error to restart the process. Eventually, the Confederate government put Bragg to work on the supply-and-draft pipeline, something he was actually good at.

Ambrose Burnside, U.S.A. There's bad, and then there's Burnside's version of bad. His problems began when this competent brigadier gained a second star. Burnside—a modest man—didn't think he had what it took to command the Army of the Potomac, but his superiors felt otherwise. Robert E. Lee spanked Burnside at Fredericksburg (Virginia, 1862), showing that Ambrose's one brilliant command judgment had been that he shouldn't command.

Burnside's Homeric error came at Petersburg (Virginia, 1864). Union engineers tunneled beneath Confederate positions and detonated explosives, breaching the lines with a big crater. Burnside sent a force commanded by a drunkard (James Ledlie) into the crater, where they halted long enough for the rebels to contain and mow them down. Burnside's solution: Send more men into the hole to die with the first group! The Battle of the Crater was one of the war's most tragic episodes.

James Ledlie, U.S.A. The charge was GWI (generaling while intoxicated). Ledlie nominally commanded one of the divisions Burnside squandered in the Crater at Petersburg. Instead of leading his men into danger, he stayed behind and got crocked. Drunkenness is one thing in a leader—a number of Civil War generals took a drink—but few deliberately ducked combat. Even incompetent Ambrose Burnside was neither a drunkard nor a coward; Ledlie was both.

Nathan Evans, C.S.A. As drunkards went, Evans had a decent generaling career, except for one incredible blunder at Kinston (North Carolina, 1862). Ordering a fighting withdrawal across a river under heavy Federal assault, Evans burned a bridge behind him. That would have worked well had he not accidentally left half his force on the far bank. Observing the scene from a safe distance, he mistook his forsaken troops' gunsmoke for Union fire and ordered his artillery to shell his own men.

Ulysses S. Grant, U.S.A. Even great generals botch now and then. Until mid-1863, the rebel fortress guns of Vicksburg dominated Mississippi River traffic; no Union vessel could safely pass. In 1862, Grant decided to dig a long ditch on the Louisiana side of the Big Muddy. He figured that the water would rise, scour out a generous channel, and let Union warships sail upriver outside Confederate gunnery range. After months of hard labor, the river leaked into the ditch—then silted it up. Grant's canal was useless.

Joseph Hooker, U.S.A. Many officers command well at one level but fail at another. "Fighting Joe" was a heck of a corps commander: fierce, brave, and popular. Promoted to army command, he managed to lose to Lee at Chancellorsville (Virginia, 1863) despite outnumbering the Southerners two to one. After this debacle, Hooker went back to corps command, where he resumed his competent ways.

George McClellan, U.S.A. McClellan might have been elected president in 1864 had he led the Army of the Potomac better in 1862. He was reportedly Caesar, Napoleon, and Hannibal rolled into one, posturing for public approval, dodging battle despite superior numbers, and whining for more troops. It's hard to avoid thinking that McClellan feared a career-spiking defeat. Abe Lincoln summed it up: "If General McClellan does not want to use the army, I would like to borrow it for a time."

George Pickett, C.S.A. No, this isn't for his Charge at Gettysburg, in which he was obeying Lee's direct orders with the only fresh division on the field. On April Fools' Day in 1865, Pickett's force suffered a terrible defeat at Five Forks (Virginia). For that he might be forgiven, except that he and some generaling cronies had decided to attend a fish fry and missed the entire battle.

Gideon Pillow, C.S.A. This doesn't seem difficult: When you blow a hole in enemy lines, you exploit the hard-won breach. You don't do what Pillow did at Fort Donelson (Tennessee, 1862)—march your guys back to their trenches, giving someone as smart as Ulysses S. Grant time to patch his lines and regroup. While Pillow's 12,000-man garrison hauled down its flag, he fled across the river, thus helping the Union again by avoiding captivity.

David Porter, U.S.A. Admirals, the seagoing version of generals, must also take their medicine. Like Grant, Porter was an outstanding officer who only once opened a jug—but Porter drank the entire thing. In 1865, the Union was trying to capture the tough Fort Fisher (North Carolina). Porter decided that Navy sailors and U.S. Marines armed with swords and pistols could "board" Fort Fisher and capture it, not realizing that the defenders' long-rifled muskets made this a suicidal proposition for the Yankee tars.

Daniel Sickles, U.S.A. His movement of III Corps to the Peach Orchard at Gettysburg—leaving a big gap in the line—has long been debated. "Boob" or "savior"? Most say the former, since he disobeyed orders and got his corps pounded doing so. Somehow the Union lines held anyway. Sickles might have been court-martialed, but he lost a leg in the fight, so he was just chewed out by George Meade, commander of the Army of the Potomac at the time.

MODERN UNITED STATES ARMY RANKS

✳ ✳ ✳ ✳

Commissioned Officers
Army Chief of Staff
General
Lieutenant General
Major General
Brigadier General
Colonel
Lieutenant Colonel
Major
Captain
First Lieutenant
Second Lieutenant

Warrant Officers
Master Warrant Officer 5
Chief Warrant Officer 4
Chief Warrant Officer 3
Chief Warrant Officer 2
Warrant Officer 1

Non-Commissioned Officers
Sergeant Major of the Army
Command Sergeant Major
Sergeant Major
First Sergeant
Master Sergeant
Sergeant First Class
Staff Sergeant
Sergeant
Corporal

Enlisted Personnel
Specialist
Private First Class
Private

GREATEST SPORTS NICKNAMES

✳ ✳ ✳ ✳

The banter-filled atmosphere of the locker room, the media's fertile imagination, and fans' wisecracks give professional sports an inexhaustible source of interesting nicknames for teams, coaches, and players. Here are some of the most apt, colorful, and/or amusing.

Hockey

Stu "The Grim Reaper" Grimson (1988–2002; eight different NHL teams): One of hockey's tougher pugilists, six-foot-five Grimson earned more than 2,100 penalty minutes during his 729-game NHL career—with only 17 career goals. When asked how he reconciled his frequent fighting with his born-again-Christian faith, Stu replied: "I don't think that Christ would be shy to shake off his gloves and protect his teammates."

André "Red Light" Racicot (1989–1994; Montreal Canadiens): For you non–hockey fans, the red light behind the net signals a goal—usually accompanied by a blaring siren or horn. For a goalie, being referred to as "Red Light" is like being called "Swiss Cheese" or "Sieve." But André was nowhere near as lousy as his unfortunate nickname suggests. He won 26 games, lost 23, and tied 8 for the Canadiens, averaging 3.50 goals against per game—not All-Star stuff, but no reason for Racicot to hang his head.

Dave "Cementhead" Semenko (1977–1988; WHA and NHL Edmonton Oilers, NHL Hartford Whalers and Toronto Maple Leafs): During Wayne Gretzky's heyday with the great Edmonton teams, Dave had one job: Keep Wayne safe. Most players didn't rough up Gretzky, preferring to avoid being punched out by someone who once acquitted himself respectably in an exhibition bout with Muhammad Ali, as Semenko had.

Football

Dick "Night Train" Lane (1952–1965; Los Angeles Rams, Chicago Cardinals, Detroit Lions): Though this defensive wizard's tackles indeed felt like locomotive hits arriving out of the night, Night Train got the odd nickname from associating with fellow Hall of Famer Tom Fears, who constantly played the record *Night Train* on his phonograph. The name became so associated with Lane that today hardly anyone remembers his first name.

William "The Refrigerator" Perry (1985–1994; Chicago Bears, Philadelphia Eagles): The 326-pound "Fridge" took up a lot of space on the defensive line. But what brought him the most attention was Chicago coach Mike Ditka's willingness to use him at fullback on goal-line plays. Although he was considered quite formidable, this reputation was mostly media hype—Fridge had only eight regular-season NFL carries for five yards and two touchdowns. Still, it was great fun for fans while it lasted.

Baseball

Burleigh "Ol' Stubblebeard" Grimes (1916–1934; seven NL/AL teams): The last pitcher legally allowed to throw the spitball under the grand-father clause when baseball outlawed ball-doctoring, Burleigh always showed up with a faceful of scruffy whiskers. On the hill, he was meaner than a bag of bob-cats, and he handily admitted this while wondering about all the "nice" guys in baseball.

Mike "The Human Rain Delay" Hargrove (1974–1985; Texas Rangers, San Diego Padres, Cleveland Indians): A lifetime .290 hitter, Hargrove got his nickname by fooling around in the batter's box: He would adjust his helmet, adjust his batting glove, pull on his sleeves, wipe his hands on his pants—and he'd do this before every pitch. If the pitcher threw instead to a base, Mike started screwing around all over again. Most pitchers like to get on with an at-bat, and it's probably no coincidence that Mike drew so many walks, inten-tional walks, and hits-by-pitch.

Pepper "The Wild Horse of the Osage" Martin (1928–1944; St. Louis Cardinals): According to teammate Leo Durocher, Oklahoman Martin played commando-style ball on more than one level: He wore no underwear, much less a protective cup. His rather wild, free-spirited baserunning got him the nickname, though it also probably referred to his love of practical jokes. Baseball historian Lee Allen summed up Pepper: "A chunky, unshaven hobo who ran the bases like a berserk locomotive, slept in the raw, and swore at pitchers in his sleep." ("Pepper" was a nickname, too. The Wild Horse of the Osage was born Johnny Leonard Roosevelt Martin.)

Basketball

Darrell "Dr. Dunkenstein" Griffith (1980–1991; Utah Jazz): This doctor was only six-foot-four but could jump as though grafted to a pogo stick. Griffith grew up in the era of George Clinton's Parliament and Funkadelic bands, and his brother and friends gave him a nickname that rhymed with Clinton's Dr. Funkenstein character— hardly knowing it would become a household name when Darrell became a pro.

Vinnie "The Microwave" Johnson (1979–1992; Seattle Supersonics, Detroit Pistons, San Antonio Spurs): Basketball fans know how important the "sixth man" can be, and Vinnie was one of the best at coming off the bench. Boston Celtic Danny Ainge hung the tag on him in 1985 after Johnson's brilliant 34-point outing off the bench: "If that guy in Chicago is 'The Refrigerator,' then Vinnie Johnson is 'The Microwave.' He sure heats up in a hurry."

"Pistol" Pete Maravich (1970–1980; Atlanta Hawks, New Orleans Jazz, Utah Jazz, Boston Celtics): Had Maravich played his full career in the era of the three-pointer, there's no telling how many this deadly long-range gunner might have racked up. Pistol Pete's nickname evoked the quick-draw shooting threat he always was, but he was also a lot of fun to watch. He used his eerie peripheral vision to pull off hotdog passes and circus shots like one of the Harlem Globetrotters. The former gym rat died playing the sport he loved, suffering a heart attack when he was just 40 years old during a pickup game of three-on-three.

Fast Facts

- The original name of the telephone was the harmonic telegraph.

- It took a year to connect the first telephone line from New York to San Francisco. Approximately 14,000 miles of copper wire and 130,000 telephone poles were needed to link the country.

- The annual revenue for the telephone industry is $210 billion, almost 8 times that of television and 23 times that of radio.

- Globally, about $1 trillion is spent annually on telecommunications products and services.

- One million threads of fiber-optic cable can fit in a tube one-half inch in diameter.

- The telephone is the most used piece of communication equipment in the world.

- The busiest organization in the world is the Pentagon, which has 34,500 phone lines and receives 1 million calls a day. It received more than 1.5 million phone calls on the 50th anniversary of D-Day.

- The busiest telephone exchange was reportedly by BellSouth at the 1996 Olympic Games, during which 100 billion bits of information were transmitted per second.

- Sweden has the greatest penetration of telephones. It has 229 phones for every 1,000 people.

- The longest phone cable is a submarine cable called Fiber-Optic Link Around the Globe (FLAG). It spans 16,800 miles from Japan to the United Kingdom and can carry 600,000 calls at a time.

- The telephone has been one of the most profitable inventions in the history of the United States.

Talk to the Expert
GOLF BALL DIVER

✳ ✳ ✳ ✳

Remember the time you duck-hooked three consecutive
tee shots into the lake before finally hitting a lousy 80 yards into
deep rough? We're asking the question for you: "What happens
to that layer of golf balls at the bottom of the lake?"

Q: How many balls does a golf ball diver fish out of a water hazard in a day?

A: At a large course, probably 2,000 or more. That's assuming I don't die in the process. In many parts of the United States, golf ball diving is an extreme sport.

Q: Because you get hit with golf balls?

A: No, though it does happen. Because I can drown, or have an encounter with an alligator, or get bit by a water moccasin—I have lots of hazards of my own. Leeches attach to me. Turtles have tried to take off my fingers. Even some fish think I'm food.

Q: Come on. Most of these lakes are less than ten feet deep, and you're fully qualified in scuba and wearing scuba gear. How could you drown?

A: You'd be sad to see how easily a diver, especially one carrying a big netlike bag full of golf balls in a dark environment, can get hung up in weeds along the bottom of a lake. I could be down there struggling to get free, running out of oxygen, while ten yards away Joe Duffer is celebrating because he just hit the green in regulation for the first time in a week. If I panic, I'm dead. The only way I live through that is if I can remain calm and methodically get myself loose.

Q: Okay, but alligators and snakes? Don't most golf courses remove dangerous reptiles?

A: In Southern states, these critters are everywhere. I don't know of any gator that can read "no trespassing" signs. Usually, where there's water, there are alligators and snakes.

Q: Threatening animals aside, how do you manage to find balls in the dark water?

A: By feel. I can't wear gloves, which is dangerous. I curse the people who have thrown beer bottles into a water hazard to a life of four-putts, because I've been cut quite a bit. I also find a lot of other junk, and stuff that's not junk. I've recovered quite a few golf clubs, often really expensive ones.

Q: Do you make good money?

A: I can. You have to love to dive, and you have to be able to work alone, because unlike the usual dives, you aren't with a buddy. I get a few cents a ball, but that adds up. Sometimes I find specialty balls that sell for a lot more—souvenir balls, really expensive premium balls. One time I pulled out a ball with the presidential logo. If I can get paid to go diving, I don't mind the occasional leech bite.

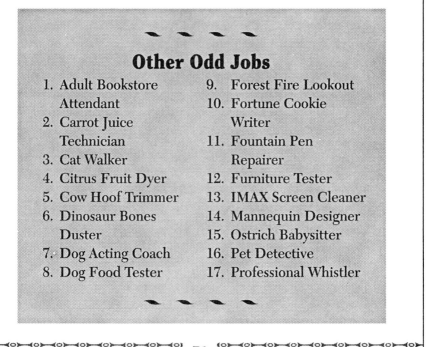

Other Odd Jobs

1. Adult Bookstore Attendant
2. Carrot Juice Technician
3. Cat Walker
4. Citrus Fruit Dyer
5. Cow Hoof Trimmer
6. Dinosaur Bones Duster
7. Dog Acting Coach
8. Dog Food Tester
9. Forest Fire Lookout
10. Fortune Cookie Writer
11. Fountain Pen Repairer
12. Furniture Tester
13. IMAX Screen Cleaner
14. Mannequin Designer
15. Ostrich Babysitter
16. Pet Detective
17. Professional Whistler

ICARUS

* * * *

In Greek mythology, a man named Daedalus built a labyrinth for King Minos. Despite this generous act, Daedalus fell out of favor with the king and was shut up in a tower with his son, Icarus. Daedalus decided he and his boy should escape. Using feathers collected from birds that flew through their tower, Daedalus and Icarus created huge wings for themselves and attached them to their backs with wax. Before they leaped out of the window to fly to freedom, Daedalus cautioned his son to stay close to him. "If you get too close to the water, the wax will stiffen up. If you get too close to the sun, it will melt." After father and son launched into flight, an exhilarated Icarus cried, "This is great!" and decided to fly higher. The wax melted and Icarus plunged into the sea, perhaps providing the genesis of the parental phrase, "Didn't I tell you...?"

Modern musicians (from Joni Mitchell to Kansas to Third Eye Blind) have embraced Icarus imagery in their music. In U2's "Even Better than the Real Thing," Bono sings, "We're free to fly the crimson sky/the sun won't melt our wings tonight."

The story of Icarus is a myth, but people throughout history have tried to improve on Icarus's plan of flight:

- In 1020, English monk Oliver of Malmesbury jumped off a tall tower with cloth wings fashioned after those of Icarus. He didn't fly and actually broke most of his bones.

- Leonardo da Vinci is actually credited with giving the world the first plans for human flight. In the 1480s, he began a serious study of the subject, amassing more than 100 drawings that represented the relationship between birds and mechanical flight.

- A French locksmith named Besnier created a glider contraption in 1678 that used rods and blades controlled by his hands and feet. Besnier's claims to have flown successfully are unsubstantiated.

IN THE YEAR...1919

✳ ✳ ✳ ✳

- Jerome David (J. D.) Salinger meets the world on January 1. His 1951 book *The Catcher in the Rye* would come to hold the simultaneous distinctions of being the most banned book in the United States and the second most taught in public schools.

- It is a big year for commercial air travel, with the advent of U.S. air passenger service and delivery of the first U.S. international airmail, transported from Seattle to Victoria, British Columbia, by pilot William Boeing.

- The Volstead Act passed by Congress enacts Prohibition in the United States.

- Congress declares the Grand Canyon a national park.

- Curly Lambeau founds the Green Bay Packers.

- The American Communist party is established.

- Henry Ford steps down as head of the Ford Motor Company, passing the job to his son Edsel.

- Carl Sandburg wins the Pulitzer Prize for his collection of poetry titled *Cornhuskers*.

- Eight members of the Chicago White Sox, along with the second baseman for the St. Louis Browns, are kicked out of Major League Baseball for "throwing," or intentially losing, games in the World Series. The term "Black Sox" is often associated with the scandal that darkened the reputation of Chicago's South Side team, but the term's origins are clouded in mystery. Some say it refers to a jab at the legendarily cheap team owner Charles Comiskey, who wouldn't cough up the change to launder the team's uniforms.

- W.E.B. DuBois organizes the first Pan-African Congress in Paris.

- More than 3,000 Chinese student protesters march on Tiananmen in support of a democratic revolution in China.

TOKYO

✳ ✳ ✳ ✳

- There are 35 million people living in Greater Tokyo, making this Japanese city the most populous metropolitan area on the planet.

- Large men known as *oshiya* ("pushers") are employed to cram commuters onto the city's overcrowded subways and trains.

- If you need to call 911 in Tokyo, you'll have to reverse the digits. To report a fire or call an ambulance, dial 119.

- Disneyland Tokyo opened in 1983, the first Disney park outside the United States. More than 17 million people visit the park each year, making it the most successful theme park in history.

- Built in 1958, the Tokyo Tower, at 1,100 feet, is the world's tallest self-supporting iron structure. So that it's clearly visible to wayward airplanes, the tower is painted orange and white.

- In 1923, a massive earthquake and subsequent fire destroyed most of Tokyo and killed more than 100,000 people. Most of the city had been rebuilt by 1930, only to suffer destruction again during World War II.

- The literacy rate in Tokyo is 99 percent, and the city has more than 150 institutions of higher learning.

- Tokyo hosted the 1964 Summer Olympics, the first time in history the Games were held in a non-Western nation.

- Tokyo boasts the world's first public monorail line, built to coincide with the 1964 Olympics. It runs between downtown and Haneda International Airport.

- The legal drinking age in Japan is 20, and there's a zero-tolerance policy for drunk driving. If you intend to drive in Japan, you are not allowed even one drink.

- Many public bathrooms do not supply toilet paper—it's a good idea to take your own when you head out of the house.

BASEBALL—THEY USED TO BE THE...

✳ ✳ ✳ ✳

What and where were some of today's major league baseball teams?
Some borrowed the names of defunct teams but have no other
continuity with the ghosts of old.

Atlanta Braves (National Association/National League): formerly the Boston Red Caps and Red Stockings (1876–1882), then the Beaneaters (until 1906), then Doves (to 1910), then Rustlers (for 1911). In 1912, they stopped the insanity, becoming the Boston Braves. After a 38–115 season in 1935, they played as the Boston Bees from 1936 to 1940. Just before the 1953 season, they lit out for Milwaukee and stayed 12 years, moving to Atlanta in 1966. In 1977, they began playing for owner Ted Turner.

Boston Red Sox (American League): founded as the Boston Americans in 1901, unconnected with the Boston Red Stockings, who became the modern Atlanta Braves. They've been playing as the Boston Red Sox since 1908. Other early names, such as Pilgrims, were in fact rarely used and not official.

Baltimore Orioles (AL): started play as the Milwaukee Brewers in 1901 (finishing last), then became the St. Louis Browns. Deciding that 52 years of bad baseball in one place would suffice, the team became the Baltimore Orioles in 1954—honoring a rough-and-tumble 1890s team by that name, though without direct succession.

Chicago Cubs (NA/NL): once the Chicago White Stockings (1876–1889), then Colts (1890–1897), then Orphans (1898–1901). In 1902, they finally settled on the name they still carry today.

Chicago White Sox (AL): grabbed the Cubs' old nickname (White Stockings) in 1901 on their founding, then took the official abbreviation of White Sox in 1904. If you want to have fun with Sox fans, just point out that their name is actually an old Cubs nickname.

Cincinnati Reds (American Association/NL): formerly the Red Stockings (1882–1889), then the Reds. During the McCarthy years (1954–1958), they quietly became the Cincinnati Redlegs, lest a team playing the American national pastime hint at a Bolshevik take-over. They soon resumed the nickname "Reds."

Cleveland Indians (AL): born the Cleveland Blues in 1901, called Broncos in 1902, then became the Naps in 1903 to honor star Nap Lajoie. After trading Lajoie in 1914, the team took its current name.

Los Angeles Angels (AL): began play in 1961, but in 1965 they became the California Angels, now playing in Anaheim. Thirty years later it was time for a change, so they became the Anaheim Angels. Since 2005, the team has officially been the Los Angeles Angels of Anaheim.

Los Angeles Dodgers (AA/NL): began as the Brooklyn Atlantics in 1884 and were often called the Trolley Dodgers. They would play as the Grays, Bridegrooms, Grooms, Superbas, Infants, and Dodgers— all before World War I! In 1914, they became the Robins (after man-ager Wilbert Robinson), then went back to Dodgers in 1932. After the 1957 season, their owner moved them to Los Angeles.

Milwaukee Brewers (AL/NL): started as the Seattle Pilots in 1969. After giving Emerald City ball fans a season of futile baseball in Sicks Stadium (today the spot is a hardware store), they fled to Milwaukee in haste for the 1970 season. When major league baseball expanded in 1998, a team had to switch leagues, and the Brew Crew moved to the National League.

Minnesota Twins (AL): began in the District of Columbia as the Washington Senators but were also periodically called the Nationals— from 1905 to 1906 the name even appeared on their jerseys. How could this nebulous situation be? Especially before 1920, nicknames were more fluid, and teams were often called by their city names: "The Bostons defeated the Detroits." In 1961, the Senators/some-time Nationals moved to their current Minneapolis home.

New York Yankees (AL): began (in 1901) as one of several Baltimore Orioles franchises in Major League Baseball. Moving to the Bronx in 1903, they became the New York Highlanders. The name Yankees gradually supplanted Highlanders, becoming official in 1913.

Oakland Athletics (AL): started play as the Philadelphia Athletics in 1901, and in 1955 they became the Kansas City Athletics, an informal Yankee farm team sending promising players to the Bronx in exchange for declining veterans. They moved to Oakland in 1968, then became a dynasty. They've also been called A's since they began.

Philadelphia Phillies (NL): started as the Philadelphia Quakers in 1883, but by 1890 the popular Phillies nickname was official. It has stayed that way except for 1943–1944, when they were called the Blue Jays.

Pittsburgh Pirates (AA/NL): Go Alleghenys! In 1882, that's how they were born—just Alleghenys, spelled thus, not Pittsburgh anything. Soon the Pittsburgh designation took over. Briefly called Innocents in 1890, they were then called Pirates for supposedly stealing a player from another team. That name sticks to this day.

St. Louis Cardinals (AA/NL): used to be the Brown Stockings (1882)—those were the days of flamboyant, creative, egomaniacal owner Chris von der Ahe. The team quickly became the Browns. In 1899, someone decided to rename them the Perfectos, but that was too dumb to stick. The next year they became Cardinals.

Texas Rangers (AL): started in 1961 as the new Washington Senators (the old Sens having run off to Minnesota) and underwhelmed the baseball world throughout the decade. The team left for Arlington, Texas, for the 1972 season and became the Rangers.

Washington Nationals (NL): started in 1969 as the *Expos de Montréal* but never quite seemed to fit there. In 1977, they took bad baseball locations to the next level by moving to *Stade Olympique*, with its dysfunctional retractable roof. Local interest got so bad that from 2003 to 2004, they played some home games in Puerto Rico. The ownership disconnected the Expos from the Montreal respirator for the 2005 season, moving to D.C. and reviving the old Nationals name.

I'm No Expert, But...
PHILOSOPHIES

✳ ✳ ✳ ✳

*To make more sense of the cosmos and human relationships
(among other curiosities), people often turn to philosophers.
But what did these guys know, anyway?*

Q: Was Machiavelli the author of new levels of conniving evil?

A: Most would say no. Niccolò Machiavelli was a patriot during the
Renaissance, when his beloved city-state of Florence was caught
between Venice, Milan, France, Spain, the Papal States, and several
other greedy enemies. He believed in using all practical methods
to further the lot of one's own people and nation, being humane
when possible and rough when necessary. His bad reputation largely
comes from the Catholic Church, which banned his writings—an act
of hippocracy, given the political climate of the time.

Q: How did Socrates view the world?

A: He didn't leave us any writings, so we only know from the words
of others. Socratic thought questioned everything: religion, politics,
dogmas, and, "things everybody knows." He questioned not merely
conclusions but the underlying assumptions, annoying the power
structure of ancient Athens.

Q: Nietzsche: proto-Nazi?

A: That would be a bold assertion, but Nietzsche certainly believed
in the morality of power; he glorified strength and despised weakness. Primarily, he advocated the development of superior beings.
But in his last years, he started to suggest outlandish things that even
Nazis wouldn't have liked, including the fact that European powers
should all invade Germany.

Q: What's Neo-Platonism?

A: Neo-Platonism arose in the third century. Since then, it has
evolved from the version advanced by the philosophers Plotinus
and Porphyry, who interpreted Plato their own way. Neo-Platonism

had a religious bent, advocating Monism—the belief that there is a transcendent one divinity immensely superior to all lesser divinities, angels, and so on. Thomas Taylor, to better distinguish Plotinus's thought from Plato's original, came up with the term "Neo-Platonism" in the 19th century.

Q: Aleister Crowley proclaimed himself the biblical "Great Beast." What did he believe?

A: Crowley liked to shock people. He founded a philosophy called Thelema (Greek for "will"), which has adherents today. Its founding and core statement: "Do what thou wilt shall be the whole of the law." That sounds anarchic, but Crowley was advocating that each person should define and seek his or her own highest purpose in life. He was only a beast to those who believed we should live strictly regimented and carefully pious lives.

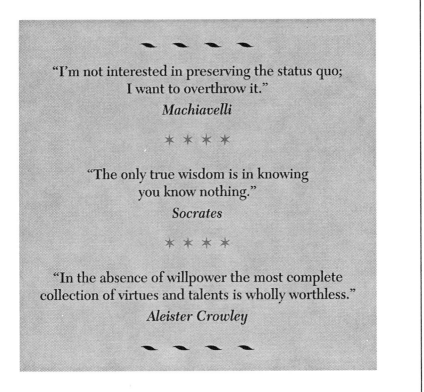

"I'm not interested in preserving the status quo; I want to overthrow it."
Machiavelli

* * * *

"The only true wisdom is in knowing you know nothing."
Socrates

* * * *

"In the absence of willpower the most complete collection of virtues and talents is wholly worthless."
Aleister Crowley

COCO CHANEL

✳ ✳ ✳ ✳

- "Coco" was the nickname for this revolutionary fashion designer. Her actual first name was Gabrielle.

- Chanel opened her first shop in Paris in 1909, where she sold hats. In 1910, she moved to the Rue Cambon, where the House of Chanel remains to this day.

- Before Chanel, black was a color of mourning only; after she began to work with it, black became synonymous with chic.

- The concept we have of the classic little black dress is credited to Coco herself, in addition to sweater sets, pleated skirts, triangular scarves, and fake pearls.

- Chanel couldn't actually sew, but she did possess a great skill for draping and pinning. She would pin the garment the way she wanted it to look and then hand it to her workers to create.

- When Coco returned from vacation with a dark tan in the 1920s, tanning quickly became a symbol of wealth and leisure. Prior to this, no proper woman would expose her delicate, pale skin to the sun. Chanel also produced the first artificial suntan lotion.

- Chanel No. 5 perfume was introduced in 1921. The number was chosen because it was the fifth sample presented to Chanel and the one she liked best.

- In 1945, Chanel lived in exile in Switzerland after she became romantically involved with a Nazi officer.

- People said of Chanel, "She knows what a woman wants to wear before the woman knows it herself."

- The average cost of a Chanel suit today is $5,000, and they are available only at Chanel boutiques or exclusive department stores.

- The haute couture House of Chanel now produces clothing designed by Karl Lagerfeld for Chanel.

ODD THINGS ABOUT THE 1900 OLYMPICS

✳ ✳ ✳ ✳

The second modern Olympic Games were held in 1900 in Paris and were billed as part of the Exposition Universelle Internationale, *the world's fair that featured the unveiling of the Eiffel Tower. It was the first Olympiad to be held outside of Greece, and there were plenty of other firsts to it, as well.*

- Despite the fact that more than a thousand athletes competed in the 1900 Olympics, spectator attendance was low. The press preferred to focus on the Paris Exposition and seldom referred to the games as actual Olympic events. Instead, they were reported variously as "International Championships," "Paris Championships," "World Championships," and even "Grand Prix of the Paris Exposition." The founder of the International Olympic Committee, Baron Pierre de Coubertin, later said: "It's a miracle that the Olympic movement survived that celebration."

- The Olympic status of the athletes was equally downplayed, to the extent that many competitors never actually knew they were participating in the Olympics. Margaret Ives Abbott, a student from Chicago who won the nine-hole women's golf tournament, died in 1955 without realizing she was America's first female Olympic champion.

- Because the Olympics were held in conjunction with the Paris Exhibition, the scheduling and locations of the sporting events were often absurd. The fencing competition, for instance, was held as a sort of sideshow in the exhibition's cutlery area, and swimmers were forced to battle the polluted waters and strong currents of the Seine River.

- After preliminary rounds, Myer Prinstein (from Syracuse University) had a clear lead in the long-jump competition and seemed poised to win. But when the final jump was scheduled on a Sunday, the official in charge of U.S. athletes disapproved of their competing on the Christian Sabbath. The athletes gave their word not to participate; Prinstein, who was Jewish, reluctantly agreed as well. On Sunday, however, Prinstein's main rival, Alvin Kraenzlein (University of Pennsylvania), broke his promise and competed, beating Prinstein's qualifying jump by a centimeter and winning the gold. Allegedly, Prinstein was so angry that he punched Kraenzlein in the face.

- Alvin Kraenzlein also won the 110-meter hurdles, the 220-meter hurdles, and the 60-meter dash—all in three days. As of 2007, he was still the only track-and-field athlete to have won four gold medals in individual events at a single Olympics.

- Women made their first appearance in the 1900 Games, albeit in small numbers: Of the thousand or so athletes participating, only 19 were women. The first female Olympic champion was Charlotte Cooper of Great Britain, who won the tennis singles and the mixed doubles. Female athletes wore the ankle-length skirts and dresses typical of the time.

- Ray Ewry of Indiana won the gold in three championships— standing high jump, standing long jump, and standing triple jump—all on the same day. A remarkable feat for any man, these victories amounted to Olympic heroism for Ewry, who had spent his childhood confined to a wheelchair because of polio.

- After the French won both gold and silver medals in the marathon, three runners from the United States contested the results, accusing the winners of taking a short cut. As proof, they submitted their observation that the new champions were the only contestants not splattered with mud. Although the objection was not sustained, the celebratory spirit had been soured.

- The 1900 Olympics saw the Games' youngest champion. On August 26, two Dutch rowers suddenly needed a replacement coxswain and chose a French boy, undoubtedly because of his small size. The pair rowed to a close victory, and the boy joined them in the victory ceremony. He then disappeared, but a photograph taken of the boy and the rowers indicates that he could have been as young as ten years old.

Fast Facts

- *There is a National Fancy Rat Society.*

- *Teddy Roosevelt kept pet rats in the White House.*

- *The average lifespan of a rat is less than three years, but one pair can produce 2,000 offspring in a year.*

- *Health officials in China feed feral rats flavored birth-control pills.*

- *A group of rats is called a mischief.*

- *One pair of rats shed more than a million body hairs each year, and a single rat can produce 25,000 droppings in a year.*

- *It's a myth that rats like cheese. In fact, they're lactose intolerant and can't digest dairy.*

- *Some rats can enter an opening as small as a half-inch wide.*

- *Each year, rats cause more than $1 billion in damages in the United States alone.*

- *Some rats can swim as far as half a mile in open water, dive through water-plumbing traps, travel in sewer lines against strong currents, and stay underwater for as long as three minutes.*

- *Rats constantly gnaw anything softer than their teeth, including bricks, wood, and aluminum sheeting.*

- *A rat can fall 50 feet without injury. What's more, rats can jump 36 inches vertically and 48 inches horizontally.*

- *Rats use their tails to regulate their temperature, to communicate, and to balance.*

- *Rats are intelligent and have excellent memories. Once rats learn a route, they never forget it.*

- *Rats are colorblind and cannot vomit or burp.*

THE EARLY DAYS OF VIDEO GAMES

✳ ✳ ✳ ✳

*Today's die-hard video gamers might chuckle at the
concept of playing a simple game of table tennis on a TV screen.
But without* Pong, *there might not be* Grand Theft Auto: Vice City.
*Read about the early history of the video game and
marvel at how far the industry has come.*

Spacewar—At MIT in 1962, Steve Russell programmed the world's
first video game on a bulky computer known as the DEC PDP-1.
Spacewar featured spaceships fighting amid an astronomically correct screen full of stars. The technological fever spread quickly, and
by the end of the decade, nearly every research computer in the
United States had a copy of *Spacewar* on it.

Pong—Nolan Bushnell founded Atari in 1972, taking the company's
name from the Japanese word for the chess term "check." Atari
released the coin-operated *Pong* later that year, and its simple, addictive action of bouncing a pixel ball between two paddles became
an instant arcade hit. In 1975, the TV-console version of *Pong* was
released. It was received with great enthusiasm by people who could
play hours of the tennislike game in the comfort of their homes.

Tetris—After runaway success in the Soviet Union in 1985 (and in
spite of the Cold War), *Tetris* jumped the Bering Strait and took over
the U.S. market the next year. Invented by Soviet mathematician
Alexi Pajitnov, the game features simple play—turning and dropping
geometric shapes into tightly packed rows—that drew in avid fans in
both countries. Many gamers call *Tetris* the most addictive game of
all time.

Space Invaders—Released in 1978, Midway's *Space Invaders* was
the arcade equivalent of *Star Wars:* a ubiquitous hit that generated a
lot of money. It also presented the "high score" concept. A year later,
Atari released *Asteroids* and outdid *Space Invaders* by enabling the
high scorer to enter his or her initials for posterity.

Pac-Man—The 1980 Midway classic is the world's most successful arcade game, selling some 99,000 units. Featuring the yellow maw of the title character, a maze of dots, and four colorful ghosts, the game inspired rap songs, Saturday morning cartoons, and a slew of sequels.

Donkey Kong—In 1980, Nintendo's first game marked the debut of Mario, soon to become one of the most recognizable fictional characters in the world. Originally dubbed Jumpman, Mario was named for Mario Segali, the onetime owner of Nintendo's warehouse in Seattle.

Q*bert—Released by Gottlieb in 1982, this game featured the title character jumping around on a pyramid of cubes, squashing and dodging enemies. Designers originally wanted *Q*bert* to shoot slime from his nose, but it was deemed too gross.

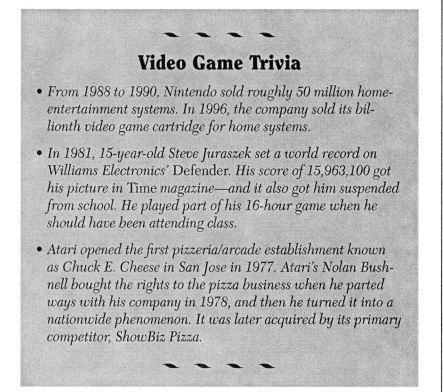

Video Game Trivia

- *From 1988 to 1990, Nintendo sold roughly 50 million home-entertainment systems. In 1996, the company sold its billionth video game cartridge for home systems.*

- *In 1981, 15-year-old Steve Juraszek set a world record on Williams Electronics' Defender. His score of 15,963,100 got his picture in Time magazine—and it also got him suspended from school. He played part of his 16-hour game when he should have been attending class.*

- *Atari opened the first pizzeria/arcade establishment known as Chuck E. Cheese in San Jose in 1977. Atari's Nolan Bushnell bought the rights to the pizza business when he parted ways with his company in 1978, and then he turned it into a nationwide phenomenon. It was later acquired by its primary competitor, ShowBiz Pizza.*

THE BIG CHEESE

✳ ✳ ✳ ✳

- Archaeological surveys show that cheese was being made from the milk of cows and goats in Mesopotamia before 6000 B.C.

- Travelers from Asia are thought to have brought the art of cheese making to Europe, where the process was adapted and improved in European monasteries.

- The Pilgrims included cheese in their supplies onboard the Mayflower in 1620.

- The world's largest consumers of cheese include Greece (63 pounds per person each year), France (54 pounds), Iceland (53 pounds), Germany (48 pounds), Italy (44 pounds), the Netherlands (40 pounds), the United States (31 pounds), Australia (27 pounds), and Canada (26 pounds).

- The United States produces more than 25 percent of the world's supply of cheese, approximately 9 billion pounds per year.

- The only cheeses native to the United States are American, jack, brick, and colby. All other types are modeled after cheeses brought to the country by European settlers.

- The top five cheese producers in the United States are Wisconsin (more than 2.4 billion pounds annually), California (2.1 billion pounds), Idaho (770.6 million pounds), New York (666.8 million pounds), and Minnesota (629.3 million pounds). These states account for 72 percent of the country's cheese production.

- Processed American cheese was developed in 1915 by J. L. Kraft (founder of Kraft Foods) as an alternative to the traditional cheeses that had a short shelf life.

- Pizza Hut uses about 300 million pounds of cheese per year.

- Someone who sells cheese professionally at a cheese shop or specialty food store is called a cheese monger.

- In 1886, the University of Wisconsin introduced one of the country's first cheese-making education programs. Today, you can take cheese-making courses through a variety of university agricultural programs, dairy farms, and cheese factories.

- Because of their ability to produce large volumes of milk, butter-fat, and protein, black-and-white (or sometimes red-and-white) Holsteins are the most popular dairy cows in the United States, making up 90 percent of the total herd.

- A one-ounce serving of cheese is about the size of four dice.

- June is National Dairy Month, and the last week in June is National Cheese Week.

- The Cheese Days celebration in Monroe, Wisconsin, has been held every other year since 1914. Highlights include a 400-pound wheel of Swiss cheese and the world's largest cheese fondue.

- Founded in 1882, the Crowley Cheese Factory in Healdville, Vermont, is the nation's oldest cheese maker still in operation.

- The Chalet Cheese Co-op in Monroe, Wisconsin, is the only cheese factory in the country that still makes the famously stinky Limburger cheese.

- Maytag Dairy Farms, maker of the award-winning Maytag Blue cheese, was founded by the same Iowa family that manufactures the popular home appliances.

- The Sargento Cheese Company in Plymouth, Wisconsin, introduced packaged shredded cheese in 1958. In 1986, the company went even further to ensure the "spread of the shred" by introducing the resealable bag.

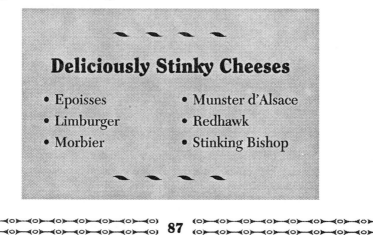

Deliciously Stinky Cheeses

- Epoisses
- Limburger
- Morbier
- Munster d'Alsace
- Redhawk
- Stinking Bishop

SILK: SOFT AS A BABY'S SKIN, STRONG AS STEEL

✻ ✻ ✻ ✻

Silk is odd stuff. It's made out of cocoons, it looks wonderful, and it's deceptively strong. If not for the cocoon part, it might be the perfect analogy to femininity. These facts explain why silk has long connoted beauty, wealth, and power.

- According to legend, a Chinese Imperial concubine named Xi Ling-Shi discovered silk more than 4,500 years ago, when Rome was a sheep pasture and Babylon a place of glory. Xi was having tea under a mulberry tree when a cocoon plopped into her cup. Its fibers magically unraveled, revealing their strength and versatility.

- The Silk Road, named for its prized commodity, was a trade route between Asia and Europe that began around 200 B.C.

- Until well after the fall of the Roman Empire, China maintained a monopoly on silk. Although death was the penalty for silkworm smuggling, people were undeterred and snuck them out anyway.

- A strand of silk is stronger than a strand of steel the same diameter. If you're tied up with silk rope, consider yourself held by steel cable.

- The silk fiber in a typical cocoon unrolls to a length of more than three football fields, or 360 yards. Some cocoons unroll to almost a mile long.

- To produce a pound of silk, you need about one-tenth of an ounce of silkworm eggs, which will hatch into 2,000 silkworms.

- The art of silk production is called sericulture.

- In proper sericulture, the sericin must be removed from the silk fiber. This substance is a natural gum that protects the fiber but attracts and holds dirt and stains. It's great for the silkworm larva but not for a bridal gown.

- Silk's density is measured in mommes, abbreviated "mm." Weigh a bolt of silk 45 inches wide and 100 yards long. The bolt's weight in pounds is the mm rating of the silk.

- Raw silk begins at a density of about 40 mm. The lightest silks may weigh 5 mm or less.

- Wild-gathered silk cocoons are less economical to work with, because the larva damages the fibers as it gnaws its way to hatching.

- When you weave copper foil in with it, silk thread can conduct electricity—a fact that may suggest computerized clothing of the future.

- Like many fabrics, silk has a back and a front. The properties of each side tell what sort of silk it is.

- As a woven fabric, silk has a warp and weft. The warp refers to the lengthwise threads; the weft describes the crosswise threads.

- That silky shimmer comes from the fibers' triangular shape. It's too small to see without magnification, but this prismatic quality bounces back incoming light at different angles.

- *Raw silk* refers to any silk without the sericin removed.

- *Charmeuse* is one of the most common kinds of silk: a shimmering weave on the front, a flattened crepe on the back.

- *Dupioni* silk comes from cocoons spun by two worms "working" together, making the thread double strength.

- In India, some sericulturists use only wild and semi-wild silkworm cocoons to produce *ahimsa* silk. The silk is extracted from the cocoon after the silkworm has metamorphosed and left the cocoon, sparing the silkworm's life.

- *Tussah* silk comes from a wild silkworm that eats oak and juniper leaves and produces a large cocoon.

- Glossy *taffeta*, a plain-weave silk, can be made with different colors for the warp and weft, creating an interesting visual effect.

- *Organza* owes its crisp texture to the tight twist of its thread.

- *Chiffon* is the lightest silk, airy, transparent, and delicate.

I'm No Expert, But...
THE UPPER ATMOSPHERE

✳ ✳ ✳ ✳

Q: What's ozone?

A: It's oxygen. Honest. The oxygen we breathe is O_2, a fairly stable chemical compound of two oxygen atoms. Ozone is O_3 and is much less stable (breaks up more easily). Passing electricity through breathable oxygen can produce ozone; it has an acrid smell and it hurts to breathe. It is toxic, even lethal in significant concentrations.

Q: Why does it help to have a layer of ozone?

A: As long as it's about 9 to 20 miles up in the stratosphere, where you won't get a lungful of it, ozone filters out the most harmful wavelengths of the sun's ultraviolet (UV) light. If pollutants react with the ozone, there's less of it to stop the incoming UVs, so you have an "ozone hole" where the UV light gets through to cause harm.

Q: Can the ozone layer recover on its own?

A: Under normal circumstances it does, with O_3 constantly changing to O_2 and back to O_3 as UVs hit it. Many of the offending pollutants are now banned, but the residue may stick around and cause trouble for 50 to 100 years. So if we leave it alone, yes, it'll recover in time.

Q: What's in the ionosphere?

A: Not much—it begins about 50 miles up and tops out at roughly 250 miles as the outermost layer of Earth's atmosphere. It varies quite a bit. We bounce radio waves off it so that you can ignore the stifling monotony of your daily commute.

Q: What's in the bathysphere?

A: We should hope it consists of people and oxygen. A bathysphere is a manmade ultra-deep-sea diving container, not part of the atmosphere. But kids can ask their parents about this one and see if they just make something up.

CURIOUS CREATURES AMONG US

* * * *

- When some types of frogs vomit, their entire stomach comes out. The frog then cleans out the contents and swallows the empty stomach.

- Pacific Island robber crabs love coconuts so much that they have developed the ability to climb trees to satisfy their cravings.

- The water-holding frog is the greatest survivor in the animal kingdom. When it rains, the frog absorbs water through the skin. It then burrows into the sand, where it can live for up to two years off its water reserve.

- The praying mantis is the only insect that can turn its head 360 degrees.

- A chameleon can focus its eyes separately to watch two objects at once. This lizard also has a tongue that is longer than its body.

- The eyes of the ostrich and the dragonfly are bigger than their brains.

- The electric eel can produce 350 to 550 volts of electricity up to 150 times per hour without any apparent fatigue.

- Spider silk is five times stronger than steel, but it is also highly elastic—a rare combination in materials. Silk stretches 30 percent farther than the most elastic nylon.

- A large parrot's beak can exert 500 pounds of pressure per square inch, enabling the bird to feast on such delicacies as Brazil nuts with a simple crunch.

- The extinct Madagascan elephant bird laid eggs as large as 13 inches in length and 9 inches in diameter. Today, ostriches lay the largest eggs, up to 8 inches in length and 6 inches in diameter.

- The arctic tern is the world's greatest migrator. During a trek between Antarctica and North America, this tiny bird will cover around 11,000 miles at an average of 120 miles per day.

- Wasps can make paper by mixing wood pulp with saliva to form a paste, which dries stiff.

THE NEW YORK TIMES

✳ ✳ ✳ ✳

- *The New York Times* newspaper has a daily circulation of more than 1 million, with a Sunday circulation of about 1.6 million.

- Since 1896, four generations of the Ochs-Sulzberger family have published *The New York Times.*

- The *Times* is often referred to as "the Gray Lady" for its sober editing style and appearance.

- The paper, originally called *The New-York Daily Times,* was founded in 1851 by politician/journalist Henry Jarvis Raymond and George Jones, a banker.

- The *Times* has won more than 90 Pulitzer Prizes (far more than any other paper in the world), some of which have included accolades for its coverage of the Vietnam War and reports on the Pentagon Papers.

- In 2003, Jayson Blair, a *Times* reporter, was found to have fabricated and/or plagarized some 36 news stories. The scandal tarnished the paper's reputation and prompted the resignation of executive editor Howell Raines, among others.

- NYTimes.com consistently ranks among the ten most popular Internet news sites on the web. The paper went online in 1996.

- It's estimated that the *Times's* editorial spending is in excess of $300 million a year.

- There are close to 1,000 reporters and editors on *The New York Times* staff.

- The *Times* might be the most respected, but it's not the top-selling paper in the United States. That distinction goes to *USA Today,* which has a daily circulation of more than 2 million.

- Papers such as the *Times* and the *Wall Street Journal* offer regional editions printed by local contractors. These are usually the editions available in airport newsstands, for example.

UTOPIAN SOCIETIES

✳ ✳ ✳ ✳

In 1516, Sir Thomas More coined the term utopia *in a book of the same name. In it he refers to an ideal, imaginary island where everything is lovely all the time. For centuries since then, groups of people (often led by fanatical figures) have broken off from society to develop their own communities intended to bring peace, harmony, and spiritual enlightenment to all their citizens—and ultimately the whole world. Unfortunately, utopian societies seldom work out as planned.*

Founder: Charles Fourier
Plan: In the mid-19th century, Fourier contacted out-of-work New Englanders with the proposition of joining communal-living groups he called "phalanxes." These groups would be arranged hierarchically according to members' trades or skills. Children are good at digging in the dirt, for example, so they would be in charge of maintaining the garbage dumps. Group members would be compensated for their contributions to the community.
Outcome: Fournier died in Paris before he saw the development of any phalanxes. In the early 1840s, a group of devotees, or Fourierists, founded the North American Phalanx and kept it going until disputes over women's rights and abolition drove many away. A fire destroyed the site in 1854.

Founder: Robert Owen
Plan: Owen called his version of utopia New Harmony and hoped his "empire of goodwill" would eventually take over the planet. His attempt at communal bliss started in Indiana in 1825.
Outcome: Hundreds of devoted followers lived according to Owen's ideals, with individual members plying their crafts and contributing to the community (even if that meant there was no one with the ability to spin the wool shorn by an abundance of sheepshearers). With no sound economic plan, New Harmony was in chaos from the start. There were five constitutions drafted in the first year alone.

Founder: The Spiritualists
Plan: The Mountain Cove Community was the Spiritualists' attempt to create their own idea of harmony. They founded their group

in Virginia in 1851 on a spot once considered to be the Garden of Eden. The group insisted that no one individual would be allowed to dictate to others; all the direction anyone needed would come from "the spirits."

Outcome: As part of their introduction into the community, members were required to give up all their possessions, again leaving issues such as finances to the spirit world. Not surprisingly, the experiment lasted less than two years.

Founder: Etienne Cabet
Plan: Cabet's *Voyage en Icarie,* written in 1840, depicted an ideal society, the Icarians, in which an elected government controlled all economic activity as well as social affairs. Cabet decided to make his dream a reality and set sail for America.
Outcome: The group landed outside New Orleans on swampland not fit for settlement. Malaria and starvation took many of this group of Icarians, and the rest deserted.

Founder: The Shakers
Plan: The Shakers were an 18th-century religious denomination of Protestants who decided to leave the immoral world behind and create a pious place in which to live and serve God.
Outcome: By the mid-1800s, the Shakers had built 19 communal settlements that attracted some 200,000 followers. Their numbers gradually dwindled, but their simple way of life continues to attract widespread interest. The Shakers are generally considered to be one of the few successful utopian societies.

"Nearly all creators of Utopia have resembled the man who has toothache, and therefore thinks happiness consists in not having toothache.... Whoever tries to imagine perfection simply reveals his own emptiness."

George Orwell, *Why Socialists Don't Believe in Fun*

THINGS YOU NEVER KNEW
ABOUT THE PENNY

✳ ✳ ✳

We collect them in jars, make them appear magically behind people's ears, and long for the days when a handful would get us a candy bar at the corner store. We handle thousands of them every year, but how much do we know about the familiar penny?

- Since they were introduced in 1787, more than 300 billion pennies have been produced. Today, there are about 150 billion pennies in circulation, enough to circle the earth 137 times.

- Since 1909, Abraham Lincoln has been the star of the penny, but it wasn't always that way. There have been 11 different designs, including the popular Indian Head penny introduced in 1859.

- The princess on the Indian Head penny was neither an American Indian nor a princess. She was, in fact, the sculptor's daughter, Sarah Longacre.

- On the 200th anniversary of Lincoln's birth, the U.S. Mint will introduce pennies that depict four different representations of his life. These will replace the Lincoln Memorial on the penny.

- Examine the faces on a penny, an original Jefferson nickel, a dime, and a quarter. All the presidents except Lincoln are facing left. People have long imagined a secret meaning behind this, but Victor David Brenner, the sculptor of the Lincoln penny, explained that he had worked from a photo of Lincoln facing to the right. Simple as that.

- If you have a strong magnifying glass, you can see the initials of the sculptors who designed the pennies. Since 1959, the initials of Frank Gasparro have been near the shrubbery to the right of the Lincoln Memorial. Pennies dated 1918 to 1958 have the initials VDB (Victor David Brenner) under Lincoln's shoulder.

- Pennies haven't been made of pure copper since 1864. During World War II, the U.S. Mint helped the war effort by recycling:

It melted shell casings to make pennies. To conserve further, it considered creating plastic pennies but settled on zinc-covered steel. After the war, the Mint returned to a zinc-and-copper combination.

- Pennies have become a popular souvenir thanks to the penny-press machines at museums, amusement parks, and family vacation spots. These machines, introduced at Chicago's World Fair in 1893, flatten and elongate a penny between two rollers and imprint a new image—anything from an octopus to the Liberty Bell to Mickey Mouse. Each year these machines roll out more than 12 million pennies into fun oval shapes.

- Money is shrinking—and not just in value. When the penny was introduced in 1787, it was about twice the size of today's version. The penny didn't reach its current size until 1857.

- See a penny, pick it up. There are about forty 1943 copper pennies in existence. One sold in 1999 for $112,500.

- You can't use pennies to pay your fare at tollbooths—unless you're in Illinois. Lincoln's home state has a soft spot for pennies.

- A coin toss isn't a game of luck if you use a penny and call heads. The penny is the only coin with the face of the same person on both sides. A magnifying glass will reveal Lincoln sitting inside the Lincoln Memorial.

- Could the penny be relegated to the endangered-coin list? Because the price of metals is rising, it now costs more than a cent to make a penny. It costs only about four cents to make a $100 bill.

- Pennies got their reputation as being lucky from the Victorian wedding saying "Something old, something new, something borrowed, something blue, and a silver sixpence in your shoe." In the United States, the penny replaced the sixpence as a guard against want for the newlywed couple.

- The nickname for a U.S. cent in 1839 was "Silly Head," because people thought the image of Miss Liberty on the front looked strange.

Talk to the Expert
COIN POLISHER

✳ ✳ ✳ ✳

Why would anyone hire someone to polish coins? Is the average person really that impressed by shiny nickels? We poked around to reveal the logic behind this peculiar practice.

Q: Who actually employs a professional coin polisher?

A: One place is the St. Francis, one of the older hotels in San Francisco. This hotel represents big money—in 2000, it sold for $243 million. The St. Francis a very luxurious hotel. When you have that kind of an image, you add little touches—such as polished coins.

Q: All right. The question is, why?

A: The practice goes back to the 1930s. Consider the type of client who could afford the St. Francis: In those days, if the patron was a woman, she might wear white gloves. You probably know how incredibly filthy money is, but also remember that coins bought more in those days, so it was more common to pay in silver and copper. Women started to complain that the hotel's coins soiled their gloves.

Q: How does one do the coin laundry?

A: It's a big operation that washes some 20,000 coins every day. If there are 50 pennies, 40 nickels, 50 dimes, and 40 quarters in their respective rolls, that's 180 coins. Multiply that by more than 100, some days almost 150, and that's how many coins get washed. The St. Francis has special machines that soak the coins, wash them with detergent and lead pellets, rinse, dry, and sort them.

Q: I wonder why coin collectors haven't thought of that.

A: Coin collectors don't clean coins, or at least they're not supposed to. St. Francis money is kind of a San Francisco trademark. You can spot them around town in a blinding flash, because a brand new coin from the bank is shiny but unworn. A flat-worn older quarter that shines like new is more than likely from the St. Francis.

LET'S SETTLE THIS: HISTORY'S SHORTEST WARS

✳ ✳ ✳ ✳

As wars grow costlier and transportation gets faster, battles compress the same level of tragedy into shorter durations. Most consider World War II to have been one big conflict, but for many smaller nations the main conflict amounted to a solo war between themselves and Nazi Germany. Here are some of the shortest conflicts in history.

Anglo-Zanzibar War (9:02–9:40 A.M., August 27, 1896, Great Britain versus Zanzibar): The British liked it when the Sultan of Zanzibar (an island off modern Tanzania) engaged in battles. When a new sultan named Khalid bin Barghash refused to, the Royal Navy gave Zanzibar a taste of British anger. Bin Barghash tapped out after just 38 minutes of shelling in what is the shortest recorded war.

Spanish-American War (April 25–August 12, 1898, United States versus Spain): Spain once had an empire, some of which was very near Florida. After months of tension, the battleship USS *Maine* blew up in Havana harbor. Though no one knew why it exploded, the United States declared war anyway. A few months later, Spain had lost Cuba, Guam, the Philippines, and Puerto Rico.

Nazi-Polish War (September 1–October 6, 1939, Nazi Germany and Soviet Union versus Poland): After Russian and German negotiators signed a secret agreement in August for the division of Poland, the Nazis invaded in vicious armored thrusts with heavy air attacks. Polish forces fought with uncommon valor, but their strategic position was impossible. Russian troops entered from the east on September 17, and Poland became the first European nation conquered in World War II.

Nazi-Danish War (4:15–9:20 A.M., April 9, 1940, Nazi Germany versus Denmark): Arguably the biggest mismatch of World War II (unless one counts Germany's invasion of Luxembourg). Sixteen Danish soldiers died before the Danish government ordered the resistance to cease.

Suez/Sinai War (October 29–November 6, 1956, Israel, Britain, and France versus Egypt): The Egyptians decided to nationalize the Suez Canal, which seems logical today given that the Suez is entirely in Egypt. British and French companies operating the canal didn't agree. The Israelis invaded by land, the British and French by air and sea. The invaders won a complete military victory, but the rest of world got so mad at them that they withdrew under international pressure.

Six-Day War (June 5–10, 1967, Israel versus Egypt, Syria, and Jordan): Israelis launched a sneak attack on the Egyptians, destroying the Egyptian air force on its airfields and sending the Egyptians reeling back toward the Suez Canal. Jordanians attacked the Israelis and immediately regretted it. The Israelis attacked Syria and seized Golan Heights.

Yom Kippur War (October 6–25, 1973, Egypt and Syria versus Israel): Egyptians and Syrians, still annoyed and embarrassed over the Six-Day War, attacked Israelis on a national religious holiday. Israeli forces were caught napping at first but soon regained the upper hand—they struck within artillery range of Damascus and crossed the Suez Canal. The United Nations' ceasefire came as a major relief to all involved, even the Israelis, who had no desire to administer Cairo and Damascus.

Soccer War (July 15–19, 1969, El Salvador versus Honduras): Immigration was the core issue, specifically the forced expulsion of some 60,000 Salvadorean illegal immigrants from Honduras. When a soccer series between the two Central American nations fueled tensions, each managed to insult the other enough to start a bloody yet inconclusive war.

Falklands War (March 19–June 14, 1982, Argentina versus United Kingdom): Argentina has long claimed the Falkland Islands as *Las Islas Malvinas*. In 1982, Argentina decided to enforce this claim by invading the Falklands and South Georgia. Although the Argentines had a surprise for the Royal Navy in the form of air-launched anti-ship missiles, the battle for the islands went heavily against Argentina. Its survivors, including most of its marines, were shipped back home minus their weaponry.

STAR WORDS

* * * *

When discussing astronomy, someone invariably mentions black holes, quasars, supernovas, or white dwarfs, among other references. Though we tend to nod knowingly, in fact, most of us haven't a clue what these terms mean. Help has arrived.

Galaxy: This is a large group of stars rotating around a central nucleus. Ours, the Milky Way, is part of a 20-fold cluster that clings together like a bunch of grapes. In 1920, we learned that the Sun was not the center of our galaxy, as we had previously assumed. Soon after that, powerful telescopes revealed a host of other galaxies, and humankind began to comprehend the immensity of the universe. Just how big is our galaxy? Traveling at the speed of light, it would take 100,000 years to cross it. The Sun, situated toward the outer edge of the galaxy, takes 200 million years to complete its orbit around the galactic center.

Nebula: This is the name given to an interstellar cloud of gas and dust. Nebulas are among the most beautiful objects in the night sky. Within nebulas, new stars are born when the diffuse matter condenses under the force of gravity into contracting regions of gas. These huge balls of gas stabilize when they reach the temperature at which nuclear reactions begin in the core of the cloud, preventing further contraction. Thus, a star is born, often in conjunction with others. Combined, these make up a star cluster.

Red giant: After a star has burned out its hydrogen supplies (which could take billions of years), the core contracts. The outer layer of the star then expands and becomes cooler, giving off a reddish glow. These red giants are up to ten times larger than our Sun. When the Sun has exhausted its hydrogen supplies (in about 5 billion years), it will become a red giant. This relatively short phase in a star's life ends with a celestial fireworks display. The star, burning any remaining helium, ejects its outer layers, forming a planetary nebula that glows because of energy received from its mother star. Eventually, the star contracts to become a faintly shining white dwarf.

White dwarf: This small white star (about the same radius as Earth) is actually the remnant core of a star that has completed fusion (nuclear collision) at its core. It is composed mainly of carbon.

Brown dwarf: A brown dwarf is larger than a planet but not as big as a star. Unlike a true star, it doesn't contain enough mass to convert hydrogen to helium. As a result, these "failed stars" have only a short period during which helium burns before they cool and fade. Brown dwarfs are often too dim to be detected easily.

Super giant: The biggest type of star, it is many times more luminous and several times larger than a red giant. Its diameter is several hundred times that of the Sun, and its luminosity is about a million times stronger. Super giants, however, have a relatively short life span and die out after only a few million years.

Supernova: A supernova is the explosion that ends the life of a star that was originally much more massive than the Sun. Huge amounts of dust and gas are spewed into space by violent shock waves at speeds of more than 6,000 miles per second. The light of the explosion is so bright that it outshines a billion suns, appearing as a sparkling diamond in the sky. The energy liberated in a single supernova explosion corresponds to the total energy that the Sun would radiate in 9 billion years.

Pulsar: A pulsar is what remains of a supernova. The once huge star has now become a fast-spinning globe approximately 20 miles in diameter. A beam of radio waves rotates with the star, like the beam of a lighthouse, appearing as a pulse to an observer (hence, the name pulsar). Pulsars are also called neutron stars because they are principally composed of tightly packed neutrons.

Black hole: Current understanding is that a black hole is simply the result of an exploded supernova. Such an event would cause the force of gravity to continue beyond the pulsar stage, so the star would actually disappear, leaving behind only its gravity and a black hole where it used to be. This hole would act as a supercharged cosmic whirlpool—ready to devour whatever comes too close.

Dark matter: This is a term used to describe celestial matter that is invisible but can be detected by the gravitational effect it exerts upon other bodies. Swiss astrophysicist Franz Zwicky first proposed dark matter in 1933, theorizing the existence of unseen mass based on the motions of galaxies. The speed of orbit he observed would have required 400 times more mass than was visible. The solution to this problem of missing mass was the existence of dark matter.

Big Bang: This theory suggests that the universe was formed from a single point in space as the result of a massive explosion some 18 billion years ago. A consequence of this explosion is that the universe continues to expand. Some astronomers suggest that the rate of expansion is slowing and will eventually come to a halt. At that point, gravity will pull the galaxies inward, back to where they began, merging in a mass of matter that will "blow up" in another big bang. Some believe this process will be repeated over and over, so that the universe "oscillates." Each cycle would take about 80 billion years—40 billion to expand, and 40 billion to contract.

Quasars: In the 1960s, strong radio signals were picked up from objects far beyond our local group of galaxies. These objects were called quasars because of their similarity to stars. But astronomers were perplexed by the prodigious energy quasars emitted. The most luminous one is approximately 10,000 times as bright as the Milky Way, and the most distant ones detected are more than 10 billion light-years away. After two decades of intensive study, astronomers have concluded that these distant quasars are very active nuclei of outlying galaxies.

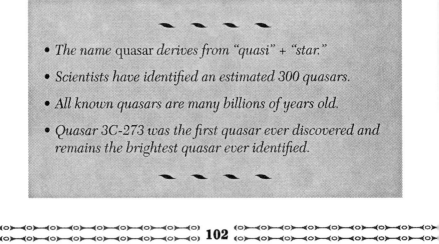

- *The name* quasar *derives from "quasi" + "star."*
- *Scientists have identified an estimated 300 quasars.*
- *All known quasars are many billions of years old.*
- *Quasar 3C-273 was the first quasar ever discovered and remains the brightest quasar ever identified.*

Folklore: Myth or Truth?
THE LADY WITH THE LAMP: FLORENCE NIGHTINGALE

✳ ✳ ✳ ✳

*Did she really invent modern nursing and then take
to her bed and become reclusive?*

- Florence was born in Florence (Tuscany, Italy) in 1820 to William and Fanny Nightingale.

- Fanny's idea was to marry off her daughter to a good "catch," but young Florence turned down all the acceptable suitors.

- Her commitment to nursing stemmed from her deep Unitarian Christianity, emphasized by a sense of divine calling from the time she was in her late teens.

- She had to go to Germany to study nursing. Her main encouragement came from Dr. Elizabeth Blackwell, the first officially qualified female doctor in the United States.

- Often forgotten: Florence Nightingale was an outstanding mathematician and statistician. She didn't invent the pie chart, but she used it and other innovative methods of data presentation.

- Only in recent generations have military hospitals become survivable; for most of history, disease was more deadly to soldiers than the spear, sword, musket, or rifle. During the Crimean War, where Florence earned her nursing stripes, cholera and malaria ran far more rampant than rifle balls and shell fragments.

- Remember the World War I "donkey generals"? Florence dealt with donkey doctors. The wounded came in caked with battlefield filth, suffering from disease and malnutrition, and instead of being given anesthesia and compassion, they were encouraged to keep stiff upper lips. Believe it or not, the donkey doctors bitterly resented Florence's objections; in so many words, they suggested that she buzz off and bake some biscuits.

- Only after media reports of the soldiers' misery did doctors relent and let Florence organize a hospital her way. Incredibly, disease and death increased! This wasn't her fault; there was a major cholera and typhus outbreak among the troops. Some nurses and doctors died as well. With major support from the British War Office, better sanitation was emphasized, and death rates from disease eventually decreased.

- Feminist irony: Florence, who had rejected a traditional gender role, ended up helping soldiers by organizing other women to bake biscuits and do laundry. One of her key complaints about military medical care was the horrid food and filthy clothing. Her kitchen and washing operations remedied that pestilential situation.

- Even as she was reforming and defining nursing, Florence Nightingale was human enough to have a considerable ego. Another enterprising woman, Mary Seacole, was also concerned about the soldiers—and she, an expert on cholera, traveled to the front to help Florence, who responded by hogging the limelight and declining Mary's help. The spurned volunteer set up her own treatment program financed by profits from a soldiers' restaurant she operated.

- Florence really did walk around with a lamp. She was the only woman allowed in the wards at night, when male orderlies were in charge of the hospital floor.

- Florence herself took ill in Crimea. It was called Crimean Fever back then; medical analysts now believe this was brucellosis—a chronic disease that also affected livestock. She recovered, but photos of her on return to England show a gaunt shadow of the vibrant young crusader she had been.

- Once back in England, Florence Nightingale campaigned for better nursing care. A meeting with Queen Victoria and Prince Albert led to the foundation of a nurse-training program. Before she began her efforts, from a social standpoint, "nurse" had barely been recognized as an occupation available to women. Now it was a legitimate and honorable profession.

- Even as an invalid—which she was for a quarter century, because of her brucellosis—she advised, watched, and assisted the growth of her profession. Never a paragon of tact, however, she became distant from family and suffered frequent depression most likely related to her illness.

- Believe it or not, she was accused of laziness after she returned home. One wonders if any of her accusers ever spent a quarter century dealing with a disease (perhaps more than one) that produced symptoms such as nausea, insomnia, depression, rapid heartbeat, weakness, inability to walk, intense spinal pain, and severe headache.

- When Florence was 60 years old, her illness and depression seem to have disappeared. The side effects of 25 years of relative isolation from humanity, except on her own terms, didn't clear up so easily. By this time, Nightingale nurses (as her program's graduates were known) were becoming authorities on the subject in their own right, and several brought their knowledge to the United States. How satisfying for Florence to see her profession take wing and know that it would survive her.

- Though Florence was an ardent women's rights advocate, some feminists felt she didn't do enough to support women who sought to make the leap from nursing to doctoring. She didn't approve of women's public speechmaking, for instance, preferring instead to work behind the scenes.

- Florence had 15 years of relatively good health until her eyesight and mind began to fail in the 1890s. It is widely speculated that she suffered from Chronic Fatigue Syndrome. Today, her birthday (May 12) is International CFS Awareness Day.

- She lingered as a blind invalid under nursing care until she died in 1910, too early to see what her efforts wrought for military medicine in World War I.

- Sadly, Florence Nightingale was never allowed to vote. British women didn't get the full vote until after World War I.

OVERTIME, IN TIME

✳ ✳ ✳ ✳

Not every goal in sudden-death overtime has been scored in highlight-reel fashion, and not always has the hero been a household name. Here are a few of the weirdest and wackiest overtime markers in the history of the National Hockey League.

Slip-Sliding Away: Cam Connor, Montreal vs. Toronto, April 21, 1979

A journeyman plugger who spent much of the 1978–1979 season nailed to the bench, Cam Connor put his name in the NHL record books during game three of the 1979 quarter-final series between the Canadiens and the Maple Leafs. Early in the second overtime period of a 3–3 tie, Connor was given a rare shift and made the most of the opportunity. He broke into the clear and was loading up for a shot on goal when the puck slipped off his stick. The change of pace completely handcuffed Toronto goaltender Mike Palmateer, and the disc slowly slid through the compunctious crease cop's legs to give Montreal a 4–3 victory. It was the only goal Connor would ever score for the Montreal Canadiens.

From Doghouse to Penthouse: Petr Klima, Edmonton vs. Boston, May 15, 1990

Pinned to the pine for most of the opening game of the 1990 Stanley Cup Finals because of undisciplined play in the early stages of the contest, Petr Klima was finally unleashed from the doghouse by Oilers coach John Muckler late in the third overtime period. Seconds into his shift, Klima corralled a pass, slowly maneuvered into the Bruins' zone, and drifted a soft shot toward the Boston cage that somehow eluded Bruins goaltender Andy Moog to give the Oilers a 3–2 victory. It was the only overtime goal of Klima's career.

Eye in the Sky: Sergei Fedorov, Detroit vs. Minnesota, April 28, 1992

Late in the opening overtime stanza of a 0–0 game between the Red Wings and the North Stars, supersniper Sergei Fedorov slipped past Minnesota defender Chris Dahlquist and blasted a bullet that buzzed by goalie Jon Casey and appeared to carom off the iron behind the cage plumber. Play continued without a whistle for several minutes until an offside call stopped the action. Both teams retired to their respective benches for a well-needed respite while the video goal judge reviewed the play. Upon further examination, it was determined that Fedorov's shot had actually struck the back bar inside the net, giving Fedorov the first overtime goal of his career and the Wings a 1–0 win. It was the first time in league history a playoff game result was determined by a video review.

I Did What?: Tony Leswick, Montreal vs. Detroit, April 15, 1954

The 1954 Stanley Cup final series between tempestuous rivals Montreal and Detroit marked only the second time in league history that overtime was required in a seventh and deciding contest. Early in the extra session, Detroit's Tony Leswick felt a moment of panic when he found the puck on his stick with a slew of Montreal attackers pursuing him. Leswick flipped the puck high into the air and retreated toward the Detroit zone. With his back turned to the play, he heard the Detroit Olympia faithful explode into a resounding roar. Leswick's little loft had deflected off the glove of Montreal's all-star defenseman Doug Harvey and floated over the shoulder of goalie Gerry McNeil, giving the Wings a 2–1 victory and possession of the Stanley Cup.

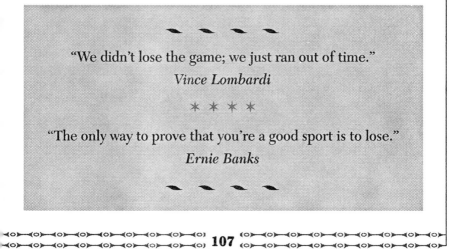

"We didn't lose the game; we just ran out of time."
Vince Lombardi

* * * *

"The only way to prove that you're a good sport is to lose."
Ernie Banks

FAULTY FORECASTS

✳ ✳ ✳ ✳

Predicting the future is seldom easy, even for people who are widely respected for their expertise and authority. Here are some serious statements that were way off the mark.

"I think there is a world market for maybe five computers."
Thomas Watson, chairman of IBM, 1943

✳ ✳ ✳ ✳

"The Americans have need of the telephone, but we do not. We have plenty of messenger boys."
Sir William Preece, chief engineer of the British Post Office, 1876

✳ ✳ ✳ ✳

"Who the hell wants to hear actors talk?"
H. M. Warner, Warner Brothers, 1927

✳ ✳ ✳ ✳

"We don't like their sound, and guitar music is on the way out."
Decca Recording Company, rejecting the Beatles, 1962

✳ ✳ ✳ ✳

"It will be years—not in my time—before a woman will become prime minister."
Margaret Thatcher, 1974

✳ ✳ ✳ ✳

"I see no good reasons why the views given in this volume should shock the religious feelings of anyone."
Charles Darwin, The Origin Of Species, *1869*

✳ ✳ ✳ ✳

"With over 50 foreign cars already on sale here, the Japanese auto industry isn't likely to carve out a big slice of the U.S. market."
Business Week, *1968*

"The bomb will never go off. I speak as an expert in explosives."
Admiral William Leahy, United States Atomic Bomb Project

* * * *

"Airplanes are interesting toys but of no military value."
Marechal Ferdinand Foch, Professor of Strategy, Ecole Superieure de Guerre, *1911*

* * * *

"Louis Pasteur's theory of germs is ridiculous fiction."
Pierre Pachet, Professor of Physiology at Toulouse, 1872

* * * *

"The abdomen, the chest, and the brain will forever be shut from the intrusion of the wise and humane surgeon."
Sir John Eric Ericksen, Surgeon-Extraordinary to Queen Victoria, 1873

* * * *

"What? Men dodging this way for single bullets? What will you do when they open fire along the whole line? I am ashamed of you. They couldn't hit an elephant at this distance!"
Last words of General John Sedgwick, spoken during the Battle of Spotsylvania, moments before he was killed by a bullet to the eye

* * * *

"Reagan doesn't have that presidential look."
United Artists executive, rejecting Reagan as lead in 1964 film The Best Man

* * * *

"Capitalist production begets, with the inexorability of a law of nature, its own negation."
Karl Marx, Das Kapital

* * * *

"Stick to driving a truck, because you're never going to make it as a singer."
Memphis musician Eddie Bond, after hearing Elvis Presley, 1954

THE A TO Z OF IM-ING

✳ ✳ ✳ ✳

Interpersonal communication keeps getting faster. Writing letters took too long, so people became adept at the quick phone call, which was largely replaced by e-mail. Instant messaging offers the speediest way to express yourself, but only if you know the lingo.

AFK: Away from keyboard
ADN: Any day now
AYTMTB: And you're telling me this because?
BRB: Be right back
BTA: But then again
BTDT: Been there, done that
CRBT: Crying really big tears
CU: See you
CUL8R: See you later
DEGT: Don't even go there!
DIKU: Do I know you?
DQMOT: Don't quote me on this
EG: Evil grin
EOM: End of message
FICCL: Frankly, I couldn't care less
FWIW: For what it's worth
FYEO: For your eyes only
GD/R: Grinning, ducking, and running
GGOH: Gotta get outta here
GMTA: Great minds think alike
HB: Hurry back
H&K: Hugs and kisses
H2CUS: Hope to see you soon
IB: I'm back
IDTS: I don't think so
IMHO: In my humble opinion
JIC: Just in case
JK: Just kidding
JMO: Just my opinion

KIT: Keep in touch
KOTL: Kiss on the lips
KWIM: Know what I mean?
LOL: Laughing out loud
LTNS: Long time no see
MOS: Mother over shoulder
MTFBWU: May the force be with you
NM: Never mind
NMU: Not much, you?
NOYB: None of your business
OMG: Oh my God
OTH: Off the hook
OTTOMH: Off the top of my head
P911: My parents are in the room
PRW: Parents are watching
PU: That stinks!
QIK: Quick
QT: Cutie
RME: Rolling my eyes
ROTFLUTS: Rolling on the floor laughing, unable to speak
SH: Same here
SMHID: Scratching my head is disbelief
SSIF: So stupid it's funny
TIC: Tongue-in-cheek
TMI: Too much info
TNSTAAFL: There's no such thing as a free lunch
UCMU: You crack me up!
UV: Unpleasant visual
VEG: Very evil grin
VSF: Very sad face
WH5: Who, what, where, when, why?
WOMBAT: Waste of money, brains, and time
X: Kiss
XLNT: Excellent
YG2BKM: You've got to be kidding me
YKWYCD: You know what you can do
ZUP: What's up?
Zzzz: Bored

NOTEWORTHY CANADIAN WOMEN

* * * *

Kim Campbell was Canada's first female prime minister. Jeanne Sauvé was the first governor-general. What have other Canadian women done lately?

Susan Aglukark: an Inuk who once worked as a linguist for the Department of Indian and Northern Affairs. This uplifting northern Manitoban musician plays guitar and sings in Inuktitut and English, hoping to encourage all people toward self-respect and strength.

Madame Louise Arbour: born in Montreal and one of Canada's most distinguished judges. She is a former prosecutor for the United Nations International Criminal Tribunal and former Justice of the Supreme Court of Canada. In 2004, she became the U.N. High Commissioner for Human Rights, raising Canada's world profile in an area important to Canadians.

Jean Augustine: born in Grenada, emigrated to Canada in 1959. Jean represents the level of opportunity available to immigrant Canadians: She started as a maid in Ontario, then became a teacher and later a principal. In 1993, she became Canada's first African Canadian member of Parliament for the Etobicoke-Lakeshore Riding (similar to a congressional district in the United States).

Dr. Roberta Bondar: from Sault Ste. Marie, Ontario. A noted researcher and professor, she began training as an astronaut in 1984. In January 1992, she became the first Canadian woman to leave the planet, spending eight days in space aboard *Discovery*.

The Honorable Jocelyne Bourgon: born in Papineauville, Quebec. As the first woman to serve as Clerk of the Privy Council, she was Canada's chief civil servant. Her reforms trimmed Canada's large civil service payroll by 47,000 jobs. She is now a member of the Queen's Privy Council for Canada (the monarchy's Canadian advisory body).

Major Deanna Brasseur: from Pembroke, Ontario. She entered the armed forces as a dental clerk and rose to become one of the first female CF-18 fighter pilots. Impressive, but perhaps more difficult was her courageous decision to tell her story of sexual abuse in the Canadian military, leading to reforms.

Rosemary Brown: emigrated to Canada from Jamaica and became the first African Canadian woman to serve in any Canadian legislature (British Columbia). Later she served on the board overseeing the Canadian Security Intelligence Service, Canada's national intelligence agency.

Major Maryse Carmichael: from Quebec City, Quebec, she became a pilot in her teens. Little did she know then that she would become the first woman to fly with the Canadian Forces' elite Snowbirds aerobatic team. She has also flown with the Forces' VIP transport squadron, trusted to fly the prime minister and governor-general around the world.

Françoise David: from Montreal, Quebec. Mademoiselle David is one of Canada's most outspoken Francophones and feminist activists. Through the *Fédération des femmes du Québec* (Quebec Women's Federation), she has campaigned tirelessly for women's rights and against poverty in Canada.

Right Honorable Ellen Fairclough: from Hamilton, Ontario. She marched in the vanguard of Canadian women assuming roles in national leadership. As Immigration Minister, she did away with racial discrimination in Canadian immigration in 1962.

Barbara Frum: a United States immigrant from Niagara Falls. She became one of Canada's most highly regarded television journalists. Her empathy and sense of humor endeared her to the viewing public. After battling leukemia for 18 years, her adopted nation mourned her loss in 1992.

Pauline Julien: born in Trois-Rivières, Quebec. One of Canada's most successful musicians was a passionate crusader for Quebec separatism. She wove her ideals and dreams for her province into her music, even declining to perform for the queen.

Chantal Petitclerc: born in Saint-Marc-des-Carrières, Quebec. Although Petitclerc was paralyzed from the waist down when she was

13, she took up swimming, then wheelchair racing. At the Athens 2004 Paralympics, she broke three world records and earned Canada five gold medals to become Canadian Female Athlete of the Year.

Dr. Buffy Sainte-Marie: a Cree from Saskatchewan. Sainte-Marie was orphaned in infancy. Her guitar and voice talent surfaced in her teens, and she became a folk-rock balladeer in Canada. She has used her fame and resources to help First Nations at every opportunity, and like most on this list, she is a member of the Order of Canada.

Muriel Stanley Venne: born in Lamont, Alberta. This Metis Canadian founded the Institute for the Advancement of Aboriginal Women. A lifetime of hard work has made her a nationally admired human rights activist and the winner of numerous awards.

Hayley Wickenheiser: born in Shaunavon, Saskatchewan. This tough, physical hockey player has helped win Canada two Olympic gold medals. Wickenheiser was only 28 when she was Canada's top forward in 2006 at the Olympics in Torino, Italy.

Sharon Wood: born in Halifax, Nova Scotia, but raised in Vancouver. She climbed Canada's highest peak, Mt. Logan (Yukon Territory), in 1977. After climbing other challenging mountains in many countries, she became the first North American woman to conquer the world's highest peak, Mount Everest.

Julie Payette: born in Montreal. Being Canada's second female astronaut is quite an honor, but Payette's multiple talents make her an outstanding Canadian. She speaks six languages, is an accomplished singer and pianist, and is certified in deep-sea diving.

> "Without knowledge the world is bereft of culture. And so we must be educators and students both."
>
> *Roberta Bondar*

YOU'RE SUCH AN ANIMAL

* * * *

*It would take lifetimes to uncover every odd detail
of the animal world, but from our human perspective,
the following creatures stand out.*

- The **fish tapeworm** reaches lengths of up to 60 feet and can infect humans as well as fish.

- The **torpedo ray** builds up an electric charge in its head, then grabs a small fish and pours in 200 volts.

- Unborn **crocodiles** make noises inside their eggs to alert the mother that it's time for them to hatch.

- The *alacran tartarus* **scorpion** has been found in caves as far as 2,600 feet below ground—that's more than eight football fields deep.

- Eggs of the **sand tiger shark** hatch within one of two womb chambers. The embryos then eat each other until only one shark survives in each chamber. Only those two are actually born.

- The **killer whale,** or orca, will actually beach itself to feast on baby seals. It then worms its way back to the water.

- A mere .002 ounce (about the volume of a very small raindrop) of venom from the **Australian small-scaled snake** can kill several adult humans.

- The **imperial scorpion,** one of Africa's many charming insects, grows up to seven inches long. It looks dangerous, but its venom isn't very toxic.

- The male **starling** will line a nesting area with vegetation that helps the baby birds resist the impact of bloodthirsty lice.

- The African **honey badger** will fight anything or anyone at any time. Its tough hide can resist penetration and most poisons, a great help when the badger's dinner includes puff adders or beehive honey.

- In the Galapagos, the **woodpecker finch** digs bug larvae out of wood with a stick, twig, or cactus spine.

- The skin of some **toads** contains poison, thus few creatures prey upon them. The skunk is an exception: It rolls the toads in wet grass to get the poison off.

- The **large-eared pika,** essentially a mini squirrel, can make its home at an altitude of 20,000 feet.

- The **shingleback lizard** of Australia has a thick, short, rounded tail that's shaped just like its head. This characteristic confuses predators and gives this slow, sleepy reptile a better chance to escape.

- The **Japanese macaque** is that rare monkey that likes cold weather. When temperatures in its mountain habitat drop below freezing (which they do regularly), the macaque lounges in natural hot springs.

- Amorous **great gray slug** couples hang from a rope of their slime as they twist around each other in the throes of slug passion.

- The **red deer** on the island of Rhum (in Scotland) kill seabird chicks and gnaw the bones to get nutrients otherwise unavailable on the isle.

- The rabbit-size **mouse deer** of Asia has long upper incisors that make it look like a miniature vampire deer. When these timid creatures encounter people, however, they quickly flee.

- An **echidna** is a spiny anteater of Australia and New Guinea that can grow to three feet long. The echidna and the duck-billed platypus are the only egg-laying mammals on earth.

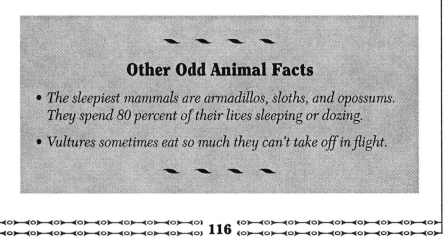

Other Odd Animal Facts

- *The sleepiest mammals are armadillos, sloths, and opossums. They spend 80 percent of their lives sleeping or dozing.*

- *Vultures sometimes eat so much they can't take off in flight.*

ATLANTIS

✳ ✳ ✳ ✳

Although it's often re-created as a popular theme resort for vacationers, the lost city of Atlantis is rich in historical lore.

- Plato claimed in his dialogues *Timaeus* and *Critias* that on a single night around 9400 B.C., the great island civilization Atlantis (named for the ocean in which it was situated) sank into the sea. Most historians believe that Plato created the myth of Atlantis to support his political theories.

- A volcanic eruption did occur about 3,600 years ago on the Santorini archipelago, located in the Aegean Sea about 125 miles southeast of Greece. The massive explosion likely didn't sink a fake city called Atlantis, but it may well have destroyed the Minoan civilization on the nearby island of Crete.

- Dan Brown's blockbuster novel *The Da Vinci Code* reignited public interest in Atlantis in a roundabout way. Brown's story referenced the Knights Templar, an early Christian military order with a dramatic history that involved bloodshed, exile, and secrets—one of which was that they were carriers of ancient wisdom from the lost city of Atlantis.

- Ulf Erlingsson, a Swedish geographer, believes that the lost city of Atlantis is actually Ireland. Erlingsson claims that Plato's measurements, geography, and landscape reports of Atlantis perfectly match those of Ireland. He claims that somewhere around 6100 B.C., Dogger Bank (an isolated shoal in the North Sea connecting Britain and Denmark) flooded, and over the centuries, the Irish have confused the sinking of the shoal with the sinking of Atlantis.

- The name Atlantis derives from Atlas, the Greek god who is said to have supported the world on his back. In Greek, Atlantis means "Daughter of Atlas."

Talk to the Expert
FOLEY ARTIST

✳ ✳ ✳ ✳

Q: Why are you called a Foley artist?

A: Adding sound to film was an industry leap that engaged a sense not previously used by the audience: hearing. A man named Jack Foley invented the fine art of background sound effects by using simple objects to create specific noises: Knocking coconut shells together mimics the sound of galloping horses, and snapping a stalk of celery sounds like a bone is being broken.

Q: You must have excellent hearing.

A: Hearing for me is like eyesight for pilots. My special talent is the ability to look at something and hear, in my mind, what sound it would make. I think of my work as audio art.

Q: Describe your work area.

A: It's the biggest collection of junk you've ever seen. My Foley stage has multiple walking surfaces, to produce the sounds of footsteps on anything from sand to snow. I have pie plates, staple guns, boxes of broken glass, crash tubes containing different materials to make particular crashing sounds, bamboo, leather gloves, boxes of cornstarch, you name it.

Q: How, exactly, do you produce some of your sounds?

A: We'll start with kissing sounds: That's me making out with the back of my hand. Someone's walking in the snow? That isn't real snow; I'm just squeezing a pouch of cornstarch. Rusty door hinges? I have an old hinge that I place against different surfaces, pouring on more water or less, depending on the creep factor involved. To create the sound of a crackling fire, I wad up cellophane. The process isn't as technical as you might think.

WHERE DID THAT NAME COME FROM?

✳ ✳ ✳ ✳

WD-40: In 1953, the Rocket Chemical Company began developing a rust-prevention solvent for the aerospace industry. The name WD-40 indicates what the product does (water displacement) and how many attempts it took to perfect it.

Starbucks: *Moby Dick* was the favorite book of one of the three founders of this coffee empire. He wanted to name the company after the story's fabled ship *Pequod*, but he and his partners reconsidered and settled instead on the name of the first mate, Starbuck.

Google: In the 1930s, mathematician Edwin Kasner asked his young nephew to think of a word that could mean a very large number (1 followed by 100 zeros). The boy, Milton Sirotta, came up with *Googol.* The creators of the world's most popular search engine varied the spelling and adopted it to represent an infinite amount of information.

M&Ms: Chocolate pellets coated in sugar were popular in Britain for decades under the brand name Smarties. When Forrest Mars (son of the founder of the Mars candy company) saw soldiers eating them during the Spanish Civil War, he and his partner, R. Bruce Murrie, bought the U.S. rights. But there was already an American candy product called Smarties, so Mars and Murrie used their initials to form the new brand name.

GAP: Don and Doris Fisher opened their first store in 1969 to meet the unique clothing demands of customers between childhood and adulthood, identified and popularized then as "the generation gap."

Adidas: This sportswear giant's name derives from the name of its founder, Adolf "Adi" Dassler.

Shell Oil: The name was appropriated by Marcus Samuel, one of the company's founders. His father ran a London retail outlet called the Shell Shop, where he sold bags decorated with seashells. This grew into an import-export business, which diversified into a business that imported oil and kerosene.

Aspirin: In 1899, the German company Bayer trade-marked the word *aspirin* as a composite of the scientific name of the drug. "A" indicates that it comes from the acetyl group, and "spir" represents its derivation from the plant genus *spiraea*. A common ending for drug names in the 19th century was "in."

Nike: In 1971, the founders of a small sports shoe business in Beaverton, Oregon, were searching for a catchy, energetic company name. Designer Jeff Johnson suggested Nike, the name of the Greek goddess of victory. Nike is now the largest sportswear manufacturer in the world.

Jeep: Eugene the Jeep, a character in a 1936 *Popeye* comic strip, was actually a dog that could walk through walls, climb trees, and fly. When U.S. soldiers were given a new all-terrain vehicle in the early 1940s, they were so impressed that they may have named it after the superdog. The Jeep trademark is now owned by Daimler Chrysler.

"I never did anything worth doing by accident, nor did any of my inventions come by accident; they came by work."

Plato

✳ ✳ ✳ ✳

"Without question, the greatest invention in the history of mankind is beer. Oh, I grant you that the wheel was also a fine invention, but the wheel does not go nearly as well with pizza."

Dave Barry

ODD EGG RITUALS

✳ ✳ ✳ ✳

Throughout the world, the egg is used for more than whipping up omelets. Here are some traditional charms, potions, and spells that make use of this seemingly innocuous breakfast staple.

- In Macedonia, an egg can mean the difference between life and death. According to local lore, if you share a birthday or even a birth month with a dying relative, your days are likewise numbered. The only way to cheat fate is to share the yolk of an egg with this relative while standing on opposite sides of a stream. Similarly, a dying man might save himself if he finds someone to share a sugared egg with him on the threshold of a house.

- In Mergentheim, Germany, if someone falls gravely ill, that person ties a white thread around an egg and places it into a fire. If the shell turns black in the flame, death is not far off.

- Swamped at work? Beset by bad luck? Craving undead company? Sneak into a Jamaican churchyard at night and visit the grave of a friend or relative—one's mother would be the most suitable. Break an egg and offer it to the deceased with some rice and rum. The ghost will rise, eat the food, and offer you help and good luck in return.

- In Morocco, a woman who has a very young son and is preparing to give birth again keeps an egg close to her during labor. After the birth, the egg is given to the newborn's brother to ensure that the siblings will like each other. But if the egg should happen to be eaten by someone other than the baby's brother, the baby will grow up to hate the mother.

- All across Europe, eggs are used to tell fortunes. The most popular method is to carefully pierce the shell and catch drops of the egg white in a glass of water. The shapes that form in the water are examined and interpreted by an unmarried woman who is looking for clues to her future husband's profession. A ship means marriage to a sailor, a shoe means she'll wed a cobbler, and so on.

- The Scottish variant of this fortune-telling technique is called "drap glasses." A group of women get together, and each one brings an egg and hands it to the woman in charge. She then separates out the whites, drops each one into a glass of water, seals the rim with her hand, and inverts it. When everyone is done interpreting the shapes, the eggs yolks are used to bake "dumb cakes," called so because the fortune-telling is done in silence.

- In rural Russia, eggs can help you make friends with supernatural forces. The house sprite (*domovoi*), a ubiquitous if usually invisible presence in every home, is said to occasionally assume the shape of a snake. If the owners of the house find this snake, they would do well to offer it some egg pancakes (*blini*). If the gift is accepted, the *domovoi*'s benevolence is secured and the household will prosper; a rejection means the house will burn down.

- Occasionally, hens lay eggs with imperfect shells or without shells altogether. In England, such eggs are traditionally called "wind eggs," from the belief that the hen laying them had been impregnated not by the rooster but by the wind. In parts of Hungary, if a black hen lays a soft-shelled egg, it is destroyed upon discovery, for it signifies the worst of omens: that the earth is softening beneath a member of the family, which is a metaphor for impending death.

- Many cultures consider unusual eggs—misshapen, empty, yolkless, shell-less, or ones with the yolk and white merged—to be laid not by hens but by roosters. This belief is likely derived from the fact that the bodies of aged roosters (seven years or older) are often found to contain a white egg-shaped globule.

- In 1474, legal proceedings were instituted at Basel against a rooster accused of laying an egg for purposes of witchcraft. The prosecutor pointed out that roosters' eggs were very valuable for mixing magic potions, and that Satan was known to employ witches for brooding these eggs. The magistrates were convinced, and the rooster was convicted as a sorcerer in the form of a bird and burned at the stake together with his egg.

Fast Facts

- *The "bones" in whalebone corsets were actually baleen—plates of "combs" in the jawbones of whales used to strain plankton from the water.*

- *Earth weighs approximately 5,940,000,000,000,000,000,000 metric tons.*

- *Geodesic domes have the highest enclosed volume-to-weight ratio of any known linear structure.*

- *Peep dueling is a popular "sport" that involves placing two Peep marshmallow confections in a microwave oven, facing each other. The duelists each insert a toothpick into their Peep and start the microwave, causing the Peeps to expand. The first Peep to deflate the other with its toothpick wins!*

- *Bouvet Island in the South Atlantic is the most remote island on Earth. It lies almost a thousand miles from the nearest land (Queen Maude Land, Antarctica).*

- *A 100-pound woman in high heels exerts more pressure per square inch (psi) when walking than a 6,000-pound elephant. The elephant clocks in at around 75 psi, but the woman can apply approximately 1,500 psi to the heel point of her shoe.*

- *Leo Tolstoy, author of* War and Peace, *left all of his possessions to the stump of a tree.*

- *The Torino Impact Hazard Scale is used to categorize the chances of an asteroid or comet hitting Earth. The scale goes from zero to ten, with zero being no risk and ten being a certain collision, with global catastrophe imminent.*

- *Asteroid 99942 Apophis was the first object to be categorized above level one on the Torino Scale—it was briefly rated as level four for a pass in 2029, but further observations have downgraded it again to level zero.*

CHARLES BUKOWSKI

✳ ✳ ✳ ✳

- This Los Angeles writer, who developed a cult following in the 1960s, was often referred to by his nickname, "Buk."

- Bukowski's column in the Los Angeles–based newspaper *Open City*, "Notes of a Dirty Old Man," garnered him notoriety early in his career. These columns were collected into a book of the same name in 1969. The first printing of 20,000 copies sold out in two months.

- Critics of Bukowski claim his writing is too simplistic, too cynical, and without nuance. Fans argue that Bukowski's style is raw, gritty, and real.

- Buk is known for his irreverent outlook on life, love, and death. The titles of many of his poems make this clear, including: *Love Is a Piece of Paper Torn to Bits, The Death of a Roach,* and *Suicide.*

- Bukowski had one child, a daughter named Marina, born in 1964.

- In 1966, Bukowski was approached by publisher John Martin, who was a fan of the writer's "Notes" column. In 1969, Martin offered to pay Bukowski $100 a month for the rest of his life on one condition: Buk had to quit his job at the post office and write full time.

- Bukowski's first published novel was titled *Post Office,* written just three weeks after he quit his job there.

- By the 1980s, Bukowski was no longer living an impoverished writer's life in West Los Angeles. He bought a home in San Pedro, upgraded his Volkswagen to a BMW, enjoyed eating in expensive restaurants, and installed a swimming pool in his backyard.

- Though never treated for it, Bukowski suffered from alcoholism and depression for most of his life. It was only after undergoing treatment for leukemia in 1993 that he quit drinking.

- Bukowski died of leukemia in 1994 at the age of 73. The inscription on his headstone reads, "Don't Try," the advice he often gave to aspiring writers.

IN THE YEAR...1929

✳ ✳ ✳ ✳

- Martin Luther King, Jr., is born.

- The Academy of Motion Picture Arts and Sciences holds its first awards ceremony, hosted by Douglas Fairbanks and William C. DeMille. The event was attended by fewer than 250 people and lasted 15 minutes. *Wings* becomes the first movie, and the only silent film in history, to win Best Picture.

- Alexander Fleming treats a staph infection with an experimental drug, wiping out nearly all of the bacteria and marking the first clinical application of penicillin.

- New York City's Museum of Modern Art opens to the public.

- On February 14, four members of Al Capone's gang (two dressed as police officers) lure seven members of the gang led by George "Bugs" Moran into a garage on Chicago's north side. Lining them up against the wall in a faux arrest, Capone's men mow down the rival gangsters.

- Archaeologist Wenzhong Pei discovers Peking Man. The discovery of the 500,000-year-old skull is a benchmark moment for evolutionary theory.

- Rosika Schwimmer, a Jewish woman who led an activist's life in her native Austria-Hungary before immigrating to the United States, is denied American citizenship by a six-to-three vote by the U.S. Supreme Court. The reason: Schwimmer, a pacifist, refused to swear that she would bear arms to defend the United States.

- The average citizen in the United States earns $28 per week.

- The Ford Motor Company introduces the station wagon.

- The Graf Zeppelin completes the first round-the-world flight of any aircraft, carrying 20 commercial passengers 19,000 miles in 21 days, 7 hours.

- The stock market crash accelerates the decline of an already unstable economy.

- Electric dishwashers are introduced in Europe.

GRAND, INCOMPLETE STRUCTURES AND MONUMENTS AROUND THE WORLD

✳ ✳ ✳ ✳

Sometimes people decide to build something huge but then get tired of it and quit. Here are some of the greatest unfinished monuments, including a few that lingered long enough to make the incomplete phase part of their legacies.

Crazy Horse Memorial (Crazy Horse, South Dakota): In 1949, the Ziolkowski family of South Dakota embarked on a multigenerational project. Having helped sculpt nearby Mt. Rushmore, Korczak Ziolkowski promised Native American leaders that he would under-take a similar monument in honor of the brilliant Oglala war leader known as Chief Crazy Horse. Ziolkowski kept that commitment until his death, and his family carries on the work.

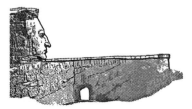

As of 2007, only the chief's head was complete. At 87 feet high, that alone is about half again the height of the heads at Mt. Rushmore. Assuming eventual comple-tion, the result will tower at 563 feet, depicting Crazy Horse's outstretched arm pointing over his horse's mane. As long as things progress at the current rate, that will likely take centuries.

Washington Monument (Washington, D.C.): Yes, it's finished now, but the nation took a 20-year break during which it conducted a Civil War, ran low on funds, and politicized the project.

The original 1848 plan called for a flat obelisk surrounded by a pillared ring (ghosted by today's flag circle), styled much like the front of the later Lincoln Memorial. Work ceased in 1856 because of money problems and a political takeover of the Washington Monument Society by the "Know-Nothing" Party. They also turned out to be the "Build-Nothing" Party, laying only 26 feet of masonry before the Civil War.

In 1876, planners decided to resume work but settled on a tall, sharp-pointed obelisk. The finished structure was dedicated in 1885 and stands today. It is 555 feet tall, and if you look carefully about 150 feet up, you'll see a difference in the color of the stone that marks the interruption in construction.

Germania (Berlin, Federal Republic of Germany): If you're a big thinker, maybe a big statue of yourself isn't enough. Maybe your entire capital should be a monument. After he subjugated the world, Adolf Hitler intended to transfigure Berlin into a monumental world capital, modestly renamed Germania. He got the Olympic Stadium built and had avenues widened to accommodate his visions. An egotistical Reich chancellor must have a humongous chancellery, so Hitler built a new one twice as long as the French Hall of Mirrors at Versailles. Soviet artillery flattened it at the end of the war.

The rest of Germania never got past plans and experiments. Hitler wanted a triumphal arch more massive than the French Arc de Triomphe. The flawed assumption, of course, was that Hitler would keep triumphing. Then there was the proposed Volkshalle (People's Hall), a dome intended to hold 180,000 people. Besides the Olympic Stadium and the street renovations, the only remnant of Germania is a big concrete pylon that was poured to see how far into the earth these structures might sink. Good thing it was tested first: The pylon sank three times deeper than Hitler had hoped.

Ollantaytambo (Ollantaytambo, Peru): Why would people build with pink granite blocks 15 feet high by 6 feet wide by 6 feet deep? Maybe the ancient Incas of this city knew that one day invaders would come. Maybe they just wanted to honor their gods. Either way, they were still working on Ollantaytambo's immense structure when Hernando Pizarro's Spaniards showed up in 1536.

The Spaniards spent a lot of time fighting with each other, but they took a break to attack Ollantaytambo. Hernando and his men encountered a multiterraced fortress made of those 15-foot pink blocks, with determined defenders raining missile weapons down on them. The Spaniards regrouped and took Ollantaytambo, ensuring that the Incas would never finish the citadel. The big blocks they left lying around indicate that more would have been in store for Ollantaytambo had the Incas been able to hold it.

Maginot Line (border of Germany/Luxembourg/Belgium/France):
Though this lengthy series of interlocking forts and bastions was
built after World War I to ensure that Germany could never again
threaten France (and we all know how that turned out), it was also
something of a monument. It embodied static defensive thinking—
the notion (true enough in World War I) that the military defense
had utterly outgrown the offense.

France originally planned to extend the Line all the way to the
English Channel, but the monstrous structure had already consumed
a large percentage of the defense budget. It was well-built, modern,
engineered to take advantage of terrain—and militarily worthless.
When the Germans invaded in 1940, they just went around the
Maginot Line, making plans for its eventual completion impractical.

Great Wall of China (northern China): Occasionally, people will
build something so vast it can't really ever be finished. The Great
Wall began as a humble series of regional walls eventually linked
together during the Qin Dynasty (around 221 B.C.). By the time one
part was "done," some other part had eroded or fallen into disre-
pair. Most of the Wall was rammed earth packed between wooden
frames, and the rest was made of stone.

Emperor Qin called this the *Wan Li Chang-Cheng*—roughly
translated, the "3,000-Mile Wall." The actual length varied depending on which part had fallen down or been added to. For the
next 2,000 years, numerous Chinese rulers ordered different degrees of repair, expansion, and upgrade work. The Ming Dynasty
(1368–1644) built much of what survives today. It is impressive that
Chinese leaders had enough human and financial resources to continue building and improving the Wall for so many centuries; it also
illustrates how greatly they dreaded invasion from the north.

> *The Great Wall is not just a wall. Features for defensive pur-
> poses, such as forts, passageways, and towers, were built along
> the structure to house auxiliary soldiers, store grain and weap-
> ons, and facilitate the exchange of military information.*

THE ROYAL DIRT

✳ ✳ ✳

Queens, kings, and mistresses—in the backstabbing world of royal courts, people got into all sorts of crazy things.

- After his first wife died, King Louis XIV secretly married his longtime mistress, Madame de Maintenon. But because of her low social status, she never became queen.

- Edward III's notorious mistress, Alice Perrers, is said to have stolen the rings off the king's fingers as he died.

- Elizabeth I lost a fortune in gold and jewel decorations that came loose and fell off her clothes as she went about her daily business. This was a common problem for nobles at the time, and attendants were often charged with watching for fallen ornaments and discretely retrieving them.

- King Charles VI of France supposedly sent the young Henry V of England a bunch of small balls, saying his age was more suited to games than to battle. Henry was not impressed and declared that he would soon play a game of ball in the French streets. He invaded France not long after.

- Jane Seymour, third wife of Henry VIII, picked out her wedding dress on the day her predecessor, Anne Boleyn, was executed.

- King Louis XV's longtime mistress, Madame de Pompadour, wielded so much power over the king she was known as "the real Queen of France."

- King Henry IV of England was a childhood friend of King Richard II, whom he later deposed.

- "Divorced, beheaded, died; divorced, beheaded, survived" is a popular rhyme to remember the fates of Henry VIII's six wives.

- Edward III was the first English king to claim the French throne. His claim was through his mother, Queen Isabella, and had been included as part of her marriage contract to Edward II. The French king's refusal to honor the contract was the spark that started the Hundred Years' War.

- Egyptian pharaohs often married their siblings because it was believed that pharaohs were gods on Earth and thus could marry only other gods.

- Queen Cleopatra of Egypt was the first ruler in 300 years who actually spoke Egyptian. The Ptolemaic pharaohs were Greeks descended from Ptolemy, one of Alexander the Great's generals, so Greek was the dominant language of their court. Cleopatra also spoke several other languages, including Latin, Hebrew, and Aramaic.

- Richard II was so upset over the death of his first wife, Anne of Bohemia, that he had the house she died in destroyed.

- Edward I grieved the death of his wife, Eleanor of Castile, by building a stone monument at each place her funeral procession stopped en route from Lincoln to London. Three of the twelve original structures, known as Eleanor crosses, still stand.

- On several occasions, Cleopatra dressed as the goddess Isis to play up the common belief that Egyptian kings and queens were the incarnations of gods.

- Henry VI of England suffered periodic mental breakdowns, during which he would respond to no one. One lasted more than a year.

- In Tudor England, being beheaded instead of hanged was considered a "favor" granted to condemned nobles.

- Emperor Augustus attempted to reform what he considered loose Roman morals. In a bit of irony, he then had to banish his daughter Julia for committing adultery.

- Eleanor of Aquitaine is known for having stormy relationships. Shortly after escaping her first marriage, to King Louis VII of France, she married Henry II, who was soon to be the king of England. Although Eleanor bore him five sons, Henri constantly flaunted his mistresses, especially Rosamund Clifford.

- The wedding of King Henri III of France was delayed by several hours when Henri insisted on dressing his bride's hair himself. He also designed her wedding gown and a number of her other dresses.

PECULIAR PRESIDENTIAL FACTS

✳ ✳ ✳ ✳

- President William Taft had a new bathtub installed in the White House that could hold four grown men. Why? His 300-pound frame wouldn't fit in the original presidential tub.

- President John Quincy Adams started each summer day with an early-morning skinny-dip in the Potomac River.

- Grover Cleveland was the first and only president to marry in the White House itself. He wed Frances Folsom in 1886.

- With 15 children from 2 marriages, President John Tyler was the most prolific chief executive.

- President George Washington never shook hands with visitors, choosing to bow instead.

- The only president never to have won a national election was Gerald Ford, who took office after President Richard Nixon resigned in 1974.

- President Jimmy Carter is said to be able to speed-read at the rate of 2,000 words per minute.

- Franklin Delano Roosevelt was related to 11 other presidents, either directly or through marriage.

- There hasn't been a bearded president since Benjamin Harrison, who left office in 1893.

- President James Garfield could write Latin with one hand and Greek with the other—at the same time.

- George W. Bush's brother Neil was scheduled to dine with John Hinckley's brother, Scott, the day after Hinckley tried to kill President Ronald Reagan.

- John Adams and Thomas Jefferson both died on July 4, 1826, 50 years to the day after the official signing of the Declaration of Independence.

- Edwin Booth, the brother of Abraham Lincoln's assassin, John Wilkes Booth, once saved the life of President Lincoln's son Robert. He kept the boy from falling off a train platform.

HOLLYWOOD'S WARPED SENSE OF HISTORY

✳ ✳ ✳ ✳

Many writers consider it "creative license." The simple truth is that sometimes facts get in the way of a good story.

- ***Alexander* (2004):** The big flaws in this biography are its omissions: The pivotal battles of Alexander's military career—the sieges of Thebes, Tyre, and Gaza—go completely unnoticed. The disastrous trek through the Gedrosian desert is barely touched on, even though it killed more of Alexander's soldiers than all of the onscreen battles combined. The three-hour epic presents a series of bloody exchanges between Greeks and Macedonians, but the audience is subjected to Irish, Scottish, and American accents.

- ***Anna and the King* (1999):** This film depicts a close relationship between British governess Anna Leonowens and King Mongkut, even hinting at a romance. The truth is that they hardly knew each other, having had only a handful of exchanges. The film also depicts Anna as playing a leading role in the reform and development of the Thai nation. This so offended the Thai people that the movie is banned in Thailand.

- ***Apocalypto* (2006):** Mel Gibson's epic adventure portrays the ancient Mayan world as an ultraviolent, religiously void civilization with few redeeming qualities. Finally, white missionaries come to save the heathens from themselves. Such a view, however, has been thoroughly discounted by historians who point to the scientific, astronomical, spiritual, agricultural, and artistic achievements of the Mayas as evidence that they were doing just fine before the arrival of Europeans.

- ***Braveheart* (1995):** The major fabrication here revolves around the relationship between William Wallace and Isabella of France, who was around ten years old when Wallace died. The two never even met, let alone had an affair or a child. Wallace's wardrobe also had historians shaking their heads: He wears a kilt even though they weren't introduced to Scotland for another 300 years.

- **Elizabeth (1998):** This movie's characters and time sequences are all over the place. Bishop Stephen Gardiner, who led the opposition to the queen in the movie, actually died three years before she was crowned. Also, the real Elizabeth was well aware that Lord Robert Dudley was married. It was only when his wife died in suspicious circumstances that the queen distanced herself from him.

- **Gladiator (2000):** Marcus and Commodus Aurelius were, of course, father and son. However, Commodus did not smother his father to death because his father wasn't going to make him emperor—the truth is he already was emperor! On November 27, 176, Marcus Aurelius gave his son the rank of Imperator, which conveyed equal ruling power upon Commodus, then 15 years old. Three years later Marcus Aurelius died (of natural causes), and Commodus continued his rule.

- **JFK (1991):** This film is guilty of hyperbole and fantasy: There were 20 people (not 51) who heard shots from the grassy knoll, the mayor of Dallas did not change the motorcade route, and David Ferrie never claimed to have inside knowledge of the killing. In addition, the "mysterious" deaths of such witnesses as Lee Bowers, David Ferrie, and "Jada" indicated no evidence of foul play.

- **The Patriot (2000):** The character of William Tavington is based on British lieutenant colonel Banastre Tarleton, who gets a bad rap in the film. In truth, he never set fire to churches full of people, nor did he die in the climactic Battle of Cowpens. Rather than the dour wallflower depicted in the film, Tarleton was a fun-loving extrovert who died in his sleep when he was 78.

- **Tombstone (1993):** Let's set the record straight: Johnny Behan was not the sheriff when Wyatt Earp arrived in Tombstone, Arizona. John Ringo was not the leader of the cowboys, who, by the way, did not wear red sashes to identify themselves. Nor did Deputy Billy Breakenridge and outlaw Curly Bill Brocius have a homosexual relationship. Regarding the famous shoot-out: In the film, there are 51 shots fired in 128 seconds in a 30-foot-wide lot. In reality, there were 30 shots fired in 30 seconds in a space just 18 feet wide.

Talk to the Expert
BANANA GASSER

❋ ❋ ❋ ❋

Q: You gas bananas?

A: That's the short version. My work is much more precise and technical than you might think, because bananas are so perishable. Have you ever wondered how bananas can make it from other continents to your grocery store in edible shape, and yet they turn black and disgusting after three days on your kitchen counter?

Q: Now that you mention it, yes. But they are refrigerated during their cross-continental trip, right?

A: By itself, refrigeration wouldn't bring home the banana, so to speak. Banana pickers harvest them when they're green, and they're shipped in chilled containers. That's where I come in. New shipments are placed in hermetically sealed chambers, where I spray the fruit with gas to catalyze ripening. If I'm on my game, they show up at your grocery store looking like something you'd want to peel and eat either on the spot or within a couple of days.

Q: What type of gas do you use?

A: Ethylene, C_2H_4, which basically is what remains of the alcohol in liquor if you take out the water. Plants naturally produce ethylene, and it causes fruit to ripen. I'm in charge of manipulating the gas vents so the fruit ripens when we want it to ripen. The gas itself doesn't harm the fruit, nor does it harm people.

Q: Not to sound critical, but how hard is it to open a gas vent?

A: There's more to it than that. Here's the reality: First I have to evaluate where the bananas came from, and how long they have been traveling. They go immediately into the chamber, and I have to decide how much gas to give them, what temperature to keep them at, and for how long. A given chamber's bananas need to have the same general characteristics, because one batch of fast-ripeners could cause the whole chamber of bananas to ripen too early.

GOING OUT TONIGHT...
FOR CANADIAN!

✳ ✳ ✳

You'd be hard pressed to find a Canadian restaurant in the United States (except for the 300 Tim Hortons franchises...we'll get to that), but Canada's cultural and geographic diversity has produced quite a few foods that can boast Canadian heritage.

Arctic char: This is the northernmost freshwater fish in North America, caught commercially since the 1940s. Char is a little like salmon in color and texture, but its unique flavor elevates it to a delicacy.

Back bacon: Also called Canadian bacon in the United States, this cut has less fat than other kinds of bacon. It has a taste and texture similar to ham. Peameal bacon is cured back bacon that's coated with ground yellow peas.

Bakeapples: These are also referred to as baked-apple berries, *chicoute*, and cloudberries. Found mostly in the Maritime provinces of Nova Scotia and Newfoundland, they taste—surprise—like a baked apple. These can be eaten raw or used in pies and jams.

Bangbelly: To ward off some of the wettest, windiest, nastiest cold on the continent, Newfoundlanders have long boiled up a pudding of flour, rice, raisins, pork, spices, molasses, and sometimes seal fat. The result is comparable to bread pudding and is commonly served at Christmastime.

Beavertails: No aquatic rodents are harmed in the making of this snack. These fried, flat pastries, shaped like a beaver's tail, are similar to that carnival staple called elephant ears. They can be topped with sugar, cinnamon, fruit, even cream cheese and salmon. An Ottawa specialty.

Bloody Caesar: Similar to the Bloody Mary, this cocktail is popular all over Canada. It's made of vodka, tomato-clam juice, Worcestershire sauce, and hot sauce, served on the rocks in a glass rimmed with celery salt.

Butter tart: Along with so many other aspects of their culture, the Scots brought these to Canada. These are little pecan pies without the pecans, perhaps with chocolate chips, raisins, or nuts. You haven't had Canadian cuisine until you've had a butter tart.

Cipaille: This layered, spiced-meat-and-potato pie is most popular in Quebec. Look for it on menus as "sea pie" in Ontario, not for any aquatic additives but because that's exactly how the French word is pronounced in English.

Cretons: Break your morning butter-and-jam routine and have some *cretons* instead! This Quebecois tradition is a seasoned pork-and-onion pâté often spread on toast.

Dulse: This tasty, nutritious, protein-packed seaweed washes up on the shores of Atlantic Canada and is used in cooking much the same ways one uses onions: chopped, sautéed, and added to everything from omelets to bread dough.

Malpeques: Many consider these Prince Edward Island delicacies the world's tastiest oysters, harvested with great care by workers who rake them out of the mud by hand. If you can find them, the "pride of P.E.I." will cost you dearly.

Maple syrup: Close to 90 percent of Canada's maple syrup comes from Quebec, and Canada is the world's largest producer of this sweet, sticky pancake topping.

Nanaimo bar: New York also claims this confection, but the thoughtful Manhattanite doesn't utter that on Vancouver Island. It's a chocolate bar layered with nuts, buttercream, and sometimes peanut butter or coconut. Nanaimo bars are well liked throughout Canada and in bordering U.S. regions (especially around Seattle).

Perogies: Canada's large waves of Slavic immigration have brought these Polish–Ukrainian delights to the True North. They're small dumplings with a variety of fillings, including cheese, meat, potatoes, mushrooms, cabbage, and more. Top with sour cream and onions.

Ployes: Acadia, the Cajuns' ancestral homeland, loves its buckwheat pancakes. But these greenish-yellow griddle cakes contain no milk or eggs, so they're not actually pancakes. Eat them with berries, whipped cream, *cretons*, or maple syrup.

Poutine: Dump gravy and cheese curds on french fries: *Voilà la poutine!* Quebec is the homeland of *poutine*, but you can get it all over the nation. Ignore your cardiologist's entreaties for greater enjoyment.

Rye: This is the Canadian name for Canadian whiskey, though it's actually made with a blend of rye, corn, and barley. Prohibition in the United States created a boom for Canadian distillers, and this unique style became part of the national identity. Rye is generally sweeter than bourbon and retains a worldwide following among liquor connoisseurs.

Tim Hortons: Horton was a solid National Hockey League defenseman of long service to the Toronto Maple Leafs, but he's best known for founding a ubiquitous chain of donut shops. Though Tim Hortons sells coffee, breakfast foods, and sandwiches, the donuts are the most popular. With more than 2,700 franchises, you have to go pretty far into the Canadian bush to be deprived of your Tim's fix.

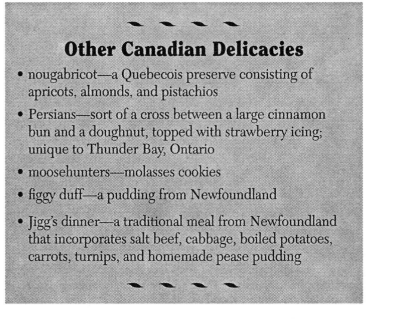

Other Canadian Delicacies

- nougabricot—a Quebecois preserve consisting of apricots, almonds, and pistachios
- Persians—sort of a cross between a large cinnamon bun and a doughnut, topped with strawberry icing; unique to Thunder Bay, Ontario
- moosehunters—molasses cookies
- figgy duff—a pudding from Newfoundland
- Jigg's dinner—a traditional meal from Newfoundland that incorporates salt beef, cabbage, boiled potatoes, carrots, turnips, and homemade pease pudding

DANGEROUS JOBS

✳ ✳ ✳ ✳

*The next time you complain about bad coffee at the office,
consult this list for some perspective. At least the threat of
death or injury doesn't hang over your head. These are the
most dangerous occupations in the United States.
(The numbers cited are per 100,000 workers.)*

Truck Drivers

Truck drivers and other workers who spend a lot of time on the road
(e.g., people in sales and deliveries) face the professional hazard of
highway crashes. In 2005, 993 road deaths occurred among workers
in this industry.

Farmers and Ranchers

The machinery, for the most part, is the biggest threat to farmers
and ranchers. Threshers, combines, and other heavy pieces of agricultural equipment cause more than 300 deaths per year.

Pilots

Pilots of smaller aircraft such as crop dusters and air taxis are far
more likely to crash than the people flying 747s. The fatality rate for
those who work among the clouds often reaches 100 deaths per year.

Roofers

Not only are roofers high above the ground and at risk of falling,
they also work with toxic chemicals at extremely high temperatures.
This combination is so perilous that some 100 roofers die on the job
each year.

Loggers

Loggers often meet their end when tree limbs fall on them or machinery chews up more than lumber. Approximately 90 loggers die
from work-related injuries every year.

Fishers

Fishers brave the perils of the sea to bring you your king crab, and
an average of 80 people die trying each year. Anglers fall overboard,

are injured by equipment, or succumb to illnesses that are difficult to treat at sea.

Taxi Drivers and Chauffeurs

Aside from the risk of being involved in traffic accidents, people who drive strangers around for a living face potentially hostile situations with each fare. Homicide and assault account for an average of 65 deaths per year among cabbies and chauffeurs.

Trash Collectors

Toxic fumes and hidden sharp objects aren't the only dangers posed to the people who pick up our garbage. More than 40 workers are hit and killed each year by drivers who try to speed past sanitation trucks.

Electrical Power Installers and Repairers

The next time your power goes out, consider the folks who risk their lives so you can get back to watching your TV shows. Electrical power installers and repairers handle lethal amounts of electricity hundreds of feet above the ground, and there are an average of 36 deaths in this line of work each year.

Steelworkers

Steelworkers hang perilously from bridges and scaffolding to execute the plans of architects. Despite safety devices that include ropes, clips, and harnesses, approximately 30 workers fall to their deaths each year.

Other Dangerous Jobs

- Animal researcher
- Bomb squad technician
- Armored-car guard
- Bounty hunter
- Astronaut
- Hurricane hunter
- Bicycle messenger
- Propulsion engineer
- Bodyguard
- Volcanologist

TOP TEN CRIME SCENE TRACES

✳ ✳ ✳ ✳

Have people learned nothing from TV crime shows?
Here's a hint: Just walk through a room, let alone commit a crime,
and you'll leave a trace that will detail your every action.

1. Tool marks: If you use any sort of object to commit your crime—a pickax on a door lock, a ladder to reach a window, a knife or a rag (for any purpose)—it will be traceable. Tools used in any capacity create tiny nicks that can be detected, identified, and tracked by a crime-scene investigator.

2. Paint: A paint chip left at a crime scene reveals volumes. If it's from the vehicle you used in committing the crime, it indicates the make and model. If paint is found on the tool you used to break into a house, it could place you at the scene. Think it's too hard to distinguish specific paint colors? There are 40,000 types of paint classified in police databases.

3. Broken glass: Microscopic glass fragments cling to your clothes and can't be laundered out easily. Crime labs examine tint, thickness, density, and refractive index of the fragments to determine their origins.

4. Dust and dirt: Even if you're a neat-and-tidy sort of criminal, dust and dirt are often missed by the most discerning eye. These particles can reveal where you live and work, and if you have a pet (and what kind). If you've trudged through fields or someone's backyard, researchers can use palynology—the science that studies plant spores, insects, seeds, and other microorganisms—to track you down.

5. Fibers: The sources include clothing, drapes, wigs, carpets, furniture, blankets, pets, and plants. Using a compound microscope, an analyst can determine if the fibers are manufactured or natural, which often indicates their value as evidence. The more specific the fiber, the easier it will be to identify (consider the differences between fibers from a white cotton T-shirt and those from a multicolored wool sweater). There are more than a thousand known fibers, as well as several thousand dyes, so if an exact match is found, you will be too.

6. Blood: A victim's blood tells investigators a lot, but they're also looking for different kinds of blood—including yours if you were injured at the scene—and the patterns of blood distribution. Detectives are well trained in collecting blood evidence to estimate when the crime occurred and who was involved. By the way, don't bother to clean up any blood, because investigators use special lights that reveal your efforts.

7. Bodily fluids: Saliva, urine, vomit, and semen are a crime-scene investigator's dream, providing DNA evidence that will implicate even the most savvy criminal. Saliva is commonly found left behind by a criminal who took time out for a beverage, a snack, or a cigarette.

8. Fingerprints: One of the best ways to identify a criminal is through fingerprints left at the scene. But you kept track of what you touched and then wiped everything down, right? It doesn't matter: You still left smeared prints that can be lifted and analyzed. Investigators enter fingerprint evidence into national databases that can point directly to you.

9. Shoe prints: If you have feet (and assuming you're not a "barefoot burglar"), you left behind shoe prints. They could be in soil or snow or perhaps on a carpet or across a bare floor. The particular treads on the soles of shoes make them easy to trace, and the bottoms of most shoes have nicks or scratches that make them easy to identify.

10. Hair: Humans shed a lot of hair from all parts of their bodies, so bald bandits have no advantage. Hairs as tiny as eyelashes and eyebrows have unique characteristics that reveal a lot about a person, including race, dietary habits, and overall health. And don't forget: While your hair is dropping all over the crime scene, the victim's hair is clinging to your clothing.

BEYOND BIGFOOT: CRYPTOZOOLOGICAL CREATURES

✳ ✳ ✳

Cryptozoology is the study of creatures that are rumored to exist. But for true believers and alleged eyewitnesses, these "cryptids" are alive and well and lurking among us.

Marozi: With a maned lion's face fronting a jaguarlike body, the Marozi (also known as the spotted lion) was reported several times in the 1930s in Kenya's mountains but hasn't been mentioned much since. The Natural History Museum in Great Britain is said to be in possession of the spotted skin of a marozi, but many experts think the specimen represents a jaguar that bred with common spotless plains lions.

Kamchatka Giant Bear: Swedish zoologist Sten Bergman, working in Russia's Kamchatka Peninsula in the 1920s, discovered a paw print that measured a full square foot, suggesting a bear of remarkable size. Similar sightings tell of an ursine almost twice the size of a typical North American grizzly bear, measuring six feet at the shoulder. Some Russian biologists believe there is a small group of Kamchatka Giant Bears that survived the most recent ice age.

Skunk Ape: Bigfoot's smelly Southern cousin has been reported a number of times in Florida's swamps, most convincingly in 2000 by a couple who took an excellent snapshot of what looked to be a six-foot-six orangutan. The picture didn't capture its scent, of course, but the couple attested to its atrocity.

Lizard Man: This scaly green hominid, the resident mysterious beast of Escape Ore Swamp in South Carolina, has long been at the center of local lore. While many consider the creature a hoax, others swear they've encountered it face to face. Lizard Man has had several brushes with fame: A local radio station once offered $1 million for a live capture, and in 1988, a South Carolina Republican leader labeled Lizard Man a staunch Democrat.

Jersey Devil: According to most reports, New Jersey's cryptozoological curiosity has wings, a horse's face, a pig's hooves, and a kangaroo's body. The legend of the Jersey Devil was born in the 1700s—based on a tale of a cursed baby-turned-demon that flew off into the night—and boomed in the early 1900s, with supposed sightings all over the state. To this day, people report Devil sightings, mostly in the spooky Pine Barrens of southern New Jersey. While some locals think the creature is truly a supernatural beast, others say it's probably a misidentified sandhill crane.

El Chupacabra: Puerto Rico's legendary "goat sucker" is a fanged and clawed beast that performs vampirism on livestock. The first accounts of its victims—often goats, chickens, horses, and cows—were reported in the 1950s by farmers who found animals drained of blood, with several large puncture marks. Some who have allegedly sighted the creature describe it as a short, kangaroolike monster with oversize teeth and an oval head, but others liken it to a large reptile or bat.

Tessie: Deep in Lake Tahoe on the California–Nevada border lurks a storied sea creature that's the Sierra Nevada cousin of the Loch Ness Monster. It's alleged that after a submarine expedition, undersea explorer Jacques Cousteau said, "The world isn't ready for what's down there." (He could, of course, have been referring to anything odd.) Popular descriptions portray Tessie as either a freshwater relative of a whale or a 20-foot sea serpent with a humped back.

Champ: Like Tessie, Champ is named for the body of water in which it purportedly lurks, in this case New York's Lake Champlain. Several hundred recorded sightings typically describe the beast as an angular black sea monster measuring about 50 feet in length. One investigative group believes the often-sighted Champ is actually a surviving plesiosaur, a dinosaur that died off 60 million years ago.

TENNIS TANTRUMS

✳ ✳ ✳ ✳

Despite its genteel history and emphasis on decorum,
a good game of tennis can provoke on-court behaviors that are
tyrannical or simply tiresome. Here are a few professional players
who lost more than their composure.

John McEnroe vs. Tom Gullikson—Wimbledon, 1981: *The New York Times* once dubbed McEnroe "the worst advertisement for our system of values since Al Capone," so it's only fitting his name should appear (twice) on this list. In addition to his usual repertoire of ranting, raving, and racquet launching, McEnroe immortalized his rebellious reputation by continuously shouting, "You cannot be serious!" at umpires and line judges. This behavior continued throughout the duration of the tournament, and despite winning the prestigious prize for the first time, McEnroe was not offered a membership to the All-England club, an honor usually afforded to every first-time victor.

John McEnroe vs. Mikael Pernfors—Australian Open, 1990: Johnny Mac should have boned up on the rulebook before unleashing one of his patented temper tantrums. In his fourth-round match against Pernfors, McEnroe was issued a warning by umpire Gerry Armstrong for intimidating a lineswoman. Later, after he was docked a point for smashing a racket, McEnroe fired off a volley of vindictive vituperations toward the official. Unaware that a new "three strikes you're out" rule had recently been inserted into the code of conduct, McEnroe was rightfully disqualified from further play, and the match was awarded to Pernfors.

Jeff Tarango vs. Alexander Mronz—Wimbledon, 1995: Talk about mixed doubles! During his third-round match against Alexander Mronz, tennis menace Jeff Tarango put on a legendary display of spoiled sportsmanship, childlike insolence, and all-round bad judgment. After chair umpire Bruno Rebeuh ruled against him on several close line calls, the feisty Tarango refused to continue the match, demanded that the accumulated throng watching the debacle "shut up," and accused the umpire of being "one of the most corrupt officials in the game." At least one denizen in the crowd supported Tarango's view of the proceedings. His wife, Benedictine, strolled up to the on-court official and delivered an overhand smash of her own. She slapped the official twice across the face before storming out of the arena with her husband, who became the first player in Wimbledon history to default a match because of a disagreement over an official's judgment. Tarango was fined a record $15,500 for his tempestuous tirade.

Serena Williams vs. Jennifer Capriati—U.S. Open, 2004: When her cross-court backhand was ruled out by chair umpire Mariana Alves, Williams was stunned but certainly not silent. She unleashed a barrage of uncomplimentary comments and emphasized her perspective on the proceedings by putting a ball on the court, pointing at it, and pouting. Williams went on to lose the match, and Alves did not umpire again during the tournament.

Greg Rusedski vs. Andy Roddick—Wimbledon, 2003: When a fan in the stands yelled "out" after a Roddick shot, Rusedski stopped playing the point, believing the call had come from chair umpire Lars Graff. After the official refused Rusedski's request that the point be replayed, Rusedski launched into an expletive-laced tirade that even commentator and noted ball brat John McEnroe found offensive. The bitter Rusedski went on to lose in straight sets and stormed off the court, refusing to shake the official's hand.

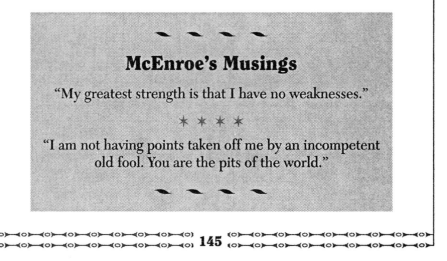

McEnroe's Musings

"My greatest strength is that I have no weaknesses."

✷ ✷ ✷ ✷

"I am not having points taken off me by an incompetent old fool. You are the pits of the world."

I'm No Expert, But...
WE KNOW THEM...OR DO WE?

* * * *

Q: Why did Lady Godiva become an exhibitionist equestrienne?
A: Sadly, she didn't—it's a myth. There was a real woman named Godgifu, wife of a powerful Briton in the 11th century, but she had nothing to do with the story about the naked tax protester. Lady Godiva was dreamed up a couple of centuries after Godgifu's death.

Q: How could someone as rich, dashing, and successful as Howard Hughes die a paranoid, disheveled hermit?
A: He started out quite differently—as a young playboy and businessman. Howard's germ phobia came from his overprotective mother; in those days of deadly epidemics (Howard was a teen during the flu pandemic of late World War I), it wasn't inherently weird to flee from disease. As he grew older, Howard became the squire of many popular Hollywood actresses before his social phobia forced him into isolation. He died in 1976 with broken needles embedded in his arms, and at six-foot-four, he weighed only 90 pounds.

Q: Okay, Abner Doubleday didn't invent baseball. Who was he, then?
A: Mainly a distinguished warrior who served in the Mexican War and the Seminole campaign and commanded a division at Gettysburg. Doubleday's obituary didn't even mention baseball. Team owners invented the connection with the national game to discredit baseball's origin in the similar English game of rounders—they wanted people to believe it was 100 percent American.

Q: Was Caligula a depraved monster or not?
A: Not for most of his life, though the last three years (A.D. 38–41) pretty well spoiled his legacy. As a child, he went on military campaigns with his famous father, Germanicus; in his little legionary's uniform, he was the army's beloved mascot. In his first year as emperor (A.D. 37–38), he did some good things for Rome, though he did just about break the treasury. After that, much of what you've heard about his excesses and insanity is credible.

HUMMINGBIRDS

✳ ✳ ✳ ✳

When early Spanish explorers first encountered hummingbirds in the New World, they called them joyas voladoras—*or "flying jewels." But the hummingbird is more than just beautiful: Its physical capabilities put the toughest human being to shame.*

- The ruby-throated hummingbird—the only hummingbird species east of Mississippi—migrates at least 2,000 miles from its breeding grounds to its wintering grounds. On the way, it crosses the Gulf of Mexico—that's 500 miles without rest. Not bad for a creature that weighs just an eighth of an ounce and is barely three inches long.

- A hovering hummingbird has an energy output per unit weight about ten times that of a person running nine miles per hour. If a person were to do the same amount of work per unit weight, he or she would expend 40 horsepower.

- A man's daily energy output is about 3,500 calories. If one were to recalculate the daily energy output of a hummingbird—eating, hovering, flying, perching, and sleeping—for a 170-pound man, it would total about 155,000 calories.

- An average man consumes about two and a half pounds of food per day. If his energy output were the same as that of a hummingbird, he would have to eat and burn off, in a single day, the equivalent of 285 pounds of hamburger, 370 pounds of potatoes, or 130 pounds of bread.

- The ruby-throated hummingbird can increase its weight by 50 percent—all of it fat—just before its winter migration. This provides extra fuel for the long, nonstop flight across the Gulf of Mexico. In comparison, a 170-pound man would have to pack on enough fat to increase his weight to 255 pounds in just a few weeks.

- The wing muscles of a hummingbird account for 25 to 30 percent of its total body weight, making it well adapted to flight. However, the hummingbird has poorly developed feet and cannot walk.

- Due to their small body size and lack of insulation, hummingbirds lose body heat rapidly. To meet their energy demands, they enter torpor (a state similar to hibernation), during which they lower their metabolic rate by about 95 percent. During torpor, the hummingbird drops its body temperature by 30° F to 40° F, and it lowers its heart rate from more than 1,200 beats per minute to as few as 50.

- Hummingbirds have the highest metabolic rate of any animal on Earth. To provide energy for flying, they must consume up to three times their body weight in food each day.

- Unlike other birds, a hummingbird can rotate its wings in a circle. It can also hover in one spot; fly up, down, sideways, and even upside down (for short distances); and it is the only bird that can fly backward.

- The smallest bird on Earth is the bee hummingbird (*Calypte helenae*), native to Cuba. With a length of only two inches, the bee hummingbird can comfortably perch on the eraser of a pencil.

- The most common types of hummingbirds include the Allen's, Anna's, berylline, black-chinned, blue-throated, broad-billed, broad-tailed, buff-bellied, Costa's, Lucifer, Magnificent, ruby-throated, Rufous, violet-crowned, and white-eared.

- Like bees, hummingbirds carry pollen from one plant to another while they are feeding, thus playing an important role in plant pollination. Each bird can visit between 1,000 and 2,000 blossoms every day.

- There are about 330 different species of hummingbirds. Most of them live and remain in Central and South America, never venturing any farther north. Only 16 species of hummingbirds actually breed in North America.

FEMALE FANG FICTION

✳ ✳ ✳ ✳

Chick literature is popular, but it doesn't compare with chick lit that features vampires. Who cares if tall, dark, and handsome has a set of fangs? Here are a few of the hottest titles and authors on the market.

Author: Mary Janice Davidson

Major Character: Elizabeth Ann "Betsy" Taylor

Transformation: After a rotten day during which she loses her job and is killed in a car accident, Betsy wakes up thirsty for the red stuff.

Bizarre Bite: She craves a new kind of Bloody Mary, and her passion for shoes is equally insatiable.

Titles: *Undead and Unpopular, Undead and Unreturnable, Undead and Unappreciated, Undead and Unwed,* and *Undead and Unemployed*

✳ ✳ ✳ ✳

Author: Charlaine Harris

Major Character: Sookie Stackhouse

Transformation: She isn't a vampire—she's a mind-reading cocktail waitress who dates a vampire.

Bizarre Bite: While Sookie and her boyfriend tackle crime, she often wonders if she'll be the next victim—his!

Titles: *Dead as a Doornail, Definitely Dead, Dead to the World,* and *All Together Dead*

✳ ✳ ✳ ✳

Author: Kim Harrison

Major Character: Rachel Morgan

Transformation: Rachel is a witch and bounty hunter whose mission is to "bring criminal night creatures to justice."

Bizarre Bite: As indicated by the novels' titles, Rachel's vigilantism evokes Clint Eastwood.

Titles: *The Good, the Bad, and the Undead; Every Which Way but Dead; Fistful of Charms; For a Few Demons More*; and *Dead Witch Walking*

✳ ✳ ✳ ✳

Author: Keri Arthur

Major Character: Riley Jensen

Transformation: She's the love child of a vampire and a werewolf who uses both sides of the family to her advantage.

Bizarre Bite: Riley manages to solve paranormal mysteries while saving plenty of time for rollicking romance.

Titles: *Full Moon Rising, Kissing Sin, Tempting Evil*, and *Dangerous Games*

✳ ✳ ✳ ✳

Author: Laurell K. Hamilton

Major Character: Anita Blake

Transformation: As if raising zombies for a living weren't weird enough, she's a powerful necromancer and a licensed vampire executioner who helps the police solve preternatural crimes.

Bizarre Bite: Anita is ruthless about surviving and protecting "her people"—not an easy task when you're neck-deep in vampires and shapeshifters most of the time. She's dangerous, which may be why the vampires' Master of the City and the local werewolf King both try to charm her!

Titles: *Guilty Pleasures, The Laughing Corpse, Circus of the Damned, Lunatic Café, Bloody Bones, The Killing Dance, Burnt Offerings, Blue Moon, Obsidian Butterfly, Narcissus in Chains, Cerulean Sins, Incubus Dreams, Danse Macabre*, and *The Harlequin*

Folklore: Myth or Truth?

LAURA SECORD: "THE YANKS ARE COMING! THE YANKS ARE COMING!"

✳ ✳ ✳

Most of you who have eaten Laura Secord candy probably don't know her story; now you will. Was she truly a Canadian Pauline Revere?

Who was she? Laura Ingersoll Secord was a homestead wife in Upper Canada (now Ontario) during the early 1800s. Modern Canadians count her among the greats of Canada for her courage during the U.S. invasion in the War of 1812. And yes, there is a brand of sweets bearing her name, which is kind of like Ethan Allen furniture or Revereware; you don't really think of the historical figure when you think of the consumer commodity.

The United States invaded Canada? For the second time, as a matter of fact. Remember the Colonial complaint about British troops quartered in people's houses? It chapped their cheeks so much that the new U.S. Constitution explicitly outlawed it. When the troops were American and the soil was foreign, that was somehow different. Laura and her husband, James, lived at Queenston, Upper Canada (near Niagara Falls), during the U.S. invasion. American officers ordered them to house and feed troops. Direct resistance would have been suicidal even had James been healthy (his leg had been shot beyond use in an earlier battle).

What did Laura supposedly do? Though it's cheap and easy to force the enemy's innocent civilians to feed and house your troops, you then can't talk about your plans over dinner. Laura overheard that U.S. troops were planning a surprise attack at Beaver Dams. According to the legend's variations, she left in slippers and walked barefoot part of the way, she took along a cow so that she would appear less suspicious, she cooked up a cover story about a sick relative, she risked accidental gunshot by an overeager sentry, and it took her hours to climb treacherous cliffs. In all variations, she met up with Mohawk warriors friendly to the British/Canadian cause. They escorted her to Lieutenant FitzGibbon, the British officer in command, and she told what she knew. Native and Anglo-Canadian forces used the information to ambush the U.S. invaders, taking most of them prisoner. This turned back the Niagara frontier offensive into Upper Canada, thus affecting the strategic overall course of the war.

What's true? Here we have a true story with minor embellishments that should not diminish its veracity. It is possible the Mohawks also figured out the U.S. plans, but we have FitzGibbon's testimony that Laura had warned him. He recounted it many years later, well removed from the heat of battle. We also have FitzGibbon's account of a conversation with his captured U.S. counterpart, confirming that Laura's information had been correct. FitzGibbon, a credible man, went on to a distinguished military and civil career. He certainly took good advantage of what he learned. Most of the troops on the British side were First Peoples, so they deserve credit for carrying out such a great ambush.

Was she rewarded? Not right away, though she did try hard to milk her deed for all it was worth. For much of her life, she and James pressured the British government for some form of official recognition, perhaps a comfortable civil service job. Finally, when she was in her 80s, she got official praise and a pension. She lived just long enough to see Canada become a Dominion.

How can she compare to the great Paul Revere? Laura walked, instead of riding, about 20 miles through dangerous, difficult country. Any way you examine the evidence, Laura Secord was a brave, loyal Canadian who answered the bell when her country needed her, despite great risk and hardship. Her act made a real difference in the outcome. Revere was only one of several riders, and he got caught; Laura won through.

ARMOR: OUTSTANDING AND INTERESTING TANKS

✳ ✳ ✳ ✳

*The 20th century saw the armored fighting vehicle (AFV)
supplant heavy cavalry as a swift, hard-hitting arm of war.
Some tanks have been a cut above their contemporaries, while
others were funny looking, or failures, or both.*

The Great

FT-17 (France, 1917; 37mm or machine gun)

Unlike most elephantine World War I armor, the small FT-17 had a
360-degree rotating gun turret, and it crossed trenches with the help
of extended rear rockers rather than oversized, diamond-shaped
treads. It was the first World War I tank that looked like World War
II tanks and the only one to see significant World War II service.

Somua S-35 (France, 1935; 47mm)

The S-35's tough, cast hull was a big leap from riveted and bolted
designs, which tended to spall (meaning "rivets, bolts, coffee cups,
and such flying around inside") when hit. Captured S-35s ended up
in German service.

Matilda II (U.K., 1937; 40mm)

If you want to stop the enemy in its tracks, bring a tank that can
barely be harmed. Mattie's crews could laugh at German tank cannons until 1942, when most Soviet Matildas were phased out in favor
of faster, more powerful tanks. Although the relatively small Matilda
waltzed slowly, her bulldog presence in the battle area commanded
respect.

KV-1 (U.S.S.R., 1939; 76mm)

This hulking brute owes its fame partly to timing. When Germany
invaded the Soviet Union, the KV was a monster only the Stuka
dive-bomber or 88mm flak gun could slay. Outside Leningrad, one
KV-1 withstood 135 German cannon hits.

T-34 (U.S.S.R., 1941; 76mm, then 85mm)

Looking for credibility around World War II zealots? Call this the
best tank of the war. Its amazing speed, sloped armor, and strong

gunnery enabled aggressive tank tactics, perfectly suited to Eastern Front warfare and deadly to Germany. The 1944 T-34 (85) model was still serving in some armies in 2000.

Panzerkampfwagen V Panther (Germany, 1943; 75mm)

Remember the guys who sneered when you heaped praise on the T-34? They have nothing on Panther advocates. Speedy and well armored up front, the Panther's hard-hitting long gun could engage at ranges that enabled few enemies to harm it.

Sherman Firefly (U.K., 1944; 77mm)

Early Shermans burned too easily and hit too gently. Then the British fitted their outstanding 17-pound cannon to Yankee-made Shermans. The result combined the Sherman's reliability with gunnery that could cook even a German Tiger or Panther.

M-60 Patton (U.S., 1960; 105mm)

For two decades, this reliable tank was NATO's mainstay—and perhaps the finest tank of the 1960s. Its variants formed the backbone of Israeli armor during the Yom Kippur War, and the U.S. Marines drove some into battle during the 1991 Gulf War. The M-60s were routinely updated until the end of the Cold War.

T-72 (U.S.S.R., 1971; 125mm)

Any tank this prolific rates mention. When introduced, the T-72's 125mm cannon raised the gunnery bar above the common 105mm. It's fast, reliable, and delivers a lot of bang for the ruble, and in 2002 it was still the world's most widely deployed tank.

Merkava (Israel, 1977; 105mm, then 120mm)

After three tank wars with the Arabs, Israel had learned the following: Tank crews experience horrifying deaths; tanks can be replaced, but crewmembers can't; and a crew that feels safe will fight boldly. The innovative Merkava ("Chariot") broke all convention by putting the engine in front, just to help shield the crew. In its first full-dressed engagement (1982), seven Merkavas became battlefield kills—but all their crewmembers lived.

The Odd

A7V (Germany, 1917; 57mm)

This clunker looked like a railroad caboose covered with a big steel drop cloth, and it fought about as well. It couldn't cross trenches, which was disappointing, because the goal of tanks was to break up trench warfare stalemates. If you romanticize German tanks, try not to look at pictures of this armored banana slug.

Fiat 2000 (Italy, 1917; 65mm)
This looked like a German A7V (see above) with a little observatory on top. While heavily armored and bristling with seven machine guns, the slow F-2000 could barely outrun a briskly marching infantryman. Fortunately for its crews, it never had to try; it only served in peacetime.

M13/40 (Italy, 1940; 47mm)
Lousy armor, weak gun, underpowered and unreliable engine, prone to stalling or catching fire when hit—what a combination. This bowser was the mainstay of Italian armor in North Africa. With equipment like this, who can blame Italian crews for bailing out of their tanks and surrendering?

Elefant tank destroyer (Germany, 1943; 88mm)
A perennial candidate for Dumbest World War II Armor Design, the glacially slow Elefant mounted the famous 88mm cannon and looked like today's self-propelled howitzers. It had no machine guns of its own, so enemy infantry were welcome to spray tags on it or use its massive front housing as a latrine.

Churchill Crocodile (U.K., 1944; 75mm, flamethrower)
Most World War II powers developed flamethrowing tanks; this was one of the best designs. The Crocodile pulled a trailer of modified gasoline "ammo" yet still mounted a standard tank cannon. Hosing flaming gas the length of a football field, the Croc was hell for dug-in defenders.

Sherman DD (U.S./U.K., 1944; 75mm)
Tanks don't swim well, which is an issue when you're planning a D-Day. Allied engineers invented a watertight skirting for the Sherman so that it could float, and then added a little propeller for instant buoyancy—at least enough for the tank to reach the beach. Ten Sherman DD battalions, the equivalent of a full division, waded ashore this way on June 6, 1944. A number swamped and sank, but on that day any Allied tank on shore was welcome.

DAYS GONE BY: PINBALL

❊ ❊ ❊ ❊

Once considered an untoward distraction, pinball survived
early disapproval and even banishment to become the popular
predecessor to today's video games.

Prohibition

Pinball was invented in the 1930s, inspired by the 19th-century
game bagatelle, which involved a billiards cue and a playing field
full of holes. Some early pinball arcades "awarded" players for high
scores, and in the mid-1930s, machines were introduced that provided direct monetary payouts. These games quickly earned pinball the
reputation as a fun diversion—and a gambling device. Thus, starting in the 1940s, New York City mayor Fiorello LaGuardia declared
pinball parlors akin to casinos ("magnets for the wrong element"),
ushering in an era of pinball prohibition. Chicago, Los Angeles, and
other major American cities followed suit with their own pinball
bans. New York's pinball embargo lasted until 1976, and city officials
destroyed 11,000 machines before it was lifted. The turning point:
Writer and pinball wizard Roger Sharpe called his shots during a
demonstration in front of the New York City Council, proving that
pinball was indeed a game of skill. The council members voted
6–0 to legalize pinball in the Big Apple.

Rise and Fall

Despite the fact that pinball was banned in the United States' three
largest cities, it became a favorite pastime among adolescents and
teens in the 1950s. This changed in 1973 with the advent of the
video game, but pinball enjoyed the first of several revivals later in
the 1970s, thanks to its association with such rock-and-roll luminar-
ies as The Who, Elton John, and Kiss. The last pinball renaissance
peaked with Bally's *The Addams Family* game, introduced in 1991 to
tie in with the release of the movie. *The Addams Family* became the
best-selling pinball game of all time, with 22,000 machines sold. In
the 1990s, the bottom dropped out of the pinball market, and as of
2007, there was only one American manufacturer, Stern Pinball.

Origin of the Flippers

Gottlieb's *Humpty Dumpty*, designed by Harry Mabs in 1947, was the first pinball game to feature flippers (three on each side) that allowed the player to use hand-eye coordination to influence gravity and chance. Many pre-flipper games were essentially dressed-up gambling contraptions, and players could just tilt the machines to rack up points. *Humpty Dumpty* and the thousands of flipper games that followed were true contests of skill. In 1948, pinball designer Steven Kordek repositioned the flippers (just two) at the bottom of the playfield, and the adjustment became the industry standard.

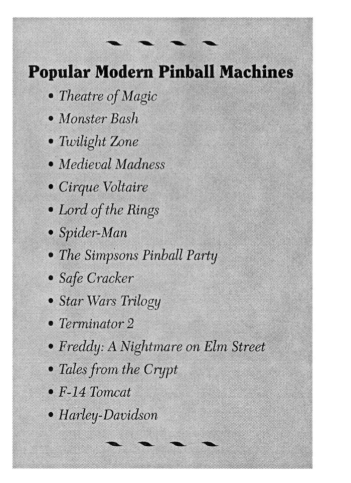

Popular Modern Pinball Machines

- *Theatre of Magic*
- *Monster Bash*
- *Twilight Zone*
- *Medieval Madness*
- *Cirque Voltaire*
- *Lord of the Rings*
- *Spider-Man*
- *The Simpsons Pinball Party*
- *Safe Cracker*
- *Star Wars Trilogy*
- *Terminator 2*
- *Freddy: A Nightmare on Elm Street*
- *Tales from the Crypt*
- *F-14 Tomcat*
- *Harley-Davidson*

Talk to the Expert
CASINO DEALER

✳ ✳ ✳

For those who pine for the bright lights of Vegas, dealing blackjack or baccarat might be a dream. One roulette dealer on the Vegas Strip told us a little more about his work.

Q: Why do some people call you a "croupier"?

A: That's a title more often used among pretentious characters, of whom there are many in Las Vegas. But in my book, "croup" refers to a bad cough, and I don't think I'd enjoy a job as a professional cougher.

Q: No offense, but your job doesn't look much more difficult than coughing. Spin a wheel, wait for a ball to stop, figure out winnings. There has to be more to it than that.

A: If you want to make your car payment, there is. Casino dealing is the ultimate people job. The game itself, whether it's roulette or blackjack, isn't very hard. People are winning or losing money, and they react to that—that's what requires me to have good social skills. People will keep playing a table partly because of the environment the dealer creates.

Q: A fortune flows across your table every workday. How much of it do you get to keep?

A: I won't tell you what I get, but if it weren't for tips, I could do just as well in retail sales. The more players I have and the more winners who come through, the more tips I make—thanks to the tradition of "winners tip."

Q: Is it hard to break into your field?

A: Easy to break in, hard to stay. You can find gambling nearly anywhere in the country, though some training helps you get hired. People don't realize how many jobs there are on a casino staff: cashiers, dealers for all the games, pit clerk, pit boss, hosting, and security—a lot of security. Most casino employees don't deal cards or craps or roulette. Some don't know how to play, and you'd be surprised how many never gamble a nickel.

Q: How's it possible to cheat at roulette?

A: I watch for that very carefully. Some people will try to manipulate the ball. People used to have an accomplice create a distraction, then blow at the wheel through a straw. Casinos ended that by putting clear shields around the wheels. Other people try bumping the table at the right time. I keep my hand on the table at all times while the wheel's going, so if someone bumps the table I'll feel it. The first time I'll use my instincts; maybe it was an accident. The second time is no accident, and we'll ask the person to leave. All casinos work diligently to spot cheaters.

Q: How easy is it for the house to cheat? The most cynical view of the gambling industry is that it's run and rigged by organized crime.

A: The house has a natural statistical advantage, with no need or reason to cheat. In theory, if the house wanted to cheat, it'd use electromagnets. I can think of quite a few ways, but if I were asked to involve myself in actually doing them—or if I knew they were going on—I'd resign without notice. I don't want to go to jail. We get inspected; I think our gambling equipment is subject to much tougher scrutiny than those new voting machines. I'm not sure this will comfort you any, but the casino business is very corporate. We get lectures on how to reduce liability. We even get retirement benefits. It isn't *The Sopranos* by a long shot.

The Venetian Resort in Macao, China, claims to be the world's largest gaming space, taking up 550,000 square feet. The casino houses 3,400 slot machines and more than 800 gaming tables.

CHUNKS OF CHEDDAR

✳ ✳ ✳ ✳

- Until 2002, cheddar was the second most popular cheese in the United States (after processed American), but the country's passion for pizza has bumped it to number three after mozzarella.

- Cheddar, England, a village in the southwestern county of Somerset, is home to the famous geological site Cheddar Gorge. Beginning in the 16th century, visitors to Cheddar Gorge tasted cheese at local inns and started taking home "cheese from Cheddar." The cheese was actually produced by local cheese makers throughout Somerset County, not just in Cheddar.

- The production of cheddar involves "cheddaring"—the repeated cutting and piling of curds to create a firm cheese.

- Cheddar is so important to the English palate that during World War II, it was illegal to commercially produce any other variety of cheese in England.

- Traditional English cheddar is produced in wheels and aged in cloth for a minimum of six months.

- "Squeaky curds" refers to fresh young cheddar in its natural shape, before it's pressed into a block and aged. Fresh curds are considered a delicacy—and they actually make a squeaking sound when you eat them.

- Cheddar cheese is naturally white or pale yellow. These days, much of it is dyed orange with seeds from the annatto plant, and early cheese makers used carrot juice and marigold petals.

- Originally, cheese was dyed to prevent seasonal color variations. Traditional cheddars had a natural orange color derived from the carotene-rich grass cows ate during spring and summer. In winter, cows ate dry feed, and the resulting cheese was white. Consumers had the misperception that orange cheese was more nutritious, so cheese makers began uniformly coloring their cheeses a "healthful" shade of orange.

- As dry feed has become more commonly used year round, dyeing now depends on regional preferences and traditions. Cheddars from Wisconsin are usually dyed orange, while New England and Canadian cheddars are typically left white.

- Prior to 1850, nearly all cheese produced in the United States was cheddar.

- You can tell the age of cheddar by its taste. Young cheddar has a mild taste; the longer it ages, the sharper and more tangy it becomes.

- "American" cheese is a young, pasteurized cheddar that undergoes additional processing to become the easy-to-melt variety.

- People in the United States eat more than nine pounds of cheddar cheese per person per year.

- The "World's Best Cheddar" is made in the United States: Cabot Creamery in Vermont took home blue-ribbon honors at the 2006 World Championship Cheese Contest.

- According to historians, President Andrew Jackson once served a 1,400-pound block of cheddar at a White House party.

- The *Guinness Book of World Records* has not officially documented the world's largest wheel of cheddar, but here are a few gigantic wheels of note:
  —In 1964, the Wisconsin Cheese Foundation created a 34,665-pound wheel of cheddar for display in the Wisconsin Pavilion at the 1964–1965 World's Fair in New York.
  —In 1988, Simon's Specialty Cheese in Little Chute, Wisconsin, made a 40,060-pound wheel of cheddar known as the "Belle of Wisconsin."
  —In 1995, a cheese maker in Quebec, Canada, claimed to have created the largest wheel of cheese—a 57,518-pound round of cheddar.

- The "World's Cheesiest Car" was constructed in 2003: It was a large-scale model of NASCAR driver Terry Labonte's number five car made out of 3,500 pounds of cheddar.

FLYING FISH

✳ ✳ ✳ ✳

- To escape predators such as swordfish, tuna, and dolphins, flying fish extend their freakishly large pectoral fins as they approach the surface of the water; their velocity then launches them into the air.

- A flying fish can glide through the air for 10 to 20 feet—farther if it has a decent tailwind. It holds its outstretched pectoral fins steady and "sails" through the air, using much the same action as a flying squirrel.

- If you'd like to catch sight of a member of the *Exocoetidae* family, you'll have to travel to the Atlantic, Indian, or Pacific oceans, where there are more than 50 species of flying fish.

- Whiskers are not an indication that a flying fish is up there in years; actually, it's the opposite. Young flying fish have long whiskers that sprout from the bottom jaw. These whiskers are often longer than the fish itself and disappear by adulthood.

- To get a taste of flying fish, stop by a Japanese restaurant. The eggs of flying fish, called *tobiko*, are often used in sushi.

- Attached to the eggs of the Atlantic flying fish are long, adhesive filaments that enable the eggs to affix to clumps of floating seaweed or debris for the gestation period. Without these filaments, the eggs (which are more dense than water) would sink.

- There are about 40 known species of flying fish. Beyond their useful pectoral fins, all have unevenly forked tails, with the lower lobe longer than the upper lobe. Many species also have enlarged pelvic fins and are known as four-winged flying fish.

- Flying fish can soar high enough that sailors often find them on the decks of their ships.

THEY SAID WHAT!?

✳ ✳ ✳ ✳

"Traditionally, most of Australia's imports come from overseas."
Australian cabinet minister Keppel Enderbery

✳ ✳ ✳ ✳

"I owe a lot to my parents, especially my mother and father."
Greg Norman, professional golfer

✳ ✳ ✳ ✳

"If it weren't for electricity, we'd all be watching television by candlelight."
George Gobel, comedian and TV personality

✳ ✳ ✳ ✳

"The Internet is a great way to get on the Net."
Bob Dole, Republican presidential candidate

✳ ✳ ✳ ✳

"Sure, there have been injuries and deaths in boxing, but none of them serious."
Alan Minter, boxer

✳ ✳ ✳ ✳

"I have opinions of my own—strong opinions—but I don't always agree with them."
President George W. Bush

✳ ✳ ✳ ✳

"We've got to pause and ask ourselves, 'How much clean air do we need?'"
Lee Iacocca, American industrialist

✳ ✳ ✳ ✳

"If you're killed, you've lost a very important part of your life."
Brooke Shields, actor and antismoking spokesperson

"We don't necessarily discriminate, we just exclude certain types of people."
Colonel G. Wellman, ROTC commander

✳ ✳ ✳ ✳

"If your parents never had children, chances are you won't either."
Talk-show host Dick Cavett

✳ ✳ ✳ ✳

"You guys line up alphabetically by height."
Bill Peterson, former Florida State football coach

✳ ✳ ✳ ✳

"It is white."
President George W. Bush, upon being asked what the White House is like by a student in East London

✳ ✳ ✳ ✳

"Underpopulated countries in Africa are vastly underpolluted."
World Bank expert Lawrence Summers on sending toxic waste to developing countries

✳ ✳ ✳ ✳

"Solutions are not the answer."
President Richard Nixon

✳ ✳ ✳ ✳

"So where's the Cannes Film Festival being held this year?"
pop singer Christina Aguilera

✳ ✳ ✳ ✳

"Computers in the future may weigh no more than 1.5 tons."
Popular Mechanics, *1949*

✳ ✳ ✳ ✳

"I have a God-given talent. I got it from my dad."
Missouri basketball player Julian Wakefield

"I like to drive with my knees; otherwise, how can I put on my lipstick and talk on the phone?"
actor Sharon Stone

* * * *

"I quit flying years ago. I don't want to die with tourists."
actor Billy Bob Thornton

* * * *

"Experts say you should never hit your children in anger. When is a good time? When you're feeling festive?"
comedian Roseanne Barr

* * * *

"China is a big country inhabited by many Chinese."
former French president Charles de Gaulle

* * * *

"Things are more like they are now than they ever were before."
President Dwight Eisenhower

* * * *

"A proof is a proof. What kind of proof? It's a proof. A proof is proof. And when you have a good proof, it's because it is proven."
Canadian Prime Minister Jean Chrétien

* * * *

"I do not like this word 'bomb.' It is not a bomb. It is a device that is exploding."
French ambassador Jacques le Blanc

* * * *

"I wish we lived in the day where you could challenge a person to a duel."
Senator Zell Miller to Chris Matthews, during a heated interview on Hardball

UNCOMMON QUALITIES OF WORLD LANGUAGES

✳ ✳ ✳ ✳

Human language is as diverse as its speakers. Grammar is the brick and mortar of language, and a given language may have grammar elements unique to its linguistic family. Non-native speakers find certain languages particularly tough, and many potential trip-ups are amusing.

- Thanks to centuries of Moorish occupation, Arabic was a major influence on Spanish—*el* (masculine "the") is directly borrowed. So is *ojalá qué* ("would that" or "may it be so"); you can see the name Allah quite easily in that wishing phrase. Students practice it by wishing that Spanish had fewer verb tenses.

- In Hebrew you don't say, "I like it"; you say, "It finds favor in my eyes." When Eliezer ben Yehuda resurrected conversational Hebrew, he used biblical forms to accommodate the needs of 20th-century language. Another was the use of the biblical "Behold..." for "Here is/are...." Even the Israeli Defense Forces picked it up, naming one tank *Sho't* ("scourge" or "lash") and another *Merkava* ("chariot"). Behold: a challenging but beautiful modern language with firm roots in antiquity!

- Each Chinese character can have several unrelated meanings depending on the pronunciation, based on the tonal (type of intonation, such as rising or falling). This isn't as confusing as it might sound; simply learn the correct tone when you learn the word and repeat it until a native speaker gives you the thumbs-up. If you get it wrong, you could say something amusing and/or embarrassing.

- Visitors to Hungary often get a rude surprise when asking directions to the city of Szeged. It's pronounced "SEGG-ed" in Magyar, but many tourists mistakenly ask the way to "SHEGG-ed," which would actually mean "your rear end." Known for their spirited sense of comedy, Hungarians have been known to answer tourists by turning around and bending over.

- Until the 1970s, there were two official variations of modern Greek: Demotic (popular) and Katharevousa. Demotic Greek is what you speak today when you stop for a friendly chat with Mr. Kypriotakis; Katharevousa was a ceremonial version incorporating classical elements for government and formal usage. Like Sweden, Greece has the luxury of sole ownership of its national language— thus, Greek is whatever the Greeks say is Greek.

- Some Semitic languages (Hebrew, Arabic, Aramaic) are written from right to left. Left-handed persons taking up Semitic language calligraphy make a happy discovery: There's no need to worry about smearing the ink as they write.

- Many languages change verbs with suffixes, but Swahili does this mostly with prefixes to the verb's root. It's not limited to verbs: Swahili calls itself *kiSwahili*, *ki-* being the prefix to denote a language. The people of the Swahili coast refer to themselves as *waSwahili*. Swahili is part of the vast Bantu language family of southern Africa, in which similar prefixing concepts are common. Now you see why the old *National Geographic*s heavy-handedly called the Tutsi "Watusi" (should have been "waTutsi")—thus burning that name into millions of teenage male brains and inspiring the 1960s dance craze and the Orlons song.

- Hebrew is gender-intensive; even verbs are conjugated by gender. In Hebrew dialogue, participants' genders become evident within a few sentences. You have to know someone's gender to ask how he or she is doing.

- In some Spanish-speaking countries, the verb *coger* means "to catch" (as in a taxi or bus). In others, it means to have sex. So in some places, if you ask where you may *coger un autobus*, you'll encounter shocked disapproval at your vulgarity. Less stuffy listeners might be greatly amused—and even guide you to a bus so they can see just how this is accomplished!

Fast Facts

- It takes the Sun between 225 million and 240 million years to complete one orbit around the galaxy. That's moving at a breakneck 137 miles per second.

- Parts of the Great Sand Dunes in Colorado tower to 700 feet above the floor of the San Luis Valley. This five-by-seven-mile patch of desert is backed in stark contrast by the snow-capped Rocky Mountains.

- Sand from storms in the Sahara can travel thousands of miles. Mineral dust from these storms has been found in huge concentrations in South America and the Caribbean.

- The deepest place on Earth is Challenger Deep in the Marianas Trench, with a depth of 35,840 feet below sea level. If you put Mt. Everest into the Deep, there would still be a mile of water between its peak and the surface.

- Because Eris, the Greek goddess of discord, was fond of causing trouble, she was chosen as the namesake for a new "dwarf planet" discovered in our solar system in 2005. The designation caused dissention in the scientific community, resulting in the reclassification of Pluto as a dwarf planet.

- Mauna Loa is the largest volcano on Earth, approximately 56,000 feet from the base at the bottom of the ocean to its peak. It's also one of the most active volcanoes, so it's still growing.

- Depending on its composition, glass will melt at between 2,600° F and 2,900° F.

- You'll need to travel at 6.96 miles per second in order to escape Earth's gravity. You'd have an easier time leaving the Moon—its escape velocity is only 1.5 miles per second.

- The oldest known European cave drawings are found in Chauvet Cave in southern France. The 416 drawings are estimated to be 32,000 to 35,000 years old. They feature horses, rhinos, buffalo, lions, and mammoths.

HAUTE COUTURE

✳ ✳ ✳ ✳

- *Haute couture* is a French term meaning "high fashion."

- In the first half of the 1800s, wealthy European women paid dress-makers to copy and personalize the dresses worn by fashionable Parisians. French designers saw great possibility in custom-made garments, and haute couture was born.

- Though often called the father of haute couture, Charles Frederick Worth was not from France. A skilled English designer, Worth was particularly known for showing his dresses to audiences at his design firm, the House of Worth. Clients made selections at the shows and then had their garments tailor-made in Worth's work-shop.

- The French are protective of their traditions, allowing only a few fashion houses to hold the distinction of designing haute couture. Each year, the *Chambre de commerce et d'industrie de Paris* creates a list of eligible designers. To be considered for couture status, a design house must (1) create custom-order items for private clients that require one or more fittings; (2) have at least one Paris-based workshop or atelier that employs at least 15 people; and (3) present a collection, twice a year, of at least 35 pieces of daywear and eveningwear.

- The houses that received the distinction of being haute couture in 2007 included Christian Dior, Christian Lacroix, Franck Sorbier, Jean-Paul Gautier, Adeline André, Dominique Sirop, Emanuel Ungaro, Givenchy, Jean-Louis Scherrer, and Chanel.

- Couture clothing is sewn by hand and utilizes the finest materials. A custom-made haute couture evening gown can cost from $10,000 to more than $100,000.

- The houses that design couture do not rely on it as a primary source of income. The labor-intensive garments aren't ordered on a daily basis, so the houses create *prêt-a-porter* ("ready-to-wear") lines that sell in shops, right off the rack.

COLLEGE MASCOTS

✳ ✳ ✳ ✳

College sports brim with colors, birds, wildcats, tigers, and bears in some form or other. Common pooches abound, from bulldogs to wolves. There are numerous ancient warriors, such as Spartans and Trojans. Some mascots deserve high marks for originality.

Aggies (Texas A&M, New Mexico State, Utah State, and others): It's worth remembering that many land-grant schools early on taught mainly agriculture, so their students—and sometimes their teams— were called Farmers. "Aggies" grew as slang for this, and many of these schools now embrace the name proudly.

Banana Slugs (University of California–Santa Cruz): If a slug suggests a lethargic or reluctant team, that's just what students had in mind when they chose the image. The bright yellow banana slug lives amid the redwoods on campus and represents a mild protest of the highly competitive nature of most college sports.

Boll Weevils/Cotton Blossoms (University of Arkansas–Monticello, men/women): When cotton ruled Dixie, the boll weevil was more fearsome than any snake. Evidently, the women's teams didn't care to be named after an invasive insect, and who can blame them?

Cardinal (Stanford): It's the color, not the bird. That sounds odd until you consider the Harvard Crimson, Dartmouth Big Green, Syracuse Orange, etc. The university's overall symbol, however, is a redwood tree. A person actually dresses up as a redwood mascot, but the effect is more like a wilting Christmas tree than a regal conifer.

Crimson Tide (University of Alabama): The school's teams have always worn crimson, but the term "Crimson Tide" seems to have been popularized by sportswriters waxing poetic about epic struggles in mud and rain.

Eutectics (St. Louis College of Pharmacy, Missouri): "Eutectic" refers to the chemical process in which two solids become a liquid, representing the school's integration of competitive athletics and rigorous academic programs. ESPN recognized the Eutectic—a furry creature dressed in a lab coat—as one of the most esoteric mascots in the country.

Governors (Austin Peay, Tennessee): This one made sense, as the school is named for the Tennessee governor who signed the bill establishing it. At least "Governors" is more inspiring than the old nickname, "Normalities." One wonders how the eminent statesman would react to the popular student cheer today: "Let's go Peay!"

Ichabods (Washburn University, Kansas, men): An Ichabod would be, at the least, a generous man. The university was established as Lincoln College, but it ran out of money. When philanthropist Ichabod Washburn bailed out Lincoln, the grateful school renamed itself. This may disappoint everyone who references the headless ghost in *The Legend of Sleepy Hollow*, but Washburn University's version is still a worthy tale. The women's teams are the Lady Blues.

Jennies (Central Missouri State, women): A jenny is a female donkey, but this name makes sense only when put in context: The school's men's teams are the Mules. Both are a big improvement on "Normals" and "Teachers," the names used before 1922.

Nanooks (University of Alaska–Fairbanks): *Nanuq* is Inupiaq (northern Arctic Eskimo) for a polar bear. Many UAF students insist that it refers to a character in the 1922 silent ethnography film *Nanook of the North*, but to avoid controversy, perhaps, the school administration sticks firmly to the *nanuq* story.

Paladins (Furman University, South Carolina): A paladin is a pious, righteous knight. The title originally belonged to the 12 peers of Charlemagne's court.

Poets (Whittier College, California): If opponents don't exactly tremble when the Whittier mascot takes the field, it's because he's a big-headed figure who dresses in colonial garb and carries a pen and pad. The school was named for poet John Greenleaf Whittier.

Ragin' Cajuns (University of Louisiana–Lafayette): The name refers, of course, to the region's feisty Cajun ethnic heritage. Fans hold up signs saying "Geaux Cajuns!" Although decidedly not French, it certainly gets the message across.

Rainbow Wahine (University of Hawaii, women): Hawaii has an interesting situation because it chose to let its teams name themselves by sport. Some men's teams are the Warriors, some are the Rainbows, and some are the Rainbow Warriors. The women have been more consistent, all using Rainbow Wahine (*wahine* is Hawaiian for "women").

The Rock (Slippery Rock University, Pennsylvania): Some believe this school is imaginary, but it's not. There is no mascot; all teams are called "the Rock." Fans nationwide have embraced the school as a sort of cult favorite, giving it perhaps the largest honorary alumni body in college sports. When reading scores, numerous football announcers will read the Slippery Rock score last—and can expect irate phone calls if they don't.

Stormy Petrels (Oglethorpe University, Georgia): The name refers to a plucky shore bird that dives straight into heavy surf to find its food.

Tarheels (University of North Carolina): There's a lot of history at UNC, the nation's first state university. A Tarheel is a North Carolinian, though some use it to refer to rural folk in general. The legend says that North Carolinian soldiers in Civil War Confederate service remained "stuck" to the ground as if they had tar on their heels. Inexplicably, the school uses a live ram as its mascot.

Toreros (University of San Diego, California): Since 1961, USD teams have gone by this Spanish name for bullfighters. Unlike "matador" (a person in a fancy suit with rapier and cape), *torero* refers to all members of a bullfighting squad—making it an appropriate team name.

Warhawks (University of Louisiana–Monroe): One of college sports' newest mascots, the Warhawk represents the World War II fighter plane used by Louisianan Claire Chennault's American Volunteer Group in China, better known as the Flying Tigers. The logo, however, depicts a bird rather than a monoplane fighter.

FAMOUS FIRST LINES

✳ ✳ ✳ ✳

The first line of a book is often its most important, having the potential to either intrigue or irk a reader from the start. Here are a few of the best first sentences from some noted novels.

"Marley was dead, to begin with. There is no doubt whatever about that."
Charles Dickens, A Christmas Carol

✳ ✳ ✳ ✳

"It is a truth universally acknowledged, that a single man in possession of a good fortune, must be in want of a wife."
Jane Austen, Pride and Prejudice

✳ ✳ ✳ ✳

"You don't know about me without you have read a book by the name of *The Adventures of Tom Sawyer*; but that ain't no matter."
Mark Twain, The Adventures of Huckleberry Finn

✳ ✳ ✳ ✳

"When he was nearly thirteen, my brother Jem got his arm badly broken at the elbow."
Harper Lee, To Kill a Mockingbird

✳ ✳ ✳ ✳

"One morning, when Gregor Samsa woke from troubled dreams, he found himself transformed in his bed into a monstrous vermin."
Franz Kafka, Metamorphosis

✳ ✳ ✳ ✳

"On the first Monday of the month of April, 1625, the market town of Meung, in which the author of 'Romance of the Rose' was born, appeared to be in as perfect a state of revolution as if the Huguenots had just made a second La Rochelle of it."
Alexandre Dumas, The Three Musketeers

"If I am out of my mind, it's all right with me, thought Moses Herzog."
Saul Bellow, Herzog

* * * *

"Happy families are all alike; every unhappy family is unhappy in its own way."
Leo Tolstoy, Anna Karenina

* * * *

"In the country of Westphalia, in the castle of the most noble Baron of Thunder-ten-tronckh, lived a youth whom Nature had endowed with a most sweet disposition."
Voltaire, Candide

* * * *

"At a village of La Mancha, whose name I do not wish to remember, there lived a little while ago one of those gentlemen who are wont to keep a lance in the rack, an old buckler, a lean horse and a swift greyhound."
Miguel de Cervantes, Don Quixote

* * * *

"I was leaning against the bar in a speakeasy on Fifty-second Street, waiting for Nora to finish her Christmas shopping, when a girl got up from the table where she had been sitting with three other people and came over to me."
Dashiell Hammett, The Thin Man

* * * *

"He was an old man who fished alone in a skiff in the Gulf Stream and he had gone 84 days now without taking a fish."
Ernest Hemingway, The Old Man and the Sea

* * * *

"It was a pleasure to burn."
Ray Bradbury, Fahrenheit 451

Fast Facts

- California boasts the oldest known living tree—a Bristlecone Pine named "Methuselah," which is estimated to be 4,767 years old.

- One ounce of pure gold can be made into a wire 50 miles long.

- The United States consumes approximately ten percent of the world's salt production each year just to salt roads.

- Though the Hope Diamond is more famous, the Cullinan is the largest diamond ever found. Unearthed in South Africa in 1905, this 3,100-carat monster was cut into several stones that are still part of the British Crown Jewels.

- There are 318,979,564,000 different ways to play the first four moves per side in a game of chess.

- The British royal family changed its name from "Saxe-Coburg and Gotha" to "Windsor" in 1917, during World War I, because its original name sounded too German. It would have been difficult to fit onto a business card, as well. The royals are still known as the House of Windsor.

- Toys for Tots began its yearly donation drive during the 1947 Christmas season.

- The first charter for the United Nations was signed in San Francisco. Fifty countries signed the document, which was written in five languages.

- In 1791, Vermont became the first state to be added to the United States since the original 13.

- Herman Melville's Moby Dick was inspired by a real event perhaps more spellbinding than the book. In 1820, the Nantucket whale ship Essex was repeatedly rammed by a large sperm whale and sank in the Pacific Ocean, leaving the 20 crewmembers adrift in three small whaleboats for 95 days. Only eight men survived.

CURIOUS HABITS OF BIRDS

✳ ✳ ✳ ✳

Approximately 10,000 species of birds make up the class Aves—*a diverse group that has long fascinated the human race with peculiar behaviors and adaptations.*

Home invader: The kea (New Zealand), the world's only cold-weather parrot, loves to swing on car antennas and sled down the snowy roofs of ski lodges. The bird's favorite sport, though, is to get inside a lodge through its chimney and then trash the joint in search of food.

Neighborhood lookout: Bright-beaked puffins (Northern seacoasts) adopt a low-profile walk to tell other puffins they are just passing through. The other puffins adopt a sentry pose to warn the tourists not to get any bright ideas.

Airborne garbage disposal: The gull-like sheathbill (Antarctic) eats dead fish, other birds' eggs and babies, even seal and bird droppings.

Mugger: Skuas (various cold aquatic climes) are gull-like seabirds that chase other birds and force them to drop or cough up their food.

Aussie storm chaser: Huge, flightless emus (Australia) run after rain clouds, hoping for water.

Poacher: The world's smallest owl (about five inches), the elf owl (Mexico and southwest United States), moves into abandoned gila woodpecker holes in cacti.

Family planner: Similar to the cockatoo, the galah (Australia) raises a larger or smaller clutch of chicks, depending on food availability.

Sponge dad: A male sand grouse (Asian and African deserts) soaks himself in water, then flies back to the nest so his chicks can drink from his feathers.

Mach 0.13 in level flight: The spine-tailed swift (Asia) can fly 106 miles per hour—without benefit of a dive.

The Stuka: These Arctic terns know little fear and will dive-bomb larger predators, often in squadrons.

Deep-sea diver: The common loon (northern North America and Greenland) can dive more than 250 feet below the water's surface.

Vermonter at heart: The widespread sapsucker bores holes in trees, then slurps up the sweet sap.

Captain Ahab: The wetlands-dwelling anhinga spears fish with a long, sharp, slightly barbed beak that keeps dinner from sliding off.

Detox dieter: The stunning scarlet macaw (South America) eats clay from riverside deposits, which may help it process toxic seeds it consumes.

Busy mom: A gray partridge hen (Europe) can lay up to 20 eggs. She has to, because many partridge chicks don't survive.

Lazy mom: A paradise whydah hen (equatorial and southern Africa) lays her eggs in a finch nest. This fools the finch, which raises the chicks as its own.

Fears nothing: The two-and-a-half-foot-tall great gray owl (northern forests) has a wingspan of five feet and fiercely attacks anything that gets too close to its nest and owlets.

Preventive measures: The southern carmine bee-eater (Africa) rubs a bee's "butt" against a tree branch to break off its stinger.

Bone-breaker: European and Asian mountains are home to the lammergeier, a high-flying vulture that drops bones repeatedly to get at the tasty marrow.

Sanitary engineer: A malleefowl (Australia) lays eggs in a nest full of rotting vegetation. The decay gives off heat to keep the eggs warm; the male bird checks the temperature often and adjusts the pile as necessary.

Sturdy swimmer: American dipper birds, also known as "water duzels," use their strong wings to "fly" under and through water to catch prey.

OPERA

∗ ∗ ∗ ∗

Murder, suicide, and corruption—the stuff of a good night's entertainment for lovers of opera. Here are some of the most frequently performed operas in the world.

Tosca by Giacomo Puccini, premiered in 1900
Floria Tosca is a celebrated singer whose lover is arrested by a corrupt police chief. She kills the police chief, but her lover is executed, and she commits suicide.

La Bohème by Puccini, 1896
This opera deals with life in the Latin Quarter of Paris and focuses on the love affair between Rodolfo, a poet, and Mimi, a seamstress. The couple tragically separates, but they reunite shortly before Mimi dies of tuberculosis.

The Magic Flute by Wolfgang Amadeus Mozart, 1791
The complicated plot of this opera tells the story of Sarastro, a wise priest who takes a woman named Pamina to his temple to remove her from the influence of her mother, the Queen of the Night. The queen persuades the young Prince Tamino to search for her daughter, and in doing so he both comes to admire Sarastro and falls in love with Pamina.

Madame Butterfly by Puccini, 1904
The first performance of this opera, in Milan, was a flop, but Puccini revised it the same year to great acclaim. *Madame Butterfly* tells of the love affair between Cio-Cio-San, a Japanese girl, and Lieutenant B. F. Pinkerton, a U.S. naval officer. The couple has a child together, but Pinkerton subsequently marries an American woman, and Cio-Cio-San commits suicide.

Don Giovanni by Mozart, 1787
The full title of Mozart's comic opera translates as *"The Rake Punished, or Don Juan."* It is the story of a nobleman with an eye for the ladies, who is ultimately punished by being sent to hell.

Otello by Giuseppe Verdi, 1887

Based on Shakespeare's play of the same name (spelled *Othello*), this opera tells the story of Otello, a Moor who is convinced that his wife, Desdemona, has been unfaithful. Otello kills Desdemona in a jealous rage, then commits suicide in grief when he discovers that he was lied to and she was faithful to him all along.

The Barber of Seville by Gioachino Rossini, 1816

This comic opera tells the story of the love affair between Count Almaviva and Rosina, and how the barber Figaro helps them defeat Rosina's guardian's attempts to separate them.

La Traviata by Verdi, 1853

After a little light relief, we're back in tragic territory with *La Traviata* (which translates as "the woman who was led astray"), the tale of a courtesan who is spurned by her respectable lover before dying in his arms.

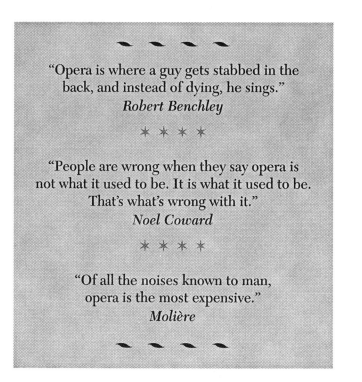

"Opera is where a guy gets stabbed in the back, and instead of dying, he sings."
Robert Benchley

✳ ✳ ✳ ✳

"People are wrong when they say opera is not what it used to be. It is what it used to be. That's what's wrong with it."
Noel Coward

✳ ✳ ✳ ✳

"Of all the noises known to man, opera is the most expensive."
Molière

IN THE YEAR...1939

* * * *

- The January 2 cover of *Time* magazine features Adolph Hitler as "Man of the Year."
- Nazis seize all enterprises of German Jews.
- *Gone with the Wind* premieres in Atlanta.
- *The Wizard of Oz* premieres in New York City.
- Marian Anderson, celebrated contralto of American opera, is refused a performance at Constitution Hall in Washington, D.C., by the Daughters of the American Revolution.
- Hewlett-Packard opens for business.
- A massive earthquake hits Chile, obliterating a surface area of 50,000 miles and killing approximately 30,000 people.
- The Borley Rectory, long reputed to be England's most haunted house, burns to the ground.
- The Spanish Civil War ends.
- Faisal II becomes King of Iraq.
- *The Grapes of Wrath* by John Steinbeck is published.
- More than 900 Jewish refugees on the SS *St. Louis* are denied entry to the United States after being rejected by Cuba, resulting in their forced return to Europe. Most later died in Nazi concentration camps.
- The National Baseball Hall of Fame and Museum opens in Cooperstown, New York.
- Siam becomes Thailand, a name that translates as "Free Land."
- The New York Yankees' Lou Gehrig, whose ill health is attributed to amyotrophic lateral sclerosis (ALS), gives his last public address, which includes the famous line, "Today, I consider myself the luckiest man on the face of the earth."
- Germany invades Poland, marking the beginning of World War II in Europe. Franklin Delano Roosevelt declares America's neutrality.

ANIMALS IN DISGUISE

✳ ✳ ✳ ✳

Polar bears waddling across arctic plains, chameleons turning from green to brown on a tree limb—images such as these come to mind when we think of animal camouflage. But there is far more to this survival behavior than just blending into the background of nature.

- Polar bears are not actually white. They appear white because their fur is made up of hollow, transparent, pigment-free hairs, which scatter and reflect visible light, much the way snow crystals do. Underneath the fur, a polar bear's skin is black, which is how the animal appears if photographed with film that's sensitive to ultraviolet light.

- The Eurasian bittern, a wading bird from the heron family, nests among tall river reeds. When alarmed, it stretches its neck and either becomes motionless or, if there is a breeze, begins to sway in time with the reeds. Because of its plumage pattern—vertical dark-brown stripes on beige—the bittern becomes extremely difficult to see.

- The purpose of camouflage is not always to hide from predators. Sometimes the best defense is to simply look as unappetizing as possible. For this reason, the caterpillars of many species of moths have evolved to look like bird droppings.

- Some species of sea horse, notably the Australian leafy sea dragon (*Phycodurus eques*), mask themselves as seaweed. Not only are these creatures green, but they also have long, tattered ribbons of skin, much like seaweed fronds, growing from their bodies.

- Some varieties of what are called "geometer" caterpillars—larvae of the *Geometridae* moths—closely resemble twigs, thanks to a combination of their grayish-brown color, humps on the body that look like tree buds, a lack of abdominal legs, and the habit of resting with their bodies stretched out at an angle from the branch. Maintaining this uncomfortable pose can be taxing, so these caterpillars often spin a supportive silk thread between their head and a leaf or twig just above it.

- In Africa, one might spot what appears to be a small, densely packed cluster of dead ants shuffling by. Close inspection reveals that the ants are being transported on the back of a large predator, *Acanthaspis petax*. After killing the ants, this bug sucks their bodies dry and covers itself with their exoskeletons. This behavior enables the *Acanthaspis petax* to avoid its own predators while infiltrating anthills for another feast.

- Eyespots on the wings of moths and butterflies serve to divert a predator's attention from the moth's vital organs to its wings, which can withstand more damage. Going a step further, the South American frog *Physalaemus nattereri* has evolved prominent black eyespots on its butt. When attacked, it heaves its backside into the air and gives the predator an "eyeful." If the predator persists, the frog surprises it with a spray of unpleasant secretions.

- It isn't necessary to look terrifying to scare away predators. Hole-nesting birds such as the European blue tit hiss like a snake if disturbed while they incubate eggs and care for small young. A dormouse does the same if something encroaches on its dark lair, and feeding termites hiss in chorus to scare off intruders.

- When threatened, a hognose snake will flatten its neck like a cobra, raise its head, and even feign strikes. If the would-be predator is not deterred by the threat, the hognose will roll over and play dead, going so far as to let its tongue hang out of its mouth while emitting a foul scent to simulate the smell of a rotting corpse.

- The saying "You are what you eat" has particular relevance to nudibranchs, commonly known as sea slugs. Some of these soft, shell-less mollusks have evolved to derive more than just nourishment from their food. If a nudibranch eats a sponge or a jellyfish, it can collect and store its prey's toxins and stinging cells in its skin to ward off predators. In addition, nudibranchs use their prey's pigments as a dazzling display of warning colors.

CURLING

* * * *

*For some people, curling is an Olympic sport; for
others it's a fun social activity. Here's some information on
a sport that's akin to shuffleboard or bowling on ice.*

History

Curling began in Scotland in the 1500s, played with river-worn
stones. In the next century, enterprising curlers began to fit the
stones with handles. With Canada's heavy Scottish influence and
northerly climate, curling was a perfect fit. The Royal Montreal
Curling Club began in 1807, and in 1927, Canada held its first national curling championship. Today, curling has millions of enthusiasts around the world. Canadian curlers routinely beat international
competition, a source of brimming national pride.

How to Curl

The standard curling rink measures 146 feet by 15 feet. At each end
are 12-foot-wide concentric rings called *houses*, the center of which
is the *button*. There are four curlers on a team. Each throws two
rocks (shoves them, rather; you don't really want to go airborne with
a 44-pound granite rock) in an effort to get as close to the button
as possible. When all eight players have thrown two rocks each, it
concludes the *end* (analogous to a baseball inning). A game consists
of eight or ten ends.

Curling Strategy

You try to knock the other team's rocks out of the house, and thus
out of scoring position, while getting yours to hang around close to
the button. After all throws, the team with the rock nearest the button scores a point for each of its rocks that's nearer the button than
the opponent's nearest rock (and inside the house).

Proper Ice-keeping

The players with the brooms aren't trying to keep the ice clear of
crud. The team *skip* (captain) determines strategy and advises the
players using the brooms in the fine art of *sweeping*. Skips can guide

the stone with surprising precision by skillfully sweeping in front of it with their brooms, but they can't touch (*burn*) that rock or any others in the process.

"Good curling!" "Thanks, you too."

Curling is a game that values good sportsmanship. Curlers even call themselves for burns. When a team is so far behind it cannot win, it is considered proper sportsmanship to concede by removing gloves and shaking hands.

Curling Jargon

Bonspiel: a curling tournament
Curler: curling player
Draw: shot thrown to score
Hack: foot brace curlers push off from, like track sprinters
Hammer: last rock of the end (advantageous)
Hog line: blue line in roughly the same place as a hockey blue line. One must let go of the rock before crossing the near hog line—and the rock must cross the far hog line—or it's *hogged* (removed from play).
Pebble: water drops sprayed on the ice between ends, making the game more interesting
Takeout: shot meant to knock a rock out of play
Up! Whoa! Off! Hurry! Hard!: examples of orders the skip might call to the sweepers
Weight: how hard one slides the rock

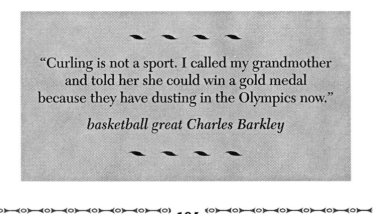

"Curling is not a sport. I called my grandmother and told her she could win a gold medal because they have dusting in the Olympics now."

basketball great Charles Barkley

BAND NAMES ONLY A MOTHER COULD LOVE

✳ ✳ ✳ ✳

Whether derived from pop culture references, or just a random pick from a book, a band's name is often as important as its music. But even a great sound can't save bands such as The Busiest Bankruptcy Lawyers in Minnesota. Here are the stories behind some interesting band names.

The Cranberries The band was originally known as "The Cranberry Saw Us," a pun on "cranberry sauce." Members soon shortened the name for simplicity.

Lynyrd Skynyrd The group is named after Leonard Skinner, an annoying gym coach some of the band members had in high school, who supposedly had them expelled for having long hair.

R.E.M. The "rapid eye movement" period in the sleep cycle is the most intense and restful. But the members of R.E.M. didn't choose the name for its symbolic connection to their aesthetic. Instead, they found it while flipping through the dictionary.

Five for Fighting The stage name for John Ondrasik came from his love of hockey. Players who fight in the National Hockey League get five minutes in the penalty box, or "five for fighting."

Three Dog Night The name is derived from an Australian Aboriginal custom of sleeping with a dog for warmth during cold nights. The colder the night, the more dogs.

No Doubt This funky, California-based "third wave" ska band was named after a favorite expression of its founder, John Spence, who ultimately committed suicide.

Toad the Wet Sprocket Members of this alt-rock band drew their name from a monologue delivered by Eric Idle on a Monty Python album from 1980.

Talk to the Expert
MUSICOLOGIST

✳ ✳ ✳ ✳

Billions of people make and love music, but few become musicologists—collegiate professors, for the most part. This will give you an idea of the inspiration behind the occupation.

Q: What's a musicologist?
A: Musicologists study the history, theory, and performance of audio art. Nearly all of us teach.

Q: Why would someone become a musicologist, as opposed to a musician?
A: Many of us are also musicians, but it takes a tremendous investment of time and energy to become a professional musician. Talent and creativity are only the beginning.

Q: Is musicology also sociology?
A: Not in the formal academic sense, because sociology relies heavily on numbers and their analysis. Musicology touches upon sociology in the more general sense of placing a finger on the pulse of humanity. I would also consider it allied with history and psychology, in that one can gain great insight into both through the study of music.

Q: How would you describe your teaching approach?
A: I ask my students to speculate: To whom does a particular style of music speak? I want them to look outside themselves, to see what the music says to others, and in so doing, to open their minds to its multiple messages. I want them to be deep listeners. Anyone who studies musicology with me and still listens to music the same way after finals week should by all rights have failed my course.

Q: Can you name someone famous you would embrace as a fellow musicologist?
A: There are many. Here's one who may surprise you: "Weird Al" Yankovic. Most people know Al as a stage performer and parody artist, but his parodies are snapshots of the pop culture of the day. There is no genre he can't touch on if he puts his mind to it.

IMPORTANT PEOPLE YOU'VE PROBABLY NEVER HEARD OF

✳ ✳ ✳ ✳

Vladimir Vysotsky (1938–1980): Russian stage and film actor, writer, poet, and singer of immense talent and productivity. In the course of his relatively brief life, Vysotsky wrote between 600 and 800 songs about every aspect of Soviet living, from labor camps to popular TV shows. When not engaged in theater performances, concerts, or movie shoots, he wrote novels, novellas, short stories, and screenplays. Although the government refused to allow him to make records, fans defiantly taped his countless live concerts and distributed the recordings all over the country. Despite Vysotsky's ruthless satirizing of the poor living conditions in the U.S.S.R., he was all but immune from political prosecution by virtue of his stardom. Vysotsky died of heart failure in 1980, when the summer Olympics were in full swing in Moscow; to avoid rioting, the state-controlled media made no mention of the star's untimely demise. But the news quickly leaked out, and huge crowds began gathering at Taganka Theatre, where Vysotsky had played Hamlet until a week before his death. It's reported that close to a million people attended his funeral.

Norman Ernest Borlaug (1914–): American microbiologist and agricultural scientist who was instrumental in developing high-yield, disease-resistant wheat varieties in Latin America, Africa, and Asia. Borlaug effectively saved billions of people from starvation and was awarded the Nobel Peace Prize in 1970. According to the Congressional Tribute to Dr. Norman E. Borlaug Act of 2006, "Dr. Borlaug has saved more lives than any other person who has ever lived."

Sir Francis Galton (1822–1911): child prodigy and cousin of Charles Darwin. Among his accomplishments are extensive exploration of the African continent; the creation of the first weather map; coining the terms "eugenics" and "nature versus nurture"; the statistical concepts of correlation and regression to the mean; the first implementation of the survey as a method of data collection; Differential Psychology, also known as the London School of Experimental

Psychology; the first scientific investigation into human fingerprints; and the biometric approach to genetics. On these and many other topics, Galton produced more than 340 papers and books throughout his lifetime. He received every major award the Victorian scientific community bestowed, and he was knighted in 1909.

Athanasius Kircher (1602–1680): German Jesuit scholar and philosopher. Nicknamed "the master of a hundred arts" and sometimes called the last Renaissance man, Kircher taught mathematics, physics, and several languages at Collegio Romano, the first Jesuit university in the world. He also pioneered the study of Egyptian hieroglyphics and was the first to put forth the idea that the plague was caused by animal microorganisms. Kircher produced more than 40 weighty tomes on a bewildering variety of subjects, from China to musical theory to fossils to magnetism. In his spare time, Kircher terrorized the superstitious peasants of the countryside around his villa by sending up hot air balloons in the shape of dragons with the words "Flee the Wrath of God" blazoned on their bellies. Kircher also constructed a great number of mechanical devices, such as speaking statues, megaphones, clocks, and musical instruments. The strangest by far was the cat piano: Caged cats with differently pitched voices were arranged side by side inside a conventional piano. When a piano key was depressed, a mechanism drove a spike into the appropriate cat's tail. "The result," wrote Kircher, "was a melody of meows that became more vigorous as the cats became more desperate. Who could not help but laugh at such music?" Who, indeed.

Eugène François Vidocq (1775–1857): French convict-turned-detective, reformer of the civil police force, and inventor of the criminal-fiction genre. After a misspent youth that left him wanted by the law for manslaughter, forgery, robbery, and numerous escapes from prison, Vidocq made the bold move of presenting himself to the prefect of police in Paris and offering his services as an insider to the criminal world in exchange for his freedom. Within a few years, Vidocq and several ex-convicts under his supervision surpassed the police proper of the entire city of Paris in the number of arrests made. This *brigade de Sureté* ("security brigade") was the beginning of a civil police occupied with the active pursuit and apprehension of criminals; before Vidocq's intervention, the activities of the police in large cities were mostly limited to political espionage and directing traffic. After resigning from the newly revolutionized police force, Vidocq published his memoirs, in which he claimed to have honestly disclosed his adventures on both sides of the law. The memoirs were a big success and formed a lasting testimonial to Vidocq's character; today they are considered the first work of criminal fiction.

Augusta Ada King, Countess of Lovelace, born Augusta Ada Byron (1815–1852): the only legitimate daughter of the poet Lord Byron and the author of the first-ever computer program. Lord Byron's wife, Annabella Milbanke, resented her husband, and to prevent her daughter from following in his professional footsteps, Annabelle gave her a rigorously mathematical education—rather unorthodox in the days when upper-class women were educated mostly in music, art, and languages. In her youth and adulthood, Ada was in close correspondence with mathematician Charles Babbage, who was highly impressed with her intellect. In 1841, Babbage gave a seminar at the University of Turin about the possibility of an "analytical engine": a mechanical calculating device capable of interpreting human instructions—in other words, a computer. After a young Italian engineer transcribed and published the lecture in French, Babbage asked Ada to translate it back into English and add her own notes to it. The notes took Ada about a year to complete and ultimately were more extensive than the paper itself; the last and longest of the seven sections describes an algorithm for the analytical engine to compute Bernoulli numbers. Because they contain the first set of instructions specifically intended for a computer, Ada Lovelace's notes are widely considered the world's first computer program, predating the first computer by about a century.

Aristarchus of Samos (310 B.C.–230 B.C.): Greek astronomer and mathematician who first proposed a heliocentric model of the solar system, placing the Sun instead of Earth at the center of the universe and arranging the other planets in correct order from the Sun. His argument for this bold theory hinged on his calculations of the relative sizes of the Sun and Earth—he found the Sun to be about 300 times larger—and a suspicion that the Sun was really a star, just positioned close to Earth. Aristarchus was criticized by laypeople for impiety and by astronomers for proposing a theory that did not account for the observable retrograde motion of the planets—periods when planets seemed to switch direction and begin to move backward in the sky over the course of several weeks or months. Thus soundly trampled, Aristarchus's theory languished until Copernicus authored his revolutionary tract *Of the Revolutions of the Heavenly Spheres* in 1543. Although he briefly mentioned Aristarchus in an early draft, Copernicus decided to cross his name out of the book before publication.

Nadezhda Andreyevna Durova (1783–1866): a woman who joined the Russian army around the time of the Napoleonic wars. Reviled by her mother, who had wanted a boy, Durova was raised primarily by her father, a cavalry officer. Brash, fearless, and accustomed from birth to horse-riding and sabre-swinging, Durova was in for a rude shock when her father gave her away in marriage at the age of 18 to a local court official. The marriage eventually ended, and Durova returned to her parents' house, leaving her ex-husband with an infant son. In 1807, she fled home dressed as a man and enlisted under a false name in a cavalry regiment. Several years later, she was discovered and brought before Czar Alexander I; Durova pleaded with him not to make her return to her intolerable life as a woman and begged to continue serving her country as a warrior. Moved by her plea, the czar gave his permission for her to remain in the army, decorated her with St. George's Cross for saving a fellow officer's life in battle, and raised her in rank. Durova retired in 1816 and wore masculine attire for the rest of her life. In her later years, she wrote of her army adventures in her widely read memoirs, *The Notes of a Cavalryman-Maiden.*

"Ötzi the Iceman" (also spelled **Oetzi**), aka **Similaun Man,** aka **"Frozen Fritz"** (ca. 3300 B.C.): a natural mummy found on the border between Austria and Italy in 1991. This spectacularly preserved specimen of a middle-aged Chalcolithic (Copper Age) European male was popularly named after the Otztal Alps where he was discovered in a glacier. He stood about five feet four inches, weighed about 84 pounds, and boasted 57 tattoos—mostly small lines. Ötzi was amazingly well-equipped for his journey across the mountains: He carried a copper axe with a yew handle, a flint knife, a quiver full of arrows, and an unfinished yew longbow. The pouch on his belt was a combined fire-starting and medicinal kit that contained flint, pyrite, tinder fungus, birch fungus (known to have antibacterial properties), two bark baskets (one containing charcoal), berries, and more than a dozen different plants. His wardrobe consisted of a cloak made of woven grass; a loincloth, leggings, vest, and belt made of leather; a bearskin hat; and waterproof shoes made of bearskin, deer hide, and tree bark, stuffed with grass for warmth. Petr Hlavacek, a Czech footwear expert from Tomas Bata University, re-created Ötzi's shoes using a prehistoric tanning process that involved boiling the liver and brains of pigs. The result, he writes, was "like going barefoot, only better."

William James Sidis (1898–1944): possibly the smartest man who has ever lived. Sidis had an IQ between 250 and 300—far beyond the range that IQ tests are capable of measuring. He was accepted to Harvard at the age of 11 after completing all of his primary and secondary schooling in seven months; he was also able to learn a new language a day and actually invented his own. However, constant media attention took its toll, and Sidis left the public eye soon after reaching adulthood, holding only menial jobs until his death from a stroke at the age of 46. The only topic to which he applied himself studiously and on which he produced a definitive text was streetcar transfers.

"There are two kinds of geniuses. The characteristic of the one is roaring, but the lightning is meager and rarely strikes; the other kind is characterized by reflection by which it constrains itself or restrains the roaring. But the lightning is all the more intense; with the speed and sureness of lightning it hits the selected particular points—and it is fatal."

Søren Kierkegaard

A BRIEF HISTORY OF UNDERWEAR

✳ ✳ ✳ ✳

*From fig leaves to bloomers to thongs, people have covered
themselves a little or a lot, depending on social preferences and
mores. Here is a brief history of the undergarment.*

- The earliest and most simple undergarment was the loincloth—
a long strip of material passed between the legs and around the
waist. King Tutankhamen was buried with 145 of them, but the
style didn't go out with the Egyptians. Loincloths are still worn in
many Asian and African cultures.

- Men in the Middle Ages wore loose, trouser-like undergarments
called braies, which one stepped into and tied around the waist
and legs about mid-calf. To facilitate urination, braies were fitted
with a codpiece, a flap that buttoned or tied closed.

- Medieval women wore a close-fitting undergarment called a
chemise, and corsets began to appear in the 18th century. Early
versions of the corset were designed to flatten a woman's bustline,
but by the late 1800s, corsets were reconstructed to give women
an exaggerated hourglass shape.

- Bras were invented in 1913 when American socialite Mary Phelps-
Jacob tied two handkerchiefs together with ribbon. She patented
the idea a year later. Maidenform introduced modern cup sizes in
1928.

- Around 1920, as women became more involved in sports such as
tennis and bicycling, loose, comfortable bloomers replaced corsets
as the undergarment of choice. The constricting corset soon fell
out of favor altogether.

- The thong made its first public U.S. appearance at the
1939 World's Fair, when New York mayor Fiorello LaGuardia
required nude dancers to cover themselves, if only barely. Thongs
gained popularity as swimwear in Brazil in the 1970s and are now
a fashionable form of underwear in many parts of the world.

ORIGINS: THE HISTORY OF THINGS

✳ ✳ ✳ ✳

*These intriguing stories offer insight into the history of some
everyday items, expressions, and endeavors—
stuff you never think to think about.*

The Latin Alphabet

People had been writing hieroglyphics (symbols that stood for objects such as *dog*, *reed*, or *pyramid*) for at least a millennium before
the first glimmer of an actual alphabet appeared. Around 2000 B.C.,
a group of Egyptian slaves (the Semitics) figured out how to communicate with one another using symbols that represented sounds, not
just things. From this system, we eventually got the Phoenician and
Aramaic alphabets, as well as the Greek and Latin alphabets. Early
Greek was written right to left, before the "ox-turning" method (in
which the direction of writing changed with every line) was adopted.
By the 5th century B.C., the left-to-right method was in place.

The Evil Eye

The language of superstition is universal. From Europe to the
Middle East, from Mexico to Scandinavia, folktales have long
warned people against the power of the "evil eye." Essentially, the
evil eye is an unintentional look of envy from a person who covets
what the recipient possesses. At the very least, it's plain old bad
vibes; at its most potent, the evil eye is blamed for bad luck, disease,
and even death in the person who receives the look. Cultures that
fear the evil eye have developed various means of protection:
A common European custom is to wear a locket containing a prayer.
In India, small mirrors are sewn into clothing to deflect an evil gaze
and reflect it to the person who gave it; similarly, the Chinese use a
six-sided mirror called a *pa kua*. The Italians have developed various
hand gestures for protection. Sometimes the defense is more elaborate: Folk healers in Mexico smear raw chicken eggs over someone's
body to keep him or her safe from the evil eye. In this case, the
person might just get a plain old dirty look.

The Face-lift

Contrary to popular belief, the "plastic" in "plastic surgery" doesn't refer to the use of petroleum-based materials; rather, it's from the Greek word *plastikos*, meaning "to mold or shape." The first facial plastic surgeries date back to ancient Rome, when they were probably performed to fix ears and noses that had been torn off during Coliseum scuffles. It wasn't until the 1900s that face-lifts, or *rhytidectomies* (literally, the surgical removal of wrinkles), were performed for cosmetic reasons. These days, plastic surgeons in the United States snip and pull the skin on men and women's faces at the rate of approximately 150,000 a year.

The Jump Rope

Skipping and jumping are natural movements of the body (especially for kids), and the inclusion of a rope in these activities dates back to A.D. 1600, when Egyptian children jumped over vines. Early Dutch settlers brought the game to North America, where it flourished and evolved from a simple motion into the often elaborate form prevalent today: Double Dutch. With two people turning two ropes simultaneously, a third, and then fourth, person jumps in, often reciting rhymes. Jumping techniques have become so complex that there are now worldwide organizations that sponsor Double Dutch competitions.

Vampires

The word *vampire* is rooted in the Hungarian word *vampyr,* a spirit who feasts on the living. The vampire archetype we recognize today (fanged, bloodsucking monsters who otherwise look normal) seems to have originated in 18th-century Eastern Europe. In the early 1700s, Serbian police investigated dozens of claims of vampirism after people died in strange, inexplicable ways—and sometimes allegedly came back to life. Most scholars attribute these claims to premature burials or rabies; nonetheless, most of Europe was already caught up in Dracula drama. Vampire lore is thousands of years old and exists in many cultures around the world. In the Old Testament, Lilith (who, according to Hebrew legend, was Adam's first wife) is described as a bloodthirsty demon. Ancient Greeks told tales of a vampire-like creature called Lamia, who was fond of the blood of children. India is rich in vampire lore. The beautiful and terrible goddess known as Kali had fangs and four arms and drank the blood of her enemies to prevent them from coming back to destroy her. Vampires in Romania are called *strigoi* (from the Latin term for screech owl), and Romanians believe that these creatures are reanimated corpses who return to suck the blood of humans and livestock. In some Eastern European regions, cemetery workers would exhume bodies years after burial to check for vampirism. If the corpse wasn't decomposed, had one foot in the corner of the casket, and had a ruddy face, it was thought to be a vampire and was quickly decapitated.

Quiche

Although similar concoctions date back to ancient Roman cheesecakes and medieval European tarts and pies, the modern quiche recipe comes from the Lorraine region of France. The original quiche Lorraine was an open-face pie filled with eggs, cream, and bacon. Cheese was later incorporated, along with any number of additions, from shallots to shellfish, depending on one's preference. In North America, quiche enjoyed its greatest popularity as a trendy 1970s food, joined by other such notable offerings as fondue and Caesar salad.

Taxicabs

Think of Cleopatra being carted around on a sedan chair, and you have the origins of the modern-day taxicab. Rickshaws replaced sedan chairs as a means of transporting people from one place to another, followed by horse-drawn carriages, which finally gave us poor humans a rest. At the end of the 19th century, automobiles started to fill the streets, and with the invention of the taximeter (an instrument that measures both the time and distance a vehicle has traveled), transport by cab became increasingly popular. Throughout the world, cab companies have painted their taxis particular colors, both for identification purposes and to cut down on the number of unofficial drivers. Today in New York City alone, taxis drive more than 200 million passengers almost 800 million miles every year.

I'm No Expert, But...
GETTING BUFF

✳ ✳ ✳

Q: What builds muscle?

A: Muscles are tissues that contract and release when they're "told to." The more they contract, the more blood flows to them and the more developed the cells become. Different types of contractions (repetitions versus strength of exertion) cause different muscle changes, which is why some people look big but aren't that strong, and others don't look huge but have handshakes that seem like the grip from a pair of channel-lock pliers.

Q: How do I work out to build endurance? Bulk? Strength?

A: It's all in the number of repetitions you do to exhaustion. If you use more resistance you can do fewer, stronger reps. Doing 1 to 5 mighty reps builds pure strength but little bulk; 6 to 12 strong reps is the range over which you go from strength to bulk. With 12 to 20 reps, strength and bulk gain little, but your endurance improves. Now you see why laborers get so strong and can work as long as they do: They're either doing a few moves with all their strength, or they're doing many moves for a long time.

Q: Why do muscles sometimes "burn" during an intense workout?

A: That burning sensation you feel is the result of temporarily high levels of lactic acid in your system. When you overload your body's ability to resupply oxygen to the muscles, they produce lactic acid. Doctors and researchers specializing in sports medicine used to consider lactic acid a sort of toxin that caused muscle fatigue and a corresponding poor athletic performance. Recent studies, however, have shown that if athletes concentrate on improving their overall endurance, their muscles can better utilize lactic acid as an energy source.

CAPTIVATING CEMETERIES

✳ ✳ ✳ ✳

Most of the world's cultures believe strongly in dignified, respectful care for the dead. The term cemetery *comes from the Greek word for "sleeping place." Here are some popular and unusual burial grounds in the United States.*

- Almost 4 million visitors a year quietly walk through the grounds of **Arlington National Cemetery** in Arlington, Virginia. There are upwards of 100 funerals each weekday throughout the year. More than 300,000 people are buried here, including Presidents William Howard Taft and John F. Kennedy and Supreme Court Chief Justices Earl Warren, Warren Burger, and William Rehnquist. The cemetery is the final resting place for veterans from all of the nation's wars. Military personnel from the American Revolution through the struggles in Iraq and Afghanistan are buried here.

- The smallest national cemetery is located at the **Veterans Administration Medical Center** in Hampton, Virginia. This .03-acre site holds 22 bodies in three short rows and is currently closed to new internments. The burial ground was used as an emergency measure in 1899 during a yellow fever epidemic at the center.

- The **National Memorial Cemetery of the Pacific** on the island of Oahu in Hawaii offers a stunning view of Honolulu and is the resting place for the recovered remains of 13,000 World War II service personnel, as well as the unidentified remains of 800 servicemembers who died in Korea. Several Medal of Honor winners from Vietnam are interred here. This cemetery has been a revered site since ancient times, when *alii* (royal) burials were held. Violators of *kapus* (taboos) were sacrificed here, as well.

- There's a wagon wheel carved into the headstone of one of dozens of circus folk buried in Showmen's Rest, a section of **Mount Olivet Cemetery** in Hugo, Oklahoma. According to circus lore, it was a practice of the day for a local sheriff to remove the nuts from one of the wheels on the office wagon of any show coming to town. This would prevent the circus from leaving before all the bills were paid. Once accounts were settled, the nuts would be returned. Hence, the show business term "making the nut," or taking in enough money to break even.

- Another Showmen's Rest section is found in Forest Park, Illinois, in a 750-plot section of **Woodlawn Cemetery**. One of the most interesting features is a mass grave of more than 50 employees of the Hagenbeck-Wallace circus who were killed in a train wreck nearby. Sometimes, neighbors around the cemetery claim they can hear the sounds of elephants trumpeting, but they probably aren't hearing ghosts. The noises likely come from the elephants in a nearby zoo.

- Barre, Vermont, is known as the granite capital of the world, and its cemeteries feature some of the most remarkable headstones in the world. Artisans praise the city's gray granite because its fine grain reflects light well and is not weathered by the elements. In Barre's **Hope Cemetery,** unique tombstones depict life-size figures, a queen-size bed, an armchair, and a giant soccer ball.

- **Mount Moriah Cemetery** in Deadwood, South Dakota, is the resting place of cowpokes, gunslingers, dance hall veterans, pioneer preachers, and assorted politicians. Side by side are the graves of legends Wild Bill Hickok and Martha Jane "Calamity Jane" Cannary. After Hickok was shot to death in 1876, Calamity Jane regularly visited Mount Moriah. It's said that just before she died in 1903, she said, "Bury me beside Wild Bill—the only man I ever loved."

- *It is considered bad luck to use areas of a cemetery for other purposes, and the disturbed deceased will likely haunt those responsible for the decision.*

- *When you experience a chill up your spine, it is said that someone has just walked across your future gravesite.*

CURIOUS WORLD CURRENCIES

✳ ✳ ✳ ✳

Paper, coins, and plastic are what we use as money today, but that wasn't always the case. Throughout history, people have used various animals, vegetables, and minerals to conduct business.

Cows represent the oldest of all forms of money, dating from as early as 9000 B.C. The words *capital, chattels,* and *cattle* have a common root, and the word *pecuniary* (meaning "financial") comes from *pecus*, the Latin word for cattle. But cattle weren't the only livestock used as legal tender: Until well into the 20th century, the Kirghiz (a Turkic ethnic group found primarily in Kyrgyzstan) used horses for large exchanges, sheep for lesser trades, and lambskins for barters that required only small change.

Cowry shells—marine snails found chiefly in tropical regions—were the medium of exchange used in China around 1200 B.C. These shells were so widely traded that their pictograph became the symbol for money in the written language. The earliest metallic money in China were cowries made of bronze or copper.

Throughout history, **salt and pepper** have been used as money, both for their value as seasonings and preservatives and for their importance in religious ceremonies. In ancient Rome, salt was used as money, and the Latin word for salt (*sal*) is the root of the word *salary*. Roman workers were paid with salt, hence the expression "worth one's salt." Pepper was also used as a form of payment. During the Middle Ages in England, rent could be paid in peppercorns, and the term "peppercorn rent" refers to the smallest acceptable payment.

The largest form of money is the **12-foot limestone coins** from the Micronesian island of Yap. The value of the coin was determined by its size—the 12-foot rounds weighed several tons. Displaying a large coin outside your home was a sign of status and prestige. Because of the coins' size and immobility, islanders would often trade only promises of ownership instead of actually exchanging them. Approximately 6,800 coins still exist around the island, though the U.S. dollar is now the official currency.

DREAD PIRATES OF HISTORY AND THEIR FATES

✳ ✳ ✳ ✳

When did piracy begin? Probably 15 minutes after the first ancient meeting of two river canoes. From the European perspective, the Golden Age of Piracy began around A.D. 1660; by 1730, the problem was largely under control. Here are some of the most notorious rascals of this era, plus noteworthy pirates from other times.

John Taylor: English. Taylor earned his fame capturing the Portuguese carrack *Nossa Senhora do Cabo* in 1721. It was one of the richest prizes of its time, consisting of diamonds and other portable loot. No idiot, Taylor then bought a pardon in Panama, where he likely retired wealthy.

"Blackbeard" Edward Teach: English. The infamous Blackbeard was a full-time drunkard who terrorized the Carolina coast, racking up captures and loot. But it wasn't all about money and rum: He once raided Charleston and took hostages until townsfolk gave him much-needed medicine for his venereal disease. In 1718, the Royal Navy ran down and killed Blackbeard just off Ocracoke Island.

Thomas Tew: English. His 1692–1694 Indian Ocean rampage made Tew rich enough to retire in New York under the protection of his friend, Governor Benjamin Fletcher. In 1695, his former crew talked him into one more voyage to raid Moghul ships. Piracy was a little like gambling: Most people lose, and winners should probably quit. Tew didn't, and in 1695 he was disemboweled by cannon fire.

Jean-David Nau: French. Also known as François l'Olonnais, Nau was a psycho in a sick line of work. Nau whittled prisoners with his cutlass, once allegedly eating a beating heart. Let us all thank the Native Central Americans for tearing him apart alive in 1668.

"Calico" Jack Rackham, Anne Bonny, and Mary Read: English, Irish, and English. The fancy-dressing Rackham got his buccaneering start under the notorious Charles Vane, whom he soon deposed in a mutiny. Rackham fell in love with Anne Bonny, who was stuck in an unhappy marriage in the Bahamas. They eloped and began a new piratical career aboard the sloop *Revenge*, where Anne's hard-living, hard-fighting style earned her respect in a male-dominated business.

Anne soon discovered another incognita in men's clothing: Mary Read, who became her close friend—and her peer in the fine arts of fighting, swearing, and drinking. When pirate hunter Jonathan Barnet caught up with *Revenge* in 1720, Mary and Anne were among the few crewmembers sober and/or brave enough to fight. As Rackham was marched off to hang, Anne showed her contempt: "If ye'd fought like a man, ye needn't hang like a dog." (One suspects that history has omitted a volley or two of choice profanities.)

Both women escaped Calico Jack's fate by revealing their pregnancies to the court. In 1721, Mary died amid disgusting jail conditions, but Anne was most likely ransomed by her father.

Charles Vane: English. When the reformer Woodes Rogers showed up to clean out the Caribbean pirates' favorite lair (New Providence, now Nassau), the wily Vane was the only captain to reject the proffered amnesty. He kept marauding—losing ships and gaining them—until his luck and cunning finally ran out. He was captured and hanged in 1720.

Edward Low: English. Low was hideously scarred by a cutlass slash to the jaw, but the tortures he inflicted upon others would have nauseated a Stalin-era KGB interrogator. It's said that he once forced a man to eat his own severed ears—with salt. According to some sources, he was last seen running from a Royal Navy warship; good thinking on his part, given his record. It is believed he was hanged by the French after 1723.

George Lowther: English. Lowther was elected captain after a mutiny aboard a slave ship. This pirate's hobbies were torture and rape. In 1723, while his ship was beached for hull maintenance, the Royal Navy showed up. Lowther decided he'd rather not dangle from the gallows and shot himself instead.

Sir Henry Morgan: Welsh. Spain was the dominant colonial power in the Americas, shipping home gold and silver by the boatload. Morgan served English foreign interests by raising merry hell with Spanish shipping and colonial interests. Moral of his story: If your piracy serves the national interest and makes you rich, your country may reward you with a knighthood and a governorship. If you're Morgan, you then gain lots of weight and drink yourself to death as a pillar of the genteel Jamaican community. He died rich of dropsy or liver failure in 1688.

Olivier "la Buze" Levasseur: French. "The Buzzard" collaborated with John Taylor and actually wore an eye patch. Unlike Taylor, though, Levasseur didn't quit while he was ahead but kept up his piratical career until his capture by French authorities at Madagascar in 1730. He was hanged.

Gráinne ni Mháille: Irish, aka Grace O'Malley. Rebel, seagoing racketeer, admiral—she was all these and more, engaging in piracy to champion the Irish cause against England. Gráinne didn't even kowtow to Queen Elizabeth I, though she did visit for tea and chitchat. She died of old age in 1603.

Howell Davis: Welsh. This sneaky rogue once captured two ships in one encounter. After the first catch, he forced the captives to brandish weapons at the second, inflating his apparent numbers. Davis was planning to seize a Portuguese island governor when the local militia recognized him and shot him in an ambush in 1719.

Rachel (Schmidt) Wall: American. She turned pirate with her husband, George, luring likely prizes with convincing distress cries. After George drowned in a storm, Rachel forsook the sea for petty thieving along the Boston docks. In 1789, she was arrested for trying to steal a woman's bonnet and was then accused of murdering a sailor. She stood trial, confessed to piracy, and was hanged.

Zheng Yi Sao, aka Ching Shih: Chinese. Hundreds of pirate ships sailed the Chinese coast under her command. Although rare in piracy, she enforced strict rules—notably, a prohibition on rape. Her fleet dominated the coasts to such a degree that in some places, it functioned as a government. Like John Taylor, Zheng quit while she was ahead, swapping her fleet for a pardon. She died of natural causes in 1844.

Fast Facts

- *The fastest wind on Earth blew through the suburbs of Oklahoma City, Oklahoma, on May 3, 1999. The 318-mile-per-hour gusts were recorded during an F5 tornado that destroyed hundreds of homes.*

- *The most rain in a three-day period fell on the tiny island of La Reunion in the South Indian Ocean. In March 2007, close to 13 feet of rain fell as Tropical Cyclone Gamede passed within 120 miles of the French-owned island.*

- *Cloud-to-cloud lightning can stretch over amazing distances. Radar has recorded at least one of these "crawlers" that was more than 75 miles long.*

- *Residents in southern Algeria were surprised by a 30-minute storm on February 18, 1979, marking the only time it has ever snowed in the Sahara.*

- *The most tornadoes recorded in one month in the United States occurred in May 2003. Experts confirmed 543 twisters, far more than the 399 recorded in June 1992.*

- *Most people evacuate when a hurricane is on the way, but some deliberately fly into the storms. The National Oceanic and Atmospheric Association's Hurricane Hunters pilot C-130s straight into a hurricane's eye to measure things such as wind speed and direction, and they are critical in predicting where a hurricane will go and how strong it is.*

- *Speaking of brave souls going into storms, tornado chasing is becoming a popular hobby in the United States. Professional meteorologists have long chased severe storms, dropping probes into tornadoes in order to learn more about how they form and helping officials send warnings so that people can take shelter. So many amateurs are starting to chase on their own that several tour companies have sprung up to give people the thrill without having to buy the equipment.*

THE ROYAL CANADIAN MOUNTED POLICE

✳ ✳ ✳ ✳

Is there an icon as visibly Canadian as the red-serge-and-Stetson dress uniform of the famous Royal Canadian Mounted Police?

- The RCMP's legal establishment began in 1873 as the North-West Mounted Police, assigned to bring law and order to western Canada. Their motto is French: *Maintiens le droit* ("Maintain the right"). A big job for a big place!

- One of the Mounties' first jobs was to banish troublemakers. By 1874, whiskey peddlers from the United States had infested southern Alberta. The Mounties believed that the native First Peoples had suffered enough without rotgut booze, and most whiskey men abandoned their fort well ahead of the arrival of the NWMP.

- Along with a force of civilian volunteers from Prince Albert, the Mounties lost a battle in the snow to the Metis at Duck Lake, Saskatchewan, in March 1885 during the Northwest Rebellion. The government forces were lucky not to be encircled and wiped out—a decision for which they could thank Metis leader Louis Riel, who urged against further bloodshed.

- The NWMP began to operate in the Yukon in 1895. Good timing, considering the characters coming up from the United States to pan, hack, dig, and sift for gold. Skagway arrivals were surprised to find NWMP constables at the Canadian border, turning back undesirables and making sure the rest brought enough food to avoid famine in Dawson.

- They became the Royal North-West Mounted Police in 1904, receiving that designation from King Edward VII. The RNWMP became the RCMP with the absorption of the Dominion Police, with law enforcement authority in every square yard of Canada (later every square meter).

- The Depression years were a time of modernization for the RCMP. The marine division was created in 1932. Police dogs became part of the force in 1935, and it began using aircraft in 1937.

- The RCMP schooner *St. Roch* was the first vessel to navigate the entire Northwest Passage (through Canada's Arctic islands from Pacific to Atlantic, or vice versa) in one season (1944).

- An era ended in 1966. Universal RCMP training in horseback riding and horse care was discontinued, though the Musical Ride carries on those traditions in ceremonial fashion.

- Only in 1969 did the RCMP discontinue use of dogsled patrols in the North.

- The first women became uniformed Mounties in 1974.

- Until 1984, the Mounties were responsible for Canada's internal counterintelligence function. The agent of change was the revelation of some unlawful covert operations concerning Quebec separatists.

- Canada has about half a million Sikh citizens and residents. Male Sikhs wear turbans, not Stetsons or billed police caps. In 1990, after a national controversy, Sikh RCMP constables were allowed to wear their turbans in uniform.

- Though a police force, the RCMP was also a regiment of dragoons (mounted rifles). It had a guidon with battle honors from the Northwest Rebellion, South Africa, and World Wars I and II.

- The Musical Ride dates back to the NWMP days. This ceremonial equestrian drill team shows off all over Canada from spring to fall. The 32 members of the Musical Ride perform in uniform (red serge and Stetson) and are armed with white lances.

- Those hoping to join the RCMP must be Canadian citizens of good character, be at least 19 years old, and have Canadian secondary school educations or better. They must be proficient in English and/or French.

TWELVE MONTHS OF FOOD

✳ ✳ ✳ ✳

Hungry for a good time? Mark your calendar, loosen your belt, and partake in a year's worth of offbeat food celebrations.

January
- Gourmet Coffee Month
- Oatmeal Month
- Soup Month
- Wheat Bread Month
- Chocolate-Covered Cherry Day (January 3)
- English Toffee Day (January 8)
- Peanut Brittle Day (January 26)

February
- Cherry Month
- Fabulous Florida Strawberry Month
- Grapefruit Month
- Macadamia Nut Month
- Sweet Potato Month
- Bubble Gum Day (February 1)
- Solo Diners Eat Out Week (February 1–7)
- Gumdrop Day (February 15)
- Chili Day (February 22)

March
- Celery Month
- Frozen Food Month
- Noodle Month
- Peanut Month
- Sauce Month
- American Chocolate Week (third week in March)

April
- Fresh Florida Tomato Month
- Grilled Cheese Sandwich Month

- Pecan Month
- Soft Pretzel Month
- Soy Foods Month
- Licorice Day (April 12)
- Jelly Bean Day (April 22)
- Egg Salad Week (the week after Easter)

May
- Asparagus Month
- Barbecue Month
- Chocolate Custard Month
- Egg Month
- Hamburger Month
- Salad Month
- Salsa Month
- Strawberry Month
- Sweet Vidalia Month
- Raisin Week (May 1–7)
- Eat Dessert First Week (May 1–7)
- Eat What You Want Day (May 11)
- Apple Pie Day (May 13)
- Chocolate Chip Day (May 15)
- Taffy Day (May 23)

June
- Candy Month
- Dairy Month
- Iced Tea Month
- Papaya Month
- Soul Food Month
- Steakhouse Month
- Turkey Lovers' Month
- Vinegar Day (June 16)
- Cheese Week (last week in June)

July
- Baked Beans Month
- Blueberry Month
- Horseradish Month
- Hot Dog Month
- Peach Month
- Gummi Worm Day (July 15)
- Lollipop Day (July 20)
- Ice Cream Day—aka Sundae Sunday (third Sunday in July)
- Drive-Thru Day (July 24)

August
- Get Acquainted with Kiwi Fruit Month
- Catfish Month
- Sandwich Month
- Watermelon Day (August 3)
- Mustard Day (August 4)
- S'mores Day (August 10)

September

- Biscuit Month
- Chicken Month
- Honey Month
- Mushroom Month
- Potato Month
- Rice Month
- Waffle Week (September 2–8)
- International Eat an Apple Day (September 15)

October
- Celebrate Sun-Dried Tomatoes Month
- Eat Country Ham Month
- Apple Month
- Caramel Month
- Chili Month
- Cookie Month
- Dessert Month

- Pasta Month
- Pickled Peppers Month
- Pizza Month
- Popcorn Poppin' Month
- Pork Month
- Pretzel Month
- Seafood Month
- Chestnut Week (second week in October)
- World Egg Day (second Friday in October)
- Candy Corn Day (October 30)

November
- Fun with Fondue Month
- Georgia Pecan Month
- Peanut Butter Lovers Month
- Pepper Month
- Pomegranate Month
- Raisin Bread Month
- Fig Week (November 1–7)
- Bundt Day (November 15)
- Homemade Bread Day (November 17)

December
- Cookie Cutter Week (December 1–7)
- Gluten-Free Baking Week (week before Christmas)
- Chocolate-Covered Anything Day (December 16)
- Candy Cane Day (December 26)

GREAT MOMENTS IN KITSCH HISTORY

✳ ✳ ✳ ✳

Kitsch is a term used to describe objects of bad taste and poor quality. But despite its bad rap, plenty of people go to great lengths to collect kitsch and keep its "charms" alive.

Pink flamingos: In 1957, Union Products of Leominster, Massachusetts, introduced the ultimate in tacky lawn ornaments: the plastic pink flamingo. Designed by artist Don Featherstone, they were sold in the Sears mail-order catalog for $2.76 a pair with the instructions, "Place in garden, lawn, to beautify landscape." Authentic pink flamingos—which are sold only in pairs and bear Featherstone's signature under their tails—are no longer on the market (Union Products shuttered its factory in 2006), but knockoffs ensure the bird's survival.

Troll dolls: Danish sculptor Thomas Damm created the popular troll doll as a handmade wooden gift for his daughter. After it caught the eye of the owner of a toy shop, Dammit Dolls were born, and plastic versions with trademark oversize hairdos hit the mass market. The dolls swept the United States in the early 1960s and were lugged around as good-luck charms by people of all ages and walks of life—including Lady Bird Johnson.

Lava Lites: In the early 1960s, Englishman Edward Craven-Walker invented the Lava Lite, and Chicago entrepreneur Adolf Wertheimer bought the American distribution rights after seeing it at a trade show. Within five years, 2 million Lava Lites had been sold in the United States.

Polyester leisure suits: Brightly colored leisure suits are actually an early 1970s interpretation of a style that took Europe by storm in the 1700s: the three-piece wool suit. Worn not to the office but on weekend outings, wool suits inspired leisure suits, which likewise never caught on as business attire but were the rage on Saturday nights at the disco.

THE WORLD'S BIGGEST INSECTS

✳ ✳ ✳

Although most people consider insects to be one of life's little annoyances, the following species are more like something out of a science-fiction movie. It's not likely you'd try to swat one of these.

South American male acteon beetle (*Megasoma acteon*): Not only is the acteon beetle regarded the bulkiest insect on the planet, it also has an impressive frame. Males can grow to be three and a half inches long by two inches wide and an inch and a half thick, with three sets of menacing tarsal claws. Its thick, smooth armor and robust thoracic horns make it look like a miniature cross between a rhinoceros and an elephant. It's commonly found in the South American tropics, where it likes to chew on tree sap and fruit.

Hercules beetle (*Dynastes hercules*): This beast can grow to be seven inches long. About half of that length is consumed by a threatening, sword-shape horn and a second smaller horn that curves back toward the head. The male Hercules is smooth and shiny with attractive green-and-black wing cases. This beetle feeds on tree sap and lives in North America.

Giant New Zealand weta (*Deinacrida heteracantha*): The Maori people of New Zealand call this insect "the God of the ugly things," an appropriate observation. It looks like a thwarted attempt to cross a cockroach with a cricket. The weta's body typically measures three inches in length, excluding its protruding legs and antennae, which can more than double its size. It eats leaves, other insects, fungi, dead animals, and fruit.

Borneo stick insect (*Pharnacia kirbyi*): At close to 13 inches in length (20 inches when it stretches its legs), this is the longest insect on the planet. It is also known as the bent twig insect, for its amazing ability to bend its body at an acute angle and stay that way for hours. The female feeds primarily on bramble during the night, and during the day she keeps very still to avoid being spotted by predators. Males are not quite as big.

Giant Brazilian ant (*Dinoponera gigantea*): The heavyweight champ of ants measures in at more than one inch, and its ability to lift 20 times its body weight makes it one of the strongest creatures on the planet. It also displays amazing skills of memory, learning, and the ability to correct mistakes. It lives in the wetlands and woodlands of the Brazilian jungle and feeds primarily on lowland plants.

South American longhorn beetle (*Titanus giganteus*): This species, also known as the titan beetle, can grow up to six inches long and has extremely powerful legs. The beetle's most prominent—and most menacing—feature is its huge mandible, which can allegedly snap pencils in half. This bug's diet consists of plants, shrubbery, and decaying organic matter.

Giant Fijian longhorn beetle (*Xixuthrus heros*): This intimidating native of the Fijian island of Viti Levu has a body length of five and a half inches and emits a frightful hissing noise when challenged. Ounce for ounce, its jaws are as powerful as those of a killer shark. Good thing for humans, it prefers to snack on tropical plants.

South American giant cockroach (*Blaberus giganteus*): The baddest of the cockroach clan lives in dark caves and can reach lengths up to four inches. It discourages predators by mimicking the color of noxious beetles and emitting a foul odor. This cockroach will eat anything but prefers fruits and vegetation.

The World's Smallest Insect

Fairyflies are tiny wasps that are cited as the smallest of all insects. Fairyflies are parasites that lay their eggs on the eggs of other insects. Their minute bodies have digestive, reproductive, respiratory, and circulatory systems, but the wasps themselves are actually smaller than a single-celled paramecium.

Emoticons:
SAYING HOW YOU FEEL WITHOUT SAYING A WORD

✳ ✳ ✳ ✳

With the right stroke of keys, you can add emotion and personality to your e-mail message—without using those irritating exclamation points and CAPITAL LETTERS!!!!

Emoticon Primer

Emoticons are usually read sideways and use the punctuation keys to elaborate on a smiley face.

(1) The colon key makes a set of eyes :

(2) The semi-colon creates a wink ;

(3) A dash is a nose -

(4) Parentheses indicate smiles) or frowns (

Combine (1) or (2) with (3) and (4), and you have a face :-)

Use these variations, or create your own and express yourself.

8-)	sunglasses
0:)	smiling angel
>-)	evil grin
{:-)	person with a toupee
:*)	drunken smile
:-&	tongue-tied
:-($)	put your money where your mouth is
#-)	partied all night
:-X	kiss
:-Y	side comment
;-D	winking and laughing
=O	surprised
:,(	crying
[:-)	wearing headphones
l(	trying to stay awake
l-D	big laugh
}:[	angry
8-P	yuck

:-E	buck teeth
:-#	braces on teeth
=====:}	snake
@>---	rose
~:-/	Elvis
=):-)=	Abraham Lincoln
*<B>	Santa Claus
:-<	pouting
:-}	embarrassed
l-)	daydreaming
=:-O	scared
!:-)	I have an idea!
:-x	I'm keeping my mouth shut.
:-P	tongue sticking out
;-)	wink
?:-l	curious
O:-*	pretending innocence
:-(	frowning/unhappy

Unrotated Emoticons

You can read these messages straight on, without getting a crick in your neck.

>_<	troubled
#^.^#	shy
^_^	smiling
^o^	happy/laughing
-_-;	"sweat"
T-T	crying
\^.^/	Yay! (arms up)
O.o;;	bug-eyed/weirded out
^*^	kiss
O_O	shocked
<.<	look left
>.>	look right
>.<	d'oh!
=^-^=	happy kitty
~_~	tired

MILITARY JARGON GETS MUSTERED OUT

✳ ✳ ✳

These interesting military phrases have seeped into civilian life so successfully that many people don't realize they started out as soldier slang.

Blockbuster: Today the word refers to a wildly successful movie, but during World War II it was a nickname used by the Royal Air Force for large bombs that could "bust" an entire city block. "Blockbuster" retired from the military in the 1950s when advertisers started using it as a synonym for *gigantic*.

Bought the Farm/Gone for a Burton: Because they face death daily, most soldiers try to avoid talking about it. During World War I, U.S. soldiers often said that someone missing or killed had "bought the farm"—what many families did with their loved one's death benefits. Heavy-hearted British soldiers in World War II would raise a glass—in this case a British beer called Burton—to a departed brother, saying he'd "gone for a Burton."

Push the Envelope: If you're tired of your boss urging you to "push the envelope," blame World War II test pilots. They listed a plane's abilities—speed, engine power, maneuverability—on its flight envelope and then did their best to get the plane to outperform its predetermined limits.

Bite the Bullet: During the Civil War, the "anesthetic" often used on wounded soldiers was a bullet or block of wood to bite down on. The patient, with no alternative, was forced to endure the procedure and excruciating pain so he could get on with the process of healing.

Show Your True Colors/With Flying Colors: Military regiments would end a victorious battle "with flying colors," or with their flag ("colors") held high. To "show your true colors," or to reveal your intentions, derives from early warships that would temporarily fly another nation's flag to deceive an enemy into feeling safe.

Over the Top: Nobody wanted to go over the top during World War I—that is, to charge over the parapets toward the enemy, a maneuver that resulted in high casualties. Soldiers who went over the top were considered incredibly—even excessively—brave.

Boondocks: In the early 1900s, U.S. troops in the Philippines fought guerillas hiding in the remote *bandok*—Tagalog (the primary language of the Philippines) for "mountains." Soldiers translated the word as *boondocks*.

Grapevine: Civil War soldiers likened telegraph wires to grapevines, the latter having a gnarled appearance. News that arrived by "grapevine telegraph" (or simply "grapevine") was eventually considered to be "twisted" or dubious.

Rank and File: Military officers lined up marching soldiers in "ranks," rows from side to side, and "files," rows from front to back. When the soldiers returned to their offices and factories after military service, "rank and file" came to represent the ordinary members of society.

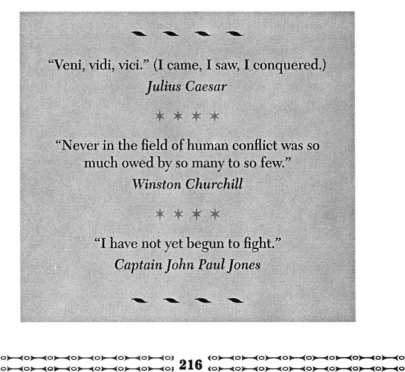

"Veni, vidi, vici." (I came, I saw, I conquered.)
Julius Caesar

* * * *

"Never in the field of human conflict was so much owed by so many to so few."
Winston Churchill

* * * *

"I have not yet begun to fight."
Captain John Paul Jones

THE DONNER PARTY

✳ ✳ ✳ ✳

*Starting around 1845, hundreds of thousands of Americans
migrated west, believing that it was their "manifest destiny" to claim
that territory and seek their fortunes. The story of the Donner Party
is one of the most tragic tales in U.S. history.*

A New Frontier

To reach Oregon and California, settlers had to cross the Great
Plains, a journey that took weeks to complete. There was little water
or shelter on this vast expanse of land, and many travelers died of
dehydration, cholera, or pneumonia.

Despite such conditions, the lure of a better life was strong. In
April 1846, George Donner formed a group of 33 people (mostly
members of his family) to head west to Sutter's Fort, California. In
May, while camped in Missouri, Donner and his group joined members from another wagon train and formed the Donner Party, named
after their elected captain. Donner predicted the journey would put
everyone in sunny California by June. He and 86 fellow travelers
were in for a big surprise.

Trouble on the Trail

The party had gotten as far as Fort Laramie in what is now Wyoming
by the end of June, when they ran into another traveler. He was
headed eastbound, having used a faster, though treacherous, route
from the west through the desert, one that he did not recommend.
Regardless, the Donner Party took the "shortcut," which put them
three weeks behind schedule. By this time, many of the travelers had
fallen ill, and most of the group's animals had either died or wandered off.

In the middle of October, when the group got stuck in a monstrous mountain blizzard, they were still more than 100 miles from
their destination.

Dwindling Supplies

The group was stranded in the Sierra Nevada mountain range for a few months. When the food supplies they had brought with them ran out, the oxen were slaughtered and eaten. Journals and letters from members of the party reveal that before very long the only "food" available consisted of twigs, the bones of decaying animals, and boiled leather hides.

Eventually, a small faction of the Donner Party set out to find help. The rest of the party was too weak to travel, and conditions for them only worsened.

Shocking Discoveries

The rescue group—the few members who remained—finally found help in California. Accounts of what the first relief team saw when they arrived at the camp depict group members who were starving, freezing, and delirious. Those who were able to make the recovery trip were taken at that point; the rest were forced to wait for a second rescue team.

As reported by the second group of rescuers, some of the remaining members of the Donner Party had resorted to cannibalism in order to make it through the winter. The survivors eventually reached Sutter's Fort more than a year after the party's departure from Independence and about six months after their expected arrival. Two thirds of the men and one third of the women and children had died on the journey.

The Aftermath

Not surprisingly, when word got out that settlers trapped in the mountains had eaten other human beings to stay alive, migration to California slowed for a while. But when gold was discovered in 1848, images of the imperiled Donner Party were replaced by dreams of newfound wealth in the West.

Today, near the eastern shore of Donner Lake, the Donner Memorial State Park commemorates the courage and the disaster that was the Donner Party's journey. The area of nearby Alder Creek, the site of the second Donner camp, is a designated National Historic Landmark.

I'm No Expert, But...
RELIGION & FOOD

✳ ✳ ✳ ✳

*As food is a universal human experience, it's not surprising
that people apply religious taboos to their diets.
To uncover the connection between food and faith,
we consulted someone in the know.*

Q: What does "kosher" mean?

A: It is an exacting series of rules for food selection (no pork or shellfish, no dairy and meat at the same meal), harvesting (specific methods of slaughter and blood removal), and preparation (separate utensils for meat and dairy dishes). Kosher Jews (typically Conservative, Orthodox, and Chasidic in ascending order of strictness) don't willingly or knowingly eat food that is *traif*—or un-kosher. The basic rules come from the Torah, with lots of arcane rabbinical clarification hashed out over the millennia.

Q: Why can't Hindus eat cheeseburgers?

A: Because cows are revered in Hinduism for their gentle nature and life-giving milk, the last thing a Hindu would do is kill one.

Q: Why do so many Catholics eat fish on Fridays?

A: It isn't so much eating fish that day as abstaining from meat. Devout Catholics make this sacrifice as an act of contrition for the sins of the past week, and Friday is chosen because it was the day of the Crucifixion—Jesus' sacrifice. Many Catholics abstain from eating meat on Fridays only during Lent.

Q: Who has the strictest dietary code?

A: Probably the Jainists. They eat according to their scripture: "Do not injure, abuse, oppress, enslave, insult, torment, torture, or kill any creature or living being." Jainist monks won't step on a bug, and they wear masks to keep from swallowing even a gnat. Some Jainists won't eat vegetables if harvesting kills the plant.

POPCORN

✳ ✳ ✳ ✳

- Aztec Indians of the 16th century used garlands of popped maize as a decoration in ceremonial dances. They were a symbol of good-will and peace.

- Native American folklore speaks of spirits that live inside each kernel of corn. When heated, or "angered," the spirits explode in a "puff," often considered an omen of bad luck.

- The oldest ears of popcorn (the variety of corn grown for this particular purpose) were discovered in the Bat Cave (in Carlsbad Caverns National Park) in west central New Mexico in 1948.

- The physics of popping: Each kernel of corn contains a drop of water in a layer of soft starch. As the kernel heats up, the water expands, building pressure against the starch. Eventually, this hard surface cracks, exploding the kernel.

- Charles Cretors invented the popcorn machine in 1885, but that was really just a peanut-roasting apparatus that happened to also pop corn kernels. Eight years later, Cretors introduced the first mobile, steam-driven popcorn machine at the Chicago World's Fair.

- During the Great Depression, popcorn was ubiquitous on city streets because it was an inexpensive way to stave off hunger.

- In 1998, the National Popcorn Board was formed as a result of the Popcorn Promotion, Research, and Consumer Information Act signed in 1996 by President Bill Clinton, a big fan of the snack.

- More than 17 billion quarts of popcorn are consumed in the United States annually; that's about 56 quarts per person every year.

- "Old maids," the unpopped kernels at the bottom of a bag or bowl of popcorn, are likely the result of dehydration. A loss of three percent of the moisture in a popcorn kernel can render it unpoppable. Store popcorn in an airtight container to keep it from drying out before it's popped.

- There's been a slight downward trend in popcorn consumption in the United States recently, but its popularity has been steadily increasing in Europe, Asia, and South America.

- According to CalorieKing.com, the average large tub (20 cups) of buttered movie theater popcorn contains 1,657 calories and 134 grams of fat. Don't worry, though: You can burn it off by walking for about seven and a half hours.

- In October 2006, the World's Largest Popcorn Ball was created in Lake Forest, Illinois, to celebrate National Popcorn Month. It weighed 3,415 pounds, was 8 feet in diameter, and had a circumference of 24½ feet.

- Colonial women poured sugar and cream on popcorn and served it for breakfast—likely the first "puffed" cereal! Some colonists popped corn in a type of cage that revolved on an axle and was positioned over a fire.

- According to the Popcorn Institute, popcorn is high in carbohydrates and has more protein and iron than potato chips, ice cream cones, pretzels, and soda crackers.

- By the time Europeans began settling in the New World, popcorn had spread to most Native American tribes in North and South America. More than 700 types of popcorn were being grown, elaborate poppers were being invented, and popcorn was sometimes worn in the hair and around the neck as jewelry. There was even a widely consumed popcorn beer.

- Most popcorn acquires one of two basic shapes when it's popped: snowflake or mushroom. Snowflake popcorn is what you eat in movie theaters and at sporting events because it looks and pops bigger. Mushroom-shaped popcorn is used to make candy confections because it doesn't crumble easily.

- If you made a trail of popcorn from New York City to Los Angeles, you would need more than 352,028,160 popped kernels!

THE STORY OF UNCLE SAM

✳ ✳ ✳ ✳

Uncle Sam may be one of the most familiar icons to people in the United States, but no one is sure of the origins of this goateed and flag-theme-attired image. Was he an actual person, or just snippets of people and images from popular culture?

- During the War of 1812, the U.S. Army needed provisions and supplies—especially protein. Samuel Wilson, a meatpacker in Troy, New York, provided the troops with barrels of preserved meat, stamped "US," likely as a stipulation of his procurement contract. In fact, "Uncle Sam" was clean-shaven, short, and pudgy, the picture of a respectable merchant of his time, and he likely did not dress up for fun.

- The Uncle Sam character we know today was born in the influential images of Thomas Nast, a prominent 19th-century political cartoonist who depicted several similar flag-themed figures.

- The most enduring Uncle Sam image—which depicts him pointing a finger and saying "I Want You"—comes from World War I recruiting posters drawn by James Montgomery Flagg, who also modeled the famous stern, craggy visage.

- Uncle Sam is actually a national personification: an image that sums up a national identity. Other countries' examples include John Bull of England—a stout, thick-necked, top-hatted guy—and *Moder Svea* (Mother Sweden), a sword-bearing woman in chain mail and a flowing skirt.

- It wasn't until 1961 that Congress recognized Samuel Wilson as the original Uncle Sam. This didn't do Wilson much good, coming more than a century after his death, but it was a good deal for Troy, New York. The city began to pitch itself as the "Home of Uncle Sam," as it does today.

- One popular beneficiary of the Uncle Sam concept was the band Grateful Dead, who used Sam's hat liberally in their imagery. Another is the New York Yankees, whose logo features Sam's top hat.

Fast Facts

- The longest cells in the human body are the motor neurons. They can be up to four and a half feet long and run from the lower spinal cord to the big toe.

- The human eye blinks an average of 3.7 million times per year.

- The longest-living cells in the body are brain cells, which can live a human's entire lifetime.

- Fifteen million blood cells are produced and destroyed in the human body every second.

- The brain requires more than 25 percent of the oxygen used by the human body.

- If your mouth was completely dry, you would not be able to distinguish the taste of anything.

- The human body has enough fat to produce seven bars of soap.

- The human head is a quarter of our total length at birth but only an eighth of our total length by the time we reach adulthood.

- Food travels from the mouth, through the esophagus, and into the stomach in seven seconds.

- The average person has 100,000 hairs on his or her head. Each hair grows approximately 5 inches per year.

- There are 60,000 miles of blood vessels in the average human.

- The pupil of the eye expands as much as 45 percent when a person looks at something pleasing.

- The human heart creates enough pressure while pumping to squirt blood 30 feet.

- The average adult body consists of approximately 71 pounds of potentially edible meat, not including organ tissue.

OUTLANDISH LAWS

✳ ✳ ✳ ✳

- Close the blinds! In Singapore, walking around in your house while nude is against the law—it's considered pornographic.

- In Arizona, it is illegal to refuse a person a glass of water. Aimed primarily at businesses, this law is meant to cut down on dehydration deaths among homeless people.

- A Virginia law states that bribery or corrupt practices are forbidden—unless you are a political candidate.

- Be careful how you break your eggs in England. Anyone caught breaking a boiled egg on the pointed end can be thrown in the "village stocks" for a day. This ordinance was put in place by King Edward VI and has yet to be overturned.

- Carrying a concealed weapon in Seattle, Washington, is illegal if it's more than six feet long. Spears don't tuck into coats very well.

- Be kind to bivalves: In Maryland, it's illegal to mistreat oysters.

- Have a duel planned in Paraguay? If you're not a legal blood donor, you could be arrested.

- In Ohio, it is against the law to get a fish drunk.

- Cursing in French may sound elegant, but it's illegal in Montreal, Canada. Swearing in English is okay, though.

- Dressing in a hurry has its hazards in Thailand, where it's illegal to leave your house unless you're wearing underwear.

- In Israel it's illegal to pick your nose on the Sabbath.

- British law mandates that if you are driving a car, you must be in the front seat.

- A law in North Carolina forbids the use of an elephant to plow cotton fields.

- According to South Korean law, traffic officers must report all bribes they receive from motorists.

- In Providence, Rhode Island, you can buy toothpaste and mouthwash on a Sunday, but you can't buy a toothbrush.

- An Australian regulation makes it illegal for fax modems to pick up on the first ring.
- Massachusetts takes its clam chowder seriously—people there are legally forbidden to put tomatoes in it.
- Members of the British Parliament are not allowed to enter the House of Commons in full armor. They can't die in Parliament, either.
- Farmers in France, be aware—you may not name your pig Napoleon.
- In Italy, a woman wearing a skirt is considered feminine. A man in a skirt can be arrested.
- Atlanta, Georgia, does not allow anyone to tie a giraffe to a telephone pole. Perhaps they're worried the pole might get jealous?
- You may not use a feather duster to tickle a girl under the chin in Portland, Maine.
- The head of any dead whale found on British shores automatically becomes the property of the king. The queen gets the tail.
- Alabama strictly forbids wearing a fake moustache in church if it could cause laughter.
- Be careful to check the clock—it's illegal to flush a toilet after 10 P.M. in Switzerland.
- Bad for business: In Sweden, prostitution is legal. Hiring the services of a prostitute, however, is not.
- California law strictly forbids hunting animals from a moving vehicle—unless your target is a whale.
- Alaska does not allow waking a sleeping bear just to take its photograph. You can hunt it, though.
- Ladies, pay attention to your wardrobe choices when in Arizona. Certain cities still have laws that make it illegal for a woman to wear pants.
- Hawaii prohibits placing coins in one's ear.
- All males in England who are older than 14 must spend at least two hours per week practicing firing a longbow.

Talk to the Expert
CHAIN PULLER

✳ ✳ ✳ ✳

No, we're not pulling your chain: This guy has pulled the chain in lumber mills for 40 years. Let's see if his job is as peculiar as it sounds.

Q: Most people probably don't understand your work. What is this chain you pull?

A: First of all, lumber mills turn logs into lumber. At a couple of points in that process, the wood has to be stacked or unstacked. Someone, or a machine, breaks the lumber load down and sends it through a series of chains about waist-high, all going the same speed, like big parallel conveyer belts. That lumber needs to be sorted, and workers called graders decide how it should be sorted. Chain pullers pull lumber off the chain and stack it by grade and length.

Q: What are the different chains?

A: Coming out of the sawmill, green chain—to divide the lumber so it'll dry right. After drying, dry chain—the dried loads are stored until the boss is ready to run them through the planer. Next is where I pull the planer chain, which sorts the boards into the stacks that will go onto trucks or train cars and eventually to your hardware store. Many mills have done away with pullers on some of the chains, replacing them with a machine, or one sorry worker pitching every board that comes down one of about 20 sorting chutes.

Q: So there's more than one chain puller on a shift?

A: One person can't do it all. Think about the different grades of lumber we could get, all out of the same drying load. We have lengths from 6 feet to 16 feet. Because you can't pile different grades or lengths together, there are a lot of lumber piles. Each puller is responsible for certain piles. The most common length and grade go to a stacking machine. In the end, it takes about three pullers to do the work of one machine.

Q: Your crew grabs boards and throws them on stacks? Sounds exhausting.

A: In fact, it's all technique. The load is below you and there are steel rollers all along the chain. Usually, the person in front of you pulls out your boards for you, to help you notice. As those come, you pull the board out farther and bear down. It whistles down the roller pretty fast, and you catch it at the end and drop it. Only at the very top of the load do you have to heave a board upward a little.

Q: How do you know when the load is full?

A: That's second-grade math. You calculate however many rows high for that thickness of lumber, and that's when it's full. You have to know when you can't pile on any more boards. No one will stop production while you count on your fingers, either. If the carrier doesn't pick up your load, you get to put the extra boards somewhere until it does.

Q: Don't you get tons of splinters from the boards?

A: Not too often, because we wear quarter-inch-thick leather aprons that get a shiny surface from all the sappy boards sliding down them, and we also wear big leather mittens. Regular work gloves don't last an hour. But you still have to watch out for hazards, such as falling off the platform or, worst of all, the lumber carrier catching the edge of the load and ramming the boards in under the chain. If you were standing in the way of that, you just lost your leg at the hip.

Working Thoughts

"It's just a job. Grass grows, birds fly, waves pound the sand. I beat people up."

Muhammad Ali

UNITED STATES NATIONAL PARKS: VACATION HIGHLIGHTS

✳ ✳ ✳ ✳

The U.S. National Park Service administers 391 sites of historic, scientific, cultural, scenic, or other interest. These include national monuments, national parks, national battlefields, national rivers, and national cemeteries. Here are some interesting details.

- Delaware is the only state with no national park territory.

- Some sites are international rather than national. St. Croix Island International Historic Site, between Maine and New Brunswick (Canada), is situated in Maine but is managed in cooperation with Parks Canada (the two nations often hold joint events on site). A similar situation exists with the International Peace Garden (North Dakota) and the Waterton-Glacier International Peace Park (Alberta/Montana).

- Although Yellowstone was the first national park (designated on March 1, 1872), it wasn't the first area set aside as a park. That honor is shared by the National Capital Parks, the White House, and the National Mall, all designated on July 16, 1790.

- National park status doesn't last forever. A couple dozen sites have been turned over to the states, or to other federal departments. For example, the Park Service transferred New Echota Marker National Memorial (a Cherokee heritage memorial) to the state of Georgia in 1950.

- In 2006, there were 272,623,980 recreational visits to national parks.

- The highest point in a national park is the summit of Denali (aka Mt. McKinley) in Alaska. At 20,320 feet, it's also the highest point on the North American landmass.

- In Alaska's Kobuk Valley National Park, there are approximately 25 square miles of rolling sand dunes, and summer temperatures can hit 100° F.

- The lowest point is Badwater Basin in California's Death Valley National Park, which is 282 feet below sea level. From 1931 to 1934, just over half an inch of rain fell there, and summer temperatures can exceed 130° F.

- Death Valley National Park also has a mountain, Telescope Peak, which tops out at 11,049 feet above sea level. From the top of this mountain to Badwater Basin it's twice the vertical drop of the Grand Canyon.

- The northernmost point in a national park is Inupiat Heritage Center at Barrow, Alaska, while the southernmost point is the National Park of American Samoa, below the equator.

- While a portion of California's Yosemite National Park has all the conveniences of a small city, 95 percent of the park is designated as wilderness.

- The farthest national park from Washington, D.C., is War in the Pacific National Historical Park in Guam. It's far closer to the Philippines than to Hawaii, let alone the continental United States.

- The Grand Canyon has a lesser-known peer: Colorado's Black Canyon of the Gunnison National Park. The dark gneiss walls of the canyon (more than a half mile deep) narrow to a quarter mile wide, presenting a majestic, shadowy abyss.

- The longest arch at Arches National Park in Utah measures 306 feet from base to base. A football field is 300 feet long.

- Oregon's Crater Lake National Park is a corpse—a volcanic corpse, that is. Ancient Mt. Mazama coughed up one last violent eruption in the earliest stages of human civilization, then its walls collapsed into the dead volcano's caldera. Precipitation fell and melted to form a shimmering six-mile-wide lake.

- Devil's Tower in Wyoming began its history buried—a tall pillar of magma that leaked or burned through the other rock in the area, then cooled underground. Millions of years of erosion laid bare the 1,267-foot tower.

Folklore: Myth or Truth?

JOHNNY APPLESEED, PIONEER TREE PLANTER

✳ ✳ ✳ ✳

The legend is almost too glib. What kind of person would run around planting trees? Didn't he need a job? It turns out that trees were Johnny Appleseed's business—but a gentler businessperson never lived. His real name was John Chapman, and he is one of those rare folk heroes whose legend is fact. What's more, he deserves the reverence his memory enjoys.

- Johnny was born in 1774, and his first memories were of the Revolution. His father, a farmer, was a Revolutionary officer and veteran of Bunker Hill; Johnny was just seven years old when Lord Cornwallis hung it up at Yorktown.

- His mother died young. Relatives raised Johnny and his sister. Perhaps with his father away at war and in the care of family members, he grew up not really thinking of any place as a permanent home—a natural roamer.

- Johnny went west in 1792. By the end of the 1790s, he was a nurseryman: He picked the seeds out of apples, planted them, grew saplings, and sold them to new settlers. Because many Continental veterans received land grants in the Ohio Valley, lots of people in Pennsylvania and Ohio wanted fruit trees.

- Johnny may have been the closest thing to a Jainist monk in U.S. frontier history. He tried hard to avoid killing any insect, much less any animal.

- He didn't just wander around tossing seeds at random. Johnny Appleseed was a smart businessperson, though he usually wore cast-off clothing and went barefoot. He would get the seeds for free from cider mills, plant a nursery, fence it, and then leave it in a neighbor's charge. Johnny would show up every so often to check on the orchards. If the neighbor had collected any payment for saplings, Johnny would pick that up.

- Chapman was a Swedenborgian. That's a religion, members of which are still around today (and they sure revere Chapman). Emmanuel Swedenborg was an 18th-century Swedish genius and Christian mystic whose church could best be described as non-mainstream Protestantism with an occult streak.

- Johnny never married and apparently had no children. When anyone asked him why he wasn't married, he told them he believed he would have two great wives in Heaven, provided he didn't marry on Earth.

- Why didn't someone else plant more trees and push him out of business? Johnny had a knack for showing up just before major population waves. Ask any skilled businessperson: It is partly about marketing, partly about finance, and all about timing and location. By the time most people arrived, Johnny's trees were ready for sale and transplant. Some are still standing today.

- As much money as Chapman earned through his business skill, he left most of it on the table. If people couldn't pay him cash, he took goods in barter or sold on credit. He tended to forgive bad debt. During his life, he tried very hard to give his wealth away.

- Along with apples, Johnny planted many and varied medicinal herbs wherever he went. Fennel, a licorice-smelling perennial often used as a spice, was referred to as "Johnny Weed" back in those days.

- In areas where relations with Native Americans could at times be tense, Johnny Appleseed walked in complete safety. Not only did the tribes respect him, some thought him touched by the Great Spirit. He seemed to be a man without an enemy.

- If you lived in the Ohio Valley and liked a drink now and then, you'd have had good reason to toast John's health. Most of his apples were made into cider. And Johnny definitely enjoyed a drink and a pinch of snuff, relaxing for an evening with a traveling or settled family, or any stranger who happened to be around.

- An early animal rescuer, Johnny would buy neglected horses and find them good homes, or put them out to graze and see if they got well. If they did, he would foster them, extracting a promise of good treatment.

- Chapman was also a Swedenborgian missionary. He donated a considerable portion of his assets to the church, spent a lot of his money on Swedenborgian literature, and tried his best to spread his faith as he traveled.

- As if all that weren't enough, John Chapman was a deeply patriotic man whose oratory would have served him well in politics, had he cared for such things. He loved Fourth of July festivals and always found time to participate.

- Johnny "Appleseed" Chapman passed away on March 18, 1845, near Fort Wayne, Indiana. And for once the folktale is less impressive than the reality.

Fun with Apples

- *Apples will ripen six times faster if you leave them at room temperature rather than refrigerate them.*

- *Apples are a member of the rose family.*

- *When the colonists arrived in North America, they found just crabapples, the only apples native to the United States.*

- *Apple trees produce fruit four to five years after they're planted. There are approximately 7,500 varieties of apples grown around the world.*

- *Early apple orchards produced very few apples because there were no honeybees. Historical records indicate that colonies of honeybees were first shipped from England and landed in the colony of Virginia early in 1622.*

Gridiron Glory:
UNLIKELY SUPER BOWL HEROES

✳ ✳ ✳ ✳

Most of the gridiron gladiators who grasped glory in the Super Bowl brought a storied and successful pedigree into the decisive game, with numerous accolades and accomplishments on their resume before they stepped into the spotlight and basked in the limelight. Most, but not all.

From the Supermarket to the Super Bowl—Kurt Warner: Before he marched the St. Louis Rams to victory in Super Bowl XXXIV, Kurt Warner was barely a name in his own household. A bench jockey throughout much of his collegiate career at Northern Iowa, Warner was signed by the Green Bay Packers in 1994 but was unceremoniously handed his pink slip before the season even began. Out of prospects and cash, he took a job at a local grocery store in Cedar Falls, Iowa, for $5.15 an hour. Undaunted by his early failures, Warner began to slowly climb the football ladder. He rode the buses in the Arena Football League and played before an average of 15,000 fans with the Amsterdam Admirals of NFL Europe, helping ensure that the experiment to introduce American football to European soccer fans was a laughable failure. Returning to the United States, Warner landed a job as the backup quarterback of the St. Louis Rams in 1998, which meant he stood on the sideline and held a clipboard on game days and took most of the hits during practices. An injury to incumbent starter Trent Green early in the 1999 campaign put the ball in Warner's hands, and he ran, threw, and excelled with it. *Sports Illustrated* immediately recognized that he was unrecognizable and put him on the cover of their October 18 edition with the caption, "Who Is this Guy?" With Warner calling the signals, the Rams became known as "The Greatest Show on Turf" and rode Warner's arm and calm grace under pressure all the way to the Super Bowl, where they dispatched the Tennessee Titans by a 23–16 score. Warner set a litany of Super Bowl records, including most passing yards and most pass attempts without an interception, and was named the game's MVP.

Hung On, Hung Over—Max McGee: In January 1967, McGee—who'd caught only four passes all season—wasn't expected to play for the Green Bay Packers in the inaugural NFL–AFL championship game, so he spent the night, and most of the morning, throwing back more than a few cool ones. As fate would have it, Boyd Dowler, the Packers' top receiver, was injured on the third play of the game, forcing McGee into the fray. After borrowing a helmet—he hadn't bothered to bring his own—McGee went on to catch nine passes, including two touchdown tosses, helping the Packers defeat the Kansas City Chiefs 35–10.

Rookie to the Rescue—Tim Smith: After rushing for only 126 yards in the regular season, Washington Redskins rookie Tim Smith set a Super Bowl record by gaining 204 yards on the ground, helping Washington down the Denver Broncos 42–10 in Super Bowl XXII.

Up Right, Right Up—Jim O'Brien: After connecting on only 19 of 34 field goal attempts during the season, the Baltimore Colts' Jim O'Brien was hardly a lock to deliver the championship-winning boot when he lined up for a 32-yard try in the waning seconds of a 13–13 tie in Super Bowl V. An early indication that the young kicker was nervous came when he tried to check the wind direction by attempting to pull up a few strands of grass from the artificial turf. Still, O'Brien popped the pigskin through the middle of the uprights to give Baltimore a 16–13 victory over Dallas in Super Bowl V.

- *Teams that have never played in a Super Bowl: Cleveland Browns, Houston Texans, Jacksonville Jaguars, Detroit Lions, New Orleans Saints, and Arizona Cardinals.*

- *Teams that have played in but never won a Super Bowl: Buffalo Bills, Cincinnati Bengals, Tennessee Titans, San Diego Chargers, Philadelphia Eagles, Minnesota Vikings, Atlanta Falcons, Carolina Panthers, and Seattle Seahawks.*

IN THE YEAR...1949

✳ ✳ ✳

- The U.S. Air Force's B-50 superfortress Lucky Lady II lands in Fort Worth, Texas, after completing the first nonstop around-the-world flight in 94 hours and 1 minute.

- Silly Putty is introduced.

- Apartheid becomes official government policy in South Africa.

- The North Atlantic Treaty Organization is established.

- Israel admitted to United Nations as its 59th member.

- David Ben-Gurion becomes prime minister in the first Israeli election.

- Arthur Miller's play *Death of a Salesman* wins the Pulitzer Prize.

- People in the United States buy an average of 100,000 television sets every week.

- The New York Yankees' Joe DiMaggio becomes the first baseball player to receive an annual salary of $100,000.

- The entire Turin football (soccer) team (except for one player who did not take the trip due to an injury) is killed in a plane crash at the Superga hill at the edge of Turin, Italy.

- Celebrities such as Helen Keller, Dorothy Parker, Danny Kaye, Fredric March, John Garfield, Paul Muni, and Edward G. Robinson are named in an FBI report as members of the Communist party.

- An earthquake in Ecuador destroys 50 towns and kills more than 6,000 people.

- George Orwell's book *1984* is published.

- Mao Tse-tung establishes the Peoples Republic of China.

- The last-known survivors of the Civil War—just six men—meet one another in Indiana.

ORIGINS OF STANDARD SYMBOLS

✳ ✳ ✳ ✳

*Removing a colon is pretty serious business—
whether you're a surgeon or a copy editor. You use punctuation
marks and other symbols on your computer keyboard every day,
and here is an explanation of their origins.*

¶—The pilcrow is a typographical character used to indicate a new
paragraph. The name may have come from *pylcraft*, a derivation of
the word *paragraph*, and the symbol that resembles a backward *P*
may have originated as a *C* for "chapter," or to represent a new train
of thought.

!—Usually used after an interjection or other word to indicate
strong feeling, the exclamation mark is a pictographic device believed
to have originated in the Roman empire. Its resemblance to a pen
over a dot was thought to represent a mark a writer might make
when surprised or overjoyed at completing a long writing project.

@—If "you've got mail," then you have seen @, or the "at" sign,
which is in the middle of every e-mail address. Before this use, the
symbol was most commonly used as an abbreviation in accounting
("3 apples @ $2 each = $6"). Its symbol may be derived from the
Norman French symbol *à*, meaning "at" in the sense of "each." It
may also have originated from the Latin word *ad*, which means "at,
toward, or by."

*—The asterisk gets its name from *astrum*, the Latin word for
"star," which the asterisk is also called. It is not an "asterix"—that's
the name of the star of a French cartoon. The asterisk was created
in feudal times when the printers of family trees needed a symbol
to indicate date of birth, which may explain why it's shaped like the
branches of a tree.

;—The semicolon was invented by an Italian printer for two main
purposes: to bind two sentences that run-on in meaning, and to act

as a "super comma" in a sentence that already contains lots of commas. Excessive use of the semicolon is considered showy by many writers, especially when employed to create long, multisegmented sentences. Author Kurt Vonnegut once said, "Do not use semicolons. All they do is show you've been to college."

?—What is the origin of the question mark? The symbol is generally thought to originate from the Latin *quaestio*, meaning "question," which was abbreviated to *Qo*, with the uppercase Q written above the lowercase o. The question mark replaces the period at the end of an interrogative sentence. There's a superstition in Hollywood that movies or television shows with question marks in the title do poorly at the box office. That may explain its absence in the title of the game show *Who Wants to Be a Millionaire,* a program that would not exist without questions!

&—The ampersand, used to replace the word *and*, has been found on ancient Roman sources dating to the first century A.D. It was formed by joining the letters in *et*, which is Latin for *and*. Through the 19th century, the ampersand was actually considered the 27th letter of the English alphabet.

%—The percent sign is the symbol used to indicate a percentage, meaning that the number preceding it is divided by 100. The symbol appeared around 1425 as a representation of the abbreviation of *P cento*, meaning "for a hundred" in Italian.

=—The equal sign is a mathematical symbol used to indicate equality and was invented in 1557 by Welsh mathematician Robert Recorde. In his book *The Whetstone of Witte*, Recorde explains that he invented it "to avoid the tedious repetition of these words: 'is equal to.'" Recorde's invention is commemorated with a plaque in St. Mary's Church in his hometown of Tenby, Wales.

GEOGRAPHIC ODDITIES

✳ ✳ ✳

The world's diverse landscapes, seascapes, and climates provide some interesting, and unusual, sightseeing opportunities.

Atacama Desert (Chile): This 600-mile stretch of coastal desert is so lung-searingly dry that if you die there, your corpse will barely decay. In some parts, no rainfall has been recorded by humanity, but a million people still live in the region.

Bay of Fundy's Tides (Nova Scotia/New Brunswick, Canada): As the water moves in and out of this bay (which is the size of Connecticut), the difference between high and low tide reaches 52 feet. Think of a four-story building at water's edge, from which you could walk out on dry land at low tide. Come high tide, the entire building would be submerged.

Black Canyon of the Gunnison (Colorado): When a river flows across hard volcanic rock for millions of years, it cuts a deep course, and its sides don't collapse much. This explains the formation of the Black Canyon, which at one point is a quarter mile across and a half mile deep—from the air it looks like a vast, dark crack in the earth.

Blue Hole of Belize (Lighthouse Reef off Belize, Central America): Sixty miles out from Belize City, there's a circular reef in the shallow water about a quarter mile across, encasing a perfectly round, 400-foot-deep pool of midnight blue.

Cliffs of Moher (County Clare, Ireland): Here you can be rained on from above and below. The sheer cliffs rise more than 600 feet above sea level, and the surf's force is violent enough to send spray all the way to the top. When it's raining, one gets the stereo effect of being thoroughly drenched from both ends.

Dead Sea (Israel/Jordan): Called *Yam Ha'maylach* ("Salt Sea") in Hebrew, the Dead Sea is eight times saltier than seawater. You can't sink unless you're weighted down (not encouraged). It's referred to as "dead" because no fish or plant life can tolerate the high salinity, though its rich mineral content draws health enthusiasts from around the world.

Devil's Bath (North Island, New Zealand): Near Rotorua is a collection of geothermal attractions. The Champagne Pool (a hot, steamy, bubbly lake) spills over to create a bright, sulfury, yellow-green pond called the Devil's Bath. It looks like a pool of molten sulfur and smells worse than one would expect.

Giant's Causeway (Antrim, Northern Ireland): Some 40,000 brown basalt columns (mostly but not all hexagonal) are packed together on and around a peninsula sticking out of Ireland. The result looks like stepping stones for a prehistoric titan and is one of the strangest and most popular sights in Ireland.

North Pacific Gyre Trash Vortex (Pacific Ocean): About a third of the way from California to Hawaii, a swirling ocean current collects garbage and doesn't easily let it go. This patch, now the size of Texas, consists mostly of floating plastic debris such as bottles and grocery bags. Unfortunately, as the pieces degrade, birds and fish eat them and die.

Punalu'u Black Sand Beach (Hawaii): Some places have beautiful beaches with sand that's white, or various shades of tan, or maybe even dark gray. Rarely, however, does one see sand that's as black as charcoal. The peculiar sand of Punalu'u is made of lava that exploded when it hit the water and has since been ground very fine. If that isn't strange enough, there are freshwater springs beneath the saltwater surf.

Uluru (Northern Territory, Australia): Formerly known as Ayers Rock, this enormous rusty sandstone monolith sticks up more than 1,100 feet from the desert floor and is about two miles wide. The rock is spiritually sacred to the Anangu (Australian Aborigines).

Uyuni Salt Flats (southern Bolivia): Roughly 25 times the size of the Bonneville Salt Flats in the United States, this saline landscape covers more than 4,000 square miles of Bolivia at an altitude of 12,500 feet. Because of brine just below the surface, any crack in the salt soon repairs itself.

LACROSSE

✳ ✳ ✳ ✳

Lacrosse is Canada's national summer sport and is the fastest growing high school and college sport in the United States. Along with basketball, it is arguably the most North American game there is—First Peoples/Native Americans invented it.

First Nations Origins

Algonquins called lacrosse *baggataway* and the Iroquois called it *teewaarathon*. Natives played the game to honor the Great Spirit or revered elders, or to celebrate. Lacrosse also served a diplomatic role. Suppose you were a Mohawk elder, and you learned that the Oneidas were fishing on your side of the lake (violating your long-standing agreement). Rather than sending your warriors to fight the Oneida, you'd send an emissary to challenge them to settle the dispute with a *teewaarathon* match. These early games, which were quite violent, took place on fields that were miles long and involved as many as 1,000 participants. We can thank French Canadians for its name: *La crosse* means "the bishop's staff," because that's what the stick looked like.

Settlers' Adoption

Europeans' first record of a lacrosse match dates to the 1630s in southern Ontario, when missionary Jean de Brébeuf watched the Hurons play. By the 1800s, the game was popular with French-Canadian settlers. In 1867, the same year Canada became a dominion, Canadian dentist W. George Beers standardized the rules of lacrosse. By 1900, the Canadian game had spread well across its native land and into the United States, with men's and women's versions.

The Game Today

There are two primary forms of lacrosse today: box (indoor) and field (outdoor). Box lacrosse is largely a Canadian sport, but Canadians also compete well in men's and women's field lacrosse. The game values speed and agility above brawn. The crosse (stick) takes skill to manipulate as players move the ball around. Play flow is similar to hockey or soccer; a team tries to control the ball and send it past a goaltender into the net. Fouls are similar to those in hockey, as is the penalty box. Lacrosse is a physical, speedy, demanding game that requires the toughness of rugby and the stamina of soccer.

First Nations in the Game

Only one First Nations team is sanctioned for international sport competition: the Iroquois Nationals, in field lacrosse. They're even sponsored by Nike!

Positions in Men's Lacrosse

Attack: There are three attackers on the field at one time. The attackers use "short-sticks" and must demonstrate good stick-handling with both hands; they must know where their teammates are at all times and be able to handle the pressure of opposing defense. Attackers score most of the goals.

Defense: Three defensive players with "long-poles" and one long-stick midfielder are allowed on the field at a time, using their sticks to throw checks and trying to dislodge the ball. One of the "long-poles" may also play midfield as a strategic defender, aka a long-stick middie. Teams usually use this to anticipate losing the face-off and to be stronger on defense.

Midfield: Three "middies" are allowed on the field at once. There are two types of midfielders, defensive and offensive. The two can rotate by running off the sidelines. Midfielders are allowed to use short-sticks and up to one long-pole. While on offense, three short-sticks are generally used for their superior stick-handling. While on defense, two short-sticks are used with one long-pole. Some teams have a designated face-off middie who takes the majority of face-offs and is usually quickly substituted after the face-off is complete.

Goalkeeper: Goalies try to prevent the ball from getting into the goal, and they also direct the team defense. A goalkeeper needs to be tough both physically and mentally, and he has to be loud enough to call the position of the ball at all times so the defense can concentrate on where the players are.

AMAZING FACTS ABOUT THE UNITED STATES

✳ ✳ ✳ ✳

- When the London Bridge (the version built in 1831) started to disintegrate, it was taken apart stone by stone, shipped to the United States, and lovingly reconstructed in Lake Havasu City, Arizona.

- Pittsburgh, Pennsylvania, has more city-maintained steps than any other city in the world. If stacked up, they would reach a height of 26,000 feet.

- Denver, Colorado, is the only city in history to turn down the Olympic Games. The 1976 Winter Games were scheduled to be held there, but residents voted against it.

- Michigan can claim the only floating post office in the world. The *J. W. Westcott II* mail ship delivers freight and correspondence to boats ferrying on the Detroit River.

- The Rockville Bridge in Harrisburg, Pennsylvania, is the longest stone arch bridge in the world. It was built in 1902 and measures 3,820 feet.

- The city of Beaver, Oklahoma, is the cow-chip-throwing capital of the world. Its annual competition is held in April.

- The 24-foot replica of Leonardo da Vinci's *Il Gavallo* in Grand Rapids, Michigan, is the largest equestrian bronze statue in the Western hemisphere.

- Middlesboro, Kentucky, is built entirely within a meteor crater.

- John Hancock was the only man to actually sign the Declaration of Independence on the Fourth of July. Most others signed on August 2, 1776.

- In the United States, there are more statues of Lewis and Clark's Native American guide Sacagawea than of any other woman.

- The world's longest shared border is the 3,987-mile boundary between the United States and Canada.

- Try this on your next vacation. If you stand at the point known as Four Corners in the Southwest United States, you can reach into four states—Utah, Colorado, New Mexico, and Arizona—without moving your feet.

- Chittenango, New York, is the childhood home of *The Wonderful Wizard of Oz* author L. Frank Baum. The town has yellow-brick-inlaid sidewalks that lead to Oz-styled businesses. The yearly highlight is the "Oz-stravaganza," featuring a Munchkins parade.

- Hawaii is the most isolated population center on Earth. It is 2,390 miles from California, 3,850 miles from Japan, and 4,900 miles from China.

- Texas is the only state in the country that has had the flags of six nations flying over it. They are: Mexico, Spain, France, the Confederate States, the Republic of Texas, and the United States.

- The eruption of Mt. St. Helens in 1980 was a disaster for many, but not for Idahoans. The great clouds of ash from the eruption drifted into Idaho and increased crop yields by an average of 30 percent throughout the 1980s.

- Maine is the only state that shares a border with only one other state—New Hampshire.

- Niagara Falls State Park in New York is the oldest state park in the United States. Approximately 140 of the park's 400-plus acres are underwater.

- The state of Florida is larger than England.

- An earthquake on December 16, 1811, caused parts of the Mississippi River to flow backward.

- Honolulu is the only place in the United States that has a royal palace.

- The only letter in the alphabet that does not appear in the name of a U.S. state is Q.

- The only mobile National Monuments are the cable cars in San Francisco.

- The United States has never lost a war in which mules were used.

THE SEGWAY

✳ ✳ ✳

- In 2001, mastermind Dean Kamen, a self-taught physicist and established inventor, developed the Segway, claiming he could make walking "obsolete." Kamen had previously developed a phonebook-sized portable dialysis machine, a non-polluting engine, and more than 150 other patented contraptions.

- Kamen's Segway is officially referred to as a "human transport device."

- Segway PTs ("personal transporters") have electric motors that drive the apparatus at speeds up to 12.5 miles per hour.

- The Segway is designed with "redundant technology." This means the device features duplicates of its important pieces of hardware. If one function fails, an internal computer uses the duplicate function to keep the machine stable long enough for the rider to hop off safely.

- Segways respond as if they're controlled by the rider's thoughts alone. The secret on newer Segways is in the control shaft, which sways in sync with the rider if he or she wants to turn.

- You operate a Segway like this: Turn it on, step onto the two-wheeled platform, grip the waist-high handle, lean forward, and off you go.

- It is illegal to use a Segway on streets, roads, or highways. They are allowed on sidewalks and bike lanes.

- The use of Segways is not permitted in public areas in the United Kingdom, but they are legal in most places in the United States. They are also legal in Austria, the Czech Republic, France, Greece, Hungary, Italy, and Portugal.

- Most Segways can travel about 12 miles before they need to be recharged.

- Despite a lot of media attention, Segways haven't sold especially well. In 2006, *Time* magazine reported that the company had sold fewer than 25,000 units since the device was unveiled.

I'm No Expert, But...
SURVIVING IN SPACE

✳ ✳ ✳ ✳

It's cold in space...or is it? Here's what it takes to survive the unforgiving conditions of vacuum.

Q: Is there anything out in space?

A: There's always something everywhere, but in space there isn't much of it. Notably, there's no air to speak of. If some mean person heaved you out of the airlock of a spacecraft, you wouldn't last long. If you were out there less than 90 seconds, you didn't hold your breath (that would rupture your lungs), and you received immediate medical care, you might survive. Linger in that environment for longer than 90 seconds, and you're a goner.

Q: Besides enabling you to stay alive, what are the functions of a space suit?

A: It supplies oxygen at a stable internal pressure, and it protects you against heat or cold by regulating temperature. Your space suit also serves as a shield against radiation and those pesky little micrometeoroids, which are things such as space pebbles, sand, and dust. They may not appear threatening, but you'll think otherwise when you realize that they're traveling at an incredibly high rate of speed.

Q: Isn't it hard to keep from freezing in space, which is pretty close to absolute zero?

A: Remember that with no air in space, things lose heat through thermal radiation (slow), not heat conduction (fast). A good contrast might be how quickly you freeze in water that's 35° F (no one can survive long) as opposed to air that's 35° F (a piece of cake for many people). Water conducts the heat right out of your body, and it does so a lot faster than air does. Thus, with solar radiation hitting astronauts in space, and a heated spacecraft, they actually need cooling. Under the suit, the astronaut wears a Liquid Cooling and Ventilation Garment with a water-cooling system, so he or she doesn't sweat like a sports mascot on a hot day.

GLACIAL LAKE MISSOULA

✳ ✳ ✳ ✳

*Around 13,000 B.C., in what is today the Pacific Northwest
of the United States, geologic time was measured
in hours and days—with all the devastation you'd expect from
such sudden geology. One minute there was a lake, then
someone pulled the plug and released a flood.*

Glacial Floods and Lakes

A glacial flood occurs when a large glacial meltwater lake gets loose.
When the continental two-mile-thick glaciers of the Cordilleran ice
sheet released an icy clasp on North America, they left large lakes at
the glaciers' melting edges. Glacial Lake Missoula was roughly the
size of Connecticut and about 2,000 feet deep. It contained 500 cubic miles of water, about the volume of Lake Ontario, perched in the
northern Montana Rockies. If it still existed today, it would be the
11th largest lake on Earth in terms of water volume.

Not the Most Glamorous Name...

Geologists named the ice dam (a finger of the ice sheet that holds
back the entire lake) the Purcell Trench Lobe. If the ice dam were
to fail, the water could only go west because of the Rockies. No one
is sure if the water undermined the dam's base, spilled over the top,
or physically floated the dam like a big iceberg. But the dam definitely failed; and when it did, Glacial Lake Missoula headed for the
Pacific Ocean at speeds approaching 80 miles per hour.

Big Lake, Big Baggage

You probably know that rivers transport sand and pebbles. Glacial
Lake Missoula transported rocks the size of large cars; they're still
lying around Palouse Country, in eastern Washington state. The
entire lake, full of icebergs and all the forest and animal debris in the
path of the water, spread out to cover the southeastern portion of
Washington—about a hundred miles across. Today, this long-lost
body of water is called Lake Lewis, and its high-water marks can be
seen far up on the region's hillsides.

It Has to Go Somewhere!

The water had only one outlet: the mile-wide canyon at Wallula Gap near the Washington–Oregon boundary. Beginning at Idaho and going west, the interstate border is a straight line until it hits the Columbia River. Wallula Gap is a brief hike from that spot.

Don't Hold Your Breath

Multiple glacial floods hit the young Columbia Basin as the ice dam re-formed and failed again. Each flood took about a week to run its course. Nobody is sure how long the re-forming took, but geologists believe there may have been more than 100 such cycles.

- *Beyond the risk to people's lives, floods destroy homes, towns, and even entire regions. In 1993, the Mississippi River Flood covered an area approximately 500 miles long and 200 miles wide. More than 50,000 homes were damaged, and 12,000 miles of farmland were washed out.*

- *A flash flood is a sudden event caused by a hydrologic response of the drainage basin. Flash floods are usually strongly localized and occur when high rates of precipitation fall in a short period of time.*

- *In 1976, the Big Thompson Canyon flood in Colorado killed approximately 140 people, many of whom tried to outrun the waters rather than climbing trees or large rocks or seeking higher ground.*

- *Sixty-six percent of people who die in floods get trapped in their vehicles while trying to navigate through surging waters.*

- *A popular story told by ancient Greeks and Romans was of Deucalion and Pyhrra, who saved their children and animals from a flood in a boat shaped like a giant box.*

Fast Facts

- Lightning can develop any time there is a major static charge in the atmosphere. Volcanic eruptions, snowstorms, and even large forest fires have been associated with lightning discharges.

- Mount Baker in Washington state is the world record holder for the most snowfall in one season. In the winter of 1998–1999, the ski resort recorded 1,140 inches of snow.

- Contrary to popular belief, tornadoes can and do hit downtown areas of major cities. Proof of this fact was shown in March 2000 when a small twister touched down in Ft. Worth, Texas, damaging numerous skyscrapers in the central business district.

- The greatest number of tornadoes to hit a downtown area occurred in St. Louis, Missouri. The city center has been flattened four times since 1871. One of those hits was an F4 monster that killed 255 people in 1896.

- Divine wind? Japan was saved from invasion twice because of storms. Both times the Mongolians tried to invade the island nation, typhoons destroyed most of their fleets.

- Weather had a huge impact on the Japanese city of Nagasaki in 1945. If not for a last-minute break in cloud cover, the atomic bomb wouldn't have been dropped there. In fact, Nagasaki wasn't the primary target for the bomb run. The bomb was originally slated to be dropped on Kokura, but cloud cover there prevented it.

- Lightning can kill people (some 3,700 deaths were recorded in the United States between 1959 and 2003) or cause cardiac arrest. It can also cause severe burns, loss of memory, changes in personality, and permanent brain damage. About 8 to 10 percent of lightning-stroke victims die, and 70 percent suffer serious long-term effects.

THE GOOD OLD DAYS OF SODA FOUNTAINS

✳ ✳ ✳ ✳

In an age when drive-through coffee shops are serving up iced mochachinos, it's easy to forget that chrome-topped soda fountains once held a place of distinction in American culture.

The Golden Age

In 1819, the first soda fountain patent was granted to Samuel Fahnestock. This nifty invention combined syrup and water with carbon dioxide to make fizzy drinks—and they caught on instantly.

The first soda fountains were installed in drugstores, which were sterile storefronts originally intended only to dispense medicines. To attract more business, pharmacists started to sell a variety of goods, including soda drinks and light lunch fare. That way, customers could come in to shop, take time out for some refreshment, and possibly do extra shopping before they left.

Typical soda fountains (the name for both the invention and the shops where the fountains could be found) featured long countertops, swivel stools, goose-neck spigots, and a mirrored back bar, all of which helped attract the attention of young and old alike. Soda fountains were also installed in candy shops and ice cream parlors. Before long, freestanding soda fountains were being built across the country.

Two of the world's most popular beverages got their start at soda fountains. In 1886, Coca-Cola was first sold to the public at the soda fountain in a pharmacy in Georgia. Pepsi's creator, Caleb Bradham, was a pharmacist who started to sell his beverage in his own drugstore in 1898.

Soda fountain drinks had to be made to order, and this was typically done by male clerks in crisp white coats. Affectionately referred to as "soda jerks" (for the jerking motion required to draw soda from the spigots), these popular, entertaining mixologists were the rock stars of the early 1900s. Think of a modern-day bartender juggling bottles of liquor to make a drink: Soda jerks performed roughly the same feats, except that they used ice cream and soda.

Birth of the Brooklyn Egg Cream

In Brooklyn, New York, candy shop owner Louis Auster created the egg cream, a fountain drink concoction that actually contained neither eggs nor cream.

You make an egg cream any way you like it, but a basic recipe combines a good pour of chocolate syrup with twice as much whole milk, along with seltzer water to fill the glass. (In New York, an egg cream isn't considered authentic unless it's made with Fox's "U-Bet" chocolate syrup.)

The foam that rises to the top of the glass resembles egg whites, which may be how the drink got its name. Some claim that the original chocolate syrup contained eggs and cream; others say "egg cream" comes from the Yiddish phrase *ekt keem,* meaning "pure sweetness"; still others believe that when kids ordered "a cream" at the counter, it sounded like "egg cream." Whatever the etymology, the drink is legendary among soda fountain aficionados. Auster claimed that he often sold more than 3,000 egg creams a day. With limited seating, this meant that most customers had to stand to drink them, prompting the traditional belief that if you want to really enjoy an egg cream, you have to do so standing up.

Several beverage companies approached Auster to purchase the rights to the drink and bottle it for mass distribution, but trying to bottle an egg cream was harder than they thought: The milk spoiled quickly, and preservatives ruined the taste. Thus, the egg cream remained a soda fountain exclusive.

Sip and Socialize

Prohibition and the temperance movement gave soda fountains a boost of popularity during the 1920s, serving as a stand-in for pubs. Booze became legal again in 1933, but by that time, fountains had become such a part of Americana that few closed shop. During the 1950s, soda fountains became the hangout of choice for teenagers everywhere.

It wasn't until the 1960s that the soda fountain's popularity began to wane. People were more interested in war protests and pooka beads than Brown Cows and lemon-lime-flavored Green Rivers. As more beverages were available in cans and bottles and life became increasingly fast-paced, people no longer had time for the leisurely pace of the soda shop.

Some fountains survived and still serve frothy egg creams to customers on swivel stools, and many of these establishments attempt to appeal to a wide audience by re-creating that old-fashion atmosphere.

Recipes

Brown Cow

4 scoops ice cream (chocolate for a Brown Cow,
   vanilla for a White Cow)
4 tablespoons flavored syrup (usually chocolate)
1½ cups milk

Whirl in a blender until smooth. Share, or not.

Green River

3 ounces lemon-lime syrup
10 ounces seltzer water

Stir. Add ice, if desired.

Hoboken

½ cup pineapple syrup
A splash of milk
Seltzer water
Chocolate ice cream

Blend and enjoy!

Catawba Flip

1 scoop vanilla ice cream
1 large egg
2 ounces grape juice
Shaved ice
Seltzer water

Blend first four ingredients until smooth.
Pour into a tall glass and fill with seltzer water.

EARLY VICE PRESIDENTS

✳ ✳ ✳ ✳

*Some vice presidents have played key roles in state affairs;
others have been primarily marginal figures.*

- John Adams (1789–1797, V.P. under George Washington): Here's
  what Adams said about his job: "My country has in its wisdom contrived for me the most insignificant office that ever the invention
  of man contrived or his imagination conceived."

- Thomas Jefferson (1797–1801, John Adams): He became vice
  president by coming in second to Adams in electoral votes, making
  the Adams administration the only one in history divided between
  two political parties. He was considered a good V.P. but was a bad
  money manager. After his death, his executors sold his remaining
  slaves to square up the large debts he left.

- Aaron Burr (1801–1805, Thomas Jefferson): After
  Burr killed Alexander Hamilton in a duel, he was
  indicted but not seriously pursued. He ran off to
  New Orleans, where he allegedly intended to raise
  a private army, conquer the Southwest, and become
  its leader. In 1834, Burr suffered a stroke and was
  debilitated until he died in 1836.

- George Clinton (1805–1812, Jefferson, then James Madison): He
  opposed ratification of the Constitution in 1788, stating that it gave
  the federal government too much power. He also disagreed with
  creation of the office of V.P., but that didn't prevent him from taking it. He was the first vice president to die in office.

- Elbridge Gerry (1813–1814, Madison): This vice president gets
  dubious credit for "gerrymandering"—redrawing legislative dis-
  tricts for optimum political advantage. After he died in office, the
  vice presidency remained vacant for three years.

- Daniel D. Tompkins (1817–1825, James Monroe): After years of
  litigation with the federal and New York state governments over

loans and money, Tompkins sought stress relief from the bottle. He survived his term by a little more than three months.

- John Calhoun (1825–1832, John Q. Adams and Andrew Jackson): During the 1760s, he was a Regulator—a member of a vigilante group attempting to impose law and order in the Carolina backwoods. While serving in James Monroe's cabinet, he urged court-martial for Andrew Jackson—under whom he would later serve as vice president. Ravaged by tuberculosis, Calhoun was the first V.P. to resign the office.

- Martin Van Buren (1833–1837, Jackson): He spent a lot of time fighting with former Speaker of the House Henry Clay. Van Buren was elected president, but the Panic of 1837 began within weeks of his inauguration. When he ran for re-election, he didn't even carry his home state, New York.

- Richard M. Johnson (1837–1841, Martin Van Buren): He was the first and only vice president chosen by the Senate, as the 12th Amendment dictated; also the first Baptist V.P.

- John Tyler (1841, William H. Harrison): Tyler was vice president for only 33 days when Harrison died, and as president, he didn't appoint a V.P. at all. He sired 15 children by 2 wives and was elected to the Confederate House of Representatives not long before his death.

- George Dallas (1845–1849, James K. Polk): After being informed of excessive alcohol use in Senate chambers, Dallas told the sergeant-at-arms to ban liquor on the Senate side of the Capitol, except for members who required it for medicinal purposes.

- Millard Fillmore (1849–1850, Zachary Taylor): Fillmore had been an indentured servant in his youth. During his short term as vice president, he had the joy of presiding over a raucous Senate in which the senior senator from Mississippi once drew a pistol. He later ran for president on the Know-Nothing Party ticket.

- William R. King (1853, Franklin Pierce): King wore a wig long after they'd gone out of style. As senator, he once challenged

Henry Clay to a duel, but the confrontation never took place. The only bachelor V.P., King took the oath of office in Cuba and died 25 days later, so he didn't accomplish a lot.

- John C. Breckenridge (1857–61, James Buchanan): Breckenridge was elected V.P. when he was just 35, and as a result, Buchanan mostly ignored him. While serving in the House, Breckenridge almost dueled another legislator with rifles, but the diplomats resolved their grievance in proper congressional style: They shook hands and had a chew together.

- Hannibal Hamlin (1861–1865, Abraham Lincoln): A former governor of Maine, Hamlin found the Senate boring and often didn't bother presiding. Lincoln didn't pick him as running mate for his second term, or he might have become President Hamlin. He did try, as had Dallas, to sober up the Senate.

- Andrew Johnson (1865, Lincoln): The morning he took the oath of office, he drank whiskey to fortify himself, then launched into an anti-Southern rant. Lincoln suddenly began to appreciate the outgoing Hannibal Hamlin (who finally managed to shut Johnson up). The new V.P. was too intoxicated to swear in the new senators; a Senate clerk had to handle it.

- Schuyler Colfax (1869–73, Ulysses S. Grant): Nicknamed "Smiler," he was always cordial and urbane. He was involved with the Know-Nothing Party (a movement hostile to immigrants and Catholics) but also campaigned actively against slavery. Late in his term, the *Crédit Mobilier* railroad scandal turned his public name to mud.

- Henry Wilson (1873–75, Grant): He abstained from alcohol and was a hard worker who annoyed many people by campaigning for racial equality. Unfortunately for one of the nation's more able V.P.s, a stroke in 1873 limited his role, and he died two years later.

- William A. Wheeler (1877–1881, Rutherford B. Hayes): Wheeler was a man of few words, and when he was nominated to run with Hayes, the future president had to ask who he was. He faded into obscurity after his term, which was unfortunate, because he actually did his job as a sincere, honest public servant.

CANADA'S MINERAL WEALTH

✳ ✳ ✳ ✳

Canada, like the United States, Russia, and Australia, enjoys an abundance of natural resources. Here's where Canada ranks in world production of key minerals, its percentage of the world's total, and who produces the most.

- Iron ore: ninth (ranked by metal content rather than gross weight), 3 percent. Leader: Brazil.
- Cobalt: fourth, 10 percent. Leader: Congo.
- Cadmium: fifth, 10 percent. Leader: China.
- Lithium: third, 9 percent. Leader: Australia.
- Magnesium: second, 1 percent. Leader: China.
- Gypsum: fourth, 8 percent. Leader: United States.
- Platinum: third, 3 percent. Leader: South Africa.
- Aluminum: third, 9 percent. Leader: China.
- Nickel: second, 13 percent. Leader: Russia.
- Zinc: third, 8 percent. Leader: China.
- Copper: eighth, 4 percent. Leader: Chile.
- Gold: seventh, 5 percent. Leader: South Africa.
- Silver: sixth, 7 percent. Leader: Peru.
- Lead: sixth, 2 percent. Leader: United States.
- Molybdenum: fifth, 4 percent. Leader: United States.
- Sulfur: second, 14 percent. Leader: United States.
- Diamonds (gemstone—industrial diamonds are a different category): fourth, 12 percent. Leader: Botswana.
- Petroleum: eighth, percent varies. Leader: Saudi Arabia.
- Natural gas: third, about 6 percent. Leader: United States.
- Salt: fifth, 7 percent. Leader: United States.

Talk to the Expert
YEOMAN

✷ ✷ ✷ ✷

If you watched the first Star Trek *series, you might think that a yeoman is a petite blonde with her hair woven in a weird crisscross style. Here's a different image of the profession:*

Q: Is there such thing as a "yeo"?

A: Yeah, it's how you get people's attention. Or how you show that you're paying attention. If you're an enlisted person in the Navy, though, and an officer calls for you, I wouldn't answer him or her with "yeo." Not good for your career. Some yeomen are called "yeo" for short, the way people say "Chief" for "Chief Petty Officer." In that case it's okay.

Q: Seriously, though, what's your title?

A: My rate is Petty Officer, Third Class, and my rating is Yeoman, so that makes me a Yeoman Third Class—usually just "Yeoman Third." I'm a personnel clerk, secretary and typist, among other things.

Q: People who have read about Robin Hood might expect you to show up with a bow and arrow. How come we use the same word for old archers as for Navy clerks?

A: The term has evolved over a thousand years in ways that kind of amaze me. It used to refer to a sturdy peasant farmer, and then it seemed to gradually rise in social class. It also came to signify someone who was stout-hearted and capable—it was always a compliment, except perhaps to a lord or some other muckety-muck. Most English farmers were also good archers, and it came to refer to that skill as well. Then it meant an attendant on higher authority, such as a Yeoman of the Guard. I think that's probably where it crossed over from a guy with a bow or pitchfork to a clerk. The Royal Navy picked it up as the name for its clerks, and, eventually, so did the United States Navy.

Q: What does it take to be a good yeoman?

A: At the top of the list is literacy. Besides journalist, yeoman is perhaps the main job in the Navy that values a liberal arts degree, because you spend a lot of time fixing officers' and petty officers' grammatical issues. And they will thank you for it, take my word, because it makes them look better to their bosses. At the same time, I think they always regard yeomen as intellectual show-offs on some level. Can't be helped.

Q: You have a political science degree. Is that why you joined the Navy, to be a yeoman?

A: I felt it would combine travel with managerial experience with core clerical and administrative skills. Plus, it beat moving back in with my parents until I got my student loans paid off. You'd be surprised how many college graduates become enlisted men and women in all the services in a tight job market.

Q: Is it true that a yeoman is the person you least want to annoy in the Navy?

A: I think I'd be more careful about annoying a SEAL or the boatswain than a yeoman. SEALs can kill you silently with an old fingernail clipping, and the boatswain can make any sailor's life miserable. But I understand why people think that. An occupational hazard of working directly with officers is dealing with big egos. Yeoman can be officious, even with each other; some are flat-out snobs. And there are some who would unscrupulously "misplace" someone's records long enough to screw them out of a promotion or some other benefit. I wouldn't, but some would.

Q: So, after the Navy, you're trained for clerical work?

A: Yes. I'm basically prepared to do anything in a company's human resources, secretarial, or administrative departments, and I'm also well trained in office management. I don't want to limit myself, though. What I'm really interested in getting into is editing or publishing. My yeoman rating has given me ample experience and information to write something really interesting!

Folklore: Myth or Truth?
AN OVERTURE TO WILLIAM TELL

✳ ✳ ✳ ✳

Most of us learned about the controversial legend as children.
This should help answer any lingering questions.

Let's go over the legend again. In 1307, Austria's Hapsburgs wanted
to clamp down on the Swiss. An Austrian official named Hermann
Gessler put his hat atop a pole, and then made a petty, ridiculous
rule: All passersby had to bow to his hat. An expert crossbowman
named William Tell refused to bow, so Gessler's police arrested him.
But Gessler wasn't satisfied with that.

In a fit of sadistic illogic, Gessler made a deal with Tell. If Tell
could shoot an apple off his son Walter's head with the crossbow,
both would be free. If Tell whiffed, or nailed his son, Gessler would
execute him. Tell hit the apple but couldn't resist a snarky comment to Gessler. The latter, not renowned for his joie de vivre, got
mad and threw Tell in jail. Eventually, Tell escaped and assassinated
Gessler. This touched off a rebellion that led to the Swiss Confederation (which is still in business today, operating banks and ski lifts).

Where's the controversy? To begin with, there is no contemporary
historical evidence for Tell or Gessler. The legend first appeared in
the late 1400s, and no one can explain the delay. What's more: The
motif of an archer shooting a target off his son's head, then slaying
a tyrant, appears in diverse Germanic literature predating 1307. It's
not that the William Tell legend is necessarily false, because we can't
prove it. The combination of faults—lack of evidence, duplication of
older legends—makes the William Tell story a tough sell as history.

How do the Swiss feel about it? It wasn't easy for Swiss patriots
to carve out and hold their own country with all the warlike tides
of Europe buffeting them. The multilingual Swiss have built and
maintained a properous Confederation that avoids warfare from a
position of strength. William Tell symbolizes Swiss love of freedom
and disdain for tyrants, domestic or foreign.

HENRY VIII'S TOWER OF LONDON VICTIMS

✳ ✳ ✳

- Queen Catherine Howard, Henry's fifth wife, was beheaded for adultery on the Tower Green. With her went her lovers, Thomas Culpepper and Francis Dereham, and her lady-in-waiting Jane Rochford.

- Jane Rochford was instrumental in the downfall of two queens. She arranged trysts for Catherine Howard, for which both were executed, and she had previously testified against her husband, George Boleyn, and sister-in-law Queen Anne, helping them to their graves by accusing them of incest.

- Desperate to marry Jane Seymour, Henry had his second queen, Anne Boleyn, executed on trumped-up charges of adultery and witchcraft. Accused and killed with her were her brother George, as well as Henry Norris, Francis Weston, and William Brereton, who had been close friends with the king. Anne's musician, Mark Smeaton, was also executed for supposed adultery with the queen.

- The royal House of Plantagenet nearly became extinct under Henry's rule. The Plantagenets were descended from earlier kings of England, primarily the profligate Edward III, and possibly had a better claim to the throne than the Tudors. Those who made this assertion publicly were often executed on petty or unfounded charges.

- Edward Stafford, Third Duke of Buckingham, was beheaded for being the leader of nobles who were openly resentful of Henry's reliance on lowborn ministers such as Cardinal Wolsey, the son of a butcher. Many historians believe he was also killed because he was part of the royal Plantagenet family and had bragged that his family was more royal than Henry's.

- King Henry's paranoia grew as he edged closer to death, and Henry Howard, Earl of Surrey and son of the Duke of Norfolk, was one of those who paid the price. The king became convinced that Norfolk and Surrey were planning to grab the throne from Henry's son Edward when he died, so both were sent to the tower. Surrey was beheaded and his father was saved only because Henry died the day before he was to be executed.

- Thomas Howard, Third Duke of Norfolk, narrowly avoided losing his head when Henry VIII died the day before he was to sign the duke's death warrant. He was released in 1553 by Mary I.

- Margaret Pole, the 67-year-old Countess of Salisbury, suffered one of the most gruesome beheadings on record. She refused to put her head on the block, saying that she was no traitor, and therefore had to be forced down. The executioner's first blow struck her shoulder. According to some accounts, she then jumped up and ran from the executioner, who struck her 11 times before she finally died.

- The longest-serving prisoner of the Tudor reign was Sir William de la Pole, who sat in the Tower of London for 37 years. Sir William was arrested by Henry VII for suspicion of treason because he was a Plantagenet and he and his brother were Yorkist heirs, the leading contenders for the English throne. Henry VIII had Sir William executed in 1513.

- Being Henry's most trusted minister provided no protection from the executioner. Thomas Cromwell rose to power in 1532 and was a major figure in the English Reformation. Like many of Henry's advisors, his fall was caused by his support for one of Henry's wives—in this case, his arrangement of the king's marriage to Anne of Cleves, whom Henry despised. Cromwell was sent to the block in 1540.

- Anne Askew's execution proved that Henry considered Protestants to be heretics. She had been arrested for preaching Protestant views and was cruelly racked to get the names of other prominent reformists. Queen Katherine Parr was nearly arrested after pleading for mercy for Anne, but her plea was rejected and Anne burned at the stake.

CURIOUS FACTS
ABOUT LANGUAGES, WORDS,
AND LETTERS

✳ ✳ ✳ ✳

- The first three Greek letters—*alpha, beta,* and *gamma*—are etymologically equivalent to the Hebrew words for *ox, house,* and *camel.* This is because both the Greek and the Hebrew alphabets evolved from ancient Phoenician script, in which each letter was named after the object originally represented by the Phoenician hieroglyph. Phoenicians were prolific maritime traders, and the Phoenician alphabet took hold along their trade routes across Europe, the Middle East, and North Africa, evolving over time into the Aramaic, Arabic, Hebrew, Greek, Cyrillic, and Latin alphabets.

- Before the 1917 Communist Revolution, letters of the Russian alphabet had names. For instance, the first three letters were called *az, buki,* and *vedi,* meaning *I, letters,* and *know.* Read in order, the alphabet composed a message, and though its precise meaning has not been clearly established, the translations vary (primarily in details). It reads some thing like this:
  > *"Knowing all these letters renders speech a virtue. Evil lives on Earth eternally, and each person must think of repentance, with speech and word making firm in their mind the faith in Christ and the Kingdom of God. Whisper [the letters] frequently to make them yours by this repetition in order to write and live according to laws of God."*

- The longest palindrome word in any language is the Finnish word *saippuakivikauppias*—"door-to-door salesman of lye for soap." If that job seems a bit specialized, consider the following outdated German term for a revenue agent: *Obertranksteuerdonativcautionszinsgelderhauptcassir,* which translates to "first main cashier of duty on drinks and bail rent moneys."

- It is said that above the entrance to the temple of Apollo at Delphi, there were three inscriptions. The first read "Gnothi seauton," or "Know thyself"; the second was "Meden agan," or "Nothing in excess." The third was merely the letter *E*: a capital epsilon. Neither ancient philosophers nor modern scholars have been able to solve the mystery of this Delphic E. (One dubious but appealing explanation is that the person charged with writing these inscriptions got discouraged from completing the third one after re-reading the second.)

- The ampersand is actually a ligature of the letters *e* and *t* in the Latin word *et*, meaning, predictably, *and*. This is why the phrase *et cetera* was often abbreviated as &c in various 18th- and 19th-century writings. The term *ampersand* itself is a convoluted corruption of "*and (&) per se and*," which literally means "(the character) & by itself (is the word) and."

- In early Russian, the pronoun *I* used to be *Az*, the first letter of the alphabet. However, at some point another letter started meaning *I*: the last letter of the Russian alphabet, *ya*. This is why Russian mothers sometimes rebuke boastful children prone to beginning sentences with *I* by saying "*I* is the last letter of the alphabet!" (The admonishment tends to lose sway after the kids learn the real story in school.)

- Despite what you may have heard, the plural of *octopus* is not *octopi*; the academically agreed-upon plural of this word is *octopuses*. However, if circumstances compel you to pluralize *octopus*, and the plain English way of going about it just doesn't satisfy, then write *octopodes*. *Octopus* is derived from the Greek—"eight legs"—and should be pluralized according to Greek rules, not Latin.

- Traditional Irish and Welsh have no word for the color blue—the word referring to that color, *glas*, also refers to certain shades of green and gray. The Navajo language also does not distinguish between blue and green but has two words for the color black. However, none of these languages has anything on the ancient Greek when it comes to odd color perception: Authors such as Homer and Euripides consistently describe the sky as bronze; the sea and sheep as wine-colored; and blood, tears, and honey as green. One wonders if the ancient Greeks may have been colorblind.

- The word *butterfly* is one of the most persistent and baffling mysteries of linguistics. All European languages, even such closely related ones as Spanish and Portuguese, have completely different words for *butterfly* (in Spanish and Portuguese, it's *mariposa* and *borboleta*, respectively). This is in stark contrast to just about all other words for everyday objects and animals—the word *cat*, for instance, varies across European languages only in details of spelling.

- Many geographical features and locales bear tautological names. For instance, the Sahara Desert literally means "Desert Desert," since *Sahara* is the word for *desert* in Arabic. Similarly, Mount Fujiyama translates from Japanese as "Mount Fuji-mount," Lake Tahoe means "Lake Lake" in Washo, and the Mississippi River is "Big River River" in Algonquin. The world's most extreme example of a tautological place-name is probably Torpenhow Hill of west England (locally pronounced *Trup-en-ah*). "Tor," "pen," and "how" all mean "hill" in different languages, the first two being Celtic and the last being Anglo-Saxon. Therefore, "Torpenhow Hill" literally means "Hillhillhill Hill."

- The word *and* can be easily used five times in a row within a single grammatically correct sentence. For instance, suppose a small-business owner were painting a sign to hang above the front door: "Stanford and Andrews." A passerby might offer the owner the following advice: *"You should adjust the spacing between 'Stanford' and 'and' and 'And' and 'rews.'"* Similarly, the verb *had* can be used 11 times in a row, given appropriate punctuation: *"In his essay, James, where John had had 'had,' had had 'had had'; 'had had' had had a better effect on the teacher."*

Dermatoglyphics, misconjugatedly, *and* uncopyrightable, *each 15 letters long, are the longest English words in which no letter appears more than once.*

A SAVORY SAMPLER OF FOOD PHRASES

✳ ✳ ✳ ✳

There's No Such Thing as a Free Lunch: In the 1840s, bars in the United States offered anyone buying a drink a "free lunch." It was really just a bunch of salty snacks that made customers so thirsty, they kept buying drinks.

Hair of the Dog that Bit You: Medieval doctors believed if a rabid dog bit you, your chance of recovery was better if a hair was plucked from the dog and placed on your wound.

The Big Cheese: In 1802, a cheese maker delivered a 1,235-pound wheel of cheese to President Thomas Jefferson. Citizens declared it the "big cheese," referring to both the wheel and its important recipient.

In a Nutshell: This saying, which indicates a lot of information conveyed succinctly, is so old that Cicero used it. He said that Homer's *Iliad* was penned in such small handwriting that all 24 books could fit "in a nutshell."

Cool as a Cucumber: Even on a warm day, a field cucumber stays about 20 degrees cooler than the outside air. Though scientists didn't prove this until 1970, the saying has been around since the early 18th century.

Bring Home the Bacon: The Dunmow Flitch Trials, an English tradition that started in 1104, challenged married couples to go one year without arguing. The winners took home a "flitch" (a side) of bacon.

Egg on Your Face: During slapstick comedies in the Victorian theater, actors made the fall guy look foolish by breaking eggs on his forehead.

Spill the Beans: In ancient Greece, the system for voting new members into a private club involved secretly placing colored beans into opaque jars. Prospective members never knew who voted for or against them—unless the beans were spilled.

Gone to Pot: Dating to pre-Elizabethan England, this phrase refers to pieces of meat that were hardened, on the verge of spoiling—and good only for the stew pot.

Cook Your Goose: In 1560, a town attacked by the Mad King of Sweden, Eric XIV, hung up a goose—a symbol of stupidity—in protest. The furious king threatened, "I'll cook your goose!"

Easy as Pie: Making a pie from scratch isn't easy; the phrase is a contraction of the late-19th-century phrase "easy as eating pie."

In a Pickle: From the old Dutch phrase *"de pikel zitten,"* which means to sit in a salt solution used for preserving pickles—sure to be an uncomfortable situation.

With a Grain of Salt: To take something "with a grain of salt" is to consider the subject in question with skepticism or suspicion. Salt was once believed to have healing properties, and to eat or drink something with a grain of salt was to practice preventive medicine against potential poisoning or illness.

Happy as a Clam: The original phrase was "happy as a clam at high tide." Because clam diggers are able to gather clams only at low tide, the clams are much safer (and happier) when the tide is high and the water is too deep to wade into.

Take the Cake: The phrase originated at cakewalk contests, where individuals would parade and prance in a circle to the audience's delight. The person with the most imaginative swagger would take home first prize, which was always a cake.

A Baker's Dozen: It was once common that English medieval bakers would cut corners and dupe customers by making loaves that contained more air pockets than bread. By 1266, authorities enacted a law that required bakers to sell their bread by weight. To avoid paying the heavy penalties, bakers started to add an extra loaf for every dozen: hence the number 13.

INTERESTING CELESTIAL OBJECTS

✳ ✳ ✳ ✳

*Some you can see with the naked eye; others we didn't
learn about until we sent exploratory probes. Here are some
of the most intriguing features of the heavens.*

Within Our Solar System

Mercury: Eons ago, the planet nearest the Sun experienced a meteor strike that blasted a crater 800 miles wide called Caloris Basin. The strike actually raised hills on the other side of the planet.

Venus: Its buttery cloud cover is mostly carbon dioxide mixed with sulfur dioxide. Atmospheric pressure at the surface is equal to being half a mile below Earth's seas. The surface temperature can reach 900° F.

Mars: Mercury has the crater; Mars has the volcano. Olympus Mons rises 16 miles above the planet's surface—three times the height of Mt. Everest—and is the size of Arizona. It's a shield volcano (like the ones in Hawaii) the result of lava flowing out over the ages. The caldera (central crater) alone is large enough to swallow a medium-sized city.

Jupiter: The largest planet has a moon collection that thus far exceeds 60, but one of the most interesting is Io. Astronomers have watched some of Io's 400-plus active volcanoes erupt, and a few of its mountains rise higher than Mt. Everest.

Saturn: If you've never seen the rings, you can do so easily with a basic telescope. Like Jupiter, Saturn has a big moon collection. Its largest, Titan, has an atmosphere (mostly nitrogen with some methane) and standing liquid on its surface. Titan is much bigger than Earth's moon and close in size to Jupiter's largest moons.

Uranus: It's the farthest planet from Earth visible to the naked eye, but you have to know exactly where to look. The odd thing about Uranus is that it's oriented on its side. Earth is tilted 23.5 degrees out of the plane of the solar system (our local "up" reference point in space). Uranus is tilted 98 degrees, so its poles are in the middle and its equator runs from top to bottom.

Neptune: You can't see Neptune without a good telescope; it's dimmer than Jupiter's larger moons. Its main moon, Triton (a little smaller than our own), is doomed. In as little as 10 million years, when Triton falls from the sky and spirals toward Neptune, the planet's gravity will crumble it into a huge ring.

Pluto: It got kicked out of the Planet Club but not out of orbit. Its orbit is off kilter—it's out of line with the solar system and elliptical enough that for periods of 20 Earth years at a time, Pluto is closer than Neptune.

Eris: It's the (non-)planet that got Pluto kicked out of the Planet Club. Given the argument that ensued, how fitting that it was named for a goddess of strife. Officially a dwarf planet, Eris is a little bigger than Pluto and has one dinky moon that we know of. It's way out there, with a year more than twice as long (557 Earth years) as Pluto's (248 Earth years).

Beyond Our Solar System

Magellanic Clouds: Earth's nearest galaxies are visible only in the Southern Hemisphere. Both are irregular blobs that appear to the naked eye as fuzzy patches. If we ever go to other galaxies, these would surely be the first objects we'd visit.

Andromeda Galaxy: Visible to the naked eye and easily enjoyed with binoculars, Andromeda is the closest spiral galaxy (like our own Milky Way). Spot it on a night and in a place with little light pollution in the Northern Hemisphere, ideally in November.

Crab Nebula: We watched this one blow itself apart (or rather, we watched the light reach us). In A.D. 1054, Arab and Chinese astronomers noted a star visible during daytime—now it has puffed out a big gas cloud. It's in Taurus (winter, mainly in the Northern Hemisphere), just above the tip of the lower "horn." You can get a reasonable view of the cloud surrounding the star's wreckage with a four-inch telescope, but binoculars will reveal something, too.

Ring Nebula: Not visible to the naked eye but fascinating in pictures or through a big telescope, this looks like a smoke ring surrounding a small star. Just south of Vega in the constellation Lyra (summer, mainly in the Northern Hemisphere) is a little parallelogram of stars, and the Nebula is in the middle of its bottom short side. Take a good look at Vega (impossible to miss), because in 14,000 years it'll be our North Star again as Earth's axis cycles around.

Coalsack Nebula: It's smack in the middle of the Milky Way and big enough to block out most of the "milk." You have to get below the equator to see it, but its position just left of and below the Southern Cross makes it easy to spot all year round. This interstellar dust cloud obscures objects behind it.

Orion Nebula: It's not at all hard to find (winter, Northern Hemisphere; summer, Southern Hemisphere) in the dagger of Orion's three-star belt, and you can easily see the haze with binoculars—great through a small telescope.

Pleiades: This star cluster is home of the aliens who will soon arrive, to hear some tell it. These are one of the highlights of binocular astronomy, easy to spot in Taurus (winter, Northern Hemisphere; summer, Southern Hemisphere). Look for a little coffee-cup shape of blue-white stars that show up sapphire in light magnification.

Algol: It's an eclipsing binary star (a bright star eclipsed at intervals by a dimmer nearby star). For folks on Earth, the star seems to vary in brightness, and you can tell with the naked eye; visibility will go from easy to difficult. The eclipses last several hours and occur every three days.

Milky Way: Our own galaxy dazzles on a dark night as it traces a broad path of light the full width of the sky. The Milky Way is a spiral galaxy that formed approximately 14 billion years ago; our solar system is just a small part of it. Most of the stars we can see are in our galaxy, which is about 100,000 light-years in diameter and 1,000 light-years thick. The Sun, along with Earth, is around 26,000 light-years from the center, halfway to the edge of the galaxy along the Orion spiral arm.

STUFF ABOUT SHARKS

* * * *

- Sharks have been around for nearly 400 million years. It's believed that larger, now extinct species used to eat dinosaurs.

- Sharks have no tongues. Their taste buds are in their teeth.

- Bull sharks, one of the most dangerous, aggressive shark species, have the highest testosterone levels of any animal in the world. They are also the only species of shark that can survive in both saltwater and freshwater.

- Sharks are well known for their "sixth sense"—the ability to sense electromagnetic pulses sent out by creatures and objects in the water. The sensors in their snouts are small pores called the Ampullae of Lorenzini.

- Scientists have discovered that a shark can be put into a catatonic state called "tonic immobility" when it's flipped onto its back, or when the Ampullae of Lorenzini are appropriately stimulated. When the contact is stopped or the animal is righted, the shark typically snaps out of the "trance" very quickly.

- Several types of sharks have demonstrated an affinity for being touched, or for being put into a state of tonic immobility. Scientists have seen Caribbean reef sharks compete with each other for a diver's attention, sometimes ignoring food in favor of being touched. Some great whites have even shown positive responses to being touched and have allowed divers to ride along on their dorsal fins. (This is, of course, very dangerous even for professionals.)

- Humans are significantly more dangerous to sharks than sharks are to humans. People kill as many as 100 million sharks every year, often when the sharks are accidentally caught in fishing nets. Many other sharks are caught only for their fins, which are cut off (to be used in shark-fin soup) before the sharks are thrown back into the sea to drown.

- The largest known shark litter was discovered in a blue shark. When examined, she carried 135 pups in her uterus.

- Tiger sharks are often called the "garbage cans of the sea" because they will eat nearly anything. They favor sea turtles, but the contents of their stomachs have revealed tires, baseballs, and license plates.

- Although short-fin mako sharks are renowned for their ability to jump out of the water, the great white shark also makes spectacular aerial breaches, particularly when hunting seals off the coast of South Africa. Occasionally, they land in passing boats, much to the surprise of passengers.

- Sharks are not the mindless killers of lore. Many species have shown extraordinary curiosity and intelligence. They migrate to new feeding grounds at the times their prey is most plentiful there, and they adapt their hunting techniques depending on their prey. Some have even been trained to push a bell to receive food.

- Great whites are frightening enough, but they have an extinct relative that makes the biggest of them look unimposing. *Carcharodon megalodon* was a huge shark that grew to 50 feet long and could easily swallow an entire person. Fortunately, they died out around a million years ago.

- Short-finned makos are the fastest sharks out there. They have been clocked at 36 miles per hour and have been estimated to swim up to 60 miles per hour. They need this extreme speed to chase down their favorite food—the lightning-fast yellow-fin tuna.

- Most sharks are solitary hunters, but others are quite social. Greater hammerheads are known to group into large schools of 100 or more off the Island of Cacos near Mexico, and blacktip reef sharks frequently hunt in packs the way wolves do, helping one another grab fish and crabs out of the coral.

- The reportedly voracious great white shark can actually go nearly three months without eating.

- Scientists have identified more than 400 species of sharks in the world, ranging from less than a foot long to 40-foot behemoths. Approximately 30 of those species are considered dangerous.

- The pygmy ribbontail catshark is the smallest shark in the world, with a maximum length of seven inches.

- Movies such as *Jaws* may make us think otherwise, but shark bites are uncommon, and fatal attacks rarely occur. A person is 1,000 times more likely to be bitten by a dog than by a shark, and dogs kill more people every year than sharks do.

- If you happen to be attacked by a shark, try to gouge its eyes and gills, its most sensitive areas. Sharks are opportunistic feeders and generally don't pursue prey that puts up a fight in which they could be injured.

- Gansbaii, South Africa, touts itself as the "Great White Capital of the World," and for good reason. Its shores host the greatest concentration of great white sharks in any ocean.

- Great white attacks are usually caused by the animals' curiosity about an unfamiliar object. They are extremely curious, and lacking hands, they "feel out" the new object with their teeth, usually in a gentle bite. Unfortunately, the sharks are so large that even a nibble can do a lot of damage. The common belief that great white bites are a case of mistaken identity is false. Great whites have sharp eyesight, and they are often placid when interacting with humans—behavior that differs greatly when they are hunting seals.

Where Are Shark Attacks Most Common?

Most shark attacks occur in North American waters. In the United States, attacks happen most often in:

1. Florida
2. California
3. Texas
4. Hawaii
5. North Carolina

In other places around the world, most shark attacks occur in:

1. Australia
2. Brazil
3. South Africa
4. Reunion Island (Indian Ocean)

Roughly tied are the Bahamas, Cuba, Egypt, Fiji, New Zealand, and Venezuela.

SUETONIUS'S TWELVE CAESARS

✳ ✳ ✳ ✳

Not only is Suetonius one of the most interesting Roman writers, but much of what he says is likely true! Here are his 12 biographical subjects, along with a quirk he reported about each.

Julius Caesar was dictator, never emperor—though he probably would have become the first emperor if Team Brutus hadn't poked him full of holes.
Oddity: Caesar was not a heavy drinker—almost a perversion among Roman politicians.

Augustus was actually titled "first citizen"; a collection of special powers gained over his lifetime worked out to the equivalent of emperorship.
Oddity: Augustus had only a few small, rotten teeth—and a unibrow.

Tiberius sent the "first citizen" concept out to sea, preferring to goof off on the Isle of Capri and have underlings and bureaucrats keep the empire humming.
Oddity: Tiberius served leftovers at formal dinners.

"Caligula" was an army-brat nickname ("Little Army Boots") that stuck, though no one would call him that when he was emperor. He did some of the psychopathic things you've heard about, and some worse; he also did good things, but those make boring history.
Oddity: Caligula was exceptionally hairy—and thin-skinned about it. He executed anyone who mentioned goats in his presence.

Claudius actually looked like a clod: He drooled, stammered, and had some sort of head twitch, likely the result of a nervous condition. What most people don't realize is how well he ran the empire (though Caligula was an easy act to follow).
Oddity: Claudius was an avid gambler who wrote a book on dice games.

Nero sang while Rome burned, but he didn't play his lyre, much less a not-yet-invented fiddle. Suetonius says Nero started the fire himself as inspiration for a song.

Oddity: Nero was doomed as a popular crooner—he was thick-necked, pot-bellied, thin-legged, and acne-prone.

Galba ushered in the Year of Four Emperors, a revolving-door era when the new guy barely had the new drapes measured before dying. Galba ruled for just six greedy months before the army butchered him.
Oddity: Galba (like other Roman leaders) drank heavily, and he was nearly crippled with arthritis, perhaps brought on by gout.

Otho managed to stick around for three months, which is about how long it took the next guy's legions to reach Italy. He wasn't in charge long enough to do anything too crazy and might have made a decent emperor had he not stabbed himself.
Oddity: Otho had all his body hair removed and put wet bread on his face to inhibit beard growth, perhaps trying to avoid the goat taunts that Caligula suffered.

Vitellius was a repugnant person, both physically and in his vulgar, loutish manner. Always eating, he'd gobble sacrificial food right off the gods' altar. He lasted eight months.
Oddity: Vitellius was the worst dinner guest imaginable. He invited himself to people's houses for impromptu banquets, forcing his unlucky hosts to squander thousands of gold pieces so Vitellius could gorge himself.

Vespasian straightened out Rome handily. Popular with the Roman military and the bane of the senatorial staff, he groomed his son Titus as a worthy successor. If you go to Rome and admire the Colosseum, thank Vespasian for having it built.
Oddity: When Vespasian instituted the infamous Public Urinal Tax, Titus complained about the sickening nature of the rule. Vespasian then produced a coin and asked his son, "Does this smell bad?"—indicating that the source of money is irrelevant.

Titus wasn't around long, but he did a good job. When Mt. Vesuvius destroyed Pompeii (near modern Naples), Titus had a disaster plan. No one is sure if Titus then fell ill or was poisoned by younger brother Domitian, but you'll soon see that Domitian was clearly capable of fratricide.

Oddity: Titus believed in a daily good deed. If at dinner he realized he hadn't done his usual favor, he called that a wasted day.

Domitian was a handful. He debased not merely Roman coinage but Rome itself, executing people in fits of paranoia, signing his name "Dominus et Deus" (Lord and God), interrogating victims by burning them on the genitals, and running a morality campaign while engaging in carnal misdeeds. His assassination was met with the army's sorrow, the Senate's glee, and the public's apathy.
Oddity: Domitian would have a slave stick his hand out with fingers spread—then shoot arrows between the fingers without harming the man.

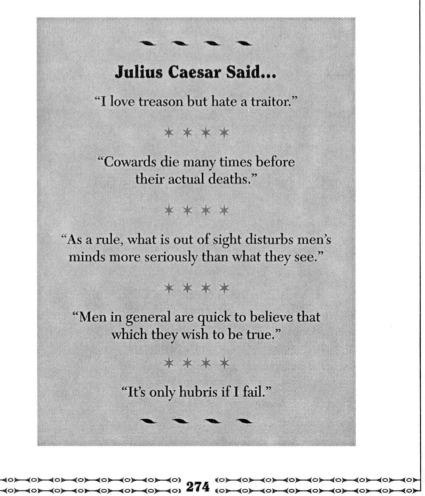

Julius Caesar Said...

"I love treason but hate a traitor."

* * * *

"Cowards die many times before
their actual deaths."

* * * *

"As a rule, what is out of sight disturbs men's
minds more seriously than what they see."

* * * *

"Men in general are quick to believe that
which they wish to be true."

* * * *

"It's only hubris if I fail."

BIG SCREEN BLUNDERS

✳ ✳ ✳ ✳

When filmmakers set out to make "movie magic," these obvious errors probably aren't what they meant.

- One of the most popular movie mistakes occurred when a storm-trooper in *Star Wars: A New Hope* hit his head on a too-short door while walking into the Death Star's control room. The digitally remastered DVDs even highlighted this goof by adding a "thunk" sound.

- In Rodgers and Hammerstein's *The King and I*, Yul Brenner's song about not being certain is consistent, but his wardrobe isn't. Pay attention to his earring: It disappears and reappears between shots.

- In *Raiders of the Lost Ark*, Harrison Ford faces off against a sword-wielding enemy in a busy marketplace. While the swords-man performs some showy maneuvers, Ford just raises his gun and shoots the man. Originally, Ford was supposed to snatch the guy's sword with his trademark whip, but he just couldn't perform the maneuver. Frustrated after many tries, he ad-libbed the shooting, and director Steven Spielberg liked it so much he used it.

- The *Star Wars* series seems to have more than its fair share of famous goofs. In the final Luke-versus-Vader battle sequence of *The Empire Strikes Back*, Luke kicks the Sith lord off a ledge in a carbonite chamber, then jumps down after him. Just before the scene cuts, Luke's head reappears as the actor bounces back up from the trampoline he landed on.

- In *The Wizard of Oz*, when the wicked witch confronts Dorothy in the apple orchard, you can clearly see a few ostriches lounging around in the background. Apparently, they had wandered away from the set of a nature film being shot next door.

- Movie vehicles seem to have a mystical ability to instantly repair themselves. In *Twister*, a tornado knocks the tailgate off Bill Paxton's pickup truck, but it's right back on in subsequent scenes. The yellow Porsche in *Commando* also seems to have an instant-fix function—its side gets completely trashed at one point, but as soon as Arnold Schwarzenegger hops in and drives off, it's pristine and shiny again.

- Other objects apparently have quick-fix skills, too. When Mary Jane is being mugged in *Spider-Man*, Spidey tosses two bad guys through the windows behind her. The camera pans away for a moment, and when it pans back, the windows are magically repaired.

- Blame it on a *Matrix* glitch? When Agent Smith seals Neo's mouth shut, Neo jumps up and walks away while trying to get it open. However, the reflection in Smith's glasses shows Neo still sitting calmly in his chair. A later glitch involves Trinity and Neo killing a bunch of soldiers on a roof while rescuing Morpheus, but moments later the bodies are gone.

- Where did that come from? When the killer shark in *Jaws* gets into the pond, the man it attacks is barefoot when he is knocked from his boat. However, when we see his severed leg sink to the bottom of the pond, it's sporting a shoe.

- James Bond always has the best toys, including what appears to be a color-changing mask. During a diving scene in *Thunderball*, 007 rips a black mask off another diver's face, but when he puts it on himself, it's suddenly bright blue.

- In another Bond movie, *Diamonds Are Forever*, tires seem to spontaneously appear out of sand dunes. Bond's car rolls during a chase, and even though all four tires are clearly still on the car, a loose tire rolls through the foreground.

- Mel Gibson needs to make up his mind. His *Braveheart* character begins an attack by running with an axe, but in the next shot he's not holding anything. In the following shot, he has a sword drawn, then he switches back to the axe before finishing with the sword. Maybe he was trying to decide which rubber weapon would wobble least.

- The Ancient Romans were technologically advanced for their time, but it's doubtful whether their knowledge extended to metal gas canisters like the one seen on the overturned chariot in *Gladiator*.

Fast Facts

- *Approximately 90 percent of crop circles in the world appear in England. The largest of these was found in Etchilhampton, Wiltshire, in 1996. The pattern formed an elongated group of circles 4,100 feet long. Another at nearby Milk Hill was made of 409 circles, the most in any one formation.*

- *The Romans worshipped some very specific gods. They had a goddess for Rome's sewer system (Cloacina) and another for thresholds and door hinges (Cardea). You just can't beat a divinely protected door hinge.*

- *There are 887 stone statues on Easter Island, though most never made it to their platforms.*

- *Galaxies often collide, and perhaps merge, with each other as they drift through the universe. Big galaxies tend to absorb smaller ones—the Milky Way Galaxy is currently merging with a tiny dwarf galaxy. Large galaxies interact, too. The Andromeda Galaxy, which is about the same size as our Milky Way, may collide with us in around 3 billion years, forming one huge elliptical galaxy.*

- *The lit end of a cigarette reaches approximately 1,292° F when the smoker inhales.*

- *Nicotine takes around eight days to leave the bloodstream completely.*

- *It's often referenced, but not everyone knows that Timbuktu is in Mali, West Africa.*

- *Ermal Fraze invented the pop-top aluminum can in 1959. In 1963, he received U.S. patent number 3,349,949 for the design.*

- *Terminal velocity for a human is approximately 124 miles per hour. To reach this speed, you would have to fall from a height of at least 158 yards—about one and a half football fields.*

THE WORLD'S OLDEST FAMILY BUSINESSES

✳ ✳ ✳ ✳

When shopping for goods and services, many people prefer companies with long, sturdy family histories. Around the world, top family businesses have been in existence for at least 500 years. Here are some of the best of the oldest.

Kongo Gumi (Osaka, Japan; contractors, founded 578): After nearly 1,400 years of Buddhist temple repair and general contracting, this family business is still going strong. Flexibility has contributed to its longevity—during World War II, the company switched its focus to coffin construction.

Chateau de Goulaine (Haute Goulaine, France; vintners and museum-keepers, founded 1000): The Goulaines have cared for this scenic castle for a thousand years. The highlight of the museum is its rare butterfly collection, but its Loire Valley wines are also prized.

Fonderia Pontificia Marinelli (Agnone, Italy; bell founders, founded around 1000): The Marinellis are still casting bronze bells, using the wax technique employed by bell masters in the Middle Ages and the Renaissance. Today, bells crafted by the Marinellis ring in some of the world's most prestigious churches.

Barovier & Toso (Murano Venezia, Italy; glassmakers, founded 1295): This family company is the world's oldest continuous maker of fine crystal. The business originally operated in Venice but later moved to the nearby island of Murano, ostensibly to guard its glass-blowing secrets.

Hotel Pilgrim Haus (Soest, Germany; hoteliers, founded 1304): The Andernach family has operated this inn through every wave of conflict and sovereignty that has washed over the Ruhr. Its survival could be attributed to its stone walls, which are three feet thick.

Richard de Bas (Ambert d'Auvergne, France; papermakers, founded 1326): When your family has supplied paper for limited-edition art by Braque and Picasso, you strive to keep up the tradition. The company produces only 200 to 300 sheets of paper per day.

Camuffo (Portogruaro, Italy; shipbuilders, founded 1438): This company, relocated from Crete, has supplied ships to many navies over the centuries, including Napoleon's. A Camuffo is to boats what a Stradivarius is to violins.

Baronnie de Coussergues (Mont Blanc, France; vintners, founded 1495): This gold-medal-draped winemaker is noted for Chardonnays, Sauvignon Blancs, Viogniers, Cabernet Francs, and Merlots. King Charles VIII was the property's original owner.

Grazia Deruta (Turin, Italy; ceramicists, founded 1500): The Grazias make majolica, a tin-glazed pottery with a surface that takes paint exceptionally well. Their customers include Neiman Marcus and Tiffany.

William Prym GmbH (Stolberg, Germany; clothing industry, founded 1530): If it's made of metal, and it's used in clothing, Prym likely started making it well before the Pilgrims landed. The company specializes in needles, fasteners, and now microelectronics.

John Brooke & Sons Holdings (Huddersfield, U.K.; formerly clothiers, now real estate, founded 1541): Brooke used to make naval and military uniforms but has recently gotten out of manufacturing. It now manages office and retail space on the site of the firm's former mill buildings.

von Poschinger Manufaktur (Frauenau, Germany; glaziers, 1568): Though glassmaking is still the priority at von Poschinger, the family has diversified into farming and forestry on their ancient lands near the Czech border. The subtle colors and artistic beauty of their glassware make von Poschinger crystal a costly collectible.

Hacienda Los Lingues (San Fernando, Chile; diversified, founded about 1575): These prestigious stables once bred fine cavalry horses. The firm also sponsors a line of well-regarded wines and operates an elegant hotel.

DON'T GO FLY A KITE!

✳ ✳ ✳ ✳

Mother Nature has a powerful arsenal to show us who's boss, and lightning is one of the most frightening. However, there are ways to avoid the danger and enjoy the spectacle. Here are some suggestions.

- If you determine that a lightning strike is within three miles of your location, anticipate that the next strike will be in your immediate area. A count of about five seconds between seeing the lightning and hearing thunder represents one mile.

- Immediately seek shelter if a storm hits your area. Move into a hard-roofed vehicle or large building.

- If you're outside away from buildings and can't get to your car, huddle on the ground at least 50 yards from the vehicle.

- Likewise, stay a good distance away from tractors, heavy road equipment, golf carts, or other vehicles.

- Do not stand in unprotected open structures such as park pavilions, rain shelters, or bus stops, and avoid clearings such as fields, ballparks, tennis courts, golf courses, and other open spaces.

- If hiking, move off ridges and summits. Avoid the tallest trees and hilltops. If you're near a tree, stay at a distance from the trunk at least equal to the tree's height. If you are in the woods, shelter yourself in a stand of smaller trees.

- If caught in the open with a group of people, spread out away from one another so everyone isn't hit by a single strike.

- If caught in the open, assume the "lightning crouch": Put your feet together, squat down, tuck in your head, and cover your ears. Insulate yourself from ground current by crouching on a sleeping pad, backpack, or coiled rope.

- If you are boating or swimming, get out of the water immediately.

- If your hair stands on end, you hear high-pitched or crackling noises, or see a blue halo (referred to as St. Elmo's fire) around objects, there is electrical activity near you.

THE OSTRICH

✷ ✷ ✷ ✷

*The ancient Roman encyclopedist and philosopher Pliny the Elder
once wrote that the ostrich, being profoundly stupid, sticks its head
into a bush at the first sign of danger and considers itself invisible.
Here's the truth about this magnificent, maligned bird.*

- To dispel the ancient libel, ostriches do not bury
their heads when faced with danger—a species
that did so would hardly be able to survive for
more than 120 million years. They do, however,
stretch their long necks flat on the ground when
they sleep; from a distance, it can look as though
their heads are buried.

- Ostriches cannot fly, but don't feel too sorry for
them. The ostrich is the fastest bipedal runner in
the world, capable of reaching speeds up to 45 miles per hour—
about twice what the fastest human can achieve. What's more, an
ostrich can maintain this speed for up to half an hour.

- Of the three main varieties of ostriches, only the African black
ostrich (*Struthio camelus domesticus*) is found in captivity. They
are farmed for meat, leather, and feathers in at least 50 countries
and just about all climatic conditions, from Alaska to equatorial
Africa. Ostriches have the best feed-to-weight ratio gain of any
farmed land animal in the world and produce the strongest commercially available leather.

- The ostrich's eyes are about the size of billiard balls. They take up
so much room in the skull that the ostrich's brain is actually smaller than either one of its eyeballs. This may be why the ostrich,
despite its tremendous running speed, is not very good at eluding
predators: It tends to run in circles.

- The ostrich's intestines are 46 feet long—about twice as long as
those of a human. This enables the bird to get the most out of the
tough plants it eats. To help with digestion, it also swallows sand
and small stones to break down food in its gizzard. Ostriches in

captivity have been known to swallow just about anything that can fit down their gullet, including coins, bicycle valves, alarm clocks, and even small bottles.

- The ostrich is the largest living bird in the world. An ostrich chick grows one foot taller each month until it is seven or eight months old. Adult ostrich roosters are six to ten feet in height and can weigh as much as 340 pounds. Because of their prodigious size, ostriches were occasionally used for riding or pulling chariots in ancient Egypt; the practice never really took off, because the ostrich has a nasty temper.

- This great bird has only two toes; all other birds have three or four. Ostriches kick forward, not backward, because that's the direction in which their knees bend. Ostriches never need to drink water—some of it they make internally, and the rest is derived from the vegetation they eat.

- Although the ostrich egg is the largest of all eggs, it is the smallest egg in relation to the size of the bird. A three-pound egg is only about 1 percent as heavy as the ostrich hen; by contrast, a kiwi's egg—the largest in comparison to the mother—is 15 to 20 percent of the mother bird's mass. An ostrich egg is equivalent in volume to two dozen chicken eggs.

- *Physiologus*, an early Christian text compiled around the second century A.D. and a popular read in the Middle Ages, asserts that the ostrich incubates its eggs by staring at them. It was widely held at the time that vision was the effect of special "seeing" rays emanating from one's eyes; thus, the heat in the gaze of the ostrich hatched its chicks. The author of *Physiologus* presents this as an allegory to inspire worshippers to keep their eyes on Christ.

- Male ostriches are polygamous, but they tend the nest with a single favored mate. This hen lays about a half-dozen eggs in a shallow depression in the sand, which takes her about two weeks. Other hens then add their own eggs to the nest, and once they are finished, the favored mate chases them off. The nest owners then incubate all the eggs: The female sits on them during the day, and the male takes a turn at night.

GREAT GOLF COURSES

✳ ✳ ✳ ✳

What differentiates golf from most other sports is that the average person can play a round where Palmer, Nicklaus, Hogan, Trevino, and Woods have played. Here are some hallowed golf temples.

St. Andrews Old Course (1400s), public, Scotland: St. Andrews represents six centuries of golf on six courses, of which the Old Course is the most famous. Storied hole: number 17, the famous Road Hole (par 4, 455 yards from the black tees), with the hungering Road Bunker awaiting anyone who overshoots the green. Stays in the Road Bunker can be so long the golfer needs a motel.

Carnoustie Championship (1842), public, Scotland: Tour players often call this "Car-nasty," mainly for its unpredictable weather. Storied hole: number 6 (par 5, 578), which is likely to involve a driver from the fairway on the second shot.

Royal County Down Championship (1889), public, Northern Ireland: This is where the famous David Feherty honed his slice. Your first three holes take you along Dundrum Bay. Storied hole: number 9 (par 4, 486 from the blacks), a blind tee shot threaded down a narrow fairway toward an undulating green.

Lahinch (1892), public, Ireland: Who wouldn't want to golf within two miles of the Cliffs of Moher and a short drive from Doolin, famous for its pubs and traditional music? Lahinch is links golf up close and personal with the North Atlantic. Storied hole: number 5 (par 3, 154 from the blues), aka The Dell, a blind shot at a foot-shaped green tucked completely behind a dune.

Oakmont (1903), private, Pennsylvania: Oakmont golfers wallow in the pain their course inflicts. If you want to get a feel for its greens, hit some practice putts on a gently sloped basketball court. Storied hole: number 3 (par 4, 428 from the green tees), where a hooked tee shot sends you to pray in the vast Church Pews—a bunker complex nearly the size of a football field.

Pinehurst No. 2 (1907), resort, North Carolina: Of Pinehurst Resort's eight courses, this is the most famous. Long, tree-lined dogleg fairways make for jungle safaris if you miss off the tee. Storied hole: number 11 (par 4, 434 from the blues), one of Ben Hogan's favorites, encouraging a slight fade off the tee.

Pine Valley (1918), private, New Jersey: Pine Valley is that rare course with no dull holes. The designer felt that a course should require every club in the bag, and Pine Valley does. Some call it the world's best. Storied hole: number 18 (par 4, 483 from the back tees), descending from an elevated tee into a steep second shot firing at a huge green flanked by perilous bunkers.

Pebble Beach (1919), public, California: If you golf, you've heard of Pebble. One of four courses clustered in the area, much of Pebble plays along the Pacific Ocean's stony shores. Storied hole: number 7 (par 3, 106 from the blues), where you hit down onto a well-bunkered peninsular green with flaky wind gusts. If the wind gets hold, "on the beach" has a literal meaning.

Royal Melbourne West (1931), semi-private, Australia: You'll have to have a letter of introduction and a respectable handicap to make a reservation, but it's worth the effort. The West Course is the highest-rated of three. Storied hole: number 18 (par 4, 433), a boomerang-shape dogleg right requiring a precise 230-yarder off the tee and a great long iron or hybrid to get home in two.

Cypress Point (1928), private, California: This Pebble Beach neighbor is known chiefly for its beauty. It has three holes that string together along the Pacific Ocean. Storied hole: number 16 (par 3, 220 yards), the second of the three oceanfront holes, where timid tee shots end up in a jumble of vines or skitter back down into the ocean inlet.

Pine Needles (1928), resort, North Carolina: This course is rated excellent for women because of its emphasis on finesse and strategy rather than cannon shots off the tee. Call it the anti–Augusta National. Often hosts the U.S. Women's Open. Storied hole: number 3 (par 3, 145 from the medal tees), a middle iron over a pond where the penalty for overshooting will likely be a three-putt.

Augusta National (1933), private and exclusive, Georgia: It hosts the annual Masters Tournament and has thus seen some of the most dramatic moments in championship golf history. Augusta's refusal to allow women to join makes it controversial. Storied hole: number 13 (par 5, 510), the Azalea Hole, with its psyche-testing drive followed by a water hazard clearance and a tough green.

Highland Links (1939), public, Nova Scotia: A contender for Canada's best golfing honors, this course has the natural beauty you'd expect in a national park. Storied hole: number 15 (par 4, 540 from the blues), where the prevailing winds and downhill play encourage you to break out your driver and hit it at the Atlantic with a fair chance to reach in two.

Bethpage Black (1935), public, New York: This is the most challenging of Bethpage State Park's five courses, as the sign near the first tee makes explicitly clear. Storied hole: number 4 (par 5, 530 from the blues), where making the green in regulation requires three great shots for most players, as the fairway passes over large bunker complexes.

Prairie Dunes (1937), private, Kansas: This project of the Carey Salt Company's founding family has more topography than most non-Kansans would expect. Storied hole: number 8 (par 4, 430 from the blues), with a green that slopes a full four feet over its length to test any golfer's putting nerves—especially if the pin is in the middle of the bisecting ridge.

TPC Sawgrass Stadium (1981), resort, Florida: Another of the world's most challenging courses. Speedy greens, if you believe Jack Nicklaus: "No, I've never been very good at stopping a 5-iron on the hood of a car." Storied hole: It could only be number 17 (par 3, 132 from the TPC tees), the dreaded Island Hole, whose surrounding lake swallows more than 100,000 golf balls each year.

Canyon Lakes (1981), public, Washington: This valleyed, varied challenger's verdancy stands in contrast to the high desert surrounding the area. Wind is common and rain is rare at this undiscovered beauty. Storied hole: number 12 (par 3, 181 from the blacks), with a vast 120-by-100-foot green most golfers have a good chance to hit.

Kiawah Island Ocean (1991), public, South Carolina: It's pretty hard to get out of sight of the ocean, so the course is well named. You're golfing in a bird sanctuary with protected wetlands. Storied hole: number 4 (par 5, 453 from the golds), a risk/reward classic requiring two swamp crossings to reach a green necklaced with bunkers and humps. If you can reach in two, you're really good.

Kapalua Plantation (1991), resort, Hawaii: Who wouldn't want to view the Hawaiian mountains and ocean while belting off elevated tees to wide fairways? You'll have to calculate club selection carefully here, but that's golf. Storied hole: number 18 (par 5, 663 from the championship tees). Despite its length, long hitters can reach the green in two with the breathtaking drop in elevation.

Bandon Dunes (1999), public, Oregon: One of three fantastic courses, it's far from urbanity but worth the long trip. Old school golf—no carts. Sometimes Bandon and its sibling Pacific Dunes will make the same top ten lists—that's how great the place is. Storied hole: number 16 (par 4, 363 from the blacks), bisected by an ocean inlet and with numerous options on the way home.

Great Miniature Golf Courses

Dolphin Mini Golf, Boothbay, Maine: You're sure to sink a putt here—the place has lots of lakes and streams that are stocked with live fish, and you will even encounter a fake dolphin or whale. On the course itself, you'll be challenged by such moving obstacles as a ship's wheel and a bobbing buoy.

Hawaiian Rumble/Hawaiian Caverns, Myrtle Beach, South Carolina: Rated two of the best by *Golf* magazine, these courses feature a 25-foot-long whale that squirts water out of its blowhole. The Rumble gets its name from a huge "active" volcano that shoots flames from its top. Hawaiian Caverns was built at the edge of a manmade mountain and lake, and grass huts positioned throughout the course provide shade. Players receive leis when they arrive and listen to music by Don Ho while they play.

I'm No Expert, But...
STATES AND CIVICS

✳ ✳ ✳ ✳

Q: What's the difference between a commonwealth and a state?

A: Kentucky, Massachusetts, Pennsylvania, and Virginia style themselves commonwealths rather than states. In practice, there is no legal difference; a commonwealth enjoys no rights that a state does not, nor vice versa. During the Revolutionary period, it implied that the entity came together by mutual consent, but that applied to numerous states that call themselves states. There really is no difference whatsoever.

Q: Why is Louisiana law based on the Code Napoleon?

A: Because the United States bought Louisiana from the famed emperor. Louisiana judges rely less on precedent and more on their own interpretation of law than judges in other states. Louisiana law students decide whether to focus on American law or the Louisiana civil code. This situation, unique in U.S. jurisprudence, definitely keeps carpetbagging out-of-state lawyers from setting up shop in the bayou—unless they can be admitted to the Louisiana bar.

Q: Why doesn't Nebraska have a state Senate?

A: The unicameral (having a single legislative chamber) Nebraska Legislature is actually more Senate than House of Representatives, but the state indeed has only one house. In the 1930s, Nebraskans felt that two legislatures wasted time and money, so they amended their state constitution to abolish the house and hand its duties to the Senate, now called simply the Nebraska Legislature. It also cut down the number of politicians: The Nebraska Legislature has 49 members, far fewer than other state legislatures.

Q: Can Texas really split itself up into five states anytime it wishes?

A: Not really. This idea comes from a provision in an 1845 compromise governing the admission of Texas to the Union, motivated by the slave state–free state debate of that day. In 1861, Texas seceded and became a Confederate state. When it was readmitted in 1870, there was no such proviso, so don't expect the Lone Star State to become the Five Star States.

Q: Wyoming was the first state to give women the vote. Which was the second?

A: Utah—but the movement, coming from out of state, was hardly motivated by altruistic concern for women's political rights. Its supporters believed that Utah's women would dispense with polygamy if given the vote. The plan backfired on two levels: Not only did senior male Mormon leaders support it, but the majority of Mormon women voters continued to vote for polygamy. The gambit having bombed, the U.S. Congress canceled the women's suffrage in 1887. They got it back in 1895.

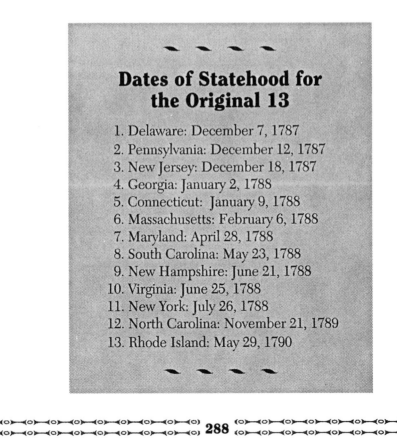

Dates of Statehood for the Original 13

1. Delaware: December 7, 1787
2. Pennsylvania: December 12, 1787
3. New Jersey: December 18, 1787
4. Georgia: January 2, 1788
5. Connecticut: January 9, 1788
6. Massachusetts: February 6, 1788
7. Maryland: April 28, 1788
8. South Carolina: May 23, 1788
9. New Hampshire: June 21, 1788
10. Virginia: June 25, 1788
11. New York: July 26, 1788
12. North Carolina: November 21, 1789
13. Rhode Island: May 29, 1790

LEADERS WHO SHAPED CANADIAN DESTINY

✳ ✳ ✳

*Canadian history would be a subtopic of U.S. history
but for key turns of the national steering wheel by determined
Canadians. Of course, not all leadership is political (or even lawful).
Here are some Canadian leaders—or outside leaders embraced by
Canadians—who shaped Canada in interesting ways.*

Air Marshal William "Billy" Bishop (1894–1956): When he flunked his first year at the Royal Military College, no one would have predicted a bright future for Cadet Bishop. Leaving the cavalry to join Britain's Royal Flying Corps, he became the second-highest-scoring Allied ace of World War I—and the highest-scoring Commonwealth ace, a fact no Canadian or Briton could ignore.

Major General Sir Isaac Brock (1769–1812): Without "the Hero of Upper Canada," it might be "Ontario, the Hudson Bay State." General Brock gets the primary credit for beating back the U.S. invasion of Upper Canada (today, Ontario) during the War of 1812. He also won his enemies' respect. He died doing his duty, and the British fired 21 guns in salute at his funeral. The nearby U.S. garrison at Fort Niagara, though a wartime enemy, fired a similar salute to General Brock that same day.

The Right Honourable Avril P. D. "Kim" Campbell (1947–): This Vancouver Island native smashed the ice ceiling, becoming Canada's first woman prime minister in 1993. Unfortunately for Campbell, her predecessor, Brian Mulroney, had poisoned the party's well in the public mind; she couldn't manage to shake that legacy. Though few characterize her brief administration as a success, she went where no Canadian woman had gone before.

Samuel de Champlain (c.1567–1635): This Frenchman founded the city of Quebec, and with it the colony of New France (later Lower Canada, still later the Province de Quebec). He did have one rough spot, siding with the Hurons against the Iroquois (thus authoring

150 years of lousy Franco-Iroquois relations), but de Champlain is still the father of French Canada—arguably, of Canada itself.

Lieutenant General Sir Arthur Currie (1875–1933): Considered by many to be Canada's greatest military man, he became its first general—and a strong advocate for keeping Canadian troops together in the World War I trenches rather than dispersing them around the front. As the commander responsible for the defining Canadian victory at Vimy Ridge in 1917, he ensured that friendly and enemy nations alike wouldn't take Canadian valor lightly.

Lieutenant General Roméo Dallaire (1946–): Dallaire was in command of the United Nations Observer Mission in Rwanda. As the 1994 genocide unfolded, he was the voice in the wilderness: First he tried to alert the United Nations to the magnitude of the problem, then attempted to halt it himself in defiance of orders. His moral courage embodied the best of Canada's national commitment to peacekeeping.

Sir Sandford Fleming (1827–1915): As railways shot across the western United States, this Scottish visionary realized that Canada must either have its own transcontinental railway or start drafting a petition for statehood. He helped with nearly every aspect of the project and was present when the last spike was driven to finish the job in Craigellachie, British Columbia (1885). He also devised the 24-zone global time system we use today.

Elijah Harper (1949–): In his view, the painfully negotiated Meech Lake Accord (1990) disregarded First Nations rights. A Cree from Manitoba, Harper rejected it in style—by standing up with an eagle feather in his hand and leading the filibuster that prevented Meech Lake's ratification. This stubborn stand may have annoyed some people, but it got Canada's undivided attention.

Sir Wilfrid Laurier (1841–1919): A Quebecois farmer's son, this gifted lawyer became Canada's first Francophone prime minister, and he helped create the Royal Canadian Navy. His passion for Canadian unity made his position difficult—the French/English divide in Canada predated him by well over a century—but his persuasive ability bridged that canyon as well as any Canadian could.

René Lévesque (1922–1987): While French Canadians have often struggled to preserve their distinct society and its language, Lévesque took it to the next level. He was the first Premier of Quebec to mount a credible bid for Quebecois independence. It didn't happen, but the national dialogue continues to this day.

Sir John A. Macdonald (1815–1891): When the British North America Act created the Dominion of Canada on July 1, 1867, Canadians elected a Parliament with Macdonald as the first Prime Minister. Sir John laid the foundations for the modern Canadian state.

William L. Mackenzie King (1874–1950): Though not always popular in or after his time, this Liberal Party stalwart established Canada's independence in foreign policy. He also invented the Canadian. That's no misprint: Until a resolution introduced by Mackenzie King's government in 1946, Canadians were technically British nationals. Fittingly, Mackenzie King received the first-ever certificate of Canadian citizenship.

Agnes C. Macphail (1890–1954): This rural Ontario schoolteacher and penal reformer—the first woman elected to Federal Parliament—would be reelected four times. As her funeral procession struggled through the snow and wind to her final rest, an old farmer gave a eulogy she might have liked: "She came in on a Grey County storm and she's bloody well going out on one."

Nellie L. McClung (1873–1951): Although this Western activist believed that women were people (as opposed to what, one might wonder), Canada's founding British North America Act wasn't specific on the matter. This made it awkward for Canadian women in politics, because most people prefer to be governed by other people. McClung's petition in 1927 began a process that led to equality (and personhood) under law for Canadian women.

Louis Riel (1844–1885): The cultural hero of Canada's Metis (mixed French and First Peoples culture), Riel was part prophet, part visionary, and part revolutionary. From the Metis perspective, he ended a martyr when authorities strung him up for his role in the failed Northwest Rebellion. His memory is a central rally point for modern Metis pride.

Jeanne Sauvé (1922–1993): In Canada's parliamentary monarchy, the governor-general represents the Crown and exercises its powers (for example, the Royal Assent to a bill of law). Sauvé was doubly important: first female governor-general (1984) and first woman speaker of the House of Commons. This also marked the first time a reigning queen had a governor-general of her own gender.

Joey Smallwood (1900–1991): Newfoundland remained a British Dominion through World War II. Smallwood, a charismatic, forceful "Newfie," was the tugboat pushing his seafaring homeland into Canada (1949). He retired from politics in 1972 as the only premier Newfoundland had ever known. Never mind his somewhat overbearing style; anyone who brings a province into Confederation is by definition an influential Canadian leader.

Superintendent and Major General Sir Samuel Steele (1849–1919): Steele's most enduring contribution to Canada was police work. During the Gold Rush, the Northwest Mounted Police under Superintendent Steele was the law in Yukon Territory. American goldseekers pouring through Soapy Smith's private thieving preserve of Skagway (Alaska) were shocked to reach the border and find NWMP constables enforcing law.

Chief and Brigadier General Tecumseh (1768–1813): Shawnee chief, orator, and general. In his effort to protect and establish free Native American territory, he allied his warriors with General Sir Issac Brock's British and Canadians in the War of 1812 and helped capture Detroit. Though a rebel from the United States' standpoint, Tecumseh is honored by Canadians as a brave, capable ally who gave his life defending Canada from U.S. invasion.

"Let us unite as brothers, as sons of one Mother Earth…. Sell our land? Why not sell the air?… Land cannot be sold."

General Tecumseh

MORE THAN YOU EVER WANTED TO KNOW ABOUT MIMES

✳ ✳ ✳ ✳

Mimes—you know them as the silent, white-faced, black-clad street performers who pretend to be trapped in boxes or walk against the wind. In case you want to know a little more ...

Greco-Roman Tradition

- *Pantomime* means "an imitator of nature"— derived from *Pan*, the Greek god of nature, and *mimos*, meaning "an imitator."

- The first record of pantomime performed as entertainment comes from Ancient Greece, where mimes performed at religious festivals honoring Greek gods. As early as 581 B.C., Aristotle wrote of seeing mimes perform.

- From religious festivals, Greek mime made its way to the stage: Actors performed pantomimic scenes as "overtures" to the tragedies that depicted the moral lesson of the play to follow.

- Greek settlers brought mime to Italy, where it flourished during the Roman Empire and spread throughout Europe as the empire expanded.

- Today, "pantomime" and "mime" are used interchangeably to refer to a mute performer, but the Ancient Romans distinguished between the two: Pantomimes were tragic actors who performed in complete silence, while mimes were comedic and often used speech in their acts.

The Rebirth of European Mime

- The Roman Empire brought pantomime and mime to England around 52 B.C., but with the fall of the Empire in the fifth century and the progress of Christianity, both were banished as forms of paganism.

- Pantomime and mime weren't really gone, though: The sacred religious dramas of the Middle Ages were acted as "dumb shows" (no words were used), and historians believe that comedic mime was used by court jesters, who included humorous imitations in their acts.

- After the Middle Ages, mime resurged during the Renaissance and swept through Europe as part of the Italian theater called the Commedia dell'arte, in which comedic characters performed in masks and incorporated mime, pantomime, music, and dance.

- The first silent mime appeared on the English stage in 1702, in John Weaver's *Tavern Bilkers* at the Drury Lane Theatre. It was really more of a "silent ballet" than silent acting.

- British actor John Rich is credited with adapting pantomime as an acting style for the English stage in 1717. His "Italian Mimic Scenes" combined elements of both Commedia dell'arte and John Weaver's ballet.

- Meanwhile, mime flourished as a silent art in 18th-century France, when Napoleon forbade the use of dialogue in stage performance for fear something slanderous might be said.

- The classic white-faced/black-dressed mime was introduced and popularized in the 19th-century French circus by Jean-Gaspard Deburau, who was deemed too clumsy to participate in his family's aerial and acrobatics act.

Mime in the 20th Century

- Mime started to fade in popularity at the beginning of the 1900s but was revitalized with the birth of silent films, in which stars such as Charlie Chaplin and Buster Keaton relied on elements of pantomime.

- In the 1920s, French performer Etienne Decroux declared mime an independent art form—different from the circus form introduced by Deburau—and launched the era of modern mime.

- In 1952, French-trained American mime Paul Curtis founded the American Mime Theatre in New York.

- In 1957, Etienne Decroux traveled to New York to teach a workshop at the Actors Studio, which inspired him to open a mime school in the city.

- Decroux's most famous student, Marcel Marceau, expanded modern mime's influence in the 1960s by touring the United States and inviting mimes to train with him.

- When he was growing up, Marcel Marceau had been greatly influenced by the actor Charlie Chaplin. In fact, Marceau's alter ego, "Bip" the clown, was inspired by Chaplin's own "Little Tramp" character.

- The San Francisco Mime Troupe (SFMT), one of the most powerful political theaters in the United States, began as a silent mime company in 1959. It was founded by Ronnie Davis, who had previously performed with the American Mime Theatre.

- Future concert promoter Bill Graham was so moved by an SFMT performance in 1965 that he left his corporate job to manage the group. That led to his career as the legendary promoter of the Rolling Stones, Grateful Dead, and Janis Joplin, among others, in the 1960s and 1970s.

- Robert Shields, a former student of Marceau's, developed the "street mime" form in the 1970s. He performed in San Francisco's Union Square, where he occasionally received traffic citations, landed in jail, and was beaten up by people for imitating them!

- Shields and his wife, fellow mime Lorene Yarnell (they married in a mime wedding in Union Square), brought Marceau's mime technique to TV in the late 1970s with the Emmy-award-winning show *Shields and Yarnell*.

- Though the popularity of mime in the United States declined after the 1970s, it still influences aspects of current culture. Urban street dances, including break dancing, incorporate aspects of mime. Most notable is the evolution of the moonwalk, universalized by Michael Jackson, who was inspired by Marcel Marceau.

ANIMALS BY THE BUNCH

✳ ✳ ✳ ✳

Everyone is familiar with the saying "It's more fun than a barrel of monkeys." But how many times have you heard, "You're as loud as a murder of magpies"? Here are the official collective names for various groups of critters.

a congregation of alligators

a shoal of bass

a smack of jellyfish

a gaze of raccoons

a clowder of cats

a cackle of hyenas

a troop of kangaroos

a leap of leopards

a fall of woodcocks

a romp of otters

a prickle of porcupines

a crash of rhinoceroses

a troubling of goldfish

a pod of whales

a charm of finches

an exaltation of larks

a murder of magpies

a watch of nightingales

a parliament of owls

a covey of partridges

an ostentation of peacocks

a colony of penguins

a bevy of quails

a business of ferrets

a wisdom of wombats

a flamboyance of flamingoes

a rhumba of rattlesnakes

a gang of elk

a tower of giraffes

a tribe of goats

a band of gorillas

a bloat of hippopotamuses

a richness of martens

a labor of moles

a pod of seals

a drove of sheep

a dray of squirrels

an ambush of tigers

a wake of buzzards

a chain of bobolinks

a gulp of cormorants

a convocation of eagles

a sedge of herons

a party of jays

a deceit of lapwings

a murder of ravens

HEAVENLY HEAVES

✳ ✳ ✳ ✳

Football fans are occasionally blessed with clutch celestial
conclusions of biblical proportions. Here are a couple.

Franco Harris—The Immaculate Reception: The
outcome looked blacker than bleak for the Pittsburgh
Steelers as the clock wound down on their 1972 AFC
divisional playoff clash with the Oakland Raiders. Se-
questered on their own 40-yard line, down by a single
point, bereft of time outs, and facing a seemingly insurmountable
fourth and ten, the supernatural was required and a miracle was delivered. With 22 seconds left, Steelers pivot Terry Bradshaw evaded
an onslaught of Oakland pass rushers, twisted, turned, and tossed a
pass toward receiver Frenchy Fuqua, who was just about to haul in
the ball when he was blindsided from behind by Raiders safety Jack
Tatum. The ball sailed over the flattened Fuqua, plunked Tatum on
the top of his shoulder pads, and caromed wildly into the air, actually moving backward as it plunged toward the pitch. Incredibly, it
was caught by Pittsburgh running back Franco Harris, who scooped
up the cascading ball just before it hit the ground and trotted
untouched the length of the field for the touchdown that gave the
Steelers a 12–7 lead. After considerable debate, including a call from
the field to the press box for a rule clarification, the play was allowed
to stand, sealing a Steelers win. Since Bradshaw's pass was thrown on
a wing and a prayer, Franco's catch was enshrined in the lexicon of
legends under the heading, "The Immaculate Reception."

Doug Flutie—Hail Mary: Although it is widely believed that former
Dallas Cowboy quarterback Roger Staubach was responsible for
concocting the catchphrase "Hail Mary," it was a stick of diminutive
dynamite named Doug Flutie who put a face on Mary's grace. At
five-foot-ten, Flutie looked more like a jockey than a jock, though his
slight stature could hardly contain his competitiveness. In his final
season with the Boston College Eagles, Flutie was leading the nation in a bevy of offensive categories and was a considered a top-line
contender for the Heisman trophy. In 1984, in a nationally televised

game against the University of Miami, Flutie captured the attention of scribes and spectators around the country. After Miami marched down the field to take a 45–41 lead in the closing moments of the game, Flutie consulted his celestial playbook and pulled out a passing prayer that would forever be dubbed the Hail Mary. Smothered deep in his own territory with only six seconds remaining on the play clock, Flutie avoided a horde of Hurricanes, scrambled to his right, and heaved a pass toward the end zone. The missile sailed through a maze of outstretched arms before settling in the grasp of Boston receiver Gerard Phelan, who fell to the field clutching the game-winning pass that delivered a 47–45 victory to the enthroned Eagles.

- *On November 17, 1968, in a game referred to as the Heidi Bowl, the New York Jets had the lead over the Oakland Raiders 32–29. With 1:05 left on the clock, television network NBC cut away to the classic children's movie Heidi, preventing millions of viewers from seeing Oakland's comeback, 43–32.*

- *Linebacker Chuck Howley was the first player voted Super Bowl MVP after playing on the losing team. It was Super Bowl V (1970), when Howley was with the Dallas Cowboys.*

- *The first regular season overtime game ever played ended in a tie. On September 22, 1974, the Steelers and Broncos played to a 35–35 tie. Oddly, the NFL instituted overtime in order to reduce the number of tied games.*

- *In 1980, Green Bay Packers kicker Chester Marcol ran in his own blocked field-goal attempt for a touchdown to beat the Chicago Bears 12–6.*

- *Early in the 1968 season, the Baltimore Colts lost Johnny Unitas to an injury. Quarterback Earl Morrall stepped up and eventually led the Colts to a 13–1 record. Morrall led the league in passing, with 2,909 yards and 26 touchdowns.*

WHAT DO YOU MEAN BY THAT?

✳ ✳ ✳ ✳

"Down in the dumps"

The word "dump" calls to mind nasty stuff, but this phrase has nothing to do with garbage or bodily functions. The origins of this expression are from the German word *dumpf*, which means "oppressive" or "heavy." To be "down in the dumps" means to feel weighted down by worry.

Loophole

If your medieval castle is under attack, we suggest you fire arrows at your enemy through the narrow windows in the castle walls. These "loops" make it hard for arrows to get in but easy for them to get out. Nowadays, the word *loophole* refers to a slick escape or a clever way out of a sticky situation.

Burlesque

If you're planning to attend a burlesque show, get ready for raunchy dialogue, biting satire, and lots of scantily clad dancers! Burlesque theater became popular in the United States around the beginning of the 20th century and has etymological roots in the Italian *burla*, which means "ridicule." Most burlesque shows feature slapstick comedy with an irreverent attitude, and though it's usually the performers who ridicule one another, the audience is fair game, too.

Marshmallow

The Proto-Indo-European root *mori* means "body of water, lake, or sea." "Marsh" comes to us by way of *mori*, and "mallow" is likely from the Latin word *malva* ("to soften"). Through translations and a good measure of miscommunication, you get "marsh mallow," the name for "a plant that grows in marshes." The root of the marsh mallow yields a thick, gluey sap that was first used for medicinal purposes; in the late 19th century, a confection was created from it. These days, the marshmallows you put in your cocoa are mostly sugar and gelatin, with no sap in sight.

"The luck of the Irish"

The roots of this phrase vary according to the person
you ask. Some say the "luck" of the people of Ireland
is anything but: They've dealt with Viking wars, English takeovers, potato famines, terrorism, etc. Others
believe that the Irish people's ability to persevere through such hardship is actually a testament to their incredibly good luck.

Nightmares

In Roman times, people thought bad dreams were caused by an
incubus or succubus, demons that slid into bed with a sleeping
victim. These spirits of ill will were later called "night hags" or "night
demons." Though "nightmare" sounds as if it describes an insomniac
horse, *mare* is the Anglo-Saxon word meaning "incubus."

"On the nose"

This term, which means to be "precisely on," comes from the early
days of radio broadcasting. Producers would use hand signals to let
their announcers (isolated in soundproof booths) know if the program was running on schedule. If it was, they'd touch their finger to
their nose.

"The whole shebang"

Walt Whitman wrote of "the whole shebang" in *Specimen Days* in
the mid-1800s, but he likely got it from the Anglo-Irish word for a
shabby—*shebeen*, or "temporary dwelling." Mark Twain liked the
sound of "shebang" and used it several times in his own works. The
expression has come to mean "all of it," as in, "That diamond thief
didn't just steal one necklace—he took the whole shebang."

"Armed to the teeth"

This phrase is said to be pirate terminology that means "to be well
equipped with weaponry." In the late 1600s, Jamaica was a British
colony surrounded by Spanish and Portuguese property, and the harbor town of Port Royal was a popular center for buccaneers engaged
in constant, heavy attacks against the Spanish. To boost their efficiency, pirates would carry many weapons at once, including a knife
held in their teeth for maximum arms capability.

Talk to the Expert
BEEF BONER

✳ ✳ ✳ ✳

*Surviving employment in the meat packing industry
is no joking matter. When people realize how dangerous
this job is, the laughter usually dies down.*

Q: Most people would call you a butcher. In any event, you make a living cutting meat away from bones, and yet you still have all your fingers.

A: Many beef boners lose fingers—or worse. There is a reason many people who grow up around meat packing plants are not interested in this line of work. I make a daily, concerted effort to be extremely attentive and careful. You have to watch for other people's knives as much as your own.

Q: Describe your boning knife.

A: It's similar to the steak knives you use at your dinner table. The blade is not very broad, it's smooth rather than serrated, and it has a very sharp tip. It's surprisingly small, considering how much animal flesh it slices up in a day. Some people imagine me waving a big meat cleaver all over the place, but that just happens in the movies.

Q: Do you cut up the whole cow?

A: Beef boners tend to specialize in one part of the animal—which is not usually a cow, but rather a steer. Whether I am working as a chuck boner, loin boner, ham boner, round boner, or blade boner, the basic work is the same: Cut out defects, bones, fat, and anything else people don't want to eat. You probably don't want me to go into too much detail here.

Q: What's the best way to avoid injury?

A: Stay alert and keep your boning knife sharp. It's true that a dull knife is more dangerous than a sharp one. Dull knives slip, and they make you work harder. The last thing I can be is fatigued.

SPIDERS

✳ ✳ ✳ ✳

Studies have shown that you're never more than ten feet away from a spider, and one estimate puts you as close as three feet. To be "spider-free" you'd have to go into space in a fumigated capsule. Rather than flee, read these facts and appreciate our amazing arachnids.

- Unlike insects, spiders cannot fly—but they can balloon! Young spiderlings pull out silk until the breeze can lift them into the sky. Most don't travel high or far, but some have been seen at altitudes of 10,000 feet and on ships more than 200 miles from land. Most ballooners are very small spiderlings, but adult spiders have been captured by planes with nets.

- Jumping spiders are smart. Studies have shown that they can solve simple 3-D puzzles; they also learn the behavior patterns of other spiders in order to capture them.

- Female wolf spiders carry their egg sacs behind them, attached to their spinnerets. After the spiders emerge, they crawl onto the mother's abdomen and hold on while she actively runs and hunts. After about a week, the spiderlings molt to a larger size and then take off to live on their own.

- While most spiders live for one year, a few may have more than one generation each year. Some spiders can live 3 to 4 years, and certain tarantulas are known to live for 25 years or longer.

- Male spiders are almost always smaller than the females and are often much more colorful. Some males are so small that they actually look like they're newly hatched.

- Male spiders are unique among all animals in having a secondary copulatory organ. While most animals spread their sperm in water or insert them into the female, mature male spiders weave a small "sperm" web. They place a drop of semen on the web, suck it up with their pedipalps (special structures on their first "arm"), and then use the pedipalp to insert the sperm into a female.

- It is estimated that up to 1 million spiders live in one acre of land—in the tropics, that the number might be closer to 3 million.

- Some spiders live underwater all of their lives. They surface to collect a bubble of air, which acts as an underwater lung. An underwater spider fills its bell-shape web with air bubbles and derives oxygen from them.

- The fisher or raft spider is able to walk across the surface of a pond or other body of water by skating like a water strider. When it detects prey (insects or tiny fish) under the surface, it can quickly dive to capture its dinner.

- Spiders are not only predators, they are often prey. Many birds and animals love to feed on them. The coatimundi, a relative of the raccoon, are fond of eating large tarantulas.

- Hummingbirds use the silk from spider webs to weave together the sticks that form their nests.

- A few species of trapdoor spiders use their abdomens to "plug" their burrows to protect themselves from wasps. The abdomen is flat on the back end and tough enough that a wasp's stinger can't penetrate it.

- Spiders eat more insects than birds and bats (combined) eat, so they should be considered another of human's best friends. They play a big role in controlling insect populations.

- The decoration in the web of some orb-weaving spiders serves a variety of purposes: It can be a warning so birds don't fly into the web, an attractant so insect-prey fly in on purpose, or an "umbrella" to shade the spider from the hot sun.

- Some orb weavers make very unusual webs. One variety greatly increases the area above the center, creating what is sometimes called a ladder web that extends eight feet above the spider.

- Bolas spiders make webs of a single line with a sticky "ball," or bola, on the end. These spiders can twirl the bolas in the air. Moths are attracted to the smell and fly toward the web until they hit it and stick. The spider then reels in its catch.

MOST MISUNDERSTOOD: REVOLUTIONARY WAR COMBAT

* * * *

*Why did the Colonies win independence from
King George III and the British?*

Most Americans chalk it up to British stupidity and Yankee ingenuity. "The boneheaded British," they might say, "marched like scarlet practice targets, not even aiming their muskets, while the clever Colonials coolly picked them off from behind rocks and trees." But that's actually hogwash and twaddle.

In fact, the British fighting system was superior in that the massed volley system forced soldiers to do everything in unison. If you let every soldier fight his own way—as most professional armies did—your force was far less effective. Some men would simply run away; others would stick around, crying and praying. More soldiers than you think would shoot blindly, even firing deliberately high so as not to kill. A few would mistakenly shoot their ramrods along with the first volley, thus rendering the musket useless past bayonet range. The remaining minority might actually harm the enemy.

In the poorly trained Colonial forces, discipline was often that bad. In the European system, everyone loaded and fired together. An officer or sergeant directed that volley where it would do some good. The British knew and followed a core principle of military science: Bash the key sector with all your might.

So where did we get this "from behind rocks and trees" notion? Small groups of Colonials indeed sniped at British troops as the Redcoats marched from place to place. Steady, harassing fire is annoying but doesn't in itself win a battle—much less a war.

The Colonials won largely because of perseverance. But there were other factors that caused a major pain in His Majesty's Royal Posterior:

• The British accounts go on endlessly about humidity, heat, cold, wind, sleet, snowdrifts, cloudbursts, and other nasty weather conditions. Most British soldiers must have wondered, "What does my

Sovereign want with this wretched hellhole? I notice he doesn't choose to live here."

- Being half-naked and short on food and ammo offers only one benefit: You travel light. The well-supplied, smartly uniformed British were slower.

- The attitude of the British domestic anti-war movement was this: "If those insane Yankees want to surrender all the benefits of membership in a great empire, good riddance! Why spend money and lives to keep them in our fold?"

- British leaders' constant indecision, infighting, and resigning undermined the cause. King George III must have wanted to crack their bewigged heads together. It wasn't always clear whose side they were on.

- The Royal Navy was (and is) the senior British service. By comparison, the army was a red-coated stepchild of sorts, often undermanned. It resorted to the help of German mercenaries (the famed "Hessian troops"), many of whom deserted. The British army lacked the means to field enough forces to pacify the Colonies.

- *The Olive Branch Petition, written by John Dickenson of Pennsylvania, was approved by the Second Continental Congress in July 1775. The document attempted to assure King George III that the colonists were loyal to him, and it requested that he respond to their complaints. Instead, he quickly declared the colonists in rebellion.*

- *The first major battle of the Revolutionary Was was the Battle of Bunker Hill, which took place in 1775. It followed the smaller opening battles at Lexington and Concord.*

- *The final major battle of the war was the Battle of Yorktown in October 1781. It ended with the surrender of the British.*

Folklore: Myth or Truth?
THE DEATH OF DAVY CROCKETT

✳ ✳ ✳ ✳

You can start fights in Texas suggesting that the Alamo fighters—Davy Crockett was prominent among them—didn't die fighting to the last man. But do we really know that they did?

First, the orthodox version: Davy Crockett grew up rough and ready in Tennessee, wrestling bears and otherwise demonstrating his machismo. He went into politics, lost an election, and moved to Texas. His homespun, informal braggadocio went over just fine in what would soon become the self-proclaimed Republic of Texas. Mexico, of course, didn't grant that Texas had the right to secede. General Antonio López de Santa Anna invaded the Republic and cornered one group of its defenders in Alamo Mission, San Antonio de Béxar (now just San Antonio). Shortly before independence, Crockett had signed on to fight for Texas.

Why question that? Most of the questions stem from the memoir of a Mexican officer who fought there, Jóse Enrique de la Peña. De la Peña says that seven captives, including Crockett, were brought before Santa Anna and murdered in cold blood after the battle. He also says that Crockett took refuge in the Alamo as a neutral foreigner rather than as a volunteer militiaman. That poses authenticity problems, because there was no logical reason for Crockett to be at the Alamo unless he planned to fight in its defense.

It's worth noting that de la Peña says he found the execution appalling. However, the Mexican officer also tells an implausible version of the death of Colonel William Travis, commander in charge of the siege of the Alamo: He claims to have seen it occur, but there's little chance de la Peña could have positively identified Travis at a distance. This was, after all, a battle with thick black-powder smoke, hand-to-hand combat, and concealment.

What evidence supports the orthodox version? Travis's slave, Joe, survived the battle and says Travis died defending the north wall (not where de la Peña has him). Joe also says he saw Crockett's body surrounded by dead Mexican soldiers, and an officer's wife who survived also testifies that Crockett died in battle. Santa Anna himself didn't say anything about executing Crockett in his after-action report; he did say that Crockett's body was found along with those of other leaders, and he didn't make a big deal of that.

Why is it contentious? The memory of the Alamo is a Texan cultural rallying point: That's why it's folklore. Opposing this view is a revisionist stance that seems so ready to dismiss tales of military valor that it dumps the orthodox account as too simple and perfect to be true. Either side has generally drawn a conclusion and seeks evidence to support it.

Do we know? So much happened at Alamo Mission between February 23 and March 6, 1836, that we will never know. It is plausible that some wounded survivors, possibly dying, were executed after the battle; that doesn't negate anyone's heroism. What's lacking is compelling, credible evidence to contradict the eyewitnesses who report no such thing. Absent that evidence, and with de la Peña's writing a questionable account well after the fact, the weight of documentation suggests that Davy Crockett went down fighting.

- *Crockett ran away from home at the age of 13.*

- *Despite having no formal education, Crockett was elected to serve in Congress three times and also served in the Tennesse legislature.*

- *The name of Crockett's rifle was "Betsy."*

- *Crockett's autobiography,* A Narrative of the Life of David Crockett, of the State of Tennessee, *was published in 1834; it is not known if it was written by ghostwriters or if he wrote it himself.*

IN THE YEAR...1959

✳ ✳ ✳ ✳

- President Dwight Eisenhower signs executive orders proclaiming Alaska and Hawaii the 49th and 50th states of the union.

- The Saint Lawrence Seaway opens North America's Great Lakes to ocean-going ships.

- Fidel Castro's forces are victorious in the Cuban revolution, and the United States recognizes the new government.

- New York City considers lobbying for statehood.

- Typhoon Vera hits Japan, causing vast destruction and the deaths of more than 5,000 people.

- The first Barbie doll is produced.

- Buddy Holly, Ritchie Valens, and the Big Bopper are killed together in a plane crash.

- The Guggenheim Museum, designed by architect Frank Lloyd Wright, opens in New York City.

- Revered jazz singer Billie Holiday dies.

- Oklahoma legalizes alcoholic beverages after 51 years.

- The Motown record label is founded in Detroit, Michigan.

- Haloid launches the first copying machine, the "Xerox 914," which is able to reproduce documents at the press of a button.

- Fleeing Chinese aggressors in Tibet, the Dalai Lama seeks and is granted refuge in India.

- Representatives of 12 nations agree to preserve the world's last undeveloped continent. The Antarctic Treaty made the continent a military-free zone for cooperative scientific research.

- After being struck in the face by a puck, Montreal Canadiens goalkeeper Jacques Plantes becomes the first player in professional hockey to wear a protective mask.

COFFEE CULTURE

✳ ✳ ✳ ✳

- Coffee is the most popular beverage in the world, with more than 400 billion cups consumed each year. More than 450 million cups of coffee are consumed in the United States every day.

- About half of the people in the United States over the age of 18 (that's 107 million) drink coffee every day. On average, each coffee drinker consumes three and a half cups each day.

- The word *coffee* comes from Kaffa, a region in Ethiopia where coffee beans may have been discovered.

- As early as the ninth century, people in the Ethiopian highlands were making a stout drink from ground coffee beans boiled in water.

- Coffee is grown in more than 50 countries in South America, Central America, Asia, Africa, and the Caribbean.

- In 1971, a group of Seattle-based entrepreneurs opened a coffee shop called Starbucks. Today there are more than 6,000 Starbucks outlets in the United States. The chain also operates stores in 36 other countries.

- Nearly 25 million farmers worldwide depend on coffee crops for their economic livelihood.

- Coffee contains caffeine, the stimulant that gives you that "lift." Caffeine is the most popular drug in the world, and 90 percent of people in the United States consume it in some form every day.

- Despite what you may believe, dark-roast coffee has less caffeine than coffee that's been lightly roasted.

- Scandinavia boasts the highest per-capita coffee consumption in the world. On average, people in Finland drink more than four cups of coffee a day.

- After oil, coffee is the world's second-most-valuable commodity exported by developing countries. The global coffee industry earns an estimated $60 billion annually.

CANADIAN SUPERLATIVES

✳ ✳ ✳ ✳

Canada is one of the largest and most livable countries on Earth and naturally has a lot of biggest, firsts, and bests.

North America's largest mall: Spread across 121 acres, the West Edmonton Mall in Alberta has more than 800 stores, an ice rink where the Edmonton Oilers practice, an indoor waterpark, miniature golf, hotels, and much more. There are spaces for 20,000 cars in what is considered the largest parking lot in the world.

World's largest bitumen deposits: Two-thirds of the world's bitumen reserves are in Alberta. Why, you might ask, would anyone not studying ancient Egyptian mummification care about bitumen? Because if you refine bitumen, it can fuel your automobile.

World's tallest totem pole: At 173 feet tall, the totem pole on Cormorant Island, British Columbia, represents the numerous tribes of the Kwakwaka'wakw nation. The artists carved all but five feet of the pole from a single tree.

Longest sea-fogs on Earth: The Grand Banks, off Newfoundland, have less than a half-mile visibility one-third of the year.

World's biggest herd of caribou: The George River herd of northern Labrador is estimated at 750,000.

Largest recorded bluefin tuna catch: A 1,496-pound beast was caught in 1979 by Ken Fraser of Auld Cove, Nova Scotia. Before he finally landed it, his depth-charge launcher failed and his harpoon gun broke.

First fully retractable stadium roof: Toronto Skydome (Ontario), 1989. *Stade Olympique* (Olympic Stadium in Montreal was supposed to be the first, but the roof didn't work correctly and was eventually replaced with a non-retractable roof, which doesn't work much better.

First recorded game of ice hockey: Some say it was played in 1855, in Kingston, Ontario (the first penalty box was probably built by the end of the first period). The first recorded public game was played in 1875 in Montreal.

World's longest skating area: On the Rideau Canal in Ottawa, Ontario, you can skate 11 miles if you wish to (many Canadians do).

North America's northernmost national park: Situated on Ellesmere Island, Nunavut, Quttinirpaaq National Park issues quite a unique advisory: "Visitors traveling in this park must carry appropriate gear, and must be self-reliant and able to handle any medical or wildlife-related emergencies on their own. Many hazards may be encountered—from dangerous river crossings to severe cold and storms. However, the biggest hazard is the profound remoteness of Quttinirpaaq and the distance from any medical or rescue assistance. There may be few if any other visitors in the park at the same time as your visit."

World's largest winter snow removal: Montreal averages 42 million metric tons of snowblowing, shoveling, plowing, and other forms of removal per year. This is the real reason behind many residents' love of french fries covered with gravy and cheese curds—it keeps them warm during the six months of this drudgery.

North America's first tidal-power-generation plant: Annapolis Tidal Generating Station, Nova Scotia, opened in 1984. It makes sense when your tides vary by 50 feet.

World's longest undersea phone cable: This runs from Port Alberni, British Columbia, to Sydney, Australia, via Hawaii and Fiji. Measuring 9,711 miles, it's more than a third of the world's circumference.

World's largest deliberate non-nuclear explosion: This event occurred on April 5, 1958, to blow up the sharp rocks of the shipping hazard at Seymour Narrows, British Columbia. This thing had snagged 120 ships since records were kept, averaging more than one per year.

First policewoman in North America: Rose Fortune of Annapolis Royal, Nova Scotia, took the position in 1830.

SCULPTOR JEFF KOONS

* * * *

- Koons rose to fame and fortune in the 1980s with his use of kitsch imagery and what some believe to be a dark sense of humor. His work is usually classified into either the "Neo-Pop" or "Post-Pop" categories of modern art.

- Koons's most famous exhibit comes from his collection of "ready-made" sculptures. *Equilibrium* consists of a collection of basketballs floating at varying levels in several aquariums, accompanied by a series of Nike advertisements painted in oil.

- *Puppy* is Koons's 43-foot topiary structure in the shape of a West Highland terrier, erected over a steel frame and covered in multicolored flowers. *Puppy* was originally exhibited in Germany in 1992 and then went on a well-received world tour. The structure now guards the Guggenheim museum in Bilbao, Spain, where it has come to be a kind of mascot for the city.

- Koons's *Popeye* painting and sculptures were priced from $500,000 to $650,000 in 2004. Prices for sculptures in Koons's epic *Celebration* series started at $1.5 million, and bids went up to $5 million for his massive stainless-steel *Balloon Dog*.

- As part of a series of work called *Banality,* Koons created a ceramic sculpture in 1988 titled *Michael Jackson and Bubbles.* Painted mostly in metallic gold and white, the sculpture depicts Jackson and his pet chimpanzee in matching outfits.

- Just before the dedication of *Puppy* to the Bilbao Guggenheim, three people attempted to plant explosives-filled flowerpots near the sculpture. They were apprehended by police before any damage was done.

- These days, Koons seldom produces any work himself. He is the self-proclaimed "idea man" and allows his foundry and assistants to create pieces for him.

Talk to the Expert
FOOD STYLIST

✳ ✳ ✳ ✳

Q: People have hair stylists, but what's a food stylist?

A: My job description is one sentence long: I get food ready for its close-up. As you may have heard, people eat first with their eyes. In Japan, in fact, people consider food presentation an art form and will hesitate to eat something if it looks unattractive. That aesthetic guides my work.

Q: Do you cook the food as well as style it?

A: Yep, everything—I have the training of a professional chef. My team shops for the ingredients, cooks the dish, and then makes sure it looks as it should on film. And filming could happen at any time, so we often have to perform a lot of maintenance to keep the dish looking fresh. When photographers have to shoot a banquet scene, I know I've done my job well if I've prepared a table full of food that is six hours old and too cold to eat—and it's still irresistible.

Q: Talk about your tool kit. What equipment does it take to style food?

A: In addition to standard kitchen utensils, I use art supplies such as palette knives and brushes, even beauty supplies such as eyebrow tweezers and bobby pins. A lot of food styling involves sculpture. I use glue, oil, cotton swabs, paper towels, and a lot of other inedible materials to create an "exhibit" that looks like a pile of food.

Q: Can people eat your styled food?

A: Some of it, some of the time—mainly when I first prepare it. Since vegetables need to look fresh, I will blanch them rather than cook them. I doubt you'd want to eat my ice cream, which is a mixture of shortening, corn syrup, and powdered sugar that doesn't melt under the lights. My clear acrylic ice cubes don't melt, but they also won't chill your drink. If I were you, I would stay away from the pancakes, because I pour motor oil on them to simulate syrup.

FOOTBALL

* * * *

*The game of football today bears little resemblance
to the disorganized brawls of the late 1800s.
As many college rivalries pass their hundredth meetings,
football has trumped baseball as America's sport.*

1861: The first documented football game (essentially rugby) is played at the University of Toronto.

1869: An era begins as Princeton travels to Rutgers for a rousing game of "soccer football." The field is 120 yards long by 75 yards wide, about 25 percent longer and wider than the modern field. It plays more like soccer than modern football, and with 25 players on a side, the field is a crowded place. Rutgers prevails 6–4.

1874: McGill University (of Montreal) and Harvard play a hybrid version of rugby. The rule changes soon affect the game in the United States.

1875: The game ball officially becomes an egg-shape rugby ball. Henceforth the field is supposed to be 100 yards long by 53.5 yards wide (though this won't be fully standard for some years), so teams are cut to 15 players per side. Referees are added to the game.

1876: With the addition of the crossbar, goal posts now look like an *H*.

1880–1885: The modern game's fundamentals are introduced. A downs system goes into use (five yards in three downs equals a first down), along with the scrimmage line and yard lines. Teams are now 11 on a side. Major changes to scoring: A field goal is worth five points, a touchdown and conversion count four points each, and a safety is two points. The first play-calling signals and planned plays come about.

1892: Desperate to beat the Pittsburgh Athletic Club team, Allegheny Athletic Association leaders create the professional football player by hiring Pudge Heffelfinger to play for their team. Heffelfinger plays a pivotal role in AAA's 4–0 victory.

1894: The officiating crew is increased to three: a referee and two bodyguards, also known as the umpire and linesman.

1896: Only one backfield man may now be in motion before the snap, and he can't be moving forward.

1897: A touchdown now counts as five points.

1902: College football is getting a little unbalanced as Michigan, having outscored its regular schedule 501–0, drubs Stanford 49–0 in the first Rose Bowl. The first African-American professional football player takes the field: Charles Follis of the Shelby (Ohio) Athletic Club.

1905: Disgusted at the mortality rate among college football players, Teddy Roosevelt tells the Ivy League schools: "Fix this blood sport, or I'll ban it." Rules Committee (forerunner of the NCAA) comes into being and legalizes the forward pass, bans mass plays responsible for brutish pileups and deaths, establishes the neutral zone along the line of scrimmage, and prohibits players from locking arms.

1909: Now a field goal is worth three points. This rule will stand, but the distances, hash marks, and goal posts will change many more times. In Canada, the first Grey Cup game is played—at this phase, it's a collegiate event.

1910: Seven players must now be on the line of scrimmage when the ball is snapped, establishing the basic offensive formation concept. The forward pass becomes commonplace in college football.

1912: Rules Committee determines that a touchdown is worth six points, and it adds a fourth down. It is now practical to punt.

1921: Fans hear the first commercially sponsored radio broadcast of a game, with University of Pittsburgh beating West Virginia 21–13.

1922: The American Professional Football Association becomes the National Football League.

1932: The NFL begins keeping statistics. Collegiate football doesn't see the benefits of official stat keeping until 1937.

1933: There is a major NFL rule change: The passer can throw from anywhere behind scrimmage. (Before this, he had to be five yards behind scrimmage.)

1934: The modern football takes its current shape after a couple of decades of gradual evolution from the egglike rugby ball.

1937: College football players must now have numbers on the fronts and backs of their jerseys.

1939: The Brooklyn Dodgers–Philadelphia Eagles game is the first to beamed into the few New York homes that can afford TV sets in this late-Depression year. Helmets become mandatory in college football, and the pros follow within a decade.

1941: It's the end of the drop-kick score. Ray McLean boots a conversion off the turf in the NFL championship game. (Actually, it wasn't the last one kicked. In 2005, Doug Flutie created a sensation by doing it again.)

1946: The NFL's first major rival league, the All-America Football Conference, begins play. It lasts four seasons, with the Cleveland Browns winning all four titles.

1950: Rules now permit unlimited free substitution, opening a hole for platoon football (exclusive offensive or defensive squads).

1951: First coast-to-coast TV broadcast of an NFL game as the Los Angeles Rams face the Cleveland Browns in the league championship game. Face masks show up in the college game.

1956: The NFL penalizes face masking (except for the ball carrier, who can be slammed to the turf by the face cage until 1960).

1958: In college football, a run or pass for conversion now counts two points.

1960: The American Football League, the NFL's new rival, begins play. Everyone derides it as inferior, just like the old AAFC.

1967: The NFL offsets goal posts with a recessed curved pole in a "slingshot" shape. Super Bowl I is played: The Green Bay Packers beat the Kansas City Chiefs, 35–10.

1970: The AFL wins the Super Bowl, then merges into the NFL, creating the biggest sports-marketing titan of all time. (Ten modern NFL teams trace heritage to the AFL.)

1974: The NFL adds sudden-death overtime for regular-season games, moves the goal posts to the back of the end zone, moves kickoffs back from the 40- to the 35-yard line, and spots the ball at the line of scrimmage for missed field goals beyond the 20. Pass defense rules now restrict defenders, opening up the air game.

1975: Kicker/quarterback George Blanda of the Oakland Raiders finally hangs up his cleats at the age of 48.

1979–1980: No more blocking below the waist on kicks, refs are to whistle a play dead when a player has the quarterback in a death grip but has not yet slammed him to the turf, and personal-foul rules tighten up.

1987: Arena Football League season starts with four teams: the Chicago Bruisers, Denver Dynamite, Pittsburgh Gladiators, and the Washington Commandos.

1988: The NFL increases the play clock to 45 seconds between plays. Eventually this is shortened to 40 seconds. College still uses the 25-second play clock.

1991: The World League of American Football—history's first non–North American league—begins in Europe as a sort of NFL minor league. Europeans prefer soccer.

1994: Professional football institutes the option of either running or passing for two points (instead of kicking for one) after a touchdown.

1999: The NFL begins using instant replay challenge system, eliminating officiating errors forever.

2007: The NFL Europa, successor to the WLAF, finally shuts down, as Europeans still prefer soccer.

DOWN COMFORTERS

✳ ✳ ✳ ✳

- Down is the layer of soft feathers closest to a bird's skin, primarily on the breast. These feathers keep ducks and geese warm during chilly flights.

- Ancient down-filled quilts have been discovered through archeological digs in Norway, leading scientists to attribute the first use of goose down to the Vikings.

- Getting down from a goose isn't particularly bird-friendly, so if you're concerned with animal well-being, go for the synthetic stuff. Some birds are killed for their down; others undergo a traumatic "live plucking" every few months.

- Because its properties enable people to regulate their natural body temperature and maintain warmth, lightweight goose down is used to fill comforters, pillows, and outerwear such as vests and coats.

- The down in these items takes the form of clusters, similar to snowflakes. The clusters have fine filaments radiating out in every direction; these filaments expand and form air pockets that trap body heat, a process called "lofting."

- The more down an item contains, the warmer (and more expensive) the product will be. The insulation down provides is rated by "fill power," which reflects the size of down clusters and their related loft. Fill power is measured as the number of cubic inches one ounce of down occupies. A good down comforter will have a fill power of at least 575; more warmth is provided by comforters with fill powers up to 800.

- A down comforter can be expensive, but with proper care it will last for years. Every morning, give it a good shake to redistribute the down. Some people prefer to protect their comforter with a duvet, or cover. Follow the manufacturer's directions for cleaning (machine wash or dry-clean); between cleanings, occasionally hang your comforter out in the fresh air.

BIBLICAL MEASUREMENTS

✳ ✳ ✳ ✳

Handbreadth—on an adult hand, three to four fingers held together, or three to four inches

A Day's Journey—roughly 20 to 30 miles, half that when traveling in a large company (with women and children)

Sabbath's Day Journey—just over a half mile, in reference to restricted travel on the day of rest

Span—the width from the end of the thumb to the tip of the little finger, fully extended, which measured about nine inches

Cubit—about 18 inches, represented by the length of an adult arm from the point of the elbow to the tip of the middle finger

Bath—between six and eight gallons, which was the largest liquid measure used by the Jews in the Old Testament

Homer—less than eight bushels; originally signified "an ass load," or the amount a donkey could carry

Talent—75 pounds, the Bible's largest unit of measurement

Farthing—approximately 1/64 of a denarius, which was the average wage a worker would receive for a day's work

Mite—the smallest Jewish coin in use, which represented only half a farthing

Shekel— approximately 58 cents

Throughout history, many people have given a tithe of their earnings to their church. According to the Bible, a tithe is one-tenth, whether it's of a crop, a herd, or money.

GOOFY PLANES

✳ ✳ ✳ ✳

In a little over a century, humans have taken powered flight from rattletrap lattices covered with canvas to spy planes that circumnavigate the globe. In the process, we have come up with some creative aviation concepts.

Kalinin K-12 (first flew 1936): It was a big flying wing with no tail to speak of and vertical stabilizers at the wingtips. Incredible fact: This twin-engine prototype was made of canvas over a steel frame!

Messerschmitt Me-163 (1941): This was the only rocket interceptor ever sent to war. The "Komet" was a flying wing with a vertical stabilizer; it dropped disposable wheels after takeoff and landed on a ski. Its noxious fuel mix gave it eight minutes of powered flight: It climbed, made a pass, climbed again, made one more pass if feasible, and glided down to land once all fuel was exhausted.

Chance Vought XF5U-1 (1942): The comical Flying Pancake was aptly named. Imagine a big saucer with two large props in front and two vertical stabilizers in back. It might have been an outstanding naval aircraft, but by the time testing was done, the age of the jet fighter was here.

Fieseler Fi-103R (1944): We're so used to thinking of the pilotless German World War II V-1 "buzz bomb," we don't realize it was technically the Fi-103 cruise missile. The R variant had a pilot. Not surprisingly, it was difficult to make a safe bailout (much less to land); the jet engine intake was directly above and behind the cockpit.

Yokosuka MXY7 (1944): The Ohka ("Cherry Blossom") was designed for suicide attacks. It could neither take off nor land; a medium bomber carried it into battle. United States warplanes tended to shoot down the bombers short of the target, forcing them to launch the Ohkas too soon. Few reached their targets and fewer still harmed them.

Bachem Ba-349 (1945): Many odd aircraft were born of German World War II desperation, such as this ungainly vertical-launch wooden rocket interceptor. It was armed only with twenty-four 73mm unguided rockets, and once those were expended, the Ba-349 was to be disassembled in the air. The pilot and engine were to parachute down. Evidently, 36 were built for battle, and only two were crewed. Those both crashed, killing the pilots.

Taylor Aerocar (1949): After World War II, some people thought that private planes would become the new family cars. Moulton B. Taylor's Aerocar was a high-wing monoplane with an upside-down vertical stabilizer and a "pusher" (rear-mounted) propeller. The wings folded up for road travel. Clever idea, except that hardly anyone bought it.

Convair YF-7A (1953): You've likely noticed that there aren't very many jet-powered flying boats. Well, it has been tried. The YF-7A looked a lot like a Cold War delta-wing jet interceptor and could land on water. It had "hydro-skis" to help it get airborne. The skis caused a lot of vibration, however, and the Navy gave up on the aquatic jet fighter.

SNECMA C.450 (1959): You won't believe this. Picture a fat aluminum barrel with four tail fins raised on silly little casters. Now cut the beaky nose off an F-14 Tomcat and mount it vertically atop the barrel, and you have the *Coléoptère* ("Beetle"). It couldn't taxi—a dump-truck-like launch trailer had to maneuver it into takeoff position. After the prototype went splat, so did the C.450 program.

Martin Marietta X-24B (1973): A rocket-powered research vehicle that looked like a big dart—something Evel Knievel would have jumped over Hell's Canyon. Long and thin with wings swept so sharply it hardly had any, it flew better than you'd think. It didn't become the next dominant fighter, but it enabled some useful testing.

Antonov An-225 (1988): This gargantuan six-jet-engine Soviet design was created to haul their space shuttle into orbit. You could barely park it on two football fields side by side. The An-225 had 32 landing wheels; it could lift a more than 550,000 pounds of cargo.

TECHNOLOGY OF THE FUTURE

✳ ✳ ✳

In case you've grown bored with the advances in technology over the past couple of decades, brace yourself for some of the breakthroughs to come.

- **Photo Tourism:** Billons of photos will be combined online so you can see objects and places in 3D from any angle in panorama. Existing software can collect images from all the different photo-sharing pages on the Web, and it's just a matter of time before it all comes together for sightseeing via computer.

- **Virtual Earth:** Real-imaging Global Positioning Systems will enable you to access any location at any time. Soon you will be able to pull up a 3D map of San Francisco, for example, made of 10 million images, including 50,000 aerial photographs as well as shots taken at street level. Unlike Google Maps, this imaging will combine the street-level pictures with aerial photos.

- **Smart Clothing:** The Laboratory on Emerging Technologies is refining the ability to package computer processors into washable clothing, thereby offering personal access to information, connectivity, and entertainment.

- **Smart Thinking:** Remote computing using brainwaves is the high-tech hit of the future. Just slide on an electrode headband and it will translate the electrical impulses from your brain into keystrokes. Once you're in sync with your computer, all you have to do is imagine moving your hands, feet, or any object, and the corresponding action will take place on the screen.

- **Virtual Keyboard:** A tiny Bluetooth laser the size of a matchbook can project a keyboard on any flat surface and make it functional! For those of us attached to our physical keyboards, it even makes simulated clicking sounds when we type.

- **Surface Computing:** This technology has been introduced by Microsoft and will soon allow us to use a touch-based, visual computer on tables, countertops, and even floors.

I'm No Expert, But...
TECHNOLOGY 101

✳ ✳ ✳ ✳

*Some folks swim in the tide of technology;
others flounder and wave their arms for help, or simply
stay on shore. These questions were posed on
behalf of technological landlubbers.*

Q: What's virtual reality?

A: The fine art of having a computer mock up a realistic environment. "Virtual" just means "fake." Someday there may be electronically created virtual worlds where one sits in the equivalent of a sensory deprivation tank and experiences artificial touch, smell, sight, taste, and hearing. For now, a good (if less comprehensive) example is the pilot-training simulator. To the extent that they involve the simulation of flight, these approach virtual reality.

Q: What is a neural network?

A: Depends what kind you mean. A biological neural network has to do with actual brain function, the connections between one's neurons. An artificial neural network creates artificial intelligence using computer software. If you can program all the natural reactions of a deer to its environment, for example, perhaps you can make a virtual deer behave realistically using an artificial neural network.

Q: Is it true that the original computer bug was a literal insect?

A: It is. Before we had transistors and diodes—we now cram many millions of transistors on a single chip—we had vacuum tubes, which looked and worked somewhat like dim incandescent light bulbs. If a moth got in, attracted by the heat and glow of the tubes, it messed up the tubes, just as a drop of water on a hot light bulb will shatter it. This actually happened in 1945, when U.S. Navy Captain Grace Murray Hopper was working on a primitive computer at Harvard University. Though the moth story was thought by many to be a myth, Hopper was able to produce the page of the log she kept at the time, to which she had taped the offending moth.

NOW YOU SEE THEM, OR MAYBE YOU DON'T

✳ ✳ ✳ ✳

Reports of UFOs have been around since the pyramids or the Inca temples, both of which were allegedly constructed by visitors from outer space needing navigational aids. Judging from the following accounts, perhaps aliens are just doing a little celebrity watching.

John Lennon's song *Nobody Told Me* touches on his experience with a UFO. In 1974, the former Beatle reported seeing a UFO outside his apartment in New York City. As he and a friend watched, the UFO drifted away, changing its shape with each rotation. Lennon took photos of the craft, but when he attempted to develop the film, it turned out blank. Lennon's friend called the police, who had received two other calls on the incident, and the *New York Daily News*, which had received five calls reporting a UFO on the East Side that night. *The New York Times* allegedly hung up on him.

Astronaut **Gordon Cooper** participated in a United Nations panel discussion on UFOs in New York in 1985. In the discussion, Cooper said, "I believe that these extraterrestrial vehicles and their crews are visiting this planet from other planets, which obviously are a little more technically advanced than we are here on Earth. I feel that we need to have a top-level, coordinated program to scientifically collect and analyze data from all over the Earth concerning any type of encounter, and to determine how best to interface with these visitors in a friendly fashion."

Heavyweight boxing champ **Muhammad Ali** has also claimed to have seen UFOs hovering over New York City. The occurrence was said to have taken place early in his career while he was working with his trainer, Angelo Dundee, in Central Park. Just before dawn, the two men observed a large, round UFO as it came out from behind the city skyline and moved slowly across the sky, a sighting that lasted about 15 minutes. Ali claimed at least 16 sightings. In one, he was a passenger in a car motoring along the New Jersey Turnpike when a cigar-shaped craft hovered briefly over his vehicle.

Ronald Reagan is considered the first president to talk about the possibility of an alien invasion. He believed that if such a situation occurred, all the nations of the world should unite to fight off the attackers. Reagan even discussed this scenario with General Secretary Mikhail Gorbachev during their first summit meeting in Geneva in 1985.

Guitarist **Jimi Hendrix** often claimed to have been followed around by UFOs and frequently referred to them in his lyrics. In addition, Hendrix allegedly was saved from freezing to death in 1965 by an eight-foot-tall angel-like alien who thawed the snowdrift in which the musician's van was stuck. He also once told a *New York Times* reporter that he was actually from Mars.

During **Jimmy Carter**'s presidential election campaign of 1976, he told reporters that he once saw what could have been a UFO in 1969, before he was governor of Georgia. "It was the darndest thing I've ever seen," he said of the incident. He claimed that the object that he and a group of others had watched for ten minutes was as bright as the moon. Carter was often referred to as "the UFO president" after being elected because he filed a report on the matter.

Infamous UFOs

- *The Roswell Incident spurred widespread controversy over the July 1947 recovery of materials thought to be debris from a crashed alien craft near Roswell, New Mexico. Proponents of this theory continue to believe in a U.S. military cover-up.*

- *The Rendlesham Forest Incident refers to a number of alleged sighting of strange lights and an extraterrestrial spacecraft in Rendlesham Forest in Suffolk, England, in late December 1980. It is considered the best-known UFO incident in the United Kingdom.*

A CHRONICLE OF KISSING

✳ ✳ ✳ ✳

Smooching, necking, spit-swapping, lip-locking—whatever you call it, kissing can be one of life's more pleasurable experiences. We've uncovered the history and naughty little secrets of the kiss.

The First Kiss

Although human nature suggests that the first kiss would have been shared much earlier, anthropologists have traced the first recorded kiss to India in approximately 1500 B.C. Early Vedic documents report people "sniffing" with their mouths and describe how lovers join "mouth to mouth."

"With This Kiss, I Thee Wed"

The tradition that inspired the phrase "You may kiss the bride" probably originated in ancient Rome. To seal their marriage contract, couples kissed in front of a large group of people. The Romans had three different categories of kisses: *osculum*, a kiss on the cheek; *basium*, a kiss on the lips; and *savolium*, a deep kiss.

The Holy Kiss

In the early Christian church, congregants would greet one another with an *osculum pacis*, or holy kiss. This greeting was said to transfer spirits between the kissers. In the 13th century, the Catholic Church provided something called a "pax board," which the congregation could kiss instead of kissing each other. Until the 16th century, the holy kiss was part of the Catholic mass, though kissing the Pope's ring is something that's still practiced.

Butterfly Kiss

The strange but sweet butterfly kiss is named for its similarity to a butterfly's fluttering wings. Simply put your eye a whisper away from your partner's eye or cheek, and bat your lashes repeatedly.

Performance High

The adrenaline rush you get when you jump out of a plane or run a marathon is essentially the same rush you get from kissing. The neurotransmitters that fire when you're kissing cause the heart to beat faster and the breath to become deeper.

Kissing Competitions

Sideshows at the Olympic games of ancient Greece included kissing competitions. How one would have judged such a thing is hard to know, but similar competitions still crop up from time to time, usually for fund-raising purposes or simply for spectacle's sake.

Germ Theory

The human mouth is coated with mucus that is chock-full of microscopic bacteria. When you lock lips with someone, between 10 million and 1 billion bacterial colonies are exchanged. The good news: Saliva also contains antibacterial chemicals that neutralize the spit, preventing the transfer of germs.

- *The scientific name for kissing is* philematology.

- *More than 5,300 couples kissed for at least ten seconds in the Phillipines on Valentine's Day in 2005.*

- *The first on-film kiss occurred between John C. Rice and May Irwin in the movie* The Kiss *(1896).*

- *In the 1927 movie* Don Juan, *Estelle Taylor and Mary Astor received a total of 127 kisses from John Barrymore.*

- *People spend an average of two weeks of their lives kissing.*

- *In Hartford, Connecticut, it's a crime for a man to kiss his wife on Sunday; in Indiana, a man with a moustache is forbidden to "habitually kiss human beings"; and in Cedar Rapids, Iowa, it's illegal to kiss a stranger.*

Folklore: Myth or Truth?
JOHN WESLEY HARDIN—THE OLD WEST'S DEADLIEST GUN?

✳ ✳ ✳ ✳

Some credit this Texan with as many as 50 kills. Some call him a misunderstood Southern folk hero. What most obscures the facts about John Wesley Hardin is Hardin himself. He wrote a self-serving autobiography late in life, taking responsibility for many killings and painting himself as a sort of avenging angel against wrong. Some of his statements have been corroborated; others can't be.

- Hardin was born a minister's son in Bonham, Texas, in 1853. His parents named him for Methodism's founder, John Wesley.

- As a child, he was outdoorsy even by rural Western standards. John was an adventuresome young man, hunting and exploring with guns and dogs at an early age. This would later stand him in good stead when he spent several years with large numbers of people from Kansas, Indian Territory, or Texas chasing him around the bush and all the way to the Florida panhandle.

- John was 12 when the Civil War ended, and postwar Texas bred desperadoes and made them into folk heroes: The average white Texan of the day looked most leniently upon anyone who showed hostility to the Yankee occupiers.

- Hardin killed his first man when he was 15. After volleys of bragging, he and a crony wrestled with a local freedman named Mage Holshousen, a mature fellow with a brawny reputation. Two teens against a big strong guy wasn't as uneven as it sounds. Hardin murdered Holshousen the next day with a .44, point blank. The spree was on.

- Though a white jury at the time probably wouldn't have convicted John, he still went on the lam. At 16, he had a brief stint teaching school while the heat died down.

- Hardin claims to have done some killing—two white soldiers, one African-American soldier—in his early adult life while working as a cowboy for relatives. During this time, he also mastered the fine arts of spitting chew, gambling, and drinking—habits that would work against him for the rest of his life.

- Hardin's killings, alleged and claimed, followed a pattern: A situation would arise involving gambling and drinking, and someone would say the wrong thing. Given the opportunity to escalate things or calm them down, Hardin would do the former. All evidence says he was the epitome of pistol wizardry, a brilliant quick-draw artist and dead shot. Likewise, no one doubts his homicidal temper. He had allegedly killed 12 men by the time he was 17.

- How did Hardin get away with so many murders? Chalk it up to the times. There was little legal infrastructure in the West during his youth, but there was a lot of vigilante justice. If you kept moving, you could probably duck the consequences. He also had an uncanny ability to make friends with law enforcement; it seems he could be a likeable guy when he wasn't drunk and losing at cards. He could also be a dangerous man to pursue—sneaky and willing to lay in wait rather than run.

- The cattle business led Hardin through Indian Territory (now Oklahoma), with more alleged killings along the way, and up to Abilene, Kansas. Abilene was a wild cattle trailhead, and J. B. "Wild Bill" Hickok was its marshal. A town full of rowdy, drunken gamblers? John Wesley Hardin? This would not end well.

- The story goes that Hickok at one point tried to confront and disarm Hardin, and that Hardin proffered the pistols, then did the "border roll" (reversing the firearms in his hands to point them, loaded and ready, at Marshal Hickok). It's possible. Reliable accounts say that Hardin was a master of this trick, which was mostly a way for kids to shoot themselves by mistake while trying to impress their friends. We can only be sure that Hickok never disarmed Hardin, because John later shot someone and hurried out of Abilene.

- By the time Hardin got back to his home state, he'd supposedly ended 23 lives, and he was 18 years old.

- Hardin married and had children. His descendants naturally still take an interest in their kinsman. That's more than can be said for Hardin, who mostly neglected his entire family. That he was usually hiding out from the law isn't a great excuse; the law might have stopped bothering him had he stopped putting holes in people.

- Back in Texas, Hardin finally killed enough people to interest the law in hunting him down. He fled across the South to Florida with a big price on his head, using the name John Swain. Lawmen subdued him in a passenger rail car at Pensacola and hauled him back home to stand trial for murder. He was convicted of second-degree murder in 1877, and the jury sentenced him to 25 years of hard labor.

- Texas governor James Hogg released Hardin several years early. Why? Hardin's wife and the mother of his children had died while he was imprisoned, and he had kept his nose clean during the later part of his sentence. Hardin had done 17 years, and at the age of 42, he was now free to become a peaceable attorney and author.

- Unfortunately, he was also free to resume his habits of drinking and gambling. This led to more confrontations, more killings, and a rapid downward spiral. A constable finally shot John Wesley Hardin dead in 1895 without warning as he played dice in the Acme Saloon in El Paso.

- According to legend, the constable who killed Hardin, John Selman, did so over an unpaid debt. Apparently, Hardin had actually hired Selman to kill another man, allegedly the husband of a woman with whom Hardin was having an affair. Although Selman carried out his end of the bargain, Hardin neglected to pay him for the job. As a result, Selman tracked Hardin to the saloon and ended his life as well.

- Hardin's death tally could be as low as 20 or could have exceeded 50. Although he went out of his way in his autobiography to claim kills and paint himself as the ultimate bad guy, there may perhaps have been murders he didn't bother to mention. Was John Wesley Hardin comfortable with or perhaps even addicted to killing? On that charge, the record is fairly clear.

WORTH A FORTUNE: VERY RARE U.S. COINS

✳ ✳ ✳

Why are certain coins so valuable? Some simply have very low mintages, and some are error coins. In some cases (with gold, in particular), most of the pieces were confiscated and melted. Better condition always adds value.

The current mints and marks are Philadelphia (*P*, or no mark), Denver (*D*), and San Francisco (*S*). Mints in Carson City, Nevada (*CC*); Dahlonega, Georgia (*D*); and New Orleans (*O*) shut down long ago, which adds appeal to their surviving coinage. Here are the most prized and/or interesting U.S. coins, along with an idea of what they're worth:

1787 Brasher gold doubloon: It was privately minted by goldsmith Ephraim Brasher before the U.S. Mint's founding in 1793. The coin was slightly lighter than a $5 gold piece, and at one point in the 1970s it was the most expensive U.S. coin ever sold. Seven known; last sold for $625,000.

1792 half-disme (5¢ piece): *Disme* was the old terminology for "dime," so half a disme was five cents. George Washington supposedly provided the silver for this mintage. Was Martha the model for Liberty's image? If so, her hairdo suggests she'd been helping Ben Franklin with electricity experiments. Perhaps 1,500 minted; sells for up to $1.3 million.

1804 silver dollar: Though actually minted in 1834 and later, the official mint delivery figure of 19,570 refers to the 1804 issue. Watch out—counterfeits abound. Only 15 known; worth up to $4.1 million.

1849 Coronet $20 gold piece: How do you assess a unique coin's value? The Smithsonian owns the only authenticated example, the very first gold "double eagle." Why mint only one? It was a trial strike of the new series. Rumors persist of a second trial strike that ended up in private hands; if true, it hasn't surfaced in more than 150 years. Never sold; literally priceless.

1870-S $3 gold piece: Apparently, only one (currently in private hands) was struck, though there are tales of a second one placed in the cornerstone of the then-new San Francisco Mint building (now being renovated as a museum). If the building is ever demolished, don't expect to see it imploded. One known; estimated at $1.2 million.

1876-CC 20-cent piece: Remember when everyone confused the new Susan B. Anthony dollars with quarters? That's what comes of ignoring history. A century before, this 20-cent coin's resemblance to the quarter caused similar frustration. Some 18 known; up to $175,000.

1894-S Barber dime: The Barber designs tended to wear quickly, so any Barber coin in great condition is scarce enough. According to his daughter Hallie, San Francisco Mint director John Daggett struck two dozen 1894-S coins, mostly as gifts for his rich banker pals. Dad gave little Hallie three of the dimes, and she used one to buy herself the costliest ice cream in history. Twenty-four minted, ten known; as high as $1.3 million.

1907 MCMVII St. Gaudens $20 gold piece: This is often considered the loveliest U.S. coin series ever. Its debut featured the year in Roman numerals, unique in U.S. coinage. The first, ultra-high-relief version was stunning in its clarity and beauty, but it proved too time-consuming to mint, so a less striking (but still impressive) version became the standard. About 11,000 minted, but very few in ultra-high relief; those have sold for $1.5 million.

1909-S VDB Lincoln cent: It's a collectors' favorite, though not vanishingly rare. Only about a fourth of Lincoln pennies from the series' kickoff year featured designer Victor D. Brenner's initials on the reverse; even now, an occasional "SVDB" will show up in change. There were 484,000 minted; worth up to $7,500.

1913 Liberty Head nickel: This coin wasn't supposed to be minted. The Mint manufactured the dies as a contingency before the Buffalo design was selected for 1913. Apparently, Mint employee Samuel W. Brown may have known that the Liberty dies were slated for destruction and therefore minted five of these for his personal gain. One of the most prized U.S. coins—and priced accordingly at $1.8 million.

1913-S Barber quarter: Forty thousand of these were made—the lowest regular-issue mintage of the 20th century. Some Barbers wore so flat that the head on the obverse was reduced to a simple outline. Quite rare in good condition; can bring up to $24,000.

1915 Panama-Pacific $50 gold piece: This large commemorative piece was offered in both octagonal and round designs. Approximately 1,100 were minted; prices range from $40,000 to $155,000.

1916 Liberty Standing quarter: This coin depicts a wardrobe malfunction...except by design! Many were shocked when the new coin displayed Lady Liberty's bared breast. By mid-1917, she was donning chain mail. Like the Barber quarter before it, the Liberty Standing wore out rapidly. With only 52,000 minted in 1916, the series' inaugural year, a nice specimen will set you back nearly $40,000.

1933 St. Gaudens $20 gold piece: This coin is an outlaw. All of the Saint's final mintage were to be melted down—and most were. Only one specific example is legal to own; other surviving 1933 Saints remain hidden from the threat of Treasury confiscation. The legal one sold in 2002 for an incredible $7.6 million.

1937-D "three-legged" Buffalo nickel: A new employee at the Denver Mint tried polishing some damage off a die with an emery stick. He accidentally ground the bison's foreleg off, leaving a disembodied hoof. No telling exactly how many were struck, but they sure look funny. Up to $30,000.

1943 bronze Lincoln cent: This was the exciting year of the steel penny—except someone flubbed and minted a few on standard bronze planchets (coin blanks) left over from 1942. Surely the dozen known examples can't be all that exist—you might find this one in your pocket! A bronze Lincoln cent sold for $112,500 in 2000.

Fast Facts

- Lightning can strike up to 20 miles away from the originating storm. These bolts, called "Positive Giants," seem to randomly come from a clear sky. They are usually much more destructive than ordinary lightning.

- A typical lightning bolt is hotter than the surface of the Sun.

- The most active hurricane season on record was in 2005. So many storms formed that year that the National Hurricane Center ran out of names on its list and had to use Greek letters for the last six storms. What's more, there were a record-breaking four category-five monsters, including the devastating Katrina.

- Low barometric pressure generally indicates stormy weather, and high pressure signals calm, sunny skies. The lowest pressure ever recorded was 25.69 inches during Typhoon Tip in 1979. The highest pressure, 32.01 inches, was measured in 1968 on a cold New Year's Eve in northern Siberia.

- Crickets make good thermometers—to get a rough estimate of the temperature, count the number of times a cricket chirps in 15 seconds and add 40.

- Despite the popular saying, nowhere on Earth does it actually get hot enough to fry an egg on the sidewalk. The pavement would need to hit at least 158° F for the egg to cook, and even blacktop has been found to heat up to only 145° F.

- Ever had your favorite shirt lose its color from too much time in the sun? It happens when ultraviolet light breaks down the chemical bonds in the dyes and causes a bleaching effect.

- The coldest temperature ever recorded on Earth was a bone-chilling −128.6° F on July 21, 1983, at Vostok Station, Antarctica. The hottest was in El Azizia, Libya, on September 13, 1922, when the mercury hit 136° F.

FEELING STRESSED?

✳ ✳ ✳ ✳

- Almost nine out of ten adults have suffered from severe stress. As many as four out of ten adults are so stressed out that it affects their health. It is reported that 75 to 90 percent of all visits to the doctor are for symptoms caused by stress.

- In the United States, tranquilizers, antidepressants, and medications for anxiety account for one fourth of all prescriptions written.

- Studies show that 60 percent of all employee absences are due to stress. The number of employees who report that they are "highly stressed" is greater than at any time in history. Stress strong enough to cause disability has doubled over the past decade.

- Job stress is estimated to cost U.S. industry $300 billion annually, as assessed by absenteeism, diminished productivity, employee turnover, and direct medical, legal, and insurance fees.

- In a 14-year study of stress among 12,500 Swedes, those who had little control over their work were twice as likely to develop heart disease. Those with little support at work were nearly three times as likely to develop heart disease.

- About a million people each day in the United States are absent from work due to stress-related disorders.

- Stress is a significant contributing factor in cardiovascular disease, gastrointestinal disorders, skin problems, neurological disease, and emotional disorders. It also attacks the immune system, causing an increase in colds, herpes, arthritis, even cancer and AIDS.

- When you're under pressure and feeling tense or angry, stress hormones such as adrenaline and cortisol pour into your system. They make your blood pressure and heart rate rise. Your muscles tense and your blood sugar increases. These physical changes affect you for hours after the stress has passed and can lead to poor health.

- Post-traumatic stress disorder (PTSD) is delayed stress that can occur when people are exposed to a disturbing or frightening experience. Any extremely stressful situation can result in PTSD, whether someone is involved or just an observer.

- Post-traumatic sress disorder is commonly experienced by people who are exposed to physical or emotional violence; a car or airplane crash; a hurricane, fire, or war; or any other imminent threat of death.

- Stress can be good for you! Eustress is the stress you feel when you play a fun game, fall in love, have a baby, ride a roller coaster, or take a vacation.

- A survey conducted by the *Detroit Free Press* showed that 45 percent of people in the United States regularly engage in stress relief, with 23 percent participating in active relaxation such as meditation and 5 percent practicing yoga.

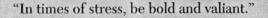

"In times of stress, be bold and valiant."

Horace

* * * *

"If you ask what is the single most important key to longevity, I would have to say it is avoiding worry, stress, and tension. And if you didn't ask me, I'd still have to say it."

George Burns

* * * *

"The life of inner peace, being harmonious and without stress, is the easiest type of existence."

Norman Vincent Peale

INVENTED BY CANADIANS

✳ ✳ ✳

Even Canadians might be surprised by how much has been discovered by sons and daughters of the North. It's a lot more than Alexander Graham Bell's telephone.

Automatic postal sorter (Dr. Maurice Levy, 1956): Revolutionizing mail delivery, his first model processed 30,000 letters an hour with an average of three errors. By 1957, a model was processing approximately 200,000 letters per hour.

Basketball (James Naismith, 1891): What most don't know is that the Ontarian invented the game to keep kids out of trouble. Teaching at a Massachusetts YMCA school, the Canadian pedagogue believed that a non-contact indoor sport would do wonders for kids' behavior.

Electric car heater (Thomas Ahearn, 1890): Like many Canadian inventions, this was a natural, considering the tender mercies of Canadian winters. It was one of this Ottawan's many patents relating to electric heat, including a hot water heater and iron.

Electric light bulb (Henry Woodward and Mathew Evans, 1874): These Canadians paved the way for Thomas Edison's later improvements to the bulb.

Flight suit (Dr. Wilbur Franks, 1941): This anti-gravity suit enabled combat pilots to withstand G-force pressure and extreme acceleration.

Hydrofoil boat (Alexander Graham Bell/Casey Baldwin, 1908): Fact: Water's drag slows down boats. In the early days of aviation, Bell and Baldwin wondered: What if you could mount a wing under a boat? The wing lifted the hull out of the water, improving both the speed and the ride.

Insulin process (Sir Frederick Banting, et. al., 1922): His team pioneered the understanding of insulin's central role in diabetes, then learned to produce it from the pancreas of a cow. Through injections, diabetics could now regulate their conditions. Banting's group deserves special credit for placing the invention into the public domain rather than making a lot of money with it.

Java (James Gosling, 1994): This Alberta native created the Java programming language. Most people think of Java as it relates to the Internet, but it's also found in devices as diverse as the Mars Rover, toasters, cars, and industrial-inventory tagging, to name a few.

Paint roller (Norman Breakey, 1940): Breakey was a victim of the legal system. He invented this useful painting method but didn't have the capital to defend his patent from those eager to make money from his idea. This may explain why he also invented a beer keg tap.

Plastic garbage bag (Henry Wasylyk, 1950): Family lore has it that Wasylyk invented it out of revenge, to compete with a company that had offered Prairie farmers (including Wasylyk) ruinously low prices for their wheat during the Depression. In any case, Union Carbide bought Wasylyk's idea, profitably.

Rotary snowplow (Dr. J.W. Elliott, 1869): Consider the difficulties in building a railroad across a country with snowy winters. How many people had to shovel off several thousand miles of track several months per year? Dr. Elliott, a dentist by trade, devised a fan to enable the locomotive to plow the snow itself.

Snowblower (Arthur Sicard, 1925): As a Quebecois farm boy, Sicard saw that snowstorm-blocked roads caused a lot of dairy spoilage. He unveiled the first "snowblowing" device in 1925, a truck with his fanlike snowblower in front. The walk-behind snowblower didn't come along until the 1950s, by which time Sicard's machines were working busily on the streets and roads of Canada.

Wonderbra (Louise Poirier, 1964): Poirier developed it while working for Canadelle, a company well known to Canadian women for more than half a century of firm support. The Wonderbra name dates back to the 1930s, but Poirier pushed the bustline maximizer version to market in 1964.

Talk to the Expert
ODONTOLOGIST

✳ ✳ ✳ ✳

"The remains were identified from dental records."
That statement requires the involvement of a forensic dentist, or
odontologist. Here's some insight into the job.

Q: You could be doing root canals on live, squirming people. But you look at the teeth of the dead and tell us about their final hours.

A: True confession: In dental school, I learned that I loved dentistry but couldn't stand inflicting pain. I got physically ill if I felt I was hurting someone, but I still had a strong interest in the science of teeth.

Q: How long has forensic dentistry been around?

A: In 1849, a Viennese opera house went up in flames, and a number of people were incinerated beyond recognition. Teeth are incredibly durable; the fact that we have the power to break a healthy tooth with our bite proves just how strong our jaws are. The fire victims' teeth enabled families to obtain the correct remains to bury and have closure. Odontology has grown with advancements in dental science and recordkeeping.

Q: This is a full-time job?

A: In larger cities it is. In smaller towns, most odontologists operate traditional dental practices and consult on the side as needed by local government. I like being near research universities, because my work also fits into archaeology.

Q: So you get to examine mummies?

A: Not quite. Bites leave patterns. What people eat and the way they chew suggests things about their diets. We can estimate age. All odontologic procedures begin with specific questions. In the case of a tooth from an ancient midden, they might include: "What species was this? From what period of time? How long did he or she live? What did this person usually eat?"

LETHAL LIGHTNING

✳ ✳ ✳ ✳

*There are about 25 million lightning strikes per year in
the United States, and for every 83,000 flashes, there's one injury.
For every 345,000 zaps, there's one death. Here are the
states with the most lightning fatalities (since 1959).*

Florida: 440
Texas: 200
North Carolina: 186
Ohio: 140
New York 136
Tennessee: 139
Louisiana: 136
Colorado: 132
Maryland: 123
Pennsylvania: 126

- In any year in the United States, the odds of being struck by lightning are 1 in 700,000. The odds of being struck in your lifetime are 1 in 3,000.

- Ice in a cloud can contribute to the development of lightning. As ice particles swirl around, they collide and cause separation of electrical charges. Positively charged ice crystals rise to the top of the storm cloud, and negatively charged particles drop to the lower parts of the storm cloud. These enormous charge differences can cause lightning.

- If your hair happens to stand on end during a storm, it could indicate that positive charges are rising through you toward the negatively charged part of the storm. If this ever occurs, get indoors immediately.

- Every year, lightning-detection systems in the United States monitor some 25 million strikes of lightning from clouds to ground during approximately 100,000 thunderstorms. It is estimated that Earth is struck by an average of more than 100 lightning bolts every second.

MEN'S SOCIETIES

✳ ✳ ✳ ✳

*A fraternal organization is a group of men who bond
through rituals, handshakes, and sometimes uniforms. They usually
have overlapping missions, whether emphasizing fellowship,
patriotism, religion, or philanthropy, and most are particularly
active in community service. Here are some of the most recognizable,
along with notable members past and present.*

Moose International, Inc. Founded in 1913, the Family Fraternity, often called the Loyal Order of Moose (and Women of the Moose), is a nonsectarian and nonpolitical organization. Moose International headquarters, in Mooseheart, Illinois, oversees 2,000 lodges, 1,600 chapters, and approximately 1.5 million members throughout the United States, Canada, Great Britain, and Bermuda. The moose was selected as the namesake animal because "it is a large, powerful animal, but one which is a protector, not a predator," according to the group's mission statement. Moose members are active in their communities, contributing nearly $90 million worth of service every year to charities and social causes in their hometowns.

Famous Moose members: presidents Franklin D. Roosevelt and Harry S. Truman, actor Jimmy Stewart, athletes Arnold Palmer and Cal Ripken, Sr., and U.S. Supreme Court Chief Justice Earl Warren.

The Benevolent and Protective Order of Elks of the United States of America was founded in 1868, making it one of the oldest fraternal organizations in the country. The order has more than 1 million members working in some 2,100 communities, with headquarters in Chicago. The Elks' mission is to promote the principles of charity, justice, brotherly love, and fidelity; encourage belief in God; support the welfare and enhance the members' happiness; bolster patriotism; cultivate good fellowship; and actively support community charities and activities. A major component of the Elks' mission is working with and mentoring youngsters.

Famous Elks: presidents John F. Kennedy and Gerald Ford, actor Clint Eastwood, football coach Vince Lombardi, and baseball greats Casey Stengel and Mickey Mantle.

Masons, also known as Freemasons, belong to the oldest fraternal organization in the world. Today, there are more than 2 million Freemasons in North America. Freemasonry, or Masonry, is dedicated to the "Brotherhood of Man under the Fatherhood of God." Masonry's principal purpose is "to make good men better." Since the origins of Masonry have been lost, no one knows how exactly old the movement is, but many historians believe it arose from the powerful guilds of stonemasons of the Middle Ages. In 1717, Masonry became a formal organization when four lodges in London formed England's first Grand Lodge. The oldest jurisdiction on the European continent is the Grand Orient de France, founded in 1728.

Famous Masons: presidents George Washington and James Monroe, composer Wolfgang A. Mozart, astronaut John Glenn, actor John Wayne, and escape artist Harry Houdini.

Lions Clubs International remains the world's largest service organization, with 45,000 clubs and 1.3 million members in 200 countries around the world. The international headquarters is in Oak Brook, Illinois. The organization was founded in 1917 in the United States and became international in 1920 when the first Canadian club was established in Windsor, Ontario. All funds raised from the general public are used for charitable purposes, and members pay all administrative costs. Since the Lions Clubs International Foundation began in 1968, it has awarded nearly 8,000 grants (totaling $566 million) to assist victims of natural disasters, fight physical and mental disabilities, and serve youth causes.

Famous Lions: President Jimmy Carter, race-car driver Johnny Rutherford, explorer Admiral Richard Byrd, and basketball star Larry Byrd.

Founded in 1957, Leo Clubs (named for their objectives of "Leadership, Experience, and Opportunity") are school- and community-based youth groups sponsored by the Lions Clubs International.

GOD'S ARCHITECT

✳ ✳ ✳

*An eccentric Spanish genius who created some of
history's strangest architecture, Antoni Gaudí's greatest work—
the world's most hallucinatory basilica—is still under
construction more than 80 years after his death.*

Antoni Gaudí was born in rural Catalan, Spain, in 1852. As a boy, he
was fascinated by the shapes peculiar to the natural environment of
his boyhood home—a lifelong inspiration that would later take form
in the irregular, fantastical designs of his buildings.

After studying architecture in Barcelona in the 1870s, he began
work on a series of commissions for private homes and commercial
buildings, some of which stand as the most shockingly innovative
architecture ever built.

In 1883, Gaudí, a devout Catholic, accepted a commission from
a wealthy publisher to build a new church in the heart of Barcelona.
Inspired by the strange mountains at nearby Montserrat, his design
for the Temple of La Sagrada Família called for 18 towers more than
300 feet tall, with a central tower that represented Jesus Christ and
stood 580 feet tall. Incorporating his distinctive use of organic shapes
and surfaces decorated with pieces of ceramic and mirror, his initial
towers soon swelled with offshoots of baroque sculpture.

As the years went on and backers balked at escalating expenses,
Gaudí sank all of his own savings into continuing the cathedral project. Work nearly ceased as Barcelona's economy collapsed and Gaudí
suffered the deep personal losses of a beloved niece and his longtime companion. He grew more reclusive and more devout, and his
appearance became increasingly eccentric. In fact, Gaudí may have
been deep in thought about his epic construction when he walked
into the path of a tram in 1926. Thousands attended his interment at
La Sagrada Família.

Work resumed on the church in the 1950s and continues today,
funded by private donations and admissions fares. During his life,
Antoni Gaudí was often ridiculed by his peers, but in death he became known as "God's Architect."

BOWLS OF CONFUSION

✳ ✳ ✳ ✳

Since the first college "bowl" game was played in 1902—fittingly enough, at the Rose Bowl in California—almost every conceivable mishap, happenstance, and circumstance has occurred. Consider this trifecta of turmoil involving a player, a coach, and, in keeping with the spirit of the endeavor, a mascot.

Wrong-Way Riegels—Rose Bowl, 1929: Perhaps the most infamous play to ever take place during a bowl game occurred during the Rose Bowl tilt between Georgia Tech and the University of California. Midway through the second quarter, Golden Bear center Roy Riegels recovered a Georgia fumble and immediately tore down the sidelines toward the end zone. There was only one problem: In his confusion after snagging the loose pigskin, Riegels ran the wrong way! The end zone he was about to reach was his own. Teammate Benny Lom, the bounciest Bear of the bunch, ran his errant buddy down, caught Wrong-Way, and tackled him on the three-yard line. Things digressed from bad to very bad after that. After failing to advance the ball from the shadow of the uprights, California tried to punt the pill from their own end zone. A surging Georgia scrum blocked the kick and recovered the ball for a two-point safety, which proved to be the margin of victory in Tech's 8–7 win.

Hothead Hayes—Gator Bowl, 1978: One of the most celebrated college coaches of all time, Woody Hayes led his Ohio State charges to 16 championships, including 13 Big Ten crowns in the 28 seasons he spent strolling the sidelines for the Buckeyes. Revered for his innovative teaching techniques, Hayes was equally renowned for his volatile temper, and it was a tantrum that eventually ended his tenure in Columbus. In the closing minutes of the 1978 Gator Bowl, the Buckeyes were trailing Clemson by a slim 17–15 margin. A last-ditch Ohio State drive was nullified when Clemson's Charlie Bauman intercepted a pass near the Buckeye bench. Bauman was forced out of bounds and into a melee of Ohio State personnel. Hayes wandered into the throng and sucker-punched Bauman in the throat, instigating a free-for-all that tarnished the reputation of both the school and its coach. The following day Hayes was dismissed by the university, bringing to an inglorious end one of the game's most illustrious careers.

Prancing Ponies—Orange Bowl, 1985: Since 1964, tradition at Oklahoma has been that every home-field score by the Sooners is commemorated with a victory lap by the Sooner Schooner, a covered wagon pulled by a pair of Shetland ponies dubbed Boomer and Sooner. However, in the 1985 Orange Bowl, it was a case of "too soon to Schooner" that proved to be the downfall of Oklahoma's bid to wipe out the University of Washington and win the Orange Bowl. With the score tied at 14–14, the Sooners drove down the field and kicked a field goal that appeared to give them a three-point cushion. In customary fashion, it was wagons-ho as Boomer and Sooner rumbled onto the field to signify the score. Unfortunately, the ponies' prance was premature, because a penalty had been called, thereby nullifing the play. Adding insult to error, the wagon's wheels became stuck in the soggy turf, and another penalty was flagged against the Oklahoma team. The Sooners missed the ensuing field goal attempt and played the remainder of the match in a lackluster slumber, eventually losing what would become known as the Sooner Schooner Game by a score of 28–17.

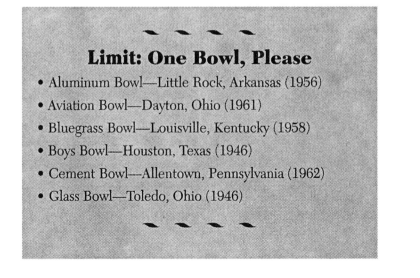

Limit: One Bowl, Please

- Aluminum Bowl—Little Rock, Arkansas (1956)
- Aviation Bowl—Dayton, Ohio (1961)
- Bluegrass Bowl—Louisville, Kentucky (1958)
- Boys Bowl—Houston, Texas (1946)
- Cement Bowl—Allentown, Pennsylvania (1962)
- Glass Bowl—Toledo, Ohio (1946)

EXPOSED TO POISON

✳ ✳ ✳ ✳

Long a favorite of mystery-novel writers and opportunistic bad guys, poison has an ancient and infamous relationship with people. Some poisons occur naturally and others are manufactured, but all of them spell bad news if you're the unlucky recipient of a dose.

Poison Plants

Deadly Nightshade, aka belladonna: Every part of this perennial herb is poisonous, but the berries are especially dangerous. The poison attacks the nervous system instantly, causing a rapid pulse, hallucinations, convulsions, ataxia, and coma.

Wolfsbane: This deadly plant was used as an arrow poison by the ancient Chinese, and its name comes from the Greek word meaning "dart." Wolfsbane takes a while to work, but when it does, it causes extreme anxiety, chest pain, and death from respiratory arrest.

Meadow Saffron: This tough little plant can be boiled and dried, and it still retains all of its poisonous power. As little as seven milligrams of this stuff could cause colic, heart failure, and paralysis.

Hemlock: This plant is probably the best known of the herbaceous poisons: It was used to knock off the Greek philosopher Socrates. Hemlock is poisonous down to the last leaf and will often send you into a coma before it finishes you for good.

Plans of Attack

There are five ways a person can be exposed to poison: ingestion (through the mouth), inhalation (breathed in through the nose or mouth), ocular (in the eyes), dermal (on the skin), and parenteral (from bites or stings).

Helpful Poison Stats

More than half of poison exposures occur in children under the age of six, and most poisonings involve medications and vitamins, household and chemical personal-care products, and plants. Eighty-nine percent of all poisonings occur at home. If you or someone in your house ingests something poisonous, stay calm and call 911 (if the person has collapsed or is not breathing) or your local poison control center (three quarters of exposures can be treated over the phone with guidance from an expert).

Good Old Arsenic

Mystery novels are filled with stories of characters choosing to off their enemies with arsenic. Colorless and odorless, this close relative of phosphorous exists in a variety of compounds, not all of which are poisonous. Women in Victorian times used to rub a diluted arsenic compound into their skin to improve their complexions, and some modern medications used to treat cancer actually contain arsenic. When certain arsenic compounds are concentrated, however, they're deadly; arsenic has been blamed for widespread death through groundwater contamination.

The Dubiously Poisoned

Napoleon Bonaparte: Many historians believe that Napoleon died of arsenic poisoning while imprisoned, because significant traces of arsenic were found in his body by forensics experts 200 years after his death. It has been argued, however, that at that time in history, wallpaper and paint often contained arsenic-laced pigments, and that Napoleon was simply exposed to the poison in his everyday surroundings.

    Vincent Van Gogh: Emerald green, a color of paint used by Impressionist painters, contained an arsenic-based pigment. Some historians suggest that Van Gogh's neurological problems had a great deal to do with his use of large quantities of emerald green paint.

    Yasser Arafat: Founder of the Palestinian liberation movement, Nobel Peace Prize winner, and politically controversial figure, Yasser Arafat died in 2004 from unknown causes. Leaders of the Islamic Resistance Movement, or Hamas, still accuse Israel of poisoning Arafat with an undetectable toxin, but there's no proof of that so far.

Food Poisoning

Unfortunately, this is a form of poisoning most of us know something about. When food is spoiled or contaminated, bacteria such as salmonella breed quickly. Because we can't see or taste these bacteria, we chomp happily away and don't realize we're about to become really sick. The Centers for Disease Control and Prevention estimates that in the United States alone, food poisoning causes about 76 million illnesses, 325,000 hospitalizations, and up to 5,000 deaths each year.

Blood Poisoning

This form of poisoning occurs when an infectious agent or its toxin spreads through the bloodstream. People actually have a low level of bacteria in their blood most of the time, but if nasty bacteria are introduced, they can cause sepsis, a life-threatening condition. The bacteria can enter the bloodstream through open wounds or from the bite of a parasite.

Snakebites

Because snakes' venom is injected, snakes them-selves are considered "venomous" rather than "poisonous." Still, an estimated 8,000 snakebites occur in the United States every year. Poisonous  snakes found in North America include rattlesnakes, copperheads, cottonmouths, and coral snakes. While most of these reptiles won't bite unless provoked, if you are bitten you have to take the antivenin fast.

Skull and Crossbones

When pirates sailed the high seas, they flew a flag emblazoned with a skull-and-crossbones symbol. When seafarers saw this Jolly Roger flag, they knew trouble was on its way. Bottles that contain poisons or other toxic substances often bear this symbol to warn anyone against drinking or even touching the contents with bare hands.

> "I would much prefer to suffer from the clean incision of an honest lancet than from a sweetened poison."
>
> *Mark Twain*

VODKA

✳ ✳ ✳ ✳

- What do screwdrivers and Bloody Marys have in common? Vodka, of course! This colorless alcohol hails from Russia, where its original name, *zhiznennaia voda*, means "water of life."

- To make vodka, vegetables (such as potatoes or beets) or grains (barley, wheat, rye, or corn) are put through a process of fermentation, distillation, and filtration. Grain vodkas are considered to be of the highest quality.

- The most expensive vodka in the world is Diaka, which comes in a crystal bottle that also contains crystals (much like the worm in some tequilas). The makers of Diaka attribute the vodka's exclusivity to its unique filtration process. It is filtered through 100 diamonds up to a carat in size.

- Vodka seems to have provided a distraction for a couple of notorious Russian czars. In 1540, Ivan the Terrible stopped fighting long enough to establish the country's first vodka monopoly, and in the late 17th century, Peter the Great explored improved methods of distillation and means of export. Anything to take their minds off human slaughter.

- During the reign of Peter the Great, it was customary that foreign ambassadors visiting the courtyard consume a liter and a half of vodka. Lightweight ambassadors began to enlist substitutes for the deed so the actual official could discuss important matters with a clear head.

- The Russian phrase *na pososhok* is a toast to the last drink given to a departing guest. It derives from the tradition that visitors traveling from afar would often facilitate their trip with a walking stick called a *pososh*, which had a hollowed-out hole on top. At the end of the visit, a glass of vodka was placed in the hole, and if the visitor could drink the vodka without touching the glass, he was likely able to get home on his own. Otherwise, it was the couch and a banging headache in the morning.

NEWS THAT'S FIT TO PRINT

✳ ✳ ✳ ✳

*Often biased and sometimes downright wrong, journalism
during the U.S. Civil War did offer some new innovations, including
bylines and wire reports from the field.*

Life was changing rapidly during the mid-19th century as modern
technology enabled journalists to report news faster than had been
possible during earlier wars. Previously, it took days or weeks for
news from the front to be read in print. Now, faster travel and the
widespread use of the telegraph meant that news could be printed
immediately. Unfortunately, speed did nothing to improve upon
accuracy—and perhaps even thwarted it. But the news had to be
published, even if it was wrong.

Credit Where Credit Is Due

General Irvin McDowell thought journalists in the field should dress
in white uniforms to show their purity and integrity. Of course, many
journalists possessed neither virtue. In fact, printing a byline—
displaying the name of the correspondent who wrote a particular
article—came about as a response to objections over inaccurate or
biased reporting. General Joseph Hooker insisted that if reporters
were going to lie about him, they needed to sign their work.

General William Tecumseh Sherman, General George Meade,
and others had even lower opinions of journalists. Sherman, upon
being informed of the death of three special correspondents in
battle, said, "Good. Now we shall have news from hell before breakfast!" Meade had a reporter drummed out of camp in humiliation—
forcing him to ride away backward on a mule to the jeers of the
soldiers—and the response of many journalists was to get revenge on
the general for the rest of the war. In fact, many news reports about
Meade were biased against him for the rest of his career.

The Business of News

Newspapers covered the war extensively. Larger papers sent multiple staff writers and artists into the field. Obviously, this became

an expensive endeavor. *The New York Herald* used 63 people in the field during the war at a cost of about $1 million. Smaller papers shared reporters, who gladly wrote for several sources to make up for the low salaries each paper paid.

Newspaper publishers used various strategies to attract readers. Often, this meant slanting the news toward the views of the intended readership or focusing on readers whose views matched those of the publisher. Other publishers focused on getting the news first. Telegraph lines and special couriers helped news travel quickly to the newspapers, but some journalists would sabotage their competitors. One reporter sent in his own dispatch and then tied up the telegraph lines by also transmitting a hefty chunk of the New Testament to make sure his competitors couldn't get through with their own reports. Speed was at such a premium that battle news was often sent in incomplete form, which sacrificed accuracy for timeliness. The early newspaper headlines about the First Battle of Bull Run, for example, described a heady Union victory. These were ultimately followed by a second edition revealing the serious defeat. Since most battles transpired in hours, while travel took days, many "eyewitness" reports were written by reporters who weren't even at the scene. Journalists sometimes did not arrive at a battle site until after the fighting had ended.

The glaringly incorrect early battle results from Bull Run and similar events caused readers and editors to demand more accurate reporting. Of course, this still didn't mean that articles were totally accurate or unbiased. All a reporter had to do to alter public impressions was to give credit selectively for victories or defeats. Even letters to the editors could affect public opinion. An example of this is a letter from a writer who used the pen name "Historicus." After the Battle of Gettysburg, the writer praised General Dan Sickles at the expense of General Meade. Despite the likelihood that Sickles wrote the letter himself, it colored the public understanding—and even the historical record, to a degree—against Meade.

The blockade of Southern ports made printing the news difficult there, because paper was in short supply. Southern newspapers dwindled in size and in a few cases were printed on wallpaper or other materials instead of newsprint.

Political Agendas

In the North, papers and politics went hand in hand. Horace Greeley's *New York Tribune* was strongly abolitionist, criticizing President Lincoln for being too moderate. (Greeley himself ran for president in 1872.) In the South, it was deemed unpatriotic to report any bad news accurately. So, bad news was sugarcoated, disguised, or omitted entirely when things were at their worst. Even foreign correspondents working in the South found it hard to produce accurate reports. Charles Mackay, Southern correspondent for *The Times* of London, repeatedly submitted reports of embarrassing inaccuracy, even writing about Lee's "impending capture of Washington" in July 1863.

The Birth of the War Correspondent

William Howard Russell was the first well-known war correspondent. He wrote the earliest widely published news account of what we now know as "The Charge of the Light Brigade." His work in the Crimean War led *The Times* of London to assign him to cover the American Civil War. Because of his reputation and international standing, Russell traveled widely and interviewed major participants on both sides. Russell's view of the war was that the Union held the moral high ground and that the Confederacy was likely to lose. His editors were pro-Confederacy, due to the English cloth industry's ties to the South, and since his opinions of the war did not match those of the paper, he was ultimately reassigned.

The most successful journalists traveled with the armies in hopes of witnessing direct action. This upset General Sherman and others, who felt that reporters often gave away military information in their columns. The most memorable reporters, including T. M. Chester, an African-American correspondent for the Philadelphia *Press*, had distinctive styles. At the siege of Petersburg, Chester wrote: "The enterprising managers of the firm of Grant & Lee take pleasure in announcing to the public in and around Petersburg that they are now prepared, and will continue until further notice, to give every evening a grand exhibition of fireworks for the benefit of their respective employees." The flamboyant Chester and other writers of the literary school of journalism often brought a lighter touch to the otherwise grim news of war.

COMMON GERMS ON YOUR TELEPHONE

✳ ✳ ✳ ✳

*We're not insinuating that you live in a dump, but there
are an estimated 25,000 germs crawling over every part of your
telephone receiver. The simple solution is to frequently wipe down
your phone with an anti-bacterial solution. If you don't,
say hello to some of these creatures.*

E. coli: Escherichia coli normally lives inside your intestine, where it assists in the breakdown of food. However, if E. coli gets into other parts of your body, it can cause major problems. Some types of E. coli are harmless; others can cause diarrhea, vomiting, cramps, stomach pain, and fever. How does E. coli get from your small intestine into other parts of the body? Well, if you don't wash your hands thoroughly after using the bathroom, there's a high likelihood that some E. coli will remain on your skin. From there, it's simply a matter of transferring it to the things you handle every day—such as the telephone. When the receiver touches your mouth, E. coli could be headed straight down your throat.

Klebsiella: Klebsiella is another bacteria that is abundant in the colon and helps keep everything functioning properly. Again, meticulous hygiene keeps it from thriving on your phone or anywhere else it shouldn't be. Klebsiella can cause real problems for a person with an already weakened immune system—including a rapid-onset illness that leads to destruction of a part of the lung. Klebsiella infection can be fatal, so be sure to wipe down that receiver with an alcohol-based solution.

Group A Streptococcus: These bacteria are commonly found in the throat and on the skin and are transferred when an infected person coughs or sneezes. The bacterium simply needs to make contact with the eyes, nose, or mouth of other people to enter into their system. Infection can cause strep throat, which is characterized by painful, difficult swallowing. Strep can cause other serious infections, such as *necrotizing fasciitis* (flesh-eating disease) and streptococcal toxic shock syndrome (which causes a dangerous drop in blood pressure).

Salmonella: Salmonella live in the intestinal tract of humans and animals. People may become infected by eating foods that have not been properly prepared or by picking up bacterium in public washrooms or from public telephones. Salmonellosis (salmonella infection) can cause diarrhea, fever, and stomach cramps, symptoms that usually last four to seven days. In some cases, though, the infection may spread from the intestines to the bloodstream, which can be fatal if the person is not treated with antibiotics.

Staphylococcus aureus: Staph resides on the skin or inside the nose, placing it at prime proximity to your phone receiver. If it enters an open wound, the resulting infection can cause irritations ranging from rashes to cellulitis (inflamed tissue). If staph enters the body orally it can cause pneumonia, meningitis, and septicemia (blood poisoning).

Campylobacter jejuni: These bacteria are commonly found in animal feces, and in homes with any type of pet, they can easily end up on your phone receiver. Infection with the bacterium can cause enteritis, a condition characterized by diarrhea, fever, stomach cramps, and a general feeling of lethargy. To avoid contamination, be sure household items are thoroughly cleaned, especially those that Fido and Kitty have access to.

Spirochetes: These distinctive bacteria are composed of long, spiraling cells that twist to facilitate motion, and they are easily distributed through the air. Spirochetes are responsible for, among other things, Lyme disease, syphilis, and leptosporosis. Spirochetes are widespread in the environment and can easily land on your phone.

Bacteroides: Bacteroides help break down food in the intestines and make up 30 to 50 percent of human feces. A contaminated phone serves as a conduit to oral contamination, which could result in periodontal disease, appendicitis due to abscess formation, and gastrointestinal infection.

Folklore: Myth or Truth?
TAMANEND, CHIEF OF THE LENNI LENAPE

* * * *

One statue that immortalizes Chief Tamanend stands in Philadelphia. Its inscription reveals the beloved leader's vision that English colonists and members of his tribe "live in peace as long as the waters run through the rivers and creeks and the stars and moon endure."

Was there really a Tamanend?

Yes. He was chief of the Native American Lenni Lenape tribe, also known as the Delaware, in the 1680s. His tribe was a member of the Unami, or Turtle clan, that lived in the Delaware River region. The name Tamanend means "pleasant," "polite," or "easy to talk to." Given these traits, it's not surprising that a missionary once described Tamanend as a long-revered figure among his people. He also allegedly sold a portion of what would become Pennsylvania to William Penn in 1683. In keeping with his name, he swore to live in peace with Penn's people forever.

What has kept his name alive?

In additioin to his own people, Tamanend made a strong impression on European colonists in America. By the time of the American Revolution, people celebrated the first of May as "Saint Tammany's Day." This holiday was a time for feasting and companionship that essentially replaced the May Day traditions of Europe. Though he was never an official saint, early Americans considered Tamanend, or "Tammany," to be a secular "patron saint" of their new home.

Who else used the name "Tammany?"

In the 1770s, the Society of St. Tammany was formed, and chapters opened across the northeast. New York City's chapter would morph into the Tammany Hall political machine, the model for government corruption and influence peddling. Tammany Hall manipulated New York City politics and patronage beginning in the 1840s until it faded away in the 1960s.

THINKING OUTSIDE
THE KNOT

* * * *

Alexander the Great was a legend in his own time, a bold
young king who conquered most of the civilized world.

In 333 B.C., Alexander, the 23-year-old Macedonian king, was a military leader to be feared. He had already secured the Greek peninsula and announced his intention to conquer Asia, a feat no Greek had
yet accomplished. His campaign eventually took him to Gordium, in
the central mountains of modern-day Turkey, where he won a minor
battle. Though undefeated, he still hadn't scored a decisive victory
and was badly in need of an omen to show his troops that he could
live up to his promise.

Conveniently, there was a famous artifact in Gordium—the
Gordian Knot. Some 100 years before Alexander arrived, a poor
peasant rode into the town on his oxcart and was promptly proclaimed king by the people because of a quirk of prophecy. He was
so grateful, he dedicated the cart to Zeus, securing it in a temple
by using a strange knot that was supposedly impossible to untie. An
oracle had once foretold that whomever loosed the knot would become the king of Asia. Because Alexander was in the neighborhood
and had just that goal in mind, he couldn't resist the temptation of
such a potentially potent omen of future success. If he could do it, it
would be a huge morale boost for his army.

Many had wrestled with the knot before, and Alexander found it
no easy task. He, too, struggled with it as a crowd gathered around
him. Irritated but not defeated, he decided to approach the problem
from a different angle. He realized that if he took the prophecy literally, it said that the person who *undid* the knot would be king. The
legend didn't specify that the knot had to be untied. Deciding that
the sword was mightier than the pen, he simply cut the knot in half.
It may have been cheating, but it certainly solved the problem.

The prophecy was fulfilled, and Alexander used it to bolster his
troops as he went on to conquer the Persian Empire and some of
India, taking the title "king of kings."

Fast Facts

- *The record for the longest filibuster is held by the late South Carolina senator Strom Thurmond, who talked against the 1957 Civil Rights Act for 24 hours and 18 minutes.*

- *The first woman senator, Rebecca Felton, was 87 years old when she was appointed to the Senate by the governor of Georgia. She served for one day: November 21, 1922.*

- *The halls of Congress are reputed to be haunted by a multitude of defunct politicians, among them John Quincy Adams and Daniel Webster. More surprising, perhaps, are the periodic sightings of a demonic cat.*

- *In the spring of 1930, the Senate almost voted to ban all dial telephones from the Senate wing of the Capitol, as the technophobic older senators found them too complicated to use.*

- *Morocco was the first country to recognize the United States as a sovereign nation, in 1777.*

- *The proud American motto "E pluribus unum"—out of many, one—was originally used by Virgil to describe salad dressing.*

- *Benjamin Franklin considered the bald eagle a "bird of bad moral character" and resented its being chosen to represent the United States of America.*

- *The founder of the Smithsonian, James Smithson, who in 1826 willed a then-staggering $508,318 to the United States "to found...an establishment for the increase and diffusion of knowledge," had never set foot in America.*

- *On September 13, 1859, California senator David Broderick established a record unlikely to ever be broken: He became the first sitting senator to be killed in a duel.*

- *Officially, the United States of America comprises only 46 states. Kentucky, Massachusetts, Pennsylvania, and Virginia designate themselves commonwealths.*

A ROSE BY ANY OTHER NAME...

* * * *

Floriography, or the language of flowers, stems from the coded messages of the Victorian era that facilitated the exchange of feelings among the simply unpoetic or those who were forbidden to verbally communicate their passions.

- Traditionally, different flowers have represented particular sentiments. These are some of a wide variety of interpretations.
  Jonquil = Your affections are returned.
  Carnation = You're fascinating. I love you.
  Peony = I'm shy, but I like you a lot.
  Ivy = Marriage and fidelity are recognized.
  Sweet pea = You give me lasting pleasure.
  Red rose = I love you.
  Iris = Thank you, or Sending sympathy.
  Lily = You're a good friend.
  Sunflower = Congratulations, or Thank you for everything.
  Gerbera daisy = Cheer up, or Thank you.
  Tulip = Happy housewarming, or You're a great host.

- Floriography has roots in Persia and Turkey. In the 1600s, Turks used a simple "language" in which flowers replaced words. Floral arrangements were used to convey a variety of messages.

- Lilies have been a significant floral symbol for centuries, appearing as a spiritual and philosophical metaphor in mythology and folklore from Egypt to Greece. These days, the stargazer lily is considered one of the most versatile and popular flowers, and the meanings behind its exchange range from purity to prosperity.

- Roses are probably the flower most imbued with meaning—and that meaning is, of course, love. Cleopatra's first romantic encounter with Antony took place atop a one-inch carpet of roses. In ancient Greece, altars were adorned with roses and offered to the gods. In the name of a good party, the Romans sprinkled dinner guests with rose water, rubbed their bodies with rose oil, and covered floors with rose petals.

- The Greeks were among the first to use flowers in weddings, representing a gift from nature to the bride, groom, and their families. Bridesmaids were in charge of the flower bouquets and garlands and often made poesies (small nosegays) for each guest as a symbol of thanks.

- While living in Paris in 1818, Charlotte de la Tour wrote the first flower dictionary, *Le Languauge des Fleurs*. Inspired by this popular tome, Miss Corruthers of Inverness later wrote the book *The Language of Flowers*, and the subject blossomed. Many other reference books were written, which sometimes caused more confusion than guidance. Depending on the writers' interpretations, the meanings behind certain flowers could vary considerably. The hydrangea, for example, could refer to either the recipient's insensitivity or an appreciation for their forgiveness, so it was important that everyone was on the same page!

- Mistletoe plays a prominent role in Norse mythology. One legend involves the death of Baldur, son of Odin and Frigga, at the hands of the wicked Loki, who used a bow made of mistletoe. When Baldur is restored to life, Frigga is so grateful that she reconsiders the offending plant, making it a symbol of love and promising to bestow a kiss upon anyone who passed under it.

- The marigold is featured in German legend inherited from Greece. It tells of a maiden, Caltha (from the Greek *kalathos,* or "cup"), who became obsessed with the sun god. She dedicated her life to seeing him, staying awake all night in order to be the first to glimpse his morning rays. In her devotion, she starved herself, and her spirit dissolved in the sun's light. The first marigold grew where she had stood for so long, representing a cup filled with the sun's rays.

- Poppies have long symbolized a sense of calm restfulness. In Roman mythology, the flower is associated with Somnus, the god of sleep. To the Greeks, the beautiful red poppy represented Hymnus, the god of rest and oblivion.

A LIFE FOR A LOAF OF BREAD— THE EDDIE SLOVIK STORY

✳ ✳ ✳ ✳

Only one American was executed for desertion during World War II. This is his tragic story.

Eddie Slovik was the fifth child of an immigrant family living in Michigan during the Depression. His father was frequently out of work, and a great deal of the financial responsibility fell upon the children. In an ill-guided effort to contribute, the otherwise shy, somewhat intimidated Eddie began stealing at a young age. When he was just 12, he became a focus of law enforcment after he and some friends broke into a factory, looking for anything they might trade for cash. Over the next few years, Eddie was arrested on several occasions and was ultimately sent to reform school. At the age of 17, he was part of a gang that, among other crimes, had stolen a car and wrecked it. On that occasion, the diminutive young criminal turned himself in to the police and received a two- to-eight-year sentence in the state reformatory.

Soon after the Second World War began, Eddie was released from prison and classified 4F (unfit for duty) because of his criminal record. Eddie got a factory job at the Montella Plumbing Company in Dearborn, Michigan, and married a working woman named Antoinette Wisniewski. During their first year of marriage, the couple saved enough money to buy a car and Antoinette became pregnant. On the day of their first anniversary, however, Eddie received a letter informing him that he had been reclassified and was to report for military service. The young man, who had so recently had nothing to lose, now had everything to lose. Moreover, Eddie knew he would not make a good soldier. He was right.

An Unwilling Soldier

During basic training in Texas, the young draftee was so nervous about handling weapons that his exasperated instructors gave him a wooden weapon for training. While Eddie was in Texas, Antoinette suffered a miscarriage—her grief-stricken young husband wrote her 376 letters during his 372 days at the camp. This trend continued after he was sent to France, where he wrote an average of two letters to his wife every day. Shortly after arriving in Europe, Eddie's unit became involved in the bloody fighting around the Hurtgen Forest, where the Allies suffered 33,000 casualties. Eddie was terrified and miserable, and he requested numerous times to be removed from the front lines, where he claimed he wasn't doing any good. Finally, after a terse exchange of words with his company commander, he deserted. Just as he did after stealing the car at age 17, Slovik turned himself in to the authorities the next day and handed the military police a written confession in which he promised he would desert again if forced to return to combat. He was imprisoned in Belgium, tried by a court-martial committee, found guilty, and sentenced to death.

"The Unluckiest Kid that Ever Lived"

Many men had been sentenced to death for desertion since the war began, but the United States had not executeed one of its own soldiers since the Civil War. Eddie and most others involved with the case assumed he would stay in jail until the end of the war. Army authorities, however, felt it was time to make an example and decided to carry out Slovik's sentence. Eddie wrote to General Dwight D. Eisenhower begging for clemency, but the letter reached the general at the height of the Battle of the Bulge and Eisenhower, perhaps bitter that a coward such as Slovik should request leniency when so many soldiers were dying, refused to rescind the order.

On January 31, 1945, Private Eddie Slovik was executed by a 12-man firing squad—many of whom probably believed the deserter deserved to die. Slovik spent his last hours rereading letters from his wife and was heard to say: "I'm Okay. They're not shooting me for deserting the United States Army—thousands of guys have done that. They're shooting me for that loaf of bread I stole when I was 12 years old."

Eddie's wife, Antoinette, lived to be an old woman and never ceased her efforts to clear her husband's name. In fact, she referred to Eddie Slovik as "the unluckiest kid that ever lived." To this day, the U.S. Army has not executed another soldier for desertion.

Folklore: Myth or Truth?
STEEL-DRIVING JOHN HENRY

✳ ✳ ✳ ✳

"But John Henry drove his steel sixteen feet…an' the steam drill drove only nine." So the song goes. We'd like to believe in John Henry. Two different towns claim him, but who's right?

Retelling the legend. It's a great one. They say that John Henry was born and raised a slave, perhaps in the 1840s. He grew up into a fortress of a man, a mighty worker, and after slavery ended he went to work for a railroad. In order to blast railroad tunnels, someone had to hammer a long steel stake deep into the rock, creating a hole where others could slide in dynamite. After workers cleared away the blasted rock, the "steel-driving men" got busy pounding more stakes. Henry was the best in the business. One day someone brought in a newfangled steam drill or steam hammer, probably suggesting in scornful tones that Henry's skill was now obsolete. John challenged the steam drill to a contest, outdrove it almost two to one, then keeled over from a heart attack.

The trouble with that story? It's a lack of evidence or conflicting evidence. No one doubts that a mighty ex-slave worked on railroad-construction gangs; many thousands of freedmen did, and it wasn't a job for the weak. It's plausible that one such man, full of heart and pride, challenged a steam drill and lost. But where and when did this happen? "John Henry" was a common enough name, appearing often in railroad employment records. Different accounts, none well corroborated, place the event in different states. If big John lived, it's unfortunate for his memory that people didn't bother keeping detailed records. But we can't make the story true by wishing it so.

Where does this scant evidence place John? Some believe that the steam drill challenge occurred at Talcott, West Virginia. Others place it near Leeds, Alabama. One historian argues that Henry was a prisoner leased out by the warden (a legal practice in those days). We don't know for sure, though both towns commemorate John Henry. All of the claims can't be right; possibly none are.

IN THE YEAR...1969

✳ ✳ ✳ ✳

- The band Led Zeppelin releases its first album, *Led Zeppelin.*

- On July 21, U.S. astronaut Neil Armstrong steps off the Apollo 11 landing craft and onto the surface of the moon.

- After 148 years, *The Saturday Evening Post* stops publishing. The weekly magazine was made famous for its cover illustrations by artist Norman Rockwell.

- Richard M. Nixon is sworn in as the 37th president of the United States.

- In Memphis, Tennessee, James Earl Ray pleads guilty to assassinating Martin Luther King, Jr. Ray would later retract his plea.

- Golda Meir becomes the first female prime minister of Israel.

- John Lennon and Yoko Ono marry.

- The Administration Building at Harvard University is seized by nearly 300 students, the majority of whom are members of the activist group Students for a Democratic Society.

- Singer and actress Judy Garland dies.

- The Woodstock Festival is held at a farm in upstate Bethel, New York, featuring more than 30 of the top musicians of the time.

- The first automatic teller machine in the United States is installed in Rockville Center, New York.

- The pilot episode of *The Brady Bunch,* starring Robert Reed and Florence Henderson, airs on U.S. television.

- After what became known as the My Lai Massacre in Vietnam, Lieutenant William Calley is charged with six counts of premeditated murder for the deaths of 109 Vietnamese civilians.

- The Boeing 747 jumbo jet debuts, carrying almost 200 people from Seattle, Washington, to New York City.

WORDPLAY

✳ ✳ ✳ ✳

Logolepts are generally defined as word maniacs, or people who love to ponder and play around with words. Creating or identifying anagrams, palindromes, oxymorons, and contronyms are just a few intriguing and humorous ways to fiddle with the English language.

Anagram: a word or phrase that exactly reproduces the letters in another word or phrase—ideally reflecting or commenting on the subject of the first

the earthquakes—that queer shake
debit card—bad credit
slot machines—cash lost in 'em
schoolmaster—the classroom
eleven plus two—twelve plus one
dormitory—dirty room
desperation—a rope ends it
the Morse code—here come dots
snooze alarms—alas, no more Zs
a decimal point—I'm a dot in place
astronomer—moon starer
the eyes—they see
payment received—every cent paid me
the public art galleries—large picture halls, I bet
election results—lies, let's recount
vacation times—I'm not as active
the detectives—detect thieves

Palindrome: a word, phrase, or sentence that reads the same forward and backward

Don't nod.
Dogma: I am God.
Never odd or even.
Too bad—I hid a boot.
Go hang a salami; I'm a lasagna hog!
Doc note: I dissent. A fast never prevents a fatness. I diet on cod.
Are we not drawn onward, we few, drawn onward to new era?

Do geese see God?
Dennis sinned.
Niagara, O roar again!
Live not on evil.
Draw, O coward!
Rise to vote, sir!
Was it Eliot's toilet I saw?
Murder for a jar of red rum.
Kay, a red nude, peeped under a yak.
Campus motto: bottoms up, Mac.
Go deliver a dare, vile dog!
Madam, in Eden I'm Adam.
Ah, Satan sees Natasha.

Oxymoron: a literary figure of speech in which opposite or contradictory words, terms, phrases, or ideas are combined to create a rhetorical effect

open secret
Advanced BASIC
act naturally
almost exactly
constant variable
same differencew
jumbo shrimp
found missing
even odds
working holiday
only choice
freezer burn
unbiased opinion
virtual reality
pretty ugly
minor crisis
genuine imitation
definite maybe
exact estimate
larger half
rolling stop

clearly confused
alone together
tragic comedy
liquid gas

Contranym: a word that is its own antonym. Contranyms are also known as homographs.

aught—all, nothing
chuffed—pleased, annoyed
cleave—separate, adhere
clip—fasten, detach
consult—ask for advice, give advice
custom—usual, special
dust—add particles, remove particles
fast—quick, unmoving
first degree—most severe (murder), least severe (burn)
fix—restore, castrate
garnish—enhance (food), curtail (wages)
give out—produce, stop production
left—remaining, departed from
liege—sovereign lord, loyal subject
mean—average, excellent ("plays a mean game")
off—off, on ("the alarm went off")
out of—outside, inside ("work out of one's home")
oversight—error, care
pit—a solid core, a hole
put out—extinguish, generate (something putting out light)
quite—rather, completely
rent—lease out, borrow
sanction—approve, boycott
screen—show, hide
seed—add seeds, remove seeds
skinned—with the skin on, with the skin removed
strike—hit, miss (in baseball)
trim—remove excess, add decoration
variety—one type ("this variety"), many types ("a variety")
weather—withstand, wear away
wind up—end, start up (a watch)

LIVING IN FEAR

✳ ✳ ✳ ✳

*Approximately 20 percent of people in the United States
have an intense, irrational fear of common things or experiences,
such as spiders, heights, or confined spaces.
Sometimes they fear something more unusual, such as
pine trees or public bathrooms.*

Acrophobia is the fear of heights. This fear is often very specific.
A person may be able to ski the Alps with no problem but be overcome with panic on a fifth-floor balcony.

Astraphobia, also known as tonitrophobia, brontophobia, or
keraunophobia, is a paralyzing fear of thunder and lightning.
As with other phobias, the reaction often causes a rapid heartbeat
or labored breathing. People, and even pets, often seek shelter in
confined spaces such as closets and basements.

Cacophobia is the fear of ugliness. Sufferers aren't just repulsed
by unattractive people or things; they actually have intense panic
attacks around them. When they see someone or something they
consider ugly, they often turn away and flee.

Coulrophobia is the fear of clowns. It is a basic survival instinct to
react with suspicion to a "person" with a painted smile and unsmiling
eyes, but people with this phobia are terror-stricken when they see
this circus staple.

Dendrophobia is the fear of trees. A child on a camping trip may be
afraid there will be bears wandering among the pines. A fear of bears
is not unusual, but the child may subsequently develop a paralyzing
fear of pine trees. People with dendrophobia usually have strange
stories about why they are terrified of a particular type of tree.

Friggatriskaidekaphobia is the fear of Friday the
13th. This fear is more typical among people who
are from England, Poland, Germany, Bulgaria, or
Portugal—countries in which the number 13 is
traditionally deemed unlucky.

Nyctophobia is an irrational fear of nightime or the dark. Rationally, an adult (the fear is common among children) may understand that there is nothing to be afraid of, but he or she still experiences heightened anxiety when the lights go out.

Trypanophobia is an exaggerated fear of injection with a hypodermic needle. This phobia has a history in genetic memory. Thousands of years ago, the people who avoided being stabbed in general were the most likely to survive.

Further Phobias

Alecktorophobia—a fear of chickens

Arachibutyrophobia—a fear of peanut butter sticking to the roof of the mouth

Basophobia—fear of standing, walking, or falling over

Catagelophobia—fear of being ridiculed

Chorophobia—fear of dancing

Didaskaleinophobia—fear of going to school

Doxophobia—fear of expressing opinions or of receiving praise

Elurophobia—fear of cats

Ergophobia—fear of work

Gamophobia—fear of marriage

Hexakosioihexekontahexaphobia—fear of the number 666

Hippopotomonstrosesquippedaliophobia—fear of long words

Iatrophobia—fear of doctors or going to the doctor

Linonophobia—fear of string

Nyctohylophobia—fear of dark wooded areas or of forests at night

Ochlophobia—fear of crowds or mobs

Paralipophobia—fear of neglecting duty or responsibility

Phengophobia—fear of daylight or sunshine

Soceraphobia—fear of parents-in-law

Xanthophobia—fear of the color yellow or the word *yellow*

STRANGE DOINGS
BENEATH THE SEA

✳ ✳ ✳ ✳

*Most sea creatures are quite comfortable with
habitats and relationships that human land-dwellers find
rather odd. They're flexible about how they look, where they live,
and even what gender they claim as their own.*

No-Brainers

Sea squirts—so named because they squirt water at whatever annoys
them—are small, blobby creatures that appear in all oceans and seas.
Many are short and fat, while others are elongated. Sea squirts can
grow to the size of an egg, though most are much smaller. Some live
alone and some form colorful colonies that look like flowers bloom-
ing on the ocean floor. Although usually found in shallow water, sea
squirts also turn up as deep as 28,000 feet.

Sea squirts are categorized as chordates, the same phylum that
humans belong to. That's because the larval stage has a notochord
(a flexible skeletal rod) and a simple nervous system. With a head,
mouth, sucker, and tail, the young sea squirt looks and moves like a
tadpole. But this adolescent goes through some major changes as it
grows up—more than a human teenager.

Attaching itself to a piling, a seashell, a sandy bottom, gravel, al-
gae, or even the back of a big crab, the youngster absorbs its own tail
and nervous system. The mature sea squirt is a spineless, sedentary,
immobile glob. Tufts University science philosopher Daniel C. Den-
nett put it this way: "When it finds its spot and takes root, it doesn't
need its brain anymore, so it eats it! (It's rather like getting tenure.)"

Sex-Shifters

Worldwide, the oceans' coral reefs harbor about 1,500 species of
fish, including some with adaptable sexual identities. Wrasses, par-
rotfish, and other reef fish start out female and eventually become
male. However, other types of reef fish change sex according to the
needs of the group. If there aren't enough males or females, the
problem is easily taken care of.

Gobies that live in Japan's coral reefs can change back and forth as need dictates. If the dominant male dies or leaves, a female will become male, changing gender in about four days. If a larger male shows up, the gobie that changed simply switches back to female. Many fish that change sex do so quickly. A particular variety of sea bass found in reefs from North Carolina to Florida and in the northern Gulf of Mexico are both female when they meet for mating. One switches to male, they mate, then both switch sex and they mate again. This toggling between sexes is accompanied by color changes; the female is blue, and the male is orange with a white stripe.

Dual Sexuality

The belted sandfish (a coastal sea bass) is a hermaphrodite, with active male and female organs. It can theoretically self-fertilize, meaning that a single individual can release eggs, then shift to its male self (in about 30 seconds) and release sperm. More often, two fish take turns fertilizing each other's eggs. Hermaphroditic sea slugs are underwater snails without shells. The *Navanax inermis* variety, found off the coast of California and Mexico and in the Gulf of Mexico, have male sex organs on one end and female sex organs on the other. They sometimes mate in chains of three or more, with suitable ends attached. The slugs in the middle of the line act as male and female simultaneously.

The Perfect Couple?

Seahorses, those bony little fish that swim upright, live in sea grasses, mangrove roots, corals, and muddy bottoms in both tropical and temperate oceans and lagoons. They keep the sex they were born with, and seahorse couples tend to remain monogamous throughout a mating season. Couples perform a little dance when they meet, joining tails, swimming around together, and circling each other. It's the male seahorse that gets pregnant. After he opens a special pouch in his body, the female aligns with the opening and lays her eggs. The male fertilizes the eggs, his pouch swells, and two weeks later he gives birth to as many as 1,500 live offspring. Male seahorses sometimes experience false pregnancies; the pouch swells but no eggs or babies are present. Males can even die of postpartum complications such as infections caused by dead, unborn ponies.

Partners Forever

Far down in the ocean, between 3,000 and 10,000 feet, is a cold, dark world of sharp-toothed hunters. There, many fish use built-in lights to confuse pursuers, to signal a mate, or to bait a trap. Among these deep-sea hunters are anglerfish that grow a "fishing rod" with deceptive "bait" dangling from it. They move about slowly, waving their glowing lures to attract potential meals toward their big toothy mouths. However, only the female anglerfish grows a lure—the male doesn't need one. He's also born without a digestive system, because he isn't going to need that either.

When a young male anglerfish is just a few inches long, he searches out a (much larger) female and sinks his teeth into her. His jaws begin to grow into her skin, and after a few weeks he is unable to let go. The male's eyes get smaller and eventually disappear. Most of his internal organs also disappear. His blood vessels connect to those of the female, so he gets nutrition from whatever she eats. The male grows a little larger, but the gain is all in testes. Finally, he's the sex object he was destined to be—a producer of sperm and little else. The female gains a mate that's literally attached to her forever. Sometimes she doesn't settle for just one but drags several males along through life.

The Sea Creature with 1,000 Stomachs

The longest of all ocean-dwellers, the praya, assigns sex to small entities that are also its body parts. A praya is a "colonial" animal called a siphonophore, made up of many individuals called polyps. Each polyp is adapted for a special duty: some breed, some swim, and some are just stomachs.

In a praya, the various kinds of polyps are strung together into a well-coordinated monster that moves through the water like a snake on a roller coaster. It roams the ocean vertically, from near the surface to depths of 1,500 feet. Though only as thick as a finger, a praya can grow to be 130 feet long. A mere six-foot siphonophore can have more than 100 stomach polyps, and a large praya might have 1,000 stomachs.

WEASEL WORDS

✳ ✳ ✳ ✳

Advertisers, politicians, and corporations are infamous for using doublespeak and euphemisms to either hide or neutralize what they're trying to sell or say. Weasel words drain the meaning from a thought or action, just as a weasel sucks the contents from an egg. Here are a few weasely words and phrases we hear every day.

bad patient outcome

between jobs

chemically tested

companion animal

complexity resolution

control technique

core strength

critical matrix

destination icon

dysfunctional family

empowerment

exit strategy

extraordinary rendition

fixer-upper

headcount reduction

human resources

immersive experience

inclusion support facilitator

lifestyle destination

limited mobility

mainstreaming

network-centric

new and improved

ongoing value creation

outside the box

partner (as a verb)

positive birth experience

pre-owned vehicle

productivity gains

quality face time

retail landscape

self-harm incident

self-regulation

touch base

vacation specialist

voluntary termination

Euphemistically Speaking

"Any euphemism ceases to be euphemistic after a time and the true meaning begins to show through. It's a losing game, but we keep on trying."
Joseph Wood Krutch

* * * *

"The more syllables a euphemism has, the further divorced from reality it is."
George Carlin

* * * *

"Euphemisms are not, as many young people think, useless verbiage for that which can and should be said bluntly; they are like secret agents on a delicate mission, they must airily pass by a stinking mess with barely so much as a nod of the head."
Quentin Crisp

* * * *

"Those comfortably padded lunatic asylums which are known, euphemistically, as the stately homes of England."
Virginia Woolf

POISONED PUDDINGS AND PURITANISM: HARVARD'S EARLY DAYS

✳ ✳ ✳ ✳

Today, Harvard is famed for a vast endowment,
but its early days were marked by a struggle to get by with
quarter-bushels of wheat donated by local farmers.

The School's Scandalous First Leader

In 1640, the tiny college of Harvard was in crisis. Founded four years before by the Massachusetts Bay Colony, Harvard had a student body of nine; a "yard" liberated from cows; and a single, hated instructor.

Harvard's 30-year-old schoolmaster, Nathaniel Eaton, was known to beat wayward students. Other students charged Eaton's wife, Elizabeth, of putting goat dung into their cornmeal porridge, or "hasty pudding." (Harvard's theatrical society is named for the dish.) Finally, Master Eaton went too far and was hauled into court after clubbing a scholar with a walnut-tree cudgel. He was also accused of embezzling 100 pounds (then an ample sum).

In 1639, Eaton and his wife were sent packing. Master Eaton returned to England, was made a vicar, then died in debtor's prison. Following the Eaton affair, Harvard's reputation lay in tatters; its operations were suspended, and its students were scattered.

The Roots of Learning

The money and work Massachusetts had put into the school seemed for naught. The colony's General Court had allotted 400 pounds for a college in what became known as Cambridge, Massachusetts—across the Charles River from Boston. The school was named for John Harvard, a clergyman from England's Cambridge University, which at the time was known to be a hotbed of Puritanism, the severe, idealistic faith opposed to the dominant Church of England.

John Harvard was a scholar whose family had known William Shakespeare. When the plague felled his brothers and his father, John inherited a considerable estate, including the Queen's Head

Tavern. After immigrating to the Boston region, he became a preacher in Charleston, but his career was short. In 1638, at the age of 31, he died of consumption, having bequeathed money and his personal library to the planned college.

Comeback Under the First President

In 1640, the colony's founders were desperate for educational cachet. They offered the post of Harvard president to Henry Dunster, a new arrival from England and another graduate of Cambridge University.

The energetic Dunster tapped into the colony's inherent educational edge. Many of the new Puritan arrivals had studied at the Oxford and Cambridge academes: Some 130 alumni of the two schools were in New England by 1646. Dunster himself was a leading scholar in "Oriental" languages, that is, biblical tongues such as Hebrew.

Led primarily by a Protestant culture that stressed reading the Bible, Boston set up the first free grammar school in 1635; within 12 years, every town in Massachusetts was required by law to have one. Harvard's new president mandated a four-year graduation requirement and rode out angry students who protested over a commencement fee. Dunster obtained Harvard's charter and authored the school's "Rules and Precepts." He bankrolled the facilities through donations of livestock and, over the course of 13 years, some 250 pounds of wheat. He took a modest salary, being underpaid through 14 years of service, and piled up personal debts. Fortunately, his wife, Elizabeth Glover, kept a printing press in their home. It was the American colonies' first press, and its profits underwrote her husband's work. Dunster managed to turn the school around. Harvard's reputation soared, and students from throughout the colonies, the Caribbean, and the mother country flocked to newly built dorms.

Religious Schisms and a President's Heresies

Yet Dunster tripped up on one of the many religious disputes roiling the Puritan colony. In 1648, it was a criminal offense to engage in "Blasphemy, Heresie, open contempt of the Word preached, Profanation of the Lord's Day"; separation of church and state was unknown.

A source of controversy was infant baptism, which the Puritan fathers required by law. Drawing on his biblical knowledge, Dunster noted that John the Baptist had baptized the adult Jesus, but he could find no biblical examples of children being baptized. In 1653, he refused to have his son Jonathan baptized. At Cambridge's Congregational Church, Dunster preached against "corruptions stealing into the Church, which every faithful Christian ought to [bear] witness against."

This put the Puritans of Boston and Cambridge in a quandary. Dunster's views made him a heretic, yet he was much liked for his work at the college. Early the next year, the colony's officers wrote that Dunster "hath by his practice and opinions rendered himself offensive to this government." They assembled a conference of 11 ministers and elders to interrogate him. Egged on by this assembly, in May 1654 the General Court forbade schools to employ those "that have manifested themselves unsound in the faith, or scandalous in their lives." Dunster resigned from Harvard.

The ex-president then petitioned the court to let him to stay in the colony until he could repay the many debts he'd accumulated from his work. Court authorities coldly responded that "they did not know of [such] extraordinary labor or sacrifices. For the space of 14 years we know of none." Dunster, with Elizabeth and their youngest child ill, then beseeched the court to at least let his family stay the winter. The magistrates agreed grudgingly, but the following spring they banished the Dunster family to the backwater town of Scituate. Harvard's first president died there four years later, at the age of 47.

"It might be said now that I have the best of both worlds. A Harvard education and a Yale degree."

John F. Kennedy

NEW YEAR'S DROPS

* * * *

New York City's ball-dropping tradition in Times Square has pretty much become synonymous with New Year's Eve. Here's how towns across the United States have gotten in on the act.

- The ball dropped in New York City weighs more than 1,000 pounds and contains hundreds of Waterford crystal triangles. The ball dropped now is more than twice as bright as the original, thanks to state-of-the-art LED lighting effects.

- The highlight of the First Night event in Atlanta, Georgia, is the dropping of an 800-pound peach.

- Celebrators in Key West, Florida, ring in the New Year in three ways: by dropping a conch shell, a pirate wench from the mast of a tall ship, and a six-foot-tall red high heel shoe carrying a drag queen.

- Port Clinton, Ohio, known as the Walleye Capital of the World, drops a 20-foot, 600-pound walleye from the sky each year at the stroke of midnight. During the celebration, the town serves walleye chowder, walleye sandwiches, walleye cinnamon chips, and walleye popcorn. A local winery has even created a "walleye white."

- In 2000, the fishing community of Point Pleasant, New Jersey, dropped a ten-foot wooden replica of an Atlantic baitfish. Mo the Millennium Mossbunker was covered with 1,500 Mylar scales.

- A sardine, the symbol of Eastport, Maine, is dropped in the easternmost city in the United States. The 22-foot structure is made of lumber and chicken wire and is decorated with silver lamé. Between appearances, it is stored in a restaurant called The Pickled Herring.

- Pennsylvania boasts an unusual lineup of New Year's Eve celebrations. Residents of Lebanon witness the dropping of a 100-pound, 16-foot stick of bologna; and in Dillsberg, it's an 8-foot-tall papier-mache pickle. The folks in Falmouth lower a stuffed goat to honor the town's goat races, and in Wilkes-Barre, a chunk of coal "transforms" into a diamond as it descends.

CANADA'S UNIQUE ETHNIC COMMUNITIES

✳ ✳ ✳ ✳

*Each of these communities can lay claim to
its portion of the Maple Leaf flag.*

- **French:** French Canadians will tell you that diversity wasn't always a Canadian hallmark. The British kicked French authority out of Canada; they tried without success to anglicize French Canadians, who maintained their language and traditions through great force of will. Some wish to form a *République Québecoise* separate from Canada, but for now French Canadians remain Canadian—23 percent of the population.

- **Acadian:** French identity in Canada is old enough to have subsets. Acadians are Francophone Canadians mainly concentrated in New Brunswick, mostly bilingual. The current population—1 percent of Canada's total—descends from the remnant that wasn't deported after 1755. Today, Acadian identity is strong and represents a great reason to visit Atlantic Canada.

- **Metis:** Canadians of mixed French and First Peoples heritage (mainly concentrated in the Prairies) have experienced discrimination in the past, and in the late 1800s they rebelled with armed force. Their fusion reflects cultural and spiritual aspects of both ancestries—a far cry from the outdated perception of mixed blood as a negative.

- **Doukhobors:** Doukhobors descend from Russian immigrants who came to Canada around 1900 after persecution in Russia for pacifist religious beliefs. They don't ⟨...⟩y often today, but in the past Doukhobors have protested in ⟨...⟩ walking around naked. Most live in British Columbi⟨...⟩ country, where it takes a tough person to protest naked.

- **Inuit:** Canada's Arctic and sub-Arctic are the home of 55,000 Inuit, many of whom live in the territory of Nunavut and speak their culture's language, Inuktitut. One-fifth of the Nunavut population lives in Iqaluit, formerly Frobisher Bay, on Baffin Island—about as far north as Nome, Alaska. Many Inuit still practice traditional subsistence methods, long proven effective in one of the world's harshest environments.

- **First Nations:** Aboriginal Canadians who are neither Inuit nor Metis—in the United States they'd be called Native Americans— are the many First Nations bands of Canada: Haida, Salish, Blackfoot, Athabascan, Cree, Ojibwa, Iroquois, and others. You'll find First Peoples in every province and territory, either on reserves or among the mainstream.

- **Sikhs:** Some 270,000 Canadians claim Sikh heritage, mostly concentrated in cities in Ontario and British Columbia. Sikhism is not only a religion but also a cultural identity. Canada allows Sikhs to wear turbans (required by their faith) and possess *kirpans,* or daggers (which male Sikhs are supposed to carry)—a Supreme Court case ensured that young Sikh males can take *kirpans* to school.

- **Chinese Canadians:** "Hongcouver" (Vancouver, British Columbia) is full of ethnic communities, but the largest is surely Chinese. More than a million Chinese Canadians have their largest concentration in this coastal, cosmopolitan city, loading it up with every variety of Chinese culture one can imagine. Pretty much every other culture of Asia is also represented in Vancouver.

- **African Canadians:** The port city of Saint John's, New Brunswick, is home to a thriving community that dates back to black Loyalists who decided not to stick around in the rebellious Colonies. More recent waves came from former slaves after the War of 1812, and later from the West Indies. While African Canadians can be found all over the country—in greater numbers in Toronto and Montreal—this community's history and continuity makes it stand out.

- **Filipinos:** The Filipinos of Manitoba are among Canada's newest and most successful ethnic communities. The first generation were mostly professionals in the medical and garment industries, but today's Manitoba Pinoy/Pinay population fits into mainstream life in true Canadian fashion: by embracing Canadian traditions and adding its own.

I'm No Expert, But...
BASEBALL PITCHES

✳ ✳ ✳ ✳

How does a pitched baseball move, and how is it thrown? Here are the tricks (as they apply to right-handed pitching).

Q: How does one throw a curveball, and how does it move?

A: Several throwing grips begin with holding the ball in a peace sign (index and middle fingers making a V, thumb below). In contrast to the fastball, which is held in the fingertips, for a curve you cram the ball deep in the hand. Deliver the ball fully overhand with mostly top-to-bottom motion, snapping the hand as though pounding a nail with a hammer. Let the ball squirt out. If done correctly, the ball will arc sharply down and to the pitcher's left. Good curveball pitchers produce dozens of annoying little curveball variants, which is important because a good hitter can see the curve coming.

Q: How about a slider?

A: Very different. Start with the peace-sign grip, but put the fingers together like a Cub Scout salute, and the thumb alongside the ball rather than below it. Cock the wrist right. Instead of extending your arm to throw, pull the ball back behind your ear the way a quarterback throws a football. As you throw, cut your fingers away viciously to the right, creating a fierce sidespin. The ball should curve away left. A great slider, thrown at the batter, breaks across the plate for a strike while the batter jackknifes away from it—now you see why it's a hated pitch. Surgeons are familiar with the slider—its effect on the elbow can be devastating. Kids should avoid throwing it.

Q: What about the famous splitter?

A: It's also known as the split-fingered fastball. Put the ball in the peace-sign fastball grip, but curve the fingers down the sides of the ball—kind of a wilted peace sign. That crams the ball between those fingers, splitting them wide apart. Now throw your normal fastball, flicking your wrist down a bit. Done right, it looks like a fastball and drops slightly just before the dish. Good hitters can hit anything they can pick up, and the splitter is hard to see coming.

Q: Many Little League coaches say speed changes are the most important pitching tool. How is a changeup thrown?

A: The changeup can be thrown many ways, but here's a mainstream approach. Add your ring finger to the peace-sign grip, thumb under the ball, but don't curl your fingers to enclose it. Throw it with all three fingers extended in a Boy Scout salute, and aim at the catcher's head (some pitchers have to aim at the umpire's head). Throw it like a fastball but with more downward motion. It should look like a fastball, but it should arrive late and tend to fall off at the end (the reason you aimed high). To upset a hitter's timing, good pitchers use different speeds.

Q: Explain how to chuck the knuck.

A: The knuckleball is difficult, but it's so easy on the arm that its masters can pitch professional ball into their late 40s. Experiment with grips; no two are alike. Start with the Boy Scout salute change-up grip described above, but curl the three fingers back on themselves so the tips dig into the ball (align them behind a lace). Stiffen your wrist and throw the ball, flicking your fingers forward. The idea is to flick just hard enough to defeat the ball's natural backspin so that it hardly spins at all, letting wind currents cause the ball to float around. Catchers like watching the batter's head bob up and down trying to follow it. You haven't lived until you've watched someone try to bunt the knuck, moving his bat up and down.

Fastballs: four-seam, two-seam, cutter, splitter, forkball, sinker

Breaking balls: curveball, knuckle curve, slider, screwball

Changeups: changeup, palmball, circle changeup

Others: knuckleball, Eephus pitch, spitball, gyroball, Shuuto

Folklore: Myth or Truth?

GREGORIO CORTEZ— TEXAS FOLK HERO

✳ ✳ ✳ ✳

The trend of lionizing fighters against lawful authority goes back to the days of Robin Hood and perhaps even earlier. More than a century ago, Tejanos (Texans of Hispanic origin) had their own legendary figure: Gregorio Cortez.

- Cortez was born in Matamoros, Mexico, in 1875. His family moved across the border when he was 12, and he began learning how to farm and be a cowboy.

- To understand why the legend of Gregorio Cortez matters to-day, one must realize the context. When he came to the United States, it had only been some 50 years since Texas had its gained independence from Mexico. Spanish-speaking people had lived in Texas for centuries before it joined the United States, but they now found themselves playing second fiddle to English-speaking Texans.

- Cortez's affable nature contributed to the way his story unfolded, and it definitely affected his esteemed place in Texas folklore. Unlike reviled outlaws such as John Wesley Hardin, Cortez was not a habitual criminal and was liked and trusted by both English- and Spanish-speakers.

- Everything went downhill for Cortez in 1901, when two county sheriffs and two deputies went hunting for a horse thief. In those days, people took a dim view of horse thieves, and if the law didn't string them up, vigilantes would do so without a second thought. Calling a man a horse thief was like calling him a liar: an insult not easily wiped away without bloodshed.

- The sheriffs contributed this precise description of the culprit: "medium-size Mexican." In Kenedy, Texas (50 miles southeast of San Antonio), in 1901, that description could have applied to virtu-ally anyone. However, a nearby resident told the deputies he had recently traded horses with Cortez and revealed where they could find him.

- According to legend, one of the deputies mistranslated Cortez's statement from Spanish to English. Cortez had said something like "you have no reason to arrest me," but the deputy believed he had said, "No white man can arrest me." It's unclear if the sheriffs took this bad translation as a "you'll-never-take-me-alive" threat or as simple disrespect for the law. Regardless, one of the sheriffs shot and wounded Cortez's brother Romuldo. Cortez then drew his gun and killed his brother's assailant.

- Now Cortez was really in hot water. He managed to escape, but his mother, wife, and children were captured. However, there is no evidence that sheriffs had any legal grounds to detain them. Cortez grew even more distrustful of law enforcement.

- County sheriffs eventually cornered Cortez at a neighboring house. By this time, Cortez probably didn't expect anything but a long rope and a short drop if he were captured, so he fought back. One deputy and the property's owner died in the resulting gunfight, but Cortez escaped again.

- Cortez then walked about a hundred miles to the home of a friend, who gave him a saddled horse and some supplies so that Cortez could proceed to the border town of Laredo.

- By now the law was after Cortez in full cry. Authorities even offered a $1,000 bounty for his capture, an enormous sum of money at the time. Hundreds of people became part of the posse to chase down the fugitive.

- As Cortez's reputation spread throughout Texas, an odd thing happened: The English-speaking press and public took a shine to him, admiring his ability to lead the authorities on such a wild chase. To elude the famous Texas Rangers was no small feat. Cortez was becoming not just a Tejano folk hero but a folk hero for all Texans.

- Even with this newfound multicultural popularity, the chase of Gregorio Cortez provoked some ugly racial violence in several Texas counties.

- A posse captured Cortez near Laredo on June 22, 1901, just ten days after the chase had begun. When he was sent back north to face trial, it became clear that not everyone admired Cortez, and the police had to face down at least one lynch mob.

- For killing the landowner in the second fight, a Gonzales County jury sentenced Cortez to 50 years in jail. Although this sentence was thrown out, he was sentenced to life in prison for killing the sheriff's deputy during the same shootout.

- While Cortez was jailed, his wife of 13 years, Leonor Díaz, divorced him, claiming that he had abused her, both physically and verbally. Less than two years later, while still imprisoned, Cortez married Estéfana Garza.

- In jail, Cortez was a model prisoner, popular with his jailers and fellow inmates of all backgrounds. Outside the walls of the jail, sentiment began to build for his release.

- Gregorio Cortez served 12 years in prison, and in 1913, Governor Oscar Colquitt pardoned him. Following his release, he went back to Mexico to fight in the Mexican Revolution. He died of pneumonia in 1916.

- Why did an accused killer and horse thief inspire such admiration from so many Texans? Surely it helped to be liked. As word spread about Cortez, many people believed that he was a good person in an unfortunate situation, rather than just a bad person. People also admired his resourcefulness. Certainly, notions of fairness played a part, as Cortez's story is one of hasty and unwarranted accusation. Most important, Cortez didn't set out looking to start a fight, but when one began, he dared to finish it.

- Gregorio Cortez has lived on in ballads, books, and film. Américo Paredes explored the legend in his 1958 book, *With His Pistol in His Hand: A Border Ballad and Its Hero,* which challenged some of the stereotypes that had surrounded the story.

- In the early 1980s, Edward James Olmos starred as Cortez in the film *The Ballad of Gregorio Cortez.*

DIFFERENT KINDS OF FUNNY

✳ ✳ ✳ ✳

With this helpful guide to humor, you'll never again be left asking, "Wait, was that a joke?" In fact, you may soon become the life of the party by throwing out a few laugh-inducing lines of your own!

Absurdism

What it is: humor based on a belief that the universe is ridiculously unreasonable and meaningless. Contradictory sayings, one-liners, and paradoxes are all forms of absurdism.

Where you've seen it: Irish writer Oscar Wilde's famous absurdism: "Always forgive your enemies—nothing annoys them so much."

Caricature

What it is: an exaggerated portrayal of a person, often with distorted distinguishing features that might include mannerisms, speech patterns, styles of dress, or hairdo.

Where you've seen it: Comedians love to do caricatures of Hollywood personalities and politicians. Will Ferrell's caricature of George W. Bush on *Saturday Night Live* played up the president's malaprops and other verbal blunders.

Farce

What it is: comedy based on mockery, with broad exaggerations and stereotypes.

Where you've seen it: It's common in Mel Brooks's films, such as *Spaceballs* (a take on *Star Wars*), and the movie *Blades of Glory* (a mockery of competitive ice skating).

Hyperbole

What it is: a conscious overstatement of facts for comedic effect.

Where you've seen it: It's often used in speech, such as when we refer to someone as "older than dirt" or say, "this box weighs a ton." Any time we exaggerate to make something seem worse—or better ("I feel like a million bucks")—than it really is, we're using hyperbole.

Irony

What it is: an incongruity between cause and effect or between what you mean and what you say. It's similar to sarcasm and is typically cutting or biting.

Where you've seen it: Science-fiction writer Robert Heinlein summed up irony nicely when he said, "The supreme irony of life is that hardly anyone gets out of it alive." The *Far Side* cartoon strip is a master at comic irony, illustrating it in such examples as a hapless cat stuck inside while watching a collision outside between a truck labeled "Al's Rodents" and another labeled "Ernie's Small Flightless Birds."

Lampoon

What it is: to ridicule or mock someone or something.

Where you've seen it: Watch Chevy Chase's film *National Lampoon's Vacation*, which makes fun of the supposed "great family vacation," and NBC's hit show *30 Rock*, which pokes fun at producing a television show at a major network.

Malaprop

What it is: a slip of the tongue that involves the substitution of a word that sounds like the one intended but means something ridiculously different.

Where you've seen it: Recall when President George W. Bush spoke of finding "weapons of mass production," or when boxer Mike Tyson said, "I just might fade into Bolivian, you know what I mean?"

Parody

What it is: a literary or musical work that mimics the style of the original.

Where you've seen it: Weird Al Yankovic's renditions of popular rock songs, such as "Fat," a parody of Michael Jackson's "Bad." Comedy Central's *The Daily Show* parodies a news broadcast to satirize political and social trends and events.

Pun

What it is: a play on words, based either on different meanings of the same word or on similar meanings of different words.

Where you've seen it: Wannabe jokesters like to tell them just for the "pun" of it. And someone once said, "A pun is a short quip followed by a long groan." While we're at it: What's the difference between a nicely dressed man on a bicycle and a poorly dressed man on a tricycle? A tire. Get it? A-tire? *Groan.*

Repartee

What it is: comedy based on one-upmanship, verbal sparring between two people who are typically trading clever insults.

Where you've seen it: The Algonquin Round Table, or "The Viscious Circle," was a group of writers, artists, and actors that included the likes of Dorothy Parker, Robert Benchley, and Alexander Woollcott. They were notorious for their witticisms and one-upmanship.

Satire

What it is: humor with a point, usually exposing some kind of social or political issue for the purpose of reform.

Where you've seen it: Comedy Central's *The Colbert Report.* Stephen Colbert is the self-righteous host who ridicules the actions of politicians and other public figures by taking all of their beliefs and statements as gospel, thus revealing their hypocrisy.

Understatement

What it is: Also called "low exaggeration," understatement treats a topic as less important than it is.

Where you've seen it: British humor is often said to be under-stated, while American humor is overstated. Comedic legend Bob Newhart is a fine example, as well as the television series *The Office*.

Wit

What it is: humor that depends on some sort of intellectual play.

Where you've seen it: Television gems *M*A*S*H* and *Sex and the City* got laughs from the quick-witted dialogue between characters. In one episode of *Sex and the City*, Miranda asks Carrie, "What happened to aging gracefully?" Carrie replies, "It got old."

SIX ANIMALS THAT ARE EXTINCT
BECAUSE OF HUMANS

* * * *

Dodo
Probably the most famous species to have been eradicated by
people, the dodo was a three-foot-tall flightless bird that lived on the
island of Mauritius in the Indian Ocean. The dodo had no natural
predators, so it was able to nest on the ground in perfect safety until
Dutch settlers arrived in the 16th century. Having never before
been bothered, the dodo had no fear of people, nor of the sheep,
dogs, pigs, and rats that accompanied them. The animals attacked
the birds, the settlers destroyed their habitat, and the species disappeared in less than a century.

European Lion
Until the first century A.D., thousands of wild lions roamed modern-
day Spain, Portugal, southern France, Italy, and the Balkans. This
was the species pitted against the gladiators in Roman arenas. In
addition to being slaughtered in amphitheaters, lions were hunted
by the Macedonians and Greeks (among others), and it wasn't long
before the Romans were forced to import lions from North Africa
and the Middle East for their entertainment.

Passenger Pigeon
At one point there were an estimated 5 billion passenger pigeons
in the United States. They gathered in enormous flocks, sometimes
consisting of as many as 2 billion birds. When European settlers
began to colonize North America in the 17th century, they hunted
the birds, mainly for food. By 1896, almost all of the flocks had been
killed for sport by hunters, and in 1914, the last remaining passenger
pigeon, known as Martha, died in the Cincinnati Zoo.

Bluebuck or Blue Antelope
This species of antelope lived on the southwestern coast of South
Africa. It was widespread during the last ice age (though its numbers
dwindled as the planet heated up again) and survived until the 17th

century. Europeans began to hunt it obsessively—purely for sport, because they didn't like the taste of its meat—until it became extinct at the beginning of the 19th century.

Alaskan Prehistoric Horse

Until recently, it was believed that these animals had died out because of climate changes long before the first people settled in Alaska. However, recent discoveries of fossil remains suggest that the horses may have been around when humans began to cross the Bering Land Bridge from Asia around 12,000 B.C. So it is likely that humankind had something to do with their extinction.

Great Auk

Similar in appearance to the penguin, the flightless Great Auk was found in great numbers in eastern Canada, Greenland, Iceland, Norway, Ireland, and Great Britain. Although it couldn't use its wings to fly, the Great Auk used them to swim underwater, and its main food was fish. In the 18th century, Great Auks began to be hunted extensively for their meat and feathers, and they became extinct in 1844.

- *Many people equate "extinction" with obliteration, but the process of extinction follows a simple rule: A species becomes extinct when its death rate is continually greater than its birthrate. The species mentioned here are goners, but there is great hope for a lot of others.*

- *Of all species that have existed on Earth, 99.9 percent are now extinct. According to a recent poll, seven out of ten biologists think we are currently experiencing another mass extinction, though many other researchers dispute this.*

THE MUSIC OF METAL

✳ ✳ ✳ ✳

The roots of heavy metal music are based in the hard rock sounds developed in the late 1960s and early 1970s by bands such as The Who, Led Zepplin, and Deep Purple. These bands created a guitar- and drum-heavy sound and layered it with distortion behind a lead male vocalist. Eventually, metal itself split into some of these genres.

Thrash Metal

Notable Purveyors: Overkill, Megadeath, Metallica

This genre features lightning-fast tempos, complex guitar riffs, and a style known as "shredding," in which the guitarist shows off his or her technical skills by playing intricate compositions really fast. Black Sabbath and Judas Priest are a couple of the bands credited with influencing thrash metal. Punk music from the 1970s also influenced thrash, because it usually featured the same quick rhythms and heavy guitar sound.

Goth Metal

Notable Purveyors: Candlemaas, Cathedral, Type O Negative

Sad, despondent tempos and melodies and a generally gloomy mood provide the soundscape of goth metal and its unholy brother, doom metal. Like most metal-offshoot genres, goth metal appeared in the 1980s. Legendary metal group Black Sabbath inspired the sound, and the hard-to-categorize group The Melvins are associated with the genre as well.

Death Metal

Notable Purveyors: Slayer, Possessed, Napalm Death

Marking the death metal genre are rapid percussion, basic chord progression from rhythm guitars, a ferocious vocal style, oft-changing time signatures, and lyrics about death, Satanism, and destruction. Death metal has its roots in thrash metal, with the majority of it coming out of Florida in the mid-1980s. A lot of death metal was also being created in Sweden at the same time.

Power Metal

Notable Purveyors: Manowar, Queensryche

Power metal employs more melody and less-intense lyrics than most metal genres, while keeping the fast-paced, chord-heavy structural basis of metal music (don't be surprised if you hear an opera singer providing backup vocals). Power metal evolved as a response to the death metal and black metal music that came before it. Emerging mostly in Europe in the mid-1990s, power metal took the energy and drive of death metal and made it more appealing to the masses.

Christian Metal

Notable Purveyors: Stryper, Theocracy, Extol

For almost every metal genre that exists, there is a Christian metal counterpart, including Christian thrash metal and Christian death metal. Everything is the same except the lyrics, of course; rather than singing about Satan, Christian metal bands sing about Jesus. Metal musicians who also identified as Christians took what they liked about metal (the chords, rhythm, and vocal style) and made it work with their ideology. Resurrection Band and Jerusalem are credited with being first on the scene in the 1970s, but it was Stryper who put Christian metal on the map when their album *To Hell with the Devil* went platinum in the 1980s.

"Nu" Metal

Notable Purveyors: Marilyn Manson, Korn, Slipknot

Anything goes in "nu" or "alternative" metal music: Hip-hop, punk, and funk sounds have all been incorporated into the music of metal in this 21st-century metal redux. Metal's mainstream success in the 1980s was blasted away with the grunge and "alternative" rock tidal wave of the 1990s. Metal has been creeping back ever since, but it sounds different this time around: Funkier bass lines, rap-inspired lyrical rhythms, and more complex production elements contribute to the mainstream metal of today.

Fast Facts

- *Skylab, the first American space station, fell to Earth in thousands of pieces in 1979. Thankfully, most of them landed in the ocean.*

- *Skylab astronauts grew one-and-a-half to two-and-a-quarter inches due to spinal lengthening and straightening as a result of zero gravity.*

- *The cosmos contains approximately 50 billion galaxies.*

- *Since 1959, more than 6,000 pieces of "space junk" (abandoned rocket and satellite parts) have fallen out of orbit, and many of these have hit Earth's surface.*

- *The surface gravity of Jupiter is more than two-and-a-half times greater than that of Earth.*

- *Uranus is unique among the planets in that its equatorial plane is almost perpendicular to the orbital plane.*

- *If you could fly across our galaxy from one side to the other at light speed, it would take 100,000 years to make the trip.*

- *Every year the Sun loses 360 million tons.*

- *If you attempted to count the stars in a galaxy at a rate of one every second, it would take about 3,000 years to complete the task.*

- *Earth is the only planet not named after a god.*

- *Neptune takes 165 Earth years to get around the Sun. It appears blue because it is made of methane gas. Winds on Neptune can reach 1,200 miles per hour. Neptune has eight moons.*

- *Objects weigh slightly less at the equator than at the poles.*

- *According to scientists, gold exists on Mars, Mercury, and Venus.*

STATEMENTS ON STUPIDITY

* * * *

Fools, ignoramuses, dimwits—it's human nature to comment on stupid behavior, and we've gathered some interesting observations on a lack of intelligence.

We are all born ignorant, but one must work hard to remain stupid.
Benjamin Franklin, U.S. founder

* * * *

A person must have a certain amount of intelligent ignorance to get anywhere.
Charles Kettering, inventor

* * * *

Two things are infinite: the universe and human stupidity; and I'm not sure about the universe.
Albert Einstein, theoretical physicist

* * * *

He was distinguished for ignorance; for he had only one idea, and that was wrong.
Benjamin Disraeli, British politican and author

* * * *

In politics, stupidity is not a handicap.
Napoleon Bonaparte, French emperor

* * * *

I do not believe in the collective wisdom of individual ignorance.
Thomas Carlyle, Scottish essayist

* * * *

A good man can be stupid and still be good. But a bad man must have brains.
Maxim Gorky, Russian author

Love is being stupid together.
Paul Valery, French poet

* * * *

He was born stupid, and greatly increased his birthright.
Samuel Butler, poet

* * * *

Anything too stupid to be said is sung.
Voltaire, French philosopher

When a stupid man is doing something he is ashamed of, he always declares that it is his duty.
George Bernard Shaw, Irish author

* * * *

A word to the wise ain't necessary—it's the stupid ones that need the advice.
Bill Cosby, comedian

* * * *

Human beings can always be relied upon to exert, with vigor, their God-given right to be stupid.
Dean Koontz, author

* * * *

Give me a smart idiot over a stupid genius any day.
Samuel Goldwyn, movie producer

* * * *

If you're poor and you do something stupid, you're nuts. If you're rich and do something stupid, you're eccentric.
Bobby Heenan, professional wrestling manager

* * * *

I'm not offended by dumb blonde jokes because I know that I'm not dumb. I also know I'm not blonde.
Dolly Parton, musician and actor

I think there's a difference between ditzy and dumb. Dumb is just not knowing. Ditzy is having the courage to ask!
Jessica Simpson, musician and actor

* * * *

If you think your boss is stupid, remember: You wouldn't have a job if he was any smarter.
John Gotti, mobster

* * * *

Some people think having large breasts makes a woman stupid. Actually, it's quite the opposite: A woman having large breasts makes men stupid.
Rita Rudner, comedian

* * * *

I may be dumb, but I'm not stupid.
Terry Bradshaw, NFL Hall of Famer

* * * *

There is more stupidity than hydrogen in the universe, and it has a longer shelf life.
Frank Zappa, musician

* * * *

Health nuts are going to feel stupid someday, lying in hospitals dying of nothing.
Redd Foxx, comedian

* * * *

No plan can prevent a stupid person from doing the wrong thing in the wrong place at the wrong time—but a good plan should keep a concentration from forming.
Charles E. Wilson, former Secretary of Defense

* * * *

I'm stupid, I'm ugly, I'm dumb, I smell. Did I mention I'm stupid?
Eminem, musician

THE FIRST FLAG RAISING ON IWO JIMA

✳ ✳ ✳ ✳

Each year, more than 30,000 people compete in the Marine Corps Marathon, which finishes next to Arlington Cemetery, the resting place of American war dead just outside Washington, D.C. As runners climb the final hill near the finish line, they're inspired by the Marines Corps War Memorial, the 60-foot-high statue of leathernecks raising a flag over Iwo Jima's Mount Suribachi. Few realize the iconic image depicts not the first but the second flag that was hoisted at Iwo Jima.

The famous emblem raising took place shortly after noon on February 23, 1945. The first happened about 90 minutes earlier.

For four days, thousands of U.S. Marines had been killed or wounded while battling toward the volcanic mount that dominated the island. Recalled 24-year-old Corporal Charles W. Lindberg, one of the first flag's raisers, "The Japs had the whole beach zeroed in. Most of the fire was coming from Suribachi."

Capturing Mount Suribachi

Lieutenant Colonel Chandler W. Johnson commanded the 2nd Battalion, 28th Regiment, 5th Marine Division. His task was to capture the top of Suribachi. The morning of February 23, after one of Johnson's companies scouted a path to the crest, he assigned the mission to 40 marines from 2nd Battalion's Company F. Johnson and gave the company commander, First Lieutenant Harold G. Schrier, an American flag, measuring 54 by 28 inches. "If you get to the top," Johnson told Schrier, "raise it."

One of the patrol's members was Sergeant Ernest Ivy Thomas. On February 21, two days before the flag was raised, Thomas had taken command of his rifle platoon when its leader was wounded. Armed with only a knife when his rifle was shot away, he repeatedly braved enemy mortars and machine guns while directing tanks against pillboxes at the base of Suribachi. Thomas was awarded the Navy Cross for his actions.

Led by Lieutenant Schrier, the patrol began its climb at 0800 hours on February 23, with Lindberg lugging his 72-pound flamethrower. They reached the top at 1015 and were attacked by a small Japanese force. While the skirmish continued, Thomas and another man scrounged up a 20-foot-long iron pipe. At 1020, recalled Lindberg, "We tied the flag to it, carried it to the highest spot we could find, and raised it." Hoisting the ensign was Lindberg, Thomas, andSchrier, along with Sergeant Henry O. "Hank" Hansen, Private First Class Louis C. Charlo, and Private First Class James Michels.

The First Photo

Sergeant Lou Lowery, a photographer for *Leatherneck* magazine, took a photo of it. While he snapped the picture, a Japanese soldier tossed a grenade nearby. Just in time, Lowery threw himself over the crater's lip. He landed 50 feet below, his camera lens smashed, yet his film intact.

After the raising, "All hell broke loose below," remembered Lindberg. "Troops cheered, ships blew horns and whistles, and some men openly wept."

"Make It a Bigger One!"

On the invasion beach was Secretary of the Navy James Forrestal, who'd arrived to watch the capture of Suribachi with Marine Commander General Holland "Howlin' Mad" Smith. Forrestal told Smith: "Holland, the raising of that flag on Suribachi means a Marine Corps for the next five hundred years." According to the book *Flags of Our Fathers* by James Bradley, Forrestal requested the emblem as a souvenir.

Battalion chief Johnson was not pleased. "The hell with that!" he reacted. He ordered an operations officer, Lieutenant Ted Tuttle, to have another patrol secure the flag and replace it with another banner. "And make it a bigger one," he told Tuttle.

Soon after, as Lowery climbed down from Suribachi, he ran into three fellow photographers going up: Marines Bob Campbell and Bill Genaust, and the Associated Press's Joe Rosenthal, whose photo of the second flag raising garnered him the Pulitzer Prize. The three photographers were considering going back down the mount, but Lowery informed them the summit offered good views, so they kept trudging up. At the top, Schrier had the first flag lowered at the same time the second 96-by-56-inch flag was raised. Down on the sands, most never noticed the switch.

The Battle Raged On

The terrible battle continued. Of the 40 marines in the first patrol, 36 were later killed or wounded on Iwo Jima. Private First Class Charlo, grandson of a noted Flathead Indian chief, was killed March 2, and Sergeant Thomas died on March 3. Photographer Genaust had taken a video of the second flag raising with imagery similar to Rosenthal's; his film was featured in a famous newsreel. He was killed March 4. Altogether, close to 7,000 marines died and 19,000 were wounded.

On March 1, Lindberg was wounded on Suribachi and was awarded the Silver Star. "I was after a mortar position up there, and I was shot, and it shattered my arm all to pieces," Lindberg said. Back in the States, he was angered by his patrol's lack of recognition. "I went on home and started talking about this," he stated. "I was called a liar and everything else. It was terrible." But "it was the truth," he said. "I mean, everyone says, 'Iwo Jima flag raising,' they look at the other one."

The Japanese were also bitter, with good reason—they lost the battle. Iwo Jima was part of the prefecture of the city of Tokyo. Its loss meant that the U.S. Marines had secured their first piece of official Japanese soil. The rest of Japan beckoned.

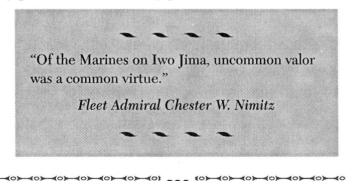

"Of the Marines on Iwo Jima, uncommon valor was a common virtue."

Fleet Admiral Chester W. Nimitz

POPULAR NOTIONS: TRUE OR FALSE?

* * * *

- **It takes seven years to digest swallowed gum.**

  False: Even though gum is indigestible, it still passes through your digestive system at a normal rate.

- **Lemmings commit suicide if their population increases too much.**

  False: This legend emerged after it was staged in the 1958 Disney animal documentary *White Wilderness*.

- **The *Titanic* was the first ship to use SOS as a distress signal.**

  False: Ships had been using SOS for at least three years before the *Titanic's* fateful voyage.

- **Charlie Chaplin once entered and lost a Charlie Chaplin look-alike contest.**

  True: He even failed to make the finals.

- **The American flag must be burned if it touches the ground.**

  False: Out of respect, it shouldn't touch the ground, but it doesn't need to be burned if this happens.

- **Boxing Day (celebrated in Canada, Great Britain, Australia, and New Zealand) was designated as a day to get rid of empty gift boxes on December 26.**

  False: Early on, wealthy people gave gifts to the lower classes the day after Christmas.

- **Two of the "Marlboro Men" featured in cigarette ads died of lung cancer.**

  True: Wayne McLaren, who became an anti-smoking activist after getting lung cancer, died in 1992 at the age of 51. David McLean, a Marlboro Man from the 1960s, died in 1995 at the age of 73.

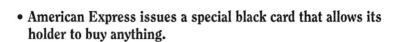

- **American Express issues a special black card that allows its holder to buy anything.**

  True: But it's still not known if the story came before the card.

- **Your dog's age in human years is its actual age multiplied by seven.**

  False: This formula works as a rough estimate in a dog's middle years, but not for its entire life.

- **Eating turkey makes you sleepy.**

  False: Turkey contains tryptophan, an amino acid that makes you sleepy, but it doesn't work unless it's consumed in large quantities.

- **The Oregon Department of Transportation once tried to get rid of a dead whale that had washed ashore by blowing it up.**

  True: Flying blubber damaged a car parked a quarter-mile away.

- **There are more suicides around Christmas than at any other time of the year.**

  False: A study conducted over more than 35 years revealed no increase during this holiday.

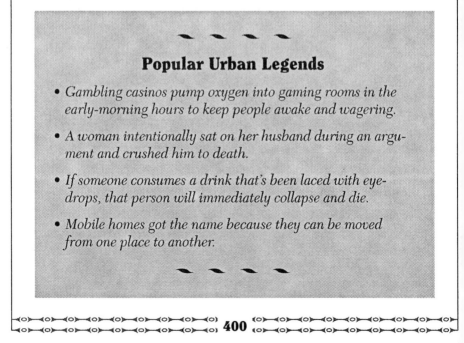

Popular Urban Legends

- *Gambling casinos pump oxygen into gaming rooms in the early-morning hours to keep people awake and wagering.*

- *A woman intentionally sat on her husband during an argument and crushed him to death.*

- *If someone consumes a drink that's been laced with eyedrops, that person will immediately collapse and die.*

- *Mobile homes got the name because they can be moved from one place to another.*

Talk to the Expert
BEST BOY

✳ ✳ ✳

This job title has nothing to do with gender or favoritism. Here's the scoop on that strange-sounding job we've seen in film credits.

Q: What does a best boy do?

A: That depends whether she's the best boy electric or the best boy grip. I'm a best boy electric, making me chief assistant to the gaffer, who's in charge of lights. A best boy grip is chief assistant to the key grip, who's in charge of camera dollies and cranes, mechanical stuff.

Q: So you rig up the lights?

A: Not usually, because my job is supervisory. I hire, fire, and oversee the people who rig up the lights. If someone has a union complaint, they bring it to me. I buy new equipment and supplies, make sure people work safely, and establish procedures. If the director or cinematographer wants something done with lighting, he might go to the gaffer or to me, but normally I'm the go-to gal. We produce the right lighting conditions for the time of day.

Q: How did you learn to be a best boy?

A: In high school, I discovered school plays and cinema and knew that's what I wanted to do. We shot our own movies on the side. I loved being up there manipulating the lights, making things work in the background. I started as a trade electrician in construction. Meanwhile, I kept putting in for film work and finally got my chance. I can tell the electricians what to do, because they know I've done it myself—and sometimes still do.

Q: It must be hard to break into your business.

A: It takes a good deal of skill and a lot of luck. When your moment comes in Hollywood, you have to perform really well. I carry spares of everything, especially fuses, because something can always go wrong.

LITTLE DEBBIE SNACKS

✴ ✴ ✴ ✴

In 1960, when O. D. McKee was contemplating a name for his company's line of snack cakes, he was inspired by a photo of his four-year-old granddaughter Debbie. Here are a few of the favorites from the line of more than 75 Little Debbie products in stores near you.

Swiss Cake Rolls
Devil Squares
Apple Flips
Nutty Bars
Banana Twins
Blueberry Muffins
Cheese Danish
Zebra Cakes
Peanut Butter Crunch Bars
Cherry Pies
Fancy Cakes
Coffee Cakes
Lemon Meringue Rolls
Mini Donuts (frosted, glazed, or powdered)
Honey Buns
Donut Sticks
Fudge Brownies
Fudge Rounds
Oatmeal Crème Pies
Marshmallow Pies
Boston Crème Rolls
P. B. & J. Oatmeal Pies
Coconut Crème Rolls
Pecan Pie
Devil Cremes
Iced Honey Buns
Pecan Spinwheels
Caramel Cookie Bars

Snow Puffs
Banana Nut Muffins
Strawberry Shortcake Rolls
Texas Cinnamon Rolls
Star Crunch
Cosmic Brownies

Little Debbie also offers seasonal treats, giving you a small window each year to gorge yourself on sweet goodness. Here are some of Little Debbie's limited-edition snacks:

Valentine's Day:
    Cherry Cordials
    Be My Valentine Cakes

Easter:
    Easter Brownies
    Easter Basket Cakes
    Easter Puffs Cookies

Fourth of July:
    Stars & Stripes Snack Cakes
    Spirit of America Marshmallow Treats

Halloween:
    Pumpkin Delights
    Fall Party Cakes

Christmas:
    Christmas Tree Cakes
    Cookie Wreaths
    Holiday Snack Cakes

THE DIRT ON GREEN ARCHITECTURE

✳ ✳ ✳ ✳

In the beginning, all architecture was environmentally friendly, or "green." Adobe houses, mud huts, dugouts, and igloos are all examples of natural homes. Newer synthetic materials lasted a lot longer than natural ones, but now we're beginning to see how such construction affects the ecosystem.

Environmental degradation, run-off, and pollution are just a few problems caused by modern-day development. To help preserve the planet, there is a growing movement to restore harmony between architecture and the environment.

Tools of the Trade

It's not just solar panels anymore. Green architecture uses a wide variety of natural, sustainable materials, including:

- recycled-rubber roofing: works just as well as shingles, no tar necessary

- insulation made of cotton or newspaper: recycled and non-hazardous

- cork flooring: recycled and inexpensive

- fiber-cement siding: recycled, durable

- photovoltaic (PV) cells: heating option that uses less energy

- wood-and-plastic-composite decking: looks the same as the real thing and is weather-resistant

- natural paints: beautiful, nonpolluting

- recycled glass: looks good, feels good

These materials, once difficult to find, are becoming more easily accessible to architects and builders. Consumers are realizing that going eco-friendly doesn't mean sacrificing quality. In fact, many green materials are more durable than their synthetic counterparts.

Compressed Earth Blocks (CEB), for example, are composite bricks made from clay, sand, and a concrete stabilizer. These bricks are uniform, economical, largely locally produced, nontoxic, non-flammable, and bug-resistant.

Location, Location, Location

If you're interested in building an environmentally sensitive home, its location is just as important as the materials you use. An adobe-brick home built in the middle of a delicate ecosystem will still affect wildlife and compromise the groundwater.

Some eco-minded architects feel that the kindest thing a person can do for the planet is to not build anything at all. Instead, they recommend "re-purposing" an existing structure, thereby using less energy and fewer resources.

If you are building from scratch, you have several "green" considerations. If you are starting a business, for example, choose a location that enables employees to bike to work or use public transportation. Building a home with a woodstove? Close proximity to a sustainable forest is prudent; burning fossil fuels to drive miles for firewood defeats the purpose.

Give Green a Go

There are lots of simple, everyday measures you can take to green-up your lifestyle.

- Buy products in recycled packaging made from recycled materials.

- Keep your heat down during colder months. Wear a sweater; layering insulates you.

- While you're sleeping, turn off computers at the power strip.

- Use rechargeable batteries or solar-powered devices.

- Turn off the lights when you leave a room.

- Clean your house with natural products, such as vinegar and baking soda.

- Take advantage of natural light by using energy-efficient glazed skylights and lightbulbs.

- Maintain an organic garden.

CATHERINE DE MEDICI

✳ ✳ ✳ ✳

*Speculation still swirls around the life of the Italian queen.
She was said to be a poisoner and a sorceress—the sole instigator of
a horrible massacre. She was also said to be a clever woman doing
the best she could in difficult circumstances. Which is true?*

- Catherine was the wife of Henri II, but she spent her entire married life overlooked in favor of Henri's lifelong mistress, Diane de Poiters, the Duchesse de Valentinois. Even at her own coronation, Catherine had to tolerate excessive attention to Diane's daughters, and Diane herself was publicly honored as well.

- Henri and Catherine didn't have children for the first ten years of their marriage, but at the insistence of Diane, the couple finally consummated their marriage and eventually had ten children.

- Catherine supposedly saw a vision of Henri's death several days before it happened. She begged him not to joust at the tournament held in celebration of their 13-year-old daughter Elisabeth's marriage to Philip II of Spain. He did so anyway and died from an infection in his eye caused by a splinter from a broken lance.

- After Henri died, Catherine wore mourning clothes for the rest of her life. She also took a broken lance as her emblem, bearing the motto "From this come my tears and my pain."

- Among Catherine's ten children were three kings of France (Francois II, Charles IX, and Henri III, respectively) and two queens: Margaret, called Margot, married Henri of Navarre, and Elisabeth became Queen of Spain.

- Francois II, Catherine's eldest son, was married to Mary, Queen of Scots. She had been raised among the French royal children, but she left France after her first husband's death.

- Despite her reputation as a persecutor of Protestants, Catherine actually tried to compromise between the Catholic and Protestant factions. She made concessions to Protestants, allowing them to worship their own way in private, but war broke out nonetheless.

- Often blamed for the St. Bartholomew's Day Massacre, it is not known what role Catherine played in the disaster. Some historians believe she intended it only to be a culling of Protestant nobles who had been leaders against her in the religious wars, but the situation got out of control.

- As was common at the time, Catherine was only 14 when she married. The match was arranged by her uncle, Pope Clement VII, and Henri's father, King Francois I.

- The daughter of Lorenzo the "Magnificent" and a French princess, Catherine was orphaned as an infant. Her mother died 15 days after Catherine's birth, and her father died six days later.

- The Medicis were overthrown in Florence when Catherine was eight years old, and she was taken hostage and moved from convent to convent around the city. She was often threatened with death or with life in a brothel to ruin her value as a bride.

- The Medici family, though very wealthy, was a merchant family rather than nobility. Catherine was reviled by many of the French because she was thought to be a commoner and therefore, in their eyes, unfit to be queen of France.

- Catherine had a great influence on fashion. As a new bride of short stature, she was desperate to make a good show at her introduction to the French court. She allegedly wore specially made high-heeled shoes to her grand entrance, impressing the fashion-obsessed nobles and sparking the style that remains popular today.

- Once out from under Henri's and Diane's influence, Catherine spread her wings and began to exercise control over her children—in fact, she dominated them. She ruled France as regent during the minority of Charles IX (and continued to rule during his adulthood, though as the king's "advisor" rather than regent), and Henri III relied heavily on her throughout his reign.

- Tragically, Catherine's large brood turned out to be sickly, and she outlived all but two of her ten children. Three had died in infancy, and only Henri and Margot were still alive when she died.

MAALOX MOMENTS:
UNEXPECTED UPSETS

✳ ✳ ✳ ✳

Notre Dame 35, Army 13—1913: Often regarded as the game that changed the face of football, the Irish attacked Army for the first time in the school's history and came away with an unlikely victory. With only 18 players on their roster and only enough cleats for 14 of them, Notre Dame used a secret weapon known as the forward pass and the combination of Gus Dorais and Knute Rockne to crush the Cadets.

Carnegie Tech 19, Notre Dame 0—1926: Irish sideline boss Knute Rockne was so confident his charges would trample the Tartans, he didn't even bother to attend the game, deciding instead to scout an Army–Navy match. While the Rock skipped, the Tech attacked, whipping the Irish with a 19–0 whitewashing.

Columbia 21, Army 20—1947: Undaunted by Army's pair of national titles and unfazed by the Cadets' 32-game unbeaten streak, Columbia rebounded from a 20–7 fourth quarter deficit to score a pair of unanswered touchdowns, including the infamous "shoestring" catch by Bill Swiacki, to squeeze past Army by a slim 21–20 score.

Miami 31, Nebraska 30—1984: In a hotly contested back-and-forth tundra tussle that many scribes describe as the most exciting college game ever played, the fifth-ranked Hurricanes shocked the top-ranked and undefeated Cornhuskers to win the Orange Bowl and claim the national championship. After Nebraska scored a last-second touchdown to pull within a single point, coach Tom Osborne decided to forgo the tie and attempt a two-point conversion. The Hurricanes held and climbed all the way to the title.

California 17, Stanford 11—1986: In the Bay area, the annual match-up between Stanford and California is known simply as "The Big Game." In most years, both schools are usually battling for Bowl positions, not bragging rights, but in 1986, the Cal team was in a state of disarray. They entered the contest with a 1–9 record, a lame duck coach who had already been fired, and an offense that hadn't been able to find the end zone in more than a month. That was then and this was now. The Bears combined a smothering sack attack that flattened Stanford pivot John Paye seven times with an opportunistic option end-around ramble by Mike Ford to send Stanford shame-faced to the sidelines.

Temple 28, Virginia Tech 24—1998: Entering the game as 35-point favorites, the 5–0 Virginia Tech Hokies learned an important lesson in the perils of overconfidence when the 0–5 Temple Owls shocked the football establishment by bouncing back from a 17–0 halftime deficit to embarrass the Hokies on their home turf. With freshman quarterback Devin Scott taking the snaps for the first time in his collegiate career and sneaking into the end zone late in the game, the Owls tutored Tech on both sides of the ball to register the biggest upset in school history.

Appalachian State 34, University of Michigan 32—2007: Dubbed "The Miracle in Michigan," Appalachian State, a Division II school, motored onto Michigan's home turf and pulled off what many pundits hail as one of the biggest upsets in the history of American sports, much less college football. After a late field goal propelled the Mountaineers into a 34–32 lead, Michigan marched down the field, eventually setting up a seemingly simple 27-yard three-pointer for the win. However, Appalachian defender Corey Lynch blocked the kick to secure the Mountaineers' victory.

> "The spirit, the will to win, and the will to excel are the things that endure. These qualities are so much more important than the events that occur."
>
> *Coach Vince Lombardi*

HYPNOSIS

✳ ✳ ✳ ✳

- Before he introduced hypnotism (aka "mesmerism") in 1775, Franz Mesmer tried to heal patients by having them swallow a drink with tiny grains of iron and then moving magnets over their bodies to sway the magnetic currents. As soon as he realized that people were actually reacting to his dramatic performance and "animal magnetism," he stopped using magnets and relied on the effect of his own voice.

- The first recorded use of hypnosis as anaesthesia took place in the 19th century. Dr. James Esdaile, a Scottish surgeon working in India, used hypnosis successfully in hundreds of limb amputations.

- People with the best imaginations are the easiest to hypnotize. Hypnosis researcher Theodore Sarbin calls hypnosis "believed-in imaginings." Those who are imaginative and creatively talented can easily visualize a hypnotist's suggestions and call to mind experiences that are colorful and compelling.

- About 10 to 15 percent of people react with either complete acceptance or outright rejection of hypnosis.

- Between 70 and 80 percent of people respond to certain hypnotic suggestions but not others. For example, they may scratch their head when a buzzer goes off if the hypnotist has told them to, but they won't go so far as to pour a bucket of water over their heads.

- Louis XVI and Marie Antoinette believed so strongly in Franz Mesmer's technique that they created the Magnetic Institute in France. At first, Mesmer had patients put their feet in buckets of magnetized water, with cables attached to magnetized trees. The French medical community—and visiting diplomat Benjamin Franklin—denounced him as a fraud.

- Falling under the power of a hypnotist was a legal defense in France in the 19th century. It was believed that a hypnotist could make someone "a toy in his hands" and that the person "could not reject the ideas of the beguiler." People who committed crimes under such influence could not be held legally or morally responsible for their acts.

- Today, hypnotists sometimes use a "mind machine" (aka "psychowalkman") to alter brainwave frequencies with light and sound. It is said to create altered states of consciousness, like meditation and shamanic rituals.

- Posthypnotic suggestions can, for instance, make people forget how to read or perceive colors where there are none or believe themselves to be capable of unusual things. Dr. Stephen M. Kosslyn, a Harvard neuroscientist, explains that this is possible because all of these experiences exist inside the brain, not in the world around us. They have always been completely in our minds.

- Stage hypnotists can make participants believe they are historical figures or celebrities. In one study in the 1960s, art students were hypnotized to believe they were Leonardo da Vinci, then asked to paint. They didn't paint like da Vinci, but, believing they were great, they painted better than they had ever done in the past.

How to Hypnotize a Chicken

Gently hold a chicken on its side on a flat surface, lightly securing its head. Move either your index finger or a small stick back and forth in front of the bird, about four or five inches from its beak. Keep the motion parallel to its head. Soon, the bird will fall into a "trance," which is easily lifted when you release the chicken.

SPEAK CANADIAN!

✳ ✳ ✳ ✳

There is, of course, no one "Canadian slang" in such a huge nation with people spread over thousands of miles. Canada has two official languages for ambitious slang-slingers to corrupt!

- **Allophone:** someone whose mother tongue is other than English or French, usually an immigrant but sometimes an Aboriginal Canadian.

- **Biscuit:** something half of Canadians pursue and the other 49 percent watch—namely, a hockey puck.

- **Bloquiste:** a member of the Bloc Quebecois, a national political party advocating the independence of Quebec.

- **Bunnyhug:** same thing as a "hoodie," that is, a hooded sweatshirt with pockets in front for your hands (or other stuff). Seems to have originated on the Prairies.

- **Deke:** a fake out, from "decoy." The term began as hockey slang for putting a move on an opponent, then went from rinks to the mainstream.

- ***Dépanneur:*** *Dep* for short, this is a convenience store. The word comes from the term for a repairperson, someone who gets you out of difficulty—as a convenience store does when you're driving from Denver to Kansas City with an intestinal ailment. Common in both English and French in Quebec.

- **Eh:** tag question roughly meaning "you see?" Canadians' signature utterance is the one folks in the United States most often kid them about—in fact, they do it so often that it long ago got old. Best not used by visitors to Canada.

- **Five-hole:** between a hockey goalie's legs. Could refer to anything passing through one's legs, or to any situation where someone got away with something at your expense.

- **Garburator:** the garbage-disposal unit under a sink.

- **Grits:** the Liberal Party, a moderate-left national political party with its main power base in Ontario. As a rule, the Grits have to screw up pretty badly to be out of power. It's a tough challenge, but they rise to it occasionally.

- **Holy!:** expression of surprise. Always emphasize the first syllable.

- **Hoser:** narrowly speaking, a clumsy, foolish, probably drunk person. Used to refer to anyone who can't cut the mustard. Thanks to Canadian comics Dave Thomas and Rick Moranis doing Bob and Doug McKenzie on *SCTV*, and much to Canadians' general chagrin, Americans have adopted it as slang for "Canadian." (Imagine if "moron" were slang for "American.")

- **Keener:** a brown-noser.

- **Molson muscle:** beer gut, apparent among sufferers of the condition known in the United States as "Dunlop's Disease" ("Your belly done lops over your belt").

- **Shebang:** a crude shelter or hut, what U.S. soldiers call a "hooch."

- **Shivaree:** a loud serenade for newlyweds, Acadian in origin, intended to chase away evil spirits.

- **Sieve:** more hockey slang, meaning a terrible goalie.

- **Skookum:** British Columbian slang for someone or something strong or sturdy, from the Chinook jargon spoken by most British Columbian and Washington state tribes of old.

- **Spud Island:** Prince Edward Island (always called P.E.I.), which is essentially Canada's own private Idaho in terms of agriculture.

- **Tory:** used to refer to the Progressive Conservatives, Canada's moderate right wing before all the shards of the right banded together in hopes of winning some federal power. Still used by some for its successor, the Conservative Party of Canada.

- **Touque:** rhymes with "Luke" and refers to a stocking cap, watch cap, etc. In most of Canada during winter, the term for one who does not wear a touque is "hypothermia fatality."

I'm No Expert, But...
SECURITIES MARKET

* * * *

In school, most students don't learn a lot to help them understand the securities markets, and a lot of misconceptions remain. Here's a little help.

Q: How does a stock transaction happen?

A: A seller and a buyer agree upon a given price for a given number of shares. Sometimes one or both parties are investors; in other cases, one is a "market maker" who deals in that security and is always willing to buy or sell it. At any given time, a stock has a current bid price (what someone is offering) and ask price (what someone will take). The distance between those is called the "spread." The transaction will occur when someone accepts someone's bid or asks for the right number of shares. A low number of shares traded daily is called "low liquidity" and is something for the investor to consider before shopping.

Q: Can daring U.S. citizens buy foreign stocks?

A: The answer is a qualified yes, depending on the foreign stock. Many foreign stocks trade on U.S. exchanges as ADRs (American Depositary Receipts); a share of the ADR represents all the privileges of X number of shares on the underlying stock's home exchange. In some cases, foreign stock trades cost extra commissions. Easy clue: For any five-letter ticker symbol ending in F or Y [examples: NIPNY (NEC Corporation), BAYZF (Bayer)], the potential buyer is crazy if he or she doesn't first investigate the way the stock is traded. Foreign stock dividends may be subject to foreign tax, so don't be impressed by gaudy double-digit yields until you see how much gets skimmed this way.

Q: How does a mutual fund work?

A: A mutual fund is simply an accumulation of invested assets in which investors own shares. The idea is that a professional can pick stocks or buy bonds more knowledgeably and wisely than you can, so you send that person your money to invest according to guidelines (clearly laid out in a prospectus). The share price of a mutual fund is called the NAV (net asset value) and fluctuates daily. The person you hired gets paid from the fund, typically collecting 1 percent of the total each year. Traditional open-end mutual funds issue and redeem shares as people buy and sell. A closed-end mutual fund issues a fixed number of shares and may trade above or below the NAV, because trades are brokered between shareholders rather than directly through the fund. An exchange-traded fund, or ETF, falls somewhere between the above.

Q: Can I buy actual bonds?

A: You can, but only if you're pretty well funded and focused. The average investor will have a much easier time buying fixed-income mutual funds (open-end or closed-end). Bonds aren't traded on an open exchange the way stocks are; dealers sell them from inventories, typically in big blocks. When looking at a bond index, keep in mind that unlike stocks, no one can buy the index to assure getting its result, because the bonds in the index aren't always available at any price.

Q: Is it actually possible for a person to make real money with stock dividends?

A: Sure, if that person is a smart investor. Very large company stocks tend to pay about 1.5 percent per year; you could beat that handily with good old bank CDs. But some smaller companies (and partnerships, and companies organized on specific models designed to pay large dividends) reliably pay 5 to 9 percent per year, which isn't chump change. The important thing is buying the shares at good prices, because dividends aren't really percentages—they're dollar amounts per share per period (often quarterly). The annual dividend divided by the stock price equals the yield percentage. Thus, if you are investing for dividends, you want a very low price because you'll get more shares, which will mean a bigger dividend check for as long as you hold the stock.

UNUSUAL U.S. ATTRACTIONS

✳ ✳ ✳ ✳

When the world-renowned, mouse-themed amusement parks lose their appeal, load your family into the car and check out some of these unique bits of Americana.

Casa Bonita
Denver, Colorado

Said to be the largest restaurant in the Western Hemisphere (at 52,000 square feet), Denver's Casa Bonita is one of the last vestiges of a regional chain of Mexican theme restaurants. The exterior, clad in pink stucco with a gilded dome tower that houses a statue of the Aztec Emperor Quahuatomec, masks an even more outrageous interior: faux cliffs, faux caverns, and long lines for cafeteria-style Mexican dinners.

The Great Stupa of Dharmakaya
Red Feather Lakes, Colorado

Tucked in the mountains northwest of Fort Collins, Colorado, this is the largest stupa—a monument to a great Buddhist teacher—in North America. Dedicated to the late Chogyam Trungpa, the 108-foot spire is a work of ornate and symbolic art. It was built with a special formulation of concrete designed to last more than 1,000 years.

The Beer Can House
Houston, Texas

What do you do with 39,000 beer cans (which, on a six-pack-a-day regimen, took 18 years to save)? You cut off the ends, flatten the sides, and rivet them together to make colorful aluminum siding. That's how John Milkovisch sided his modest home at 222 Malone Street. Fortunately, the motif complemented his yard, which he had already paved over with concrete embedded with marbles and pieces of metal. Soon, however, the hammering Houston sun assailed the siding and over-heated the house. So John recycled the lids and pull-tabs, creating curtains, mobiles, and fences to shade the house. When a warm Texas breeze blows, the effect is like a giant wind chime.

Bishop Castle
Beulah, Colorado

Jim Bishop is a man on a mission. Using rocks from the surrounding forest, he started building a one-room stone cottage in 1969 and never stopped. He now has what he describes as "the largest one-man construction project in the country, quite possibly the world!" Highlights include a tower that ascends high into the sky and a fire-breathing steel dragon that crowns the main structure.

Forbidden Gardens
Katy, Texas

Built by a Hong Kong tycoon as a testament to Chinese history, this Houston-area attraction features a one-third-scale model of one of China's greatest archeological finds: Emperor Qin's tomb and its resident army of 6,000 terra-cotta soldiers. The Gardens also include an elaborate model of the Forbidden City.

World's Second-largest Fire Hydrant
Beaumont, Texas

Painted white with black spots to promote the video release of Disney's *101 Dalmatians*, this 24-foot-tall hydrant was a gift from the movie studio to the Fire Museum of Texas, where it is on permanent display. The waterworks within the mottled shell are capable of blasting 25 gallons a second. Just two years after the Beaumont hydrant was erected, a 29½-foot fire hydrant was unveiled in Elm Creek, Manitoba, Canada, taking over honors as the world's largest.

Coral Castle
Homestead, Florida

After his beloved fiancée called off their wedding at the last minute, Ed Leedskalnin spent 28 years building an ornate castle as a monument to his lost love. Leedskalnin used only hand tools to cut massive blocks of coral—1,100 tons in all—that form the castle walls. Between moving and carving the giant chunks of coral, Leedskalnin gave visitors tours and sold pamphlets that expressed his famously eccentric views on love, politics, and magnetic currents. Three days after leaving a note on the castle door—"Going to Hospital"—he passed away in 1951, leaving the castle to his nephew. His nephew sold the place, and the new owners found Ed's life savings soon thereafter: thirty-five $100 bills, collected a dime (and later a quarter) at a time—the price of admission.

Carhenge
Alliance, Nebraska

For his family reunion, engineer Jim Reinders organized a project that became the stuff of legend: the construction of a scale model of Stonehenge using junked cars instead of slabs of stone. With the help of a backhoe, Reinders and his kin put together this lasting tribute to a much more mysterious landmark halfway around the world.

The Also Ran Gallery
Norton, Kansas

The mezzanine of Norton's First State Bank is home to the only museum in the United States dedicated to those who lost presidential elections, with a framed picture and a short biography of each person. The gallery features such famous faces as Thomas Jefferson and John Kerry alongside distinguished lesser-known losers as General Lewis Cass and Rufus King.

Forevertron
North Freedom, Wisconsin

Dr. Evermor (retired junk collector Tom Every) started building the Forevertron in 1983, and the 400-ton curiosity is now considered the world's largest sculpture. Evoking a Victorian view of the far future, Evermor used scrap metal of all kinds to build the monolith with the hope of using it to personally rocket into the cosmos.

Fountain of Youth
St. Augustine, Florida

The site of a natural spring that Spanish explorer Juan Ponce de León mistook for the legendary Fountain of Youth in 1513 is now a kitschy attraction with touristy diversions of all kinds. The spring's water is free for the taking—but you have to buy the souvenir bottle in which to take it home.

World's Largest Ball of Paint
Alexandria, Indiana

In 1977, Mike Carmichael started applying layer after layer of paint to an ordinary baseball. Since then, the ball has seen an average of two coats a day, earning the title "The World's Largest Ball of Paint." After more than 20,000 coats, the ball measures about 3 feet in diameter and weighs well over 1,300 pounds.

House on the Rock
Spring Green, Wisconsin

Capping a 60-foot geological formation named Deer Shelter Rock is one of the best-known architectural oddities in the United States. The House on the Rock (a parody of Frank Lloyd Wright's work) is the creation of Alex Jordan, who started building it in the 1940s as a vacation home. He kept on building, furnishing it with art, a three-story bookcase, and anything else that captured his fevered imagination. Jordan sold the house in the late 1980s, but subsequent owners have since made the place bigger and stranger than it has ever been. The structure now has 14 lavishly decorated rooms—including the Infinity room, which has 3,264 windows—and a surrounding complex that houses a miniature circus, one of the world's largest carousels, and a resort.

Original American Kazoo Company
Factory and Museum
Eden, New York

The Original American Kazoo Company began cranking out those crazy kazoos in 1916 and is now the world's only maker of metal kazoos. At the museum, visitors can experience the entire  kazoo-making process and view the original factory equipment. Displays include rare silver and gold kazoos, as well as kazoos of many shapes and sizes. A big metal kazoo—said to be the world's largest—adorns the roof of the museum.

WHAT'S IN A PHRASE?

✳ ✳ ✳ ✳

*They're part of our everyday language, but what are
the origins some of these popular phrases?*

Blue Bloods—In the Middle Ages, the veins of the fair-complexioned
people of Spain appeared blue. To distinguish them as untainted by
the Moors, they referred to themselves as blue-blooded.

Catherine Wheel—This popular firework was named after
St. Catherine, who, according to legend, was martyred by being
tied to a spiked wheel and rolled down a hill.

Rob Peter to Pay Paul—In the mid-1550s, estates in St. Peter's,
Westminster, were appropriated to pay for the new St. Paul's
Cathedral. This process revived a phrase that preacher John Wycliffe
had used 170 years before in *Select English Works*.

Humble Pie—While medieval lords and ladies dined on the finest
foods, servants had to utilize leftovers (the "'umbles" or offal) when
preparing their meals. To eat humble pie means to exercise humility
or self-effacement.

Men of Straw—In medieval times, men would hang around English
courts of law, eager to be hired as false witnesses. They identified
themselves with a straw in their shoe.

White Elephant—Once upon a time in Siam, rare albino elephants
were to receive nothing but the best from their owners. Therefore,
no one wanted one.

Touch and Go—English ships in the 18th century would often hit
bottom in shallow water, only to be released with the next wave.
The phrase indicated that they had narrowly averted danger.

By Hook or by Crook—This phrase describes a feudal custom that
allowed tenants to gather as much wood from their lord's land as
they could rake from the undergrowth or pull down from the trees
with a crook.

Folklore: Myth or Truth?
KAMEHAMEHA I, HAWAIIAN KING

✳ ✳ ✳ ✳

*Kamehameha was a strong peacetime leader
and an outstanding general. One might even call him
Hawaii's George Washington.*

- His given name at birth was Pai'ea. It is said that Pai'ea was born on Hawaii's Big Island shortly after an appearance of Halley's Comet, which occurred in 1758. Legend had it that a bright light in the skies would herald the birth of a great unifier. Depictions of him in later life support this timeframe. A portrait from 1810 shows a hearty, gray-haired individual, which seems about right for a man with a proud warrior youth now in his 50s.

- As he got older, Pai'ea earned the name "Kamehameha" (meaning "lonely one") because of his solitary, stern disposition.

- In 1779, he would meet his first Europeans when Captain Cook and his men arrived in Hawaii. At first, the Hawaiians thought Cook was a representative of Lono, the harvest god. However, they grew skeptical when Cook's ship floated back into the bay with storm damage. The battered ship hardly seemed like a godly vessel anymore. Some speculate that Cook's arrival prompted Kamehameha to believe that Hawaii's islands should be strengthened through unification.

- Kamehameha gained a reputation as a feared warrior. During a raid in 1782, his foot became stuck in a crevice, and while he was trapped, a couple of fishermen broke a paddle over his head. Fortunately for Hawaii, they didn't cut Kamehameha's throat before fleeing. Their small show of mercy would later inspire a crucial policy decision from Kamehameha.

- Kamehemeha worked his way up the royal chain of command of the Big Island. The path to kingship was treacherous, but the warrior was a savvy political operative who maneuvered his way through the deadly waters of royal favor. By 1790, he was well on his way to consolidating the Big Island under his rule as ali'i nui, or supreme chief.

- In 1794, Kamehameha remembered the fishermen who had knocked him on the head and ordered that they be brought before him. Instead of punishing them, though, Kamehameha put the blame on himself for having assaulted noncombatants. In a gesture of apology, he granted them land and set them free. Also, a new kapu, or law, was enacted that forbade harming civilians. It was called mamalahoe kanawai, "the law of the splintered paddle," and it decreed, "Leave the elderly, women, and children in peace."

- By 1795, with the Big Island firmly under control, Kamehameha assembled a large army and thousands of war canoes to invade the rest of the Hawaiian islands. He overtook Maui and Molokai without much trouble, and soon his forces landed on Oahu's beaches. Unfortunately, Oahu's defenders had European cannons to fire down on the invading forces from a mountain ridge. This held Kamehameha up until he sent a couple of battalions to flank the artillery. Soon, Oahu fell to Kamehameha as well.

- After the capture of Oahu, Kamehameha ran into some snags. He was getting ready to invade Kauai and Niihau when a rebellion back on the Big Island forced him to return and shore up his power base. In 1803, he attempted another invasion, which was cut short by an epidemic among his troops. Kamehameha also became ill but managed to survive.

- When he finally came for Kauai in 1810, Kamehameha had European schooners equipped with cannons to supplement his war canoes. The ali'i nui of Kauai took one look at that armada and surrendered. Kamehameha was now king of all of the Hawaiian islands with the individual rulers of each island acting as his vassals.

- The great king ended the tradition of human sacrifice but remained a devout follower of traditional Hawaiian religion. Christianity didn't impress him, though he let its followers live in peace. Regardless of religion, he would execute anyone who violated kapu.

- A figure closely associated with Kamehameha I is his favorite wife, Queen Ka'ahumanu. Traditional kapu was fairly harsh for women, with numerous gender-biased rules and restrictions. Ka'ahumanu could be called an early feminist. She used her strong influence to end most of the kapu that treated women unfairly, thereby expanding Hawaiian women's rights.

- Kamehameha's law of the splintered paddle has remained in force since it was enacted and even today is part of Hawaii's state constitution.

- In 1816, he introduced another lasting tradition, Hawaii's flag. Kamehameha's banner, with the Union Jack in the upper left corner and one horizontal stripe for each of the eight major islands, is now the state flag.

- The king loved to fish. When he didn't have more important things to do, he could be found angling off the Kailua coast. He even scheduled affairs of state around the prime fishing seasons.

- King Kamehameha I died in 1819. During his illness, tradition dictated that human sacrifice was necessary to save the king, but Kamehameha refused to bend his kapu, even to save his own life. After he died, a close friend hid his body, and his burial site remains unknown to this day. This was done intentionally, as the body of a king was believed to contain mana, or spiritual force. This mana could be stolen if someone were to possess the king's remains.

- Kamehameha's dynasty lasted through eight rulers between 1810 and 1893. Unfortunately for Hawaii, this was also an unhappy time of exploitation and loss of independence. The dynasty ended in 1893, when Americans overthrew Queen Lili'uokalani and took the first steps toward creating the Republic of Hawaii. From the start, this republic served the interests of U.S. businesses in Hawaii rather than those of Hawaii's native people. In 1898, Hawaii was incorporated as a U.S. territory.

- Every year in Hawaii on June 11, people celebrate King Kamehameha Day in honor of the visionary leader and hero.

Fast Facts

- *The gag rule was instituted in the Senate in 1836 in order that the senators would not have to accept, debate, or vote on anti-slavery petitions.*

- *The eagle on the United States Great Seal faces the olive branch in its right paw. However, until 1945 the eagle on the Presidential Seal faced the arrows gripped in its left paw.*

- *Both the GOP and the Democratic Party owe the popularization of their respective mascots—the elephant and the donkey—to a political cartoonist of the 1870s, Thomas Nast of* Harper's Weekly.

- *George Washington was a distant relation of King Edward I, Queen Elizabeth II, Sir Winston Churchill, and General Robert E. Lee.*

- *One of the U.S. presidents was not a U.S. citizen at his time of death: John Tyler, a Virginia native, died on January 18, 1862, a citizen of the Southern Confederacy.*

- *West Virginia is the only state to have formed by seceding from a pre-existing state.*

- *The original Library of Congress was burned down by the British in 1814 along with the Capitol. To replace it, the Congress bought Thomas Jefferson's personal book collection, which consisted of approximately 6,500 volumes.*

- *The middle initial "S" in Harry S. Truman's name does not actually stand for anything—his parents could not agree on a middle name.*

- *The first time John F. Kennedy and Richard Nixon locked in public debate was not as presidential candidates in 1960 but as young congressmen in 1947, when a political club invited them to discuss the pros and cons of a labor bill.*

NEW YEAR'S TRADITIONS

✳ ✳ ✳ ✳

New Year's celebrations worldwide focus on hope for prosperity and health in the future. Whether you throw dishes at your friends or free your tortured goldfish, may your tradition bring you good luck.

- In Cambodia, people roam the streets with squirt guns full of tinted water (red, pink, or yellow) in search of friends to anoint with a "colorful" future.

- In Wales, young men soak evergreen branches (symbols of good luck) in water and use them to sprinkle their friends' and relatives' homes.

- In Burma, you stand a good chance of being doused with water for good luck—by the bucketful.

- In Puerto Rico, celebrants toss a pan full of water out their windows in the belief that they're also tossing out evil spirits.

- South American celebrants hang dummies stuffed with newspaper and firecrackers off the front of their homes. At midnight, someone strikes a match and...kaboom! New Year's definitely begins with a bang.

- In an interesting gesture of good will, Danish citizens throw old dishes at their friends' front doors. A large pile of porcelain pieces indicates a wide circle of friends.

- In Vietnam, New Year's Eve is celebrated with the planting of a tree in the family garden. The tree is decorated with red streamers and lots of bells in an effort to ward off evil spirits.

- For days prior to the New Year in China, the family home must be meticulously cleaned. On New Year's Day, all cleaning activities must cease (and cleaning equipment such as brooms and dust pans must be put away) in the belief that any accumulated good fortune might be swept away and disposed of.

- The New Year's Eve dinner is the biggest celebration of the Chinese New Year and typically features vast quantities of food. In northern China, a central feature of the dinner is dumplings, which are thought to symbolize the promise of wealth because they have a shape similar to a Chinese gold nugget.

- In Thailand, people release their birds from cages and their goldfish from bowls for good luck.

- In the southern United States, Hoppin' John (black-eyed peas and rice) is prepared on New Year's Day for luck and wealth. Some families also include collard greens—the peas represent coins, and the greens represent paper money.

- Many people in Cuba and Mexico eat 12 grapes at midnight to ensure 12 happy months.

- In the Philippines, tables are piled high with food at midnight to ensure abundance for the coming year. Some also have a center-piece of seven round fruits. The round shape symbolizes money, and seven is a lucky number.

- Tradition in Anglo-Saxon countries has been that the first visitor after midnight brings the household luck for the coming year. Dark-haired men, recognized as the luckiest, often offer their neighbors a token gift of money, bread, or coal.

- The Scots eagerly anticipate a visitor who recently had good luck—new mothers, new brides, and people born on January 1 are the most popular.

- On New Year's in Germany, people tell fortunes by dropping molten lead into cold water. The lead takes a shape, and each shape represents something different. A heart or circle indicates an impending wedding, a ship means a journey, and a pig guarantees plentiful food.

- In Japan, many New Year's parties are festooned with paper lobster decorations. These are a symbol of longevity, because the crustacean's curved back resembles a hunched elderly person.

OUT TO LUNCH

✳ ✳ ✳ ✳

*Human beings are social creatures, and what brings
us together most often is food. Our early ancestors shared their
kill around a fire, but when we don't feel like cooking, we just
run out for a bite. Here a few nuggets of knowledge on
restaurants and restaurant culture.*

Oldest Restaurant: Casa Botin. Situated on *Calle de Cuchilleros* in
the heart of Madrid, Spain, Casa Botin was founded in 1725 and
still cooks up such famous food as roast pig, baby eels, and caramel
custard in its 18th-century stove.

Number of Restaurants in the United States in 2007: 935,000

Sales Projections for U.S. Restaurants in 2007: $537 billion

Most Expensive Sandwich: a McDonald's. No, not that McDonald's.
This sandwich, named after its creator, Scott McDonald, was available
for a brief time in 2006 at Selfridges in London. At a cost of
$175, this was no grilled cheese. Its ingredients included Kobe beef,
foie gras, black truffle mayonnaise, brie, mustard confit, and aged
sourdough bread.

Most Expensive Restaurant: Aragawa. Admission to this tiny steak
house in Tokyo, Japan, is by invitation only. The succulent, locally
raised Kobe beef is presented simply (with pepper and mustard
only) at the price of nearly $400 per person.

Most Popular Occasion for Dining Out: a birthday. Mother's Day
follows close behind, and Valentine's Day takes third place.

Percentage of an Individual's Meals Eaten in Restaurants: 24
percent. Though restaurants continue to beckon more people to
their tables, the average family still consumes the majority of its
meals at home.

Number of Restaurant Employees in the United States: 12.8 million.
Only the government employs more people.

HERE A GERM, THERE A GERM

✳ ✳ ✳ ✳

*All those products designed to rid our homes—and even
our air—of germs and bacteria aren't much good unless you know
where to use them. Here's a rundown of the most germ-infested areas
on the body and in the home, workplace, and around town.*

The Body is a Temple—for Germs

While most of the body is germ-free, the skin, intestines, mouth,
respiratory tract, and other areas may be really germy. The mouth
often contains more than 100 million bacteria, the skin more than
300 million, and the large intestine 200 trillion to 300 trillion! Most
of these are "good bacteria" because they help protect the body from
harmful bugs and improve the immune system.

Even Good Bacteria Can Be Bad

While most of the good bacteria in the large intestine keep the
digestive system working well, some can cause problems. People
who are lactose intolerant cannot digest the milk sugar in their small
intestine, so the lactose moves into the large intestine. There, the
bacteria are able to break down the lactose, but the process creates a
lot of acid and gas. Alcoholic sugars (the sugar found in "sugar free"
products), Olestra (fake fat), and even starch from legumes may end
up causing a person to have painful gas and diarrhea.

Germs That Cause Food Poisoning

Salmonella are bacteria usually associated with chicken and eggs.
These organisms, which can cause severe food poisoning and even
death, are found in the majority of kitchen sinks and often on
sponges and dishcloths (items that contain the most germs in the
home). Salmonella is also common on, and in, dogs, cats, turtles,
lizards, and nearly every domesticated pet.

The Most Dangerous Germs

"Bad" bacteria can cause a variety of necrotic (dead-tissue) skin
lesions. Community-Acquired-Methicilin-Resistant Staphylococcus,
known as CA-MRSA, not only damage the skin but are also resistant

to most antibiotics. *Staphylococcus aureus* are common and danger-ous bacteria that cause pimples, boils, food poisoning, and toxic shock syndrome. They are a major cause of hospital-acquired infections.

Workplace Germs

Where is the germiest place at work? Not communal lunch tables, most of which are wiped down a number of times. Not even the office bathrooms—these are also cleaned frequently. The most germ-infested area is your desktop and phone: They're probably not washed often, and your hands, which touch a lot of other germy things, are all over them.

Breathe Deep?

Is a deep breath of fresh air good for us? In fact, people breathe in at least 100,000 bacteria every day. The air that presents the great-est hazard is near a toilet (flushing causes droplets to float into the air) or sink (splashing water has the same effect), or within six feet of anyone who sneezes or coughs. Some cold and flu viruses can survive for more than 72 hours on dust.

Man's Best Friend Has a Dirty Mouth

Many people say that they would rather kiss a dog than a person, claiming that the canine mouth is cleaner than the human mouth. In reality, both contain billions of similar or identical bacteria and disease-causing agents. Moreover, many dogs eat fecal matter or rotten meat and therefore carry a variety of diseases and parasites.

Wash and Dry the Right Way

Most people believe that washing their hands with hot water will make them clean or even sterile. However, studies show that hot water causes the hands to sweat slightly, which brings more germs to the skin surface. Washing hands in cool or warm water is best. Another misconception is that hot-air hand dryers are more sanitary than towels.

Studies have shown that hand dryers actually blow bacteria off the floor and shoot them into the air, increasing the number of bac-teria on the hands by up to 162 percent. The spread of bacteria isn't limited to our hands—the germs are now everywhere.

THEY NEEDED MORE THAN AN APPLE A DAY

✳ ✳ ✳ ✳

Civil War medicine was certainly crude, but doctors in battle learned and developed new procedures at an astonishing rate.

A Civil War battlefield was not a good place to get wounded. If your injury didn't kill you immediately, the inexperienced surgeon hacking off your damaged limb probably would. But if you survived that, the infection you'd get from the filthy field hospital would do you in.

America's medical establishment was not ready to deal with a major war, so its ineffectiveness was no surprise. However, it's easy to overlook the fact that the Civil War was a vast training ground and laboratory for physicians, nurses, and other medical personnel.

Not So Spick-and-Span

When thousands of young men from around the country gathered in training camps, their bodies were assaulted by pathogens of all types. Most soldiers had never been away from their family farms and had no immunity to dysentery, cholera, malaria, and countless other diseases. There was also no plumbing in camp, so troops relieved themselves in pits dug for that purpose or randomly out in the woods. This bred hordes of flies that spread disease. Eventually the medical establishment attempted to remedy the situation, and proper sanitation was probably the first medical contribution of the Civil War.

Surgery in the Fields

Camps were not the only places that needed better sanitation; field operating stations were crude places where doctors regularly operated on soldier after soldier without washing their hands or cleaning their instruments. Infections in wounds after surgery were so common that doctors considered them part of the healing process.

While never fully curbing the spread of infection, surgeons did start to understand how to use anesthetics to clean wounds and equipment. Doctors today still fight infection after surgery, and they can look back to their Civil War counterparts as their forebears in infection prevention.

A Smooth Ride

Another vital advancement in medicine occurred in how the wounded were moved. At the beginning of the war, soldiers who performed poorly were assigned to stretcher duty. They were often poor stretcher-bearers as well, and many wounded died on the battlefield for lack of quick transport to field hospitals. Eventually, medical authorities established designated ambulance teams with attendants trained to do the job correctly and special wagons designed to hold the stretchers. Farther down the line, specially equipped trains transported the wounded to field hospitals behind the lines.

Recovery Room

Possibly the most important advancement was the establishment of better hospitals. Because of the vast number of wounded pouring off the battlefields, small civilian hospitals were practically worthless. At first, doctors commandeered schools, warehouses, and other buildings as substitutes. Eventually, though, doctors learned that disease quickly spread through these cramped, dank places, and they began building "pavilion hospitals," which featured long, wide, airy bays for patients. Ventilation kept a steady stream of fresh air moving through. Toilets with running water kept human waste—and the resulting flies—away from patient areas. Efficient design ensured that supply rooms, operating rooms, and kitchens were conveniently situated.

Nursing Back to Health

Another essential medical development was the growth of the role of female nurses. Nursing was already a profession, but during the war it became an important way for a woman to help the war effort. Nurses weren't prevalent in the war's early months, but news of wounded soldiers' suffering elicited a call for volunteers. About 2,000 women served as nurses during the war. They attended to the wounded, assisted doctors, maintained sanitary conditions, and generally helped keep order. The most famous Civil War nurse was Clara Barton, who organized volunteers and traveled to the front lines of many battles. She formed the American Red Cross in 1881.

Much has been written about the dire medical conditions during the Civil War, but underneath the horrors, important developments took place—developments that still reverberate in modern medicine.

Talk to the Expert
SPECIAL FORCES MEDIC

✳ ✳ ✳ ✳

A U.S. Army Special Forces medic isn't your garden variety hospital woker or battlefield medic. Here's what sets this job apart.

Q: How did you end up a Special Forces medic?

A: First I was with the 82nd Airborne; then I signed up for Special Forces, which you likely know as the Green Berets. Medic is one of the hardest specialties in Special Forces, but it's the most rewarding.

Q: In what way?

A: For one thing because we train for more than a year. I'm legally allowed to perform just about any medical procedure I think is necessary, short of opening up the braincase. But if enemy action opens up someone's braincase, I'll even have to do my best in there. While I am not yet a medical doctor, in field situations from sanitation to trauma to veterinary care, I do much of what an M.D. would do—and much that goes beyond what an M.D. would do. I don't know of many family practitioners who tell a family where to dig their well.

Q: Why do Special Forces teams need medics trained to that level?

A: Our primary mission is to work with indigenous people in combat zones—to learn their language and customs, earn their trust and allegiance, help them help themselves. I could be on another continent next week, delivering babies and teaching a tribe why it's a bad idea to let the goats urinate in the water supply. From their perspective, that obviously can't be harmful because the tribe hasn't died out yet. So I may have some convincing to do.

Q: Do you carry a weapon in war zones or are you unarmed?

A: Unarmed? Not Special Forces medics. I'm cross-trained in demolition, for example. Most of our likely adversaries would just laugh if you told them that they weren't supposed to shoot at medics or ambulances. I usually carry a Swedish K submachinegun on ops.

IN THE YEAR...1979

✳ ✳ ✳ ✳

- Vietnam and Vietnam-backed Cambodian insurgents announce the fall of Cambodian capital Phnom Penh and collapse of the Pol Pot regime.

- Margaret Thatcher becomes new British prime minister, the first woman in history to hold the post.

- Ugandan dictator Idi Admin is deposed.

- The Shah of Iran flees his country, and Ayatollah Khomeini seizes power when he returns to Tehran after 15 years in exile.

- Saddam Hussein becomes president of Iraq.

- Sony introduces the Walkman.

- Rap enters the popular music scene when the Sugar Hill Gang releases "Rapper's Delight."

- The partial meltdown of an overheated reactor at the Three Mile Island nuclear facility in Harrisburg, Pennsylvania, results in the evacuation of nearly 144,000 residents in nearby Middletown.

- Snow falls for 30 minutes in the Sahara.

- Egyptian president Anwar Sadat and Israeli prime minister Menachem Begin sign a peace treaty during a ceremony at the White House.

- An American Airlines DC-10 crashes shortly after takeoff at Chicago's O'Hare International Airport, killing 271 people on board and two on the ground.

- The cable sports network ESPN launches its first broadcast in the United States.

- Dustin Hoffman and Meryl Streep star in *Kramer vs. Kramer,* which goes on to win the Academy Award for Best Picture, as well as Oscars for its two stars, its director, and its screenplay.

TIPS FOR AVOIDING A MOUNTAIN LION ATTACK

✳ ✳ ✳

Mountain lions, also known as cougars, pumas, and panthers, are the largest cats in North America and live in a vast area from the Yukon Territory in Canada to the Pacific coast, the Rocky Mountains, and even Florida. Mountain lions are more plentiful than most people realize, and, though they generally avoid people, attacks do occur.

- Hike in groups. Mountain lions avoid crowds and noise, and the more people on the lookout, the better. If there are children in the group, make sure they are supervised.

- Be aware of your surroundings, paying particular attention to what's behind and above you in trees and on rocks and cliffs.

- Don't back the animal into a corner—give it a way out. It would much rather run off and survive to hunt again.

- If you encounter a mountain lion, stand still rather than try to run away. Running may cause the animal to chase you, and it's much faster than you are. Stand still while facing the mountain lion, but avoid looking it in the eye, which it takes as a sign of aggression. Watch its feet instead.

- Do things that make you appear larger and bigger than the cat, such as raising your arms over your head or holding up a jacket, a backpack, or even your mountain bike.

- Make loud noises. Growling can make you sound like something the cat would prefer not to mess with.

- Don't crouch down or bend. This makes you appear smaller and, therefore, an easy target. Don't move a lot but don't play dead. To a mountain lion, a perfectly still human looks like an entrée.

- Remain calm and don't act afraid. Like many animals, mountain lions can detect fear.

FUGITIVES WHO HAVE SPENT THE LONGEST TIME ON THE FBI'S TEN MOST WANTED LIST

* * * *

In 1950, J. Edgar Hoover founded the FBI's Ten Most Wanted Fugitives program that still exists today. Since the list was established, 484 fugitives have appeared on it and 455 have been apprehended or located. Here are the criminals who have spent the most time on the list.

1. **Donna Jean Willmott spent close to eight years on the Top Ten list before surrendering on December 6, 1994.**
    In 1985, Willmott purchased 36 pounds of explosives from an undercover FBI agent. She planned to use the material to free the leader of a Puerto Rican leftist terrorist group from prison.

2. **Claude Daniel Marks appeared on the list the same number of years as Willmott, down to the day.**
    The two were partners in the prison-escape plan, purchasing the explosives and eventually surrendering together.

3. **Benjamin Hoskins Paddock spent eight years on the list.**
    A bank robber who escaped from a Texas prison, Paddock is one of only five fugitives to be removed from the list without being captured, found dead, or surrendering. The FBI removes fugitives from the list under two conditions: The federal process against them is dismissed, or they no longer fit the Top Ten criteria. Paddock was put on the list on June 10, 1969, and was removed on May 5, 1977.

4. **Glen Stewart Godwin has been on the Top Ten list since December 7, 1996, for a string of crimes and prison escapes.**
    In 1987, he escaped from Folsom State Prison in California, where he was serving time for murder. He was arrested later that year for drug trafficking in Mexico. He was convicted and sent to prison in Guadalajara, where he allegedly murdered a fellow inmate and escaped five months later. He remains at large.

5. **Arthur Lee Washington spent 11 years on the Top Ten list before being removed on December 27, 2000.**
He remains at large, wanted for the attempted murder of a New Jersey state trooper during a traffic stop.

6. **Leo Joseph Koury spent 12 years on the list before being found dead on June 16, 1991.**
Koury, who was placed on the list on April 20, 1979, was wanted for murder, extortion, mail fraud, and attempted kidnapping.

7. **Katherine Ann Power was on the list for close to 14 years before being removed on June 15, 1984.**
As a student at Brandeis University in 1970, Power was part of a group that fire-bombed and stole arms from a National Guard armory before robbing a bank a few days later. A police officer was shot during the bank robbery, prompting Power to go into hiding for 23 years. In 1993, she turned herself in, pled guilty to manslaughter, and was sentenced to 8 to 12 years in prison.

8. **Charles Lee Herron racked up 18 years, 4 months, and 9 days of Top Ten status.**
He stood accused of the 1968 murder of two Tennessee police officers when he was placed on the list on February 9, 1968. He was captured on June 18, 1986, at home in Jacksonville, Florida.

9. **Victor Manuel Gerena has been on the list for 23 years, since May 14, 1984, wanted in connection with the 1983 armed robbery of a Connecticut bank where he was a security guard.**
He has been linked to Los Macheteros, a Puerto Rican terrorist group that advocates for independence from the United States. After making off with $7 million, Gerena disappeared and is thought to be living in Cuba.

10. **Donald Eugene Webb holds the record for longest time spent on the FBI Top Ten list at 25 years and counting.**
In 1980, Webb was being sought as a suspect in a burglary when he was pulled over for running a stop sign in Saxonburg, Pennsylvania. A fight ensued, and Webb allegedly shot and killed the police officer. Webb was also shot during the incident, leading the FBI to believe that he may have died from his injuries.

I'm No Expert, But...
GAMBLING

✳ ✳ ✳ ✳

Most people would cheat Las Vegas blind if they could get away with it—but few bother to try. We asked some questions about the fine art of betting, and its shady side.

Q: How would someone mark cards?

A: You need two things: very sharp eyes, and a deck with a repeating pattern on the back—Bicycles, Bees, and Aviators are great, but corporate logo decks are terrible. Ideally, use cards with backs printed in a color matching a fine-tip permanent marker. Then decide what mark will encode each suit and rank, and very carefully mark the cards. Since cards can be upside-down, and since most people fan them so as to view the upper left corners, mark both the upper left and lower right of each card. Wear prescription sunglasses so people can't see you staring at the backs of the cards they're holding.

Q: Does card counting really work in blackjack?

A: Depends how many decks there are, first of all. The more decks are used at once, the less fruit card counting can bear. There are two types of card counting: in your head, and mechanically assisted. The casino can't stop you from counting cards in your head; it can only make it more difficult for you. Some states have laws against mechanical assistance, and if you're caught with it, expect a quick blackball from every casino in the region.

Q: Is anyone getting away with counting cards?

A: Have no doubt of that. You'll never hear of them, because they will never be caught. Pigs get fat; hogs get slaughtered, as tax accountants say. They make reasonable money, they go to different places, they lose sometimes, they act like your everyday gambling addict or hobbyist. They don't give the game away by placing suspicious bets; they know how to behave, be friendly, flirt with employees. They stay under the radar. When the numbers are in their favor, they bet more; when numbers aren't good, they bet less, but they don't overdo it.

Q: How do casinos battle card counters?

A: First of all, from the pit boss to the security office, people are watching. When gambling you should consider yourself under surveillance from head to toe. I wouldn't put it past casinos to have night-vision cameras underneath the tables. They have a lot of experience and know what to look for. Free drinks are another tool, because hardly anyone's counting skills improve with alcohol intake. If the boss thinks you're counting, he or she may "flat bet" you—ask you to make the same wager on every hand, which is the opposite of what a counter is trying to do. What they're looking for is your reaction to that request. If you don't follow it, they'll ask you to leave.

Q: What are the best and worst games in terms of payout?

A: Casino poker, blackjack card counting, and video poker generally pay best. Slot machines are terrible, as are live keno and Wheel of Fortune. House payouts tend to range from 85 to 95 percent overall, so on the whole, the game favors the casino. Do you think all those pyramids, sphinxes, complimentary buffets, and neon lights come from the money people have won?

"At that point I ought to have gone away, but a strange sensation rose up in me, a sort of defiance of fate, and a desire to challenge it, to put out my tongue at it. I laid down the largest stake allowed—four thousand gulden—and lost it. Then, getting hot, I pulled out all I had left, staked it on the same number, and lost again, after which I walked away from the table as though I were stunned. I could not even grasp what had happened to me."

Fyodor Dostoyevsky, The Gambler

GREAT CANADIAN VACATIONS & ADVENTURES

* * * *

Everyone's heard that Montreal is charming, Victoria is quaint, and Blue Jays games are fun, but here are a variety of Canadian roads (and places lacking roads) less traveled.

Dempster Highway (Yukon Territory/Northwest Territory): This 417-mile gravel road will take you from Dawson, Yukon Territory (of gold rush fame), to Inuvik, Northwest Territory. You'll cross the Arctic Circle after the halfway point. Take two spare tires, fuel up at every opportunity, and ideally go in late August or early September, when the mosquitoes and blackflies ease up and the fall colors are in.

Churchill (Manitoba): For the moment, you can still see polar bears and beluga whales (July through August) near this Hudson Bay community and seaport. It's not a big place (pop. 923), and you'll have to fly or take the train from Winnipeg or Thompson, because no road extends to Churchill. There's kayaking, an old Hudson's Bay Company stone fort, birdwatching, and more.

Jasper National Park (Alberta): Many people go to Banff yet never venture up the spine of the Canadian Rockies to take in this gem. Walk the trail of Maligne Canyon, golf at Lac Beauvert, take the tram up to Whistler's Mountain (not to be confused with Whistler ski resort in British Columbia), or just stare in awe at Stutfield Glacier.

Charlottetown (Prince Edward Island): One used to have to boat or fly to Prince Edward Island, Canada's smallest province; now there's a toll bridge. If you love to golf, take the sticks: There are 20 courses within an hour of Charlottetown where you can slice tee shots into the rough. Otherwise, enjoy the historic architecture, friendly atmosphere, and unspoiled natural beauty.

Acadian Coast (New Brunswick): Acadian culture is not Quebecois culture, though it does involve French language; it is not militant but does involve pride of heritage. New Brunswick's north coast is the Acadian part. Walk the long, snaking boardwalk along the odd *Dune* *de Bouctouche* (a big sandbar with dunes), and go the short distance to Caraquet for immersion in Acadian history.

Quebec City Winter Carnival (Quebec): North America has one walled city: historic Quebec, a Francophone city far smaller than Montreal. Go in February and with kids—that's Winter Carnival time. While French is the first language of locals, during *le Carneval de Québec*, you can surely find English-spoken help if needed. Take in the Ice Palace, competitions on the Plains of Abraham, and views of the lighted, snowy city at night.

Toronto (Ontario): Toronto is Canada's cleaner, smaller, and safer version of New York City, and one-quarter of Canadians live in the surrounding region. Highlights include the CN Tower, the Ontario Science Center, the Toronto Zoo, the Art Gallery of Ontario, the Gardiner Museum of Ceramics, Fort York historic site, and the Hockey Hall of Fame. There are plenty of quality hotels, good transportation, and fine dining—with dress codes, so pack appropriately.

Vancouver to Kamloops (British Columbia): The Canadian San Francisco, Vancouver is a large port city full of great dining and ethnic diversity. Take the freeway up the Fraser Valley past Bridal Veil Falls, past Hope (with its Hell's Gate tram across the river), and up the gorgeous Coquihalla Highway to the ruggedly Western 'Loops. Go in late September or October to catch a Kamloops Blazers game—until you've seen a junior hockey game in a smaller town, you haven't quite touched the soul of Canada.

Cape Breton (Nova Scotia): For the full maritime experience, you must go to sea. Combine that with a boat outing to the stony Bird Islands, where in season you'll see puffins, guillemots, cormorants, kittiwakes, bald eagles, and even gray seals. Stay in a seaside cottage where you can visit the Louisbourg fortress or explore the Cabot trail. Canada's great inventor, Alexander Graham Bell, did his later research here. This is an island, but there's a bridge. If you fail to listen to Celtic music during the drive, go back to the bridge and do it over correctly.

ANIMALS THAT TASTE BAD TO PREDATORS

* * * *

*Many animals have a bad taste that protects them
from predators. That taste may come from poisonous venom,
special glands, or even a diet of foul-tasting bugs.
Here are a few crummy-tasting critters.*

Slow Loris

This primate, which lives in China and Southeast Asia, has a special gland in its elbow that secretes a toxin that it mixes with saliva. Before leaving to search for food, a mother applies this toxin to her babies to keep them safe from predators.

Poison Dart Frog

This species of frog is native to Central and South America, and one variety has been introduced to the Hawaiian Islands. The name originates from South American tribes that smear the poison from the skin of the frog on their arrows or blow-gun darts. Just touching the skin of the golden poison dart frog species with your tongue can be fatal. Evidence suggests that the toxin in poison dart frogs comes from their diet, which is primarily ants, mites, and beetles that also contain the poison, but in much smaller doses.

Eurasian Water Shrew

This shrew is highly territorial and can be found from Great Britain to North Korea. It has venomous saliva that can quickly kill its natural enemy, the vole.

Platypus

Native to eastern Australia and Tasmania, the platypus is one of the few species of mammals that lay eggs. It's also one of the few venomous mammals. The male platypus has a spur on his hind feet that delivers a poison that isn't powerful enough to kill other animals but does cause severe pain. Scientists believe the platypus uses this poison to assert dominance over rival males during the mating season.

Cane Toad

This large toad is native to Central and South America. An adult cane toad averages four to six inches in length; however, the largest recorded specimen measured 15 inches long and weighed nearly six pounds. The cane toad has large poison glands behind its eyes that make it highly toxic to predators.

Puffer Fish

The puffer fish, also called the blowfish, gets its name from its ability to inflate itself to several times its normal size by swallowing water or air when threatened. Some puffer fish produce a powerful neurotoxin in their internal organs, making them an unpleasant and possibly lethal meal for any predator, including humans. In Japan and Korea, specially trained chefs prepare puffer fish for adventurous diners who consider it a delicacy.

Monarch Butterfly

The monarch is foul-tasting and poisonous due to the toxic chemicals it ingests when feeding on milkweed during the caterpillar stage. The monarch shares this defense mechanism with the even more-unpleasant-tasting viceroy butterfly, which looks like a small monarch.

Ladybugs

Most people like ladybugs, but the same can't be said of the predators that swallow them. Adult ladybugs are able to force themselves to bleed from their leg joints, releasing an oily yellow toxin with a strong repellent smell that's poisonous to small birds and lizards. Don't worry if you accidentally swallow one, because humans have to ingest several hundred before feeling any effects of the poison.

Skunk

The best-known feature of the skunk is its anal scent glands, which produce a mixture of sulfur-containing chemicals that give off an offensive smell strong enough to ward off bears, wolves, foxes, badgers, and other potential attackers. Skunks also use their spray during mating season.

VOLUPTUOUS VELVET

✳ ✳ ✳ ✳

Velvet offerings range from the sublime to the ridiculous. Members of European royalty were fond of it, Santa Claus's suit is said to be made of it, and Elvis has been immortalized on it. Here's the story behind this super-soft and shiny fabric.

- Velvet is a closely woven fabric with a thick, short pile on one side. The highest-quality velvet, made from silk, is luxuriously soft and beautiful and can be used for apparel, home fashions, and as a canvas for paint, as well as for numerous other purposes.

- The first evidence of velvet weaving comes from the Far East, sometime in the 14th century, but velvet really made a name for itself when medieval Italians began using it. By doubling the pile, weaving in brocade and other ornaments, artisans of the time created rich tapestries that hang in museums today.

- The word *velvet* comes from the ancient French *veluotte,* and *velouté* is a term in French cooking that describes a smooth, silky texture, typically a rich white sauce thickened with cream and egg yolks.

- A velvet canvas takes paint surprisingly well. Most artists use black velvet, which allows the paint colors to "pop" from the background. From the 1950s to the 1970s, velvet paintings gained popularity for their kitsch factor, reflected in the many velvet paintings that feature dogs playing poker or likenesses of Elvis Presley.

- Is it velvet or velour? Authentic velvet is made from silk. Velour (popularly used in fashion-oriented "track suits") is a fabric with a similar feel, but it's made from cotton, not silk.

- Developed in the 18th century, corduroy was originally known as "poor man's velvet." The warp of this heavy cotton fabric is higher than its weft, producing a look similar to velvet but at a significantly lower price.

- To avoid permanent creases in this delicate fabric, velvet should be hung when stored rather than folded.

Folklore: Myth or Truth?

HIGH JOHN THE CONQUEROR, AFRICAN-AMERICAN LEGEND

✳ ✳ ✳ ✳

Africans brought a great deal to America, including vastly rich folklore. It's been said that High John the Conqueror arrived with an unbridled spirit that no person or peril could break.

Who was he?

Most likely, High John the Conqueror was a mythical creation, but his myth offers excellent insight into history. African-American culture first developed under slavery, mixing the customs of the new, African-born captives with that of their American-born counterparts. This synthesis created a diverse ethnic identity that has long retained traces of the ancestral homeland.

Many African-American folktales are believed to have origins in Africa, including the stories of High John the Conqueror. He is often portrayed as an ingenious individual who was captured in Africa and brought to America, where his new masters attempted to put him to work as a slave. However, he never embraced his new position and rebelled in a number of clever ways. In some versions of the legend, the slaveowner's barn mysteriously burned down, or John's mule team "accidentally" trampled the cotton. John always remained above his master's suspicion, yet every slave knew what had really happened.

Why were his stories so popular?

The everyday life of a slave was one of many commands and few personal decisions. Anything, including family, could be taken away at any time. The one safe place that was fully sheltered from authority was within the mind. Tales of High John the Conqueror, and of the unnamed slaves whose real-life defiance and clever deeds probably built the legend, reminded slaves of their humanity and intelligence, the very traits that their masters hoped to suppress. John was a spark of individuality and creativity in a strictly controlled world.

BASIC LAWS OF THE RICHTER SCALE

✳ ✳ ✳

In 1934, Charles F. Richter developed a way to measure an earthquake's magnitude based on the seismic waves that radiate from it. Because most big earthquakes are followed by smaller quakes called aftershocks, the Richter scale can indicate the size of these potential secondary tremors.

Magnitude 2.0 and below: You usually can't feel the effects of a quake this size, and the majority of the world's earthquakes have a magnitude of 2.5 or lower. During the earthquake "swarm" in Arkansas in 1982, there were 88 earthquakes between June 24 and July 5. From then until 1985, there were 40,000 quakes of this magnitude in the state.

Magnitude 2.0–2.9: Known as "very minor," earthquakes of magnitude 2.0–2.9 are recorded, though they're generally not felt. Worldwide, there are on average 1.3 million of these per year.

Magnitude 3.0–3.9: Called a "minor" earthquake, rumblings of magnitude 3.0–3.9 are often felt, but they rarely cause damage. In 1938, Lake Charles, Louisiana, shook from a magnitude 3.8 earthquake, and there are about 130,000 quakes of this magnitude per year worldwide.

Magnitude 4.0–4.9: Often felt but seldom damaging, occurrences of these "light" earthquakes average about 13,000 per year worldwide. In 1947, Michigan had a magnitude 4.6 earthquake, and in 1986, a 5.0 quake occurred in Ohio, with aftershocks felt in eight states.

Magnitude 5.0–5.9: Known as "moderate" earthquakes, these can cause major damage to poorly constructed buildings but present little threat to sturdy structures. There are about 1,300 of these per year worldwide. Kentucky had a 5.1 magnitude earthquake in 1980; New Brunswick, Canada, had a 5.7 in 1982; Indiana had a 5.9 in 1983; and in 1987, Illinois had a 5.1 quake.

Magnitude 6.0–6.9: There are approximately 135 "strong" earthquakes in the world each year. They can be destructive to areas as far as 60 miles from the epicenter. One of the most notable earthquakes in recent years was a 6.9 shocker that hit near Santa Cruz, California, just as the 1989 World Series was getting underway in nearby Candlestick Park.

Magnitude 7.0–7.9: These "major" earthquakes can cause serious damage over larger areas, and there are about 17 such quakes each year worldwide. In 1811 and 1812, New Madrid, Missouri, endured three earthquakes estimated to have been between 7.2 and 8.3, with 203 aftershocks. But the most noteworthy of earthquakes in the magnitude 7 range was on April 18, 1906, in downtown San Francisco. Estimated at magnitude 7.8, this quake and the subsequent fire left more than 400,000 people homeless and 3,000 dead.

Magnitude 8.0–8.9: The earth averages one "great" earthquake per year. These can cause serious damage in areas several hundred miles from the epicenter. In February 1965, a magnitude 8.7 quake shook the Aleutian Islands in the northern Pacific, west of Alaska. One of the deadliest earthquakes of all time—an estimated 8.7 magnitude—struck Lisbon, Portugal, in 1755, killing nearly 70,000 people.

Magnitude 9.0 and above: Also known as "great" earthquakes, the planet endures one of these monster quakes about every 20 years. They can cause devastation several thousands of miles from the epicenter. In 1964, the Good Friday Earthquake rocked Prince William Sound, Alaska, at a whopping 9.2 magnitude, making it the largest North American earthquake on record. Chile holds the record for the strongest earthquake in the 20th century: A massive 9.5 magnitude quake struck on May 22, 1960.

Possibly the deadliest earthquake in history was recorded in July 1201 in the eastern Mediterranean. Approximately 1.1 million people were killed.

UNEXPLAINED MYSTERIES OF THE UNIVERSE

✳ ✳ ✳ ✳

Unidentified flying objects are old hat compared with these popular supernatural mysteries, unexplained phenomena, and unsolved puzzles. Read on and see if we can make a believer out of you.

Bermuda Triangle

This area in the Atlantic Ocean between Bermuda, Miami, and San Juan is legendary as the site from which an astoundingly high number of ships, small boats, and airplanes have allegedly disappeared. Although the United States Coast Guard does not officially recognize the Bermuda Triangle or maintain any data on the area, conspiracy theorists have spent countless hours documenting the mysteries of the region. Some researchers estimate that more than 2,000 boats and 125 planes have been lost there, including the famous Flight 19, five Navy bombers that disappeared in 1945, followed by their search-and-rescue seaplane. Explanations for the disappearances include extraterrestrials that captured the boats and planes, deep-water earthquakes that caused freak waves, and time warps that took vessels to a different time or dimension.

Easter Island

One of the most remote areas on Earth, Easter Island is in the southern Pacific Ocean, 1,400 miles from any other island. So how is it that more than 800 giant, centuries-old stone statues line the island's coast? Who built them? How did they get there? These questions have baffled enthusiasts for decades. The island was discovered in 1722 by a Dutch explorer who found it uninhabited, except for the numerous *moai*, as the statues are known. The most popular explanation for the statues suggests that Polynesian seafarers arrived on the island between A.D. 400 and 1600 in canoes carried by ocean currents. Unable to paddle against the currents to leave the island, the new inhabitants carved the statues out of a volcanic wall and placed them around the island using simple machines. But when the island's resources began to give out, the people resorted to cannibalism, wiping out the population by the time the Dutch landed.

Area 51

Officially, Area 51 is a remote strip of land about 90 miles north of Las Vegas that the Air Force uses to test new military aircraft. Unofficially, it's a storage and examination site for crashed alien spaceships, a meeting spot for extraterrestrials, a breeding ground for weather control and time travel technology, and possibly the home of a one-world political group. Because the U.S. government won't discuss what goes on at Area 51, inquiring minds have had to develop their own theories. In 1989, Bob Lazar, a former government scientist, told a Las Vegas TV station that he worked on alien technology at a facility near Area 51. Millions believed Lazar's story and Area 51's mysterious reputation was sealed.

Nostradamus

Whether you believe his predictions or not, 16th-century French philosopher Nostradamus was an impressive guy. After all, how many authors' books are still in print 450 years after their first editions? *Les Prophéties,* first published in 1555, is a series of poems that predict major world events in a vague, timeless manner that leaves much room for interpretation. Nostradamus's followers credit him with predicting the rise of both Napoleon and Hitler, the French Revolution, the Great Fire of London, both World Wars, the death of Princess Diana, the Apollo moon landings, and the terrorist attacks of September 11, 2001, among other things. Skeptics say the links between his prophecies and world events are the result of misinterpretations or mistranslations, or are so vague that they're laughable.

Stonehenge

Situated near Amesbury, England, Stonehenge is a collection of giant stones standing in a circular formation. Archaeologists estimate that the stones were erected between 3000 and 1600 B.C. in three separate phases. Visitors to the site have been hypothesizing as to its origins for centuries, but various academics have credited the Danes, the Druids, the Romans, the Greeks, and the Egyptians, among others. Just as many theories exist regarding its purpose: a predictor of solar phenomena, a means of communicating with heaven, a pre-historic computer, a sacred place of worship, and more. Some people even believe it's an extraterrestrial landing site and claim to have seen UFOs in the area.

Crop Circles

Art exhibit, practical joke, or universal mystery, crop circles have been captivating observers for decades. They occur when crops are flattened to form geometric patterns most visible from the sky. Crop circles are usually found in England but have also been spotted in Australia, South Africa, China, Russia, and other countries. In 1991, two men admitted they had created a number of the crop circles identified in England since 1978 by marking out circles with a length of rope and flattening the crops with iron bars and wooden planks. But "croppies," a group of scientists and paranormal enthusiasts, ar-gue that some of the designs are far too complex for humans to cre-ate with simple tools. Croppies believe that some of the circles are the result of flying saucers that land in fields, freak wind vortexes, or ball lightning—a brief flash of light usually the size and shape of a basketball that's not always associated with a thunderstorm.

Edinburgh Castle

Thought to be one of Scotland's most haunted sites, Edinburgh Castle is reputedly home to ghosts, a headless drummer boy, and a lone piper. The castle, which once housed prisoners from the Napoleonic Wars, has been the subject of much speculation over the centuries. As recently as 2003, builders renovating the structure complained about sharing quarters with ghosts. Workers say mysteri-ous blue orbs appeared to float above their heads in photos they took each week to record their progress. In 2001, a group of scientists measured temperature, air movement, magnetic fields, and light levels in the castle in an attempt to find evidence of paranormal activity. The results were inconclusive, but believers point to the investigation as further indication that the castle is indeed haunted.

GRIDIRON GRAMMAR

✳ ✳ ✳ ✳

Football has always had a language all its own, and it has adopted many terms and truisms from commonplace sources outside of sports.

Considering that the quarterback is often referred to as the general and his players are known as troops, it's not surprising that many football terms, such as *blitz, bomb, trenches,* and *gunners,* have been borrowed from the military. The blitz, like its wartime connotation, is a bombardment, but not from the air. It is an all-out frontal attack, bolstered by 300-pound behemoths intent on planting the quarterback face first into the turf. The football bomb is also an aerial assault, but instead of an explosive-laden shell, this weapon is a perfectly delivered spiral carried triumphantly into the opposition's end zone. The trenches, much like their World War I counterparts, are pungent places, replete with sweat, spit, mud, and blood. Football's trenches are found along the line of scrimmage, an all-man's land where hand-to-hand combat determines who wins the day. Like their combative comrades, gridiron gunners are responsible for neutralizing the enemy and thwarting its attack. On the battle lines that are drawn between the boundaries, these gunners set their sights on the kickoff and punt-return specialists.

Now, it's doubtful that too many pigskin pundits would equate the quaint image of a sewing circle with the hard-nosed ferocity of the football field, but why else would words such as *patterns, buttonhooks,* and *seams* be instrumental entries in the gridiron lexicon? Tailors depend on patterns to guide them, much like a well-tuned offense on the football field depends on well-executed play patterns to methodically move the ball toward the opposition's end zone. The buttonhook is an important tool for a tailor and a nifty maneuver for a receiver, who races down field and then hooks back toward the line of scrimmage, throwing havoc and confusion into the defensive schemes of the enemy. Anyone who has ever picked up a needle and thread knows that working along the seams takes a delicate touch. In football, the seam is a narrow gap in the defense that must be worked to "sew up" a reception.

Talk to the Expert
METEOROLOGIST

✳ ✳ ✳ ✳

*It's one of the most misleading job titles
there is, because it has nothing to do with meteors.
Here's what it's really about.*

Q: "Meteorologist" just means "weather forecaster," doesn't it?

A: That oversimplifies it a lot, because there are so many specialties that fall under the umbrella of meteorology. Most of us aren't the smiling person in the business suit on the local TV news, telling you that it's going to be partly cloudy with partial clearing later. For one thing, a lot of my colleagues are way too ugly for TV and yet are outstanding at their work.

Q: Describe some of the specialties—especially yours.

A: I'm an agricultural meteorologist, which incorporates a little bit of agronomy and geology. I'm concerned with temperature and precipitation and wind as they relate to wheat, corn, sorghum, pasture grasses, and whatever else companies cultivate. The Air Force has aviation meteorologists, who study weather's effect on flight. There are research meteorologists, who are currently arguing about whether global warming is going to submerge our coastal cities, or they're trying to gain a better understanding of how the global weather puzzle fits together.

Q: Why can't meteorologists predict the weather more accurately?

A: There are two answers to your question. The first is that we do predict it more accurately, and farther out, with every passing year. In tornado-alley states, any time we see a cumulonimbus (thunderstorm) cloud possibly forming, we have our eyes on it because those clouds can create cyclones. You've seen the pictures: total devastation, yet few lives are lost. That's because we get the word out, and people take cover.

Q: You said two answers, though.

A: Sure did. Weather is a naturally chaotic system, tending to defy predictability. Our work is to beat that chaos. Sometimes we expect one result and another happens—it's that simple. Predicting weather is like predicting the result of a college football game. If a mid-major team plays the numer-three-ranked team in the country, you'll probably bet on the ranked team. But the scrappy mid-major opponent might just pull off the upset. No one could or would have called that one in advance. Same with meteorology.

Q: Can you get a college degree in meteorology?

A: You can get one in atmospheric sciences or meteorology. A typical career path would be to go into the Air Force or Naval ROTC on a scholarship, like I did, and get experience in the armed forces. Of course, if Uncle Sam has too many weatherpeople at that time, there's the risk you could spend your service running a bulldozer platoon or a shore-patrol detachment.

Q: So as an agricultural meteorologist, how do you spend your days?

A: There's data gathering, and the interpretation of that data. In the old days, everything was in the farmer's head: when to plant, how to plant, cultivation tips, how to guess the weather, accounting, etc. Today's agribusinesses replace the farmer's brain with a bunch of experts who make those calls. I'm whichever lobe of the corporate brain decides how much precipitation we'll get, the likelihood of hail, when conditions will be ideal to plant the winter wheat, that kind of thing.

Q: What's the question you get asked most often?

A: "Why do the weather people get it wrong so often?" Sometimes, it's as if I'm the complaint department for all meteorology, and folks think I have the power to fix it. I answer: "The weather people always get it right. Unfortunately, nature changes its mind." In the time it takes them to consider the answer, I'm out of there.

FACTS OF SLEEP

✳ ✳ ✳ ✳

- On average, humans sleep three hours less than other primates. Chimps, rhesus monkeys, and baboons sleep ten hours per night. Maybe that's because they don't have to get up and go to work!

- When we sleep, we drift between rapid-eye-movement (REM) sleep and non-REM sleep in alternating 90-minute cycles. Non-REM sleep starts with drowsiness and proceeds to deeper sleep, during which it's harder to be awakened. During REM sleep, our heart rates increase, our breathing becomes irregular, our muscles relax, and our eyes move rapidly beneath our eyelids.

- Elephants stand while they're dozing in non-REM sleep, but once REM sleep kicks in, they lie down. Ducks are constantly at risk of being attacked by predators, so they keep half their brain awake while they sleep.

- Studies have shown that our bodies experience diminished capacity after we've been awake for 17 hours, and we behave as if we were legally drunk. After five nights with too little sleep, we actually get intoxicated twice as fast.

- The longest recorded period that a person has gone without sleep is 18 days, 21 hours, and 40 minutes. It took place in a rocking-chair marathon. By the end, the winner was experiencing paranoia, hallucinations, blurry vision, slurred words, and an inability to concentrate.

- During their first year, babies cause between 400 and 750 hours of lost sleep for parents.

- At least 10 percent of all people sleepwalk at least once in their lives, and men are more likely to sleepwalk than women.

- Sleepwalking occurs most commonly in middle childhood and preadolescence (11 to 12 years of age), and it often lasts into adulthood.

- It is a myth that snoring is harmless. It can be a sign of sleep apnea, a life-threatening sleep disorder. As many as 10 percent of people who snore have sleep apnea. It causes them to stop breathing as many as 300 times every night and can lead to a stroke or heart attack.

- REM sleep was initially discovered years before the first studies that monitored brain waves overnight were conducted in 1953, though scientists didn't understand its significance at first.

- When we sleep, our bodies cool down. Body temperature and sleep are closely related. That's why it's hard to sleep on a hot summer night. We sleep best in moderate temperatures.

- Caffeine can overcome drowsiness, but it actually takes about 30 minutes before its effects kick in, and they are only temporary. It is better to get adequate sleep before driving all night than to rely on caffeine to keep you alert.

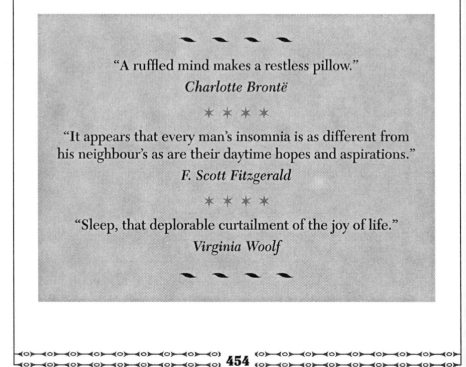

"A ruffled mind makes a restless pillow."
Charlotte Brontë

* * * *

"It appears that every man's insomnia is as different from his neighbour's as are their daytime hopes and aspirations."
F. Scott Fitzgerald

* * * *

"Sleep, that deplorable curtailment of the joy of life."
Virginia Woolf

FAD INVENTIONS

✳ ✳ ✳

*If we could figure out the next hottest trend, we'd all
be millionaires, right? Here are some seemingly crazy ideas
that turned out to be both lasting and lucrative.*

- **Hacky Sack**—Mike Marshall created this version of the footbag in 1972 to help his friend John Stalberger rehabilitate an injured leg. After they marketed it, the Hacky Sack rehabilitated their bank accounts as well. In Oregon in 2006, Tricia George and Paul Vorvick set a doubles record of 1,415 footbag kicks in ten minutes.

- **Hula Hoop**—Its origins date back some 3,000 years, when children in ancient Egypt made hoops out of grapevines and twirled them around their waists. Wham-O introduced the plastic version of the toy in 1958, and 20 million were sold in the first six months.

- **Pet Rock**—Its genesis makes sense when you consider the occupation of its inventor. In the mid-1970s, advertising executive Gary Dahl packaged ordinary beach stones in an attractive box and sold them with instructions for their care and training. They cost a penny to manufacture and sold for $3.95, and though the fad lasted less than a year, it made Dahl millions.

- **Rubik's Cube**—Enrico Rubik introduced his puzzle cube in 1974, and it became popular in the 1980s, confounding millions of people worldwide with its 43 quintillion (that's 43 followed by 18 zeros) solutions.

- **Sea Monkey**—It was Harold von Braunhut who came up with a simple three-step kit that allowed youngsters to breed their own aquatic creatures. The wee serpents are actually a unique species of brine shrimp.

- **Slinky**—In the early 1940s, a torsion spring fell off marine engineer Richard James's desk and tumbled end over end across the floor. He took it home to his wife, Betty, who gave it the cute name. Since then, more than a quarter-billion Slinkys have been sold worldwide.

- **Super Soaker**—The giant water gun was invented in 1988 by aerospace engineer Lonnie Johnson. An intriguing feature was the incorporation of air pressure, which enabled more water to be sprayed at greater distances. Some of today's pump-action models can "shoot" water accurately as far as 50 feet.

- **Twister**—The Milton Bradley Company released this unique game in 1966, and it was the first one in history to use the human body as an actual playing piece. Worldwide, approximately 65 million people have entwined in a game of Twister.

- **View-Master**—The View-Master is a device for viewing 3-D images, presented on reels that contain 14 small slides of film. It was introduced at the New York World's Fair in 1939 as a "modernized" version of the scenic postcard. The View-Master was so prevalent during World War II that the U.S. military purchased 100,000 viewers and more than 6 million reels for training purposes.

- **Yo-Yo**—The first historical mention of the yo-yo dates to Greece in 500 B.C., but it was a man named Pedro Flores who brought the yo-yo to the United States from the Philippines in 1928. American entrepreneur Donald Duncan soon bought the rights from Flores. Sales of the toy peaked in 1962, when more than 45 million units were sold.

    ~   ~   ~   ~

Chindogu is a Japanese term that refers to the strange art of creating seemingly useful yet ultimately useless inventions—useless because no one would want to be seen with one in public. An example is the hay-fever hat, which consists of a roll of toilet paper secured to the head by a chinstrap. There are many others.

    ~   ~   ~   ~

POSITIVELY CONFOUNDING

✳ ✳ ✳

Prefixes such as un- *or* de- *create an antonym, or opposite,
of the word they're attached to. But some words that appear to be
negated with prefixes or suffixes have no positives. The opposite of*
inane *is not* ane—*actually, there is no such word as* ane.

Words with No Positive Forms

defenestrate	impromptu	inhibited	nonpareil
dejected	inane	insidious	nonplussed
disconsolate	incessant	insipid	unbeknownst
disdain	inchoate	insouciant	ungainly
disgruntled	incognito	intact	unswerving
disheveled	incommunicado	invert	untold
dismayed	indomitable	misgivings	untoward
disrupt	ineffable	misnomer	
feckless	inept	nonchalant	
gormless	inert	noncommittal	
impetuous	infernal	nondescript	

Words with Uncommon Positive Forms

disconcerting	incorrigible	interminable	unmitigated
immaculate	innocent	unbridled	unrequited
impeccable	inscrutable	unflappable	unruly
inadvertent	insensate	unfurl	unthinkable
incapacitated	insufferable	unkempt	unwieldy

Fast Facts

- Approximately one out of a thousand baby sea turtles survives after hatching.

- Sea turtles absorb a lot of salt from the sea water in which they live. They excrete excess salt from their eyes, so it often looks as though they are crying.

- In Paris, France, there are more dogs than people.

- The large cats of the world are divided into two groups—those that roar, such as tigers and African lions, and those that purr. Mountain lions purr, hiss, scream, and snarl, but they cannot roar.

- Giraffes not only have long necks—they also have very long tongues. A giraffe can clean its ears with its 21-inch tongue.

- Most elephants weigh less than the tongue of a blue whale.

- Crocodiles and alligators are surprisingly fast on land, but they lack agility. If you're being chased by one, run in a zigzag line.

- In ancient China and parts of India, mouse meat was considered a great delicacy.

- In ancient Greece, where the mouse was sacred to the god Apollo, mice were sometimes devoured by temple priests.

- Ants stretch when they wake up. They also appear to yawn in a very human manner before taking up the tasks of the day.

- Bees have five eyes. There are three small eyes on the top of a bee's head and two larger eyes in front.

- A newborn turkey chick has to be taught to eat, or it will starve.

- The body of a typical spider has approximately 600 silk glands, which it uses to spin webs.

- A hippopotamus can open its mouth wide enough to accommodate a four-foot-tall child.

WOMEN RULE!

✳ ✳ ✳ ✳

- Queen Elizabeth I was taught caution early in life. She learned mistrust of men from her mother Anne Boleyn's fate and was nearly executed for treason by her half-sister Mary I. Mary couldn't prove that Liz was involved in that plot, though, and transferred her from the Tower of London to house arrest in Woodstock.

- The famous Queen Cleopatra of Egypt was once booted from the throne and exiled to the desert by her coruler, younger brother Ptolemy XIII. When Julius Caesar came to Alexandria to mediate the sibling rivalry, she had herself smuggled into her own palace in a rug in order to meet him.

- A legendary warrior, Queen Boudicca rebelled against Roman rule in eastern Britain around A.D. 60. She raised an army and trashed several Roman cities, including Londinium (London), in retribution for crimes against herself and her daughters, and nearly caused Emperor Nero to pull the Romans out of Britain entirely. She was later defeated, however, and like Cleopatra, she committed suicide rather than be captured.

- A master of propaganda, Pharaoh Hatshepsut is said to have dressed as a male king and even wore a false beard in the traditional style of pharaohs to ease common fears of a female in power. At least, that's how she was depicted in art. She ruled ancient Egypt for 20 years until she died and her stepson took over.

- Mary I was desperate to have a child to secure the Catholic religion in England instead of her Protestant half-sister Elizabeth taking the throne. She twice thought she was pregnant, but was humiliated when both pregnancies proved false and her husband left for his native Spain.

- Princess Elizabeth was on an official trip to Kenya when her father, King George VI, died, making her the new sovereign, Queen Elizabeth II. She was at a state dinner in the Treetops Hotel, and it is often said that she "went up the tree a princess and came down a queen."

- Nicknamed "the Dragon Lady," Empress Dowager Tzu Hsi was often blamed for China's humiliating losses to western powers, since her policies strongly resisted modernization. This former concubine rose to power because she was the only one to give the emperor a surviving son. Tzu Hsi took supreme power as regent for the child emperor when his father died.

- Queen Anne of Britain helped her older sister depose their Catholic father, and after Anne took the throne she passed the Act of Unification, officially joining Scotland and England into one country—Great Britain. Though she was pregnant 18 times, none of her children survived. In order to preserve Protestant rule, Anne approved the Act of Settlement, which allowed only Protestants on the throne, and cut several senior members from the succession due to their Catholicism. This led to later uprisings by the disinherited royals.

- The mother of Marie Antoinette, Empress Maria Theresa of Austria, was one of the dominant figures in European politics for nearly 40 years in the 18th century. A strong ruler in her own right, her influence spread greatly as she married most of her surviving children into various European royal families.

- Don't blame me! Queen Victoria's reign is famous for being an era of sexual repression. However, these standards weren't instituted by the queen, but by her prudish husband, Albert.

- One of the great "Catholic Monarchs," Queen Isabella of Castile was a fiercely religious woman who united much of Spain when she married Ferdinand of Aragon. Together, the two drove the "heretic" Moors out of the country and began the Spanish Inquisition.

- Queen Joanna "the Mad" of Castile (now part of Spain) was devastated by her beloved husband's death. She insisted that his coffin travel with her wherever she went, though she didn't travel much—she was imprisoned for the rest of her life, first by her father, then by her son.

- Eleanor of Aquitaine was queen of not one, but two major European powers. As the independently wealthy sovereign duchess of

Aquitaine in the 12th century, she was first married to Louis VII of France, and later Henry II of England. A fiery and active woman, she led her own troops on a crusade with Louis, encouraged her sons in their revolt against their father, Henry, and wielded enormous power during the reigns of sons Richard I and John.

- For all her reputed beauty, men were the downfall of Mary, Queen of Scots. The former Queen of France was implicated in the murder of her philandering second husband and forced to abdicate after she married the prime suspect in the assassination only three months later. After 18 years of imprisonment, Mary's connection to the Babington Plot convinced Queen Elizabeth that Mary's continued existence was too dangerous, and Mary was executed, though her actual involvement in the plot is still uncertain.

- Though not a queen in her own right, the highly intelligent Marguerite of Navarre wielded great power as a key advisor for her brother, Francois I of France, during the 16th century. She was also a famous patroness of art and literature and published several works of her own.

- In nearly 2,000 years of history, Japan has had only eight reigning empresses. The first was Empress Suiko, who held the throne from 593 to 628, and Empress Go-Sakuramachi was the last. From 1762 to 1771, she ruled Japan, but she eventually abdicated in favor of her nephew. Female rulers were officially outlawed in the Imperial Household Law of 1889.

"If particular care and attention is not paid to the ladies, we are determined to foment a rebellion, and will not hold ourselves bound by any laws in which we have no voice or representation."

Former First Lady Abigail Adams

CANADA'S LITERARY LEGACIES

* * * *

*Beyond the natural breadth of literary effort found in
any diverse society, Canadian literature tends to focus on themes
important to Canadians: multiculturalism, the allure and
adventure of taking on the unforgiving North, relations with the
United States, Canada's frontier history, and especially satire.
Here are some of the North's bright literary lights.*

Margaret Atwood is perhaps Canada's most famous living novelist. This Ottawan has written with power and eloquence on feminist themes, and her dystopian *The Handmaid's Tale,* which examines an American theocracy, sends chills up the spine.

Napoléon Aubin was a Swiss immigrant who pioneered Canadian literature in the 1800s with the political satire periodical *Le Fantasque.* Although his work is difficult to find now, he was important in shaping Canadian literature and French-Canadian identity.

Yves Beauchemin, of Noranda, Quebec, has mastered the challenge of writing about Quebec in ways that don't require direct experience with Quebec to be understood. Read *Le Matou* (*The Alley Cat*), a story of the individual struggle against an unfair society.

Maria Campbell wrote *Halfbreed*, an autobiographical story of Metis life that conveys the sad, cold realities without coming off bitter. Not many Metis have so effectively conveyed their experiences to their Canadian countryfolk.

Lynn Coady hails from Cape Breton, Nova Scotia, and her fiction has won high praise for its subtlety and insight into human thought and environment. Her first novel, *Strange Heaven*, was nominated for a Governor-General's Award.

Robertson Davies was from Ontario. His greatest success came in the field of fiction, in which he won numerous awards; he held 23 honorary degrees as well. The Deptford trilogy, beginning with *Fifth Business*, explores materialism and spirituality.

Réjean Ducharme is a reclusive Quebecois playwright and novelist who specializes in writing about young people confounded by and battling the contradictions and hypocrisies of the adult world. Read *L'Avalée des avalés* (*The Swallower Swallowed*).

Stephen Leacock, whose family settled in Ontario in the 1800s, became best known for his satiric humor, but he was also a professor of economics at McGill University. *Sunshine Sketches of a Little Town* pokes fun at rural Ontario life.

Ann-Marie MacDonald, who has lived most of her life in Toronto, is a successful actress, novelist, and playwright whose theatrical experience shows in such titles as *Fall on Your Knees*, a tale of four sisters.

Alice Munro, known as the "Canadian Chekhov," is a short-story writer from Ontario who focuses on how women experience life. Three Governor-General's Awards attest to her enduring popularity. Read *Lives of Girls and Women*.

Michael Ondaatje is Sri Lanka's gift to Canada. The multicultural author's family settled in Ontario in his youth. His poetry, fiction, and memoir of his childhood have wide followings in Canada's literary circles. *The English Patient*, a novel set in the Mediterranean theater of World War II, won a Governor-General's Award and the Booker Prize.

Mordecai Richler, a Jewish iconoclast from Quebec, said what he thought and didn't care whom he annoyed. As you might expect, his comedy could pack quite a sting. Groups tried to ban *Oh Canada! Oh Quebec!,* a nonfiction look at ethnic relations and law.

Robert J. Sawyer, a son of Toronto, is the only Canadian to win all three top international science fiction awards. His fascination with paleontology and metaphysics is easy to see in his writing. Read *The Terminal Experiment*, about a determined scientific attempt to discover the soul.

Michel Tremblay, a Quebecois playwright and novelist, has produced numerous stories about gay life using *joual*, a working-class dialect of Quebecois French. His play *Les Belles-soeurs* (*The Sisters-In-Law*) is a balance of tragedy and comedy.

Talk to the Expert
PROFESSIONAL NOSE

✳ ✳ ✳ ✳

Not too many jobs are named for a body part.
But if you're a professional nose, your schnoz could
make a bloodhound envious.

Q: So, take a sniff.

A: You needn't ask, because it's what I do naturally. You are wearing Lancôme's dependable *Poême*, which features poppy and datur, along with notes of vanilla and rose. It's a totally reliable and affordable fragrance. It complements your body chemistry, and, thankfully, the pasta alfredo you had for lunch doesn't ruin it. Oh, and pardon my unsolicited advice, but, on you, the fragrance isn't really appropriate for everyday wear. It would be much better as an accompaniment or would work a lot better with evening wear.

Q: How in the world do you know what scent I have on?

A: I'm a nose. I create perfumes, colognes, and fragrances of every kind. If I were unable tell you what you were wearing, it would be like a carpenter who can't pound a nail straight, or a chef with a dull sense of taste.

Q: Do you have a background in chemistry?

A: I attended the Sorbonne, just like Madame Curie. But that was only the beginning. I am gifted, or sometimes afflicted, with an outstanding sense of smell. I can identify nearly any scent while blindfolded, and if you mix scents, I can sort them out and tell you how much of each there is.

Q: How long did it take you to become a full *perfumière*?

A: After college, I worked for six years as an apprentice. In that time, I learned the essential ideas and procedures of fragrance design from the experts. My professional advancement now depends entirely on the commercial success of my fragrances.

ANIMALS THAT KEEP HAREMS

✳ ✳ ✳ ✳

When we hear the word harem, we envision an exotic den that housed the concubines of a wealthy sultan. In the animal kingdom, however, harems are so common that some scientists believe monogamy to be unusual. Here are a few animals that keep harems.

Elephant Seals

Male elephant seals, found in the Antarctic and along the California coast, are enormous creatures that can reach up to 18 feet long. Their harems start off as a form of female bonding; toward the end of their 11-month pregnancies, females go ashore to give birth in groups. The males follow, fighting among themselves for the right to mate with the females once they've given birth.

Elk

Elk live in the Rocky Mountain region of the western United States and Canada, as well as in the Appalachian region of the eastern United States. Each fall, male elk fight with one another to win the females that will form their harems, which usually consist of one male and six females. The females leave the harems in the spring and form small groups to care for their young before rejoining other elk in herds of up to 400 for the summer. This time, however, the tables are turned, with herds structured as a matriarchy, with one female leader.

Hamadryas Baboons

Most species of baboon form harems, though these are generally informal groupings. By contrast, male hamadryas baboons, which live in Africa, guard their harems fiercely and will attack any female that appears to be wandering away from the group. Males will also attempt to raid another male's harem to capture his females.

Shrimp

These crustaceans are found in most seas of the world, and they all form harems, usually consisting of one male and as many as ten females. The interesting thing about shrimp harems is that when the male leader dies, he may be replaced by a young female shrimp that is able to change her gender to take his place.

American Buffalo

American buffalo, or bison, live on plains, prairies, in river valleys, and sometimes forests. During breeding season—between July and October—males will fight for control of harems by charging at each other until one of them gives up. Harems generally include only three or four females, but during breeding season they keep the males so busy that they have little time to even eat.

Sperm Whales

A harem is just one option for the sperm whale, which will take part in a number of social groupings over its lifetime. Young whales often form coed schools that gradually split up as dominant males drive off smaller ones until just one male is left with as many as 25 females.

Lions

All species of lion form harems (commonly known as prides), usually consisting of one or two adult males, plus six to eight females and their cubs. Because they are smaller, quicker, and more agile than males, females do the hunting. While the lionesses are at work, the males patrol the area and protect the pride from predators.

Bats

Depending on the species, a male bat may have as many as 30 females in its harem. Female bats seek out males, drawn by their scents or, in some cases, their mating calls. Male African hammer-headed fruit bats can produce a symphony of loud, low-frequency honks by banding together in groups. When a female approaches, the calls become more frantic as each male battles to outdo the others.

Wild Horses

American feral horses, found on the East Coast and in the western part of the country, form harems that typically consist of one or two dominant males with five or six mares. A dominant male horse can be dictatorial, keeping his females in line by biting their necks and flanks. Adult mares will rarely leave a harem, and the groups tend to stay together even if the dominant male dies or is replaced.

TOP REASONS FOR EMERGENCY ROOM VISITS

✳ ✳ ✳ ✳

1. **Injury and poisoning**
   Injuries include burns, foreign bodies in tissue or cavities, fractures, intracranial injuries, open wounds, sprains and strains, surgical and medical complications, and unspecified injuries.

2. **Symptoms and signs of ill-defined conditions**

3. **Diseases of the respiratory system**
   These include asthma, bronchitis, emphysema, and pneumonia.

4. **Diseases of the digestive system**
   Diseases include appendicitis, food poisoning, and ulcers.

5. **Diseases of the musculoskeletal systems and connective-tissue system**
   These include osteomyelitis (bone infection), septic arthritis, and Lyme disease.

6. **Diseases of the nervous system and sense organs**
   Diseases include bacterial or viral meningitis, encephalitis (inflammation of the brain), and detachment of the retina.

7. **Diseases of the genitourinary system**
   These include bladder infection, kidney infection, and kidney failure.

8. **Diseases of the circulatory system**
   These include heart attacks, hypertension/high blood pressure, and pulmonary embolisms (blockage of arteries in the lungs).

9. **Diseases of the skin and subcutaneous tissue**
   Diseases include cellulitis and severe sunburn.

10. **Mental disorders**
    These include bipolar disorder, dementia, and schizophrenia.

HOLLYWOOD GOES TO WAR

✳ ✳ ✳ ✳

*Polls in the late 1930s showed that most Americans
favored staying out of what was perceived as a European conflict.
The movie industry was more prescient and went to
war years before the rest of the United States. From simple prewar
patriotism to the combat films troops tagged "flag-wavers,"
Hollywood played a vital role in the war effort.*

As the United States' entry into World War II became more likely,
Hollywood, largely on its own initiative, began to wean the country
from its isolationist stance. Some of the films were gentle calls to
patriotism, such as 1941's *Sergeant York*. This film offered a senti-
mental look back at one courageous American from the last war who
had initially resisted the call to duty, but who overcame his doubts
and went on to become a hero. It couldn't have come at a more
appropriate time for a reluctant nation.

Other films were more contemporary, giving audiences a glimpse
of the future offered by the Nazis. Jack Warner, head of the Warner
Bros. Studios, hated the regime ever since a friend and employee of
his had been beaten to death in Germany for not showing the proper
respect for Hitler. As a result, he fast-tracked the 1939 production
of *Confessions of a Nazi Spy,* featuring a warning that German-
American groups might be fronts for Fascist activity. The film was
denounced by those groups, but Warner was unconcerned. His
intention was to make a film that would "hurt Herr Goebbels." The
result was one of the first explicitly anti-Nazi movies to be shown in
the United States.

Films of this sort may have inspired average citizens, but they
drew the ire of isolationists in Congress, who in September 1941
launched investigations into the output of the movie studios, accusing them of using propaganda in an attempt to draw the country into
war. Anticipating the course of events, Hollywood largely stood up
to the investigations. Studio executive and film producer Darryl F.
Zanuck testified that the movies were valuable not just for America,

but for selling the "American way of life … to the entire world."
He claimed that the first thing dictators did when taking control of
a country was to remove Hollywood movies from the cinema, since
such people "wanted no part of the American way of life." The
investigations didn't last long, and after Pearl Harbor, Washington
and Hollywood worked in partnership for the rest of the war.

The Battle of Beverly Hills

The attack at Pearl Harbor had an immediate effect on the movie
industry. Humphrey Bogart was shooting a script called *Across the
Pacific* about just such a Japanese attack; the film was immediately
canceled. James Cagney, who was only one day away from shooting
a movie about the "damnedest patriotic man in the whole world,"
listened to FDR's announcement about the strike from the set of
Yankee Doodle Dandy, and the broadcast inspired the cast and crew
for the duration of the movie.

The war came to Hollywood both literally and figuratively. Actor
Leslie Howard (best known for his role as Ashley Wilkes in *Gone
with the Wind*) was killed when the airplane in which he was traveling was shot down by the Germans. Clark Gable enlisted as a private, saying he had "no interest in acting as long as the war is going
on." The army commandeered the Walt Disney studio property to
set up antiaircraft guns for the defense of Los Angeles. More endur-
ingly, all the studios were affected by the new regulatory authority
given to federal agencies, such as the Office of War Information
(OWI), the Bureau of Motion Pictures, and the Production Code
Administration. While not always legally binding, negative comments and thematic suggestions from these groups had the practical
effect of determining the content of movies throughout the war. The
OWI issued a list of suggested topics they believed would benefit the
American public, such as the joys of "curtailing pleasure spending in
favor of war bond purchase." Other directives had longer-ranging
effects. For instance, security restrictions on filming factories and
other locations led to a stylistic shift in camera technique. The
resulting extreme close-up shots and dim lighting paved the way for
the rise of film noir.

Documentaries as "Properly Directed Hate"

Besides following the production codes, Hollywood directors and actors put their talent to use at the government's request, doing everything from shooting newsreels and victory films—short movies offering tips on how average citizens could help with the war, such as collecting scrap metal—to documentaries or just agreeing to give their normal feature films a particular spin. Many of Hollywood's elite played a part in the effort.

Particularly notable among the nonfiction films was Frank Capra's *Why We Fight* series. Initially reluctant to produce a documentary, a genre in which he had never worked before, Capra personally promised Chief of Staff George C. Marshall that he would make the "best damned documentary films ever made" for the war effort. The result was a sequence of seven pictures documenting the arguments for taking up arms against Japan and Germany, tackling topics from the philosophic differences between democracy and Fascism to the histories of individual battles. Capra was also one of the first to turn the German propaganda machine back on itself, using clips from Leni Riefenstahl's 1934 landmark *Triumph of the Will* to attack, rather than deify, the Nazi machine. By extracting sections of Riefenstahl's work, Capra was able to show audiences visions of oppressive Fascism rather than give the impression of unstoppable Teutonic supermen, as was originally intended. The technique was widely copied in other movies to great effect. The short newsreel *Hitler Assumes Command* manipulated German footage to turn goose-stepping Nazis parading in front of Hitler into a dance troupe doing a tap routine accompanied by the lighthearted British dance tune "The Lambeth Walk." The film reportedly sent Joseph Goebbels storming from his screening room in a cursing fit.

Along with giving Americans a reason to fight, Hollywood sought to portray an image of whom they were fighting against. The OWI was of the opinion that "properly directed hatred is of vital importance to the war effort." Hollywood complied and generally portrayed America's enemies in broad caricature. Germans were often played as militaristic Übermensch; Louis B. Mayer instructed William Wyler to portray the villain in *Mrs. Miniver* as a "typical Nazi son of a bitch." In Alfred Hitchcock's *Lifeboat*, the single Nazi passenger is more than a match for the other passengers individually, only being defeated when they band together and overcome him. The Japanese fared no better: They were portrayed as butchers in many films. The American public needed little encouragement to seize on the images and cheer on John Wayne in *The Fighting Seabees* when he called the Japanese enemy "Tojo's bug-eyed monkeys." America's allies naturally received better treatment, and the OWI explicitly encouraged production of films that would build sympathy for their plight. However, some of those films came back to haunt their creators: *Mission to Moscow, The North Star,* and *Song of Russia,* all of which attempted to portray the then-Allied Soviet Union in a positive light, were later investigated by the House Un-American Activities Committee as examples of communist propaganda.

The Big Picture

Documentaries were one thing, but Hollywood's forte was the big motion picture, and Tinseltown didn't ignore that format during the war. The conflict itself provided all the elements required for a breathtaking drama, and the studios rushed out an incredible number of explicit depictions of the war. *Wake Island* showed U.S. Marines fighting the Japanese in the South Pacific. *Thirty Seconds Over Tokyo* starred Spencer Tracy leading General Doolittle's famous bombing raid on Japan. *Sahara* depicted Bogie battling Nazi tanks in the desert, and John Wayne blasted the Japanese out of the sky in *Flying Tigers.* These semifictional portrayals of current events seemed to be natural material for wartime audiences. Those audiences included the troops overseas—the military made great efforts to get films to the troops, setting up outdoor projectors mere miles from the front or on the decks of ships.

It turned out, though, that realism was the last thing the audiences wanted to see. Veteran troops would become boisterous to the point of riot when shown a high-handed war film—they, along with the spectators at home, demanded lighter fare. Escapism was the order of the day, and Hollywood began playing to this demand. The war years yielded a surprising number of comedies—advertised as having "no message, no mission, no misfortune"—and big-budget musicals experienced a resurgence, having fallen out of favor in the prewar years.

Comedies were a particularly tricky subject given the innate seriousness of the war. Some attempts at humor are absolutely painful in retrospect: 1942's *Once Upon a Honeymoon* had stars Cary Grant and Ginger Rogers exclaim, upon being detained by the Nazis, "Now they think we're Jewish—this could be serious!" However, some films of the time endure as masterpieces. Charlie Chaplin put his well-known mustache to good use when he lampooned Hitler in 1940's *The Great Dictator.* The film featured Chaplin in a dual role as a simple barber who gets confused with a dictator named Adenoid Hynkel. In the most famous scene, the obsessive tyrant expresses his dreams of world domination by dancing with a large globe that eventually explodes in his face. After the war, Chaplin said that had he known about the Nazi atrocities he could never have made the film, but at the time he believed it was important that "Hitler must be laughed at." But not all comedies were so allegorical. The Three Stooges, who all happened to be Jewish, offered a number of anti-Nazi films, including *You Natzy Spy!* and *I'll Never Heil Again,* with Moe Howard as the dictator of Moronica, in what he always remembered as his favorite role. In an incident illustrative of war-time paranoia, a still-costumed Moe rushed home from the movie set to attend his daughter's birthday party, resulting in a flood of calls to the police from concerned residents convinced they had seen Hitler running red lights in the streets of Los Angeles.

"December 7, 1941, is a date that will live in infamy. The United States was suddenly and deliberately attacked by naval and air forces of Japan."

Franklin D. Roosevelt

DREAMLAND

✳ ✳ ✳ ✳

- In an average lifetime, people spend approximately 2,100 days (almost 6 years) dreaming. Everyone dreams every night, though some of us can't remember our dreams.

- Blind people dream. If they became blind after having sight, visual images appear in their dreams. If they were born blind, their dreams, like their lives, are made up of feelings, smells, movements, and sounds.

- Developmental psychologists say that toddlers never dream about themselves. Children are not believed to appear in their own dreams until a developmental stage that occurs when they are three or four years old and realize they are separate from other people.

- Rapid eye movement (REM) sleep is the stage during which we have our most vivid dreams, characterized by bizarre plots involving unlikely people or things. In contrast, non-REM dreams are more like waking thoughts. They have less imagery and tend to repeat a thought obsessively (for example, "I've lost my keys!").

- It was once believed that dreams occurred only during REM sleep. Improved technology has allowed researchers to discover that dreams are less frequent in non-REM sleep phases but still exist. In fact, it is likely that we dream during every single moment of sleep.

- Color in dreams is a constant source of speculation. Some monochrome dreams can have a single image that's in color, such as a bright pink poodle. Other dreams seem to speak a language of colors (e.g., red or blue lights) and shapes (repeated circles or squares). Sometimes, natural colors pervade the dream, as in waking life.

- In the late 1950s, scientists proved that external stimuli can be incorporated into dreams. When researchers sprinkled water on sleeping volunteers and woke them up seconds later, 14 out of 33 subjects said they had dreamed of water.

- It is believed that we rarely feel pain in dreams. When we do, though, our bodies perceive it as a signal that something is wrong, and we react by waking up.

- Studies conducted by Harvard University reveal that dreams exhibit five strange features. They have the qualities of hallucinations (seeing things that don't exist), delusions (believing something imaginary), emotional intensity (extreme feelings about a situation), amnesia (forgetting our lives and even who we are in those lives), and cognitive abnormalities (having thoughts that differ from the waking norm).

- What is the purpose of dreams? Some experts speculate that the primitive part of the brain is overloaded during the day and cannot process all of our experiences. Dreaming gives us a way to sort through our memories and eliminate the ones that aren't useful for our growth.

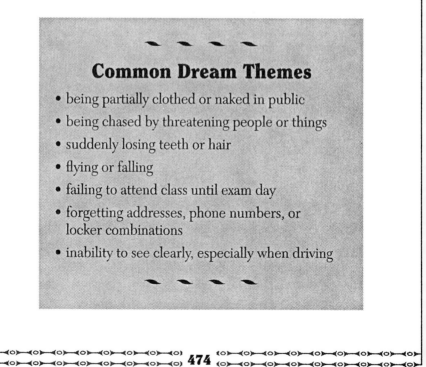

Common Dream Themes

- being partially clothed or naked in public
- being chased by threatening people or things
- suddenly losing teeth or hair
- flying or falling
- failing to attend class until exam day
- forgetting addresses, phone numbers, or locker combinations
- inability to see clearly, especially when driving

SEVENTY-PLUS-POINT SCRABBLE WORDS

✳ ✳ ✳ ✳

Word and Definition	Points
quixotry: quixotic (extremely idealist) action or thought	77
muzhiks: a Russian peasant in czarist times	75
bezique: a card game	77
caziques: native chiefs of West Indian aborigines	77
oxazepam: a tranquilizing drug	77
mezquit: same as mesquite, which is a spiny tree or shrub	77
zombify: to turn into a zombie	76
quizzers: those who quiz	75
whizbang: slang term for a highly explosive shell or firecracker	76
quetzal: a bird with brilliant plummage	75
highjack: same as hijack, to seize a vehicle while in transit	78
musquash: a British expression for the fur of the muskrat	72
packwax: same as paxwax, a strong ligament that supports the back of the head	75
squeezer: one who squeezes or presses forcibly together	76
quartzy: same as quartzose, resembling quartz or taking on the qualities of it	78
quickly: with speed, rapidly, very soon	76
asphyxy: the condition that results from interruption of respiration	75
zinkify: to zincify, which is to coat with zinc	76
jukebox: an automated phonograph that is usually coin-operated	77

THE WORLD'S MOST DANGEROUS ANIMALS

✳ ✳ ✳ ✳

The world's most dangerous animal has a legacy of death that stains history, and it seems incapable of ever being tamed. What is this ravenous, bloodthirsty beast? A human, of course. After people themselves, here are the most dangerous animals in the world.

Mosquitoes

They bite 270 million people each year, killing as many as 2 million. The seemingly innocuous mosquito is in fact the deadliest non-human on the planet, spreading up to a dozen  diseases, including malaria. With more than 3,500 different species, mosquitoes inhabit every corner of the globe, but only a handful carry diseases. The species that live in Africa, Asia, and the Americas are the deadliest.

Venomous Snakes

Snake attacks account for close to 125,000 deaths per year, making these reptiles the deadliest on the planet. Only about 450 of the 3,000 snake species are venomous, and the deadliest live in Africa, Asia, and Australia. Depending on the species of snake and the severity of the bite, death can ensue in a matter of hours if no treatment is given.

Scorpions

The scorpion is a highly compact killing machine that takes more than 1,500 human lives every year. Just 25 of the 1,500 species of scorpions are deadly to humans, and the most venomous live in Africa, the Americas, and Central Asia. The most lethal is the fat-tailed scorpion of North Africa.

Lions

Responsible for several hundred human deaths each year, mostly in African and Indian villages, the king of the jungle is certainly worthy of our respect and fear. The strength of full-grown lions is remarkable. They have been known to kill animals weighing more than 3,000 pounds. Lions can reach speeds of 36 miles per hour, but because they cannot sustain that speed for long, lions employ stalk-and-ambush techniques to obtain their meals.

Crocodiles

The Nile crocodile is the most dangerous to humans, followed by the crocs that inhabit Australia. With more than 60 teeth of various sizes, crocodiles are active, vicious, and treacherous brutes that kill hundreds of people each year. But crocs don't just capture prey with their lethal teeth; with an incredibly swift twist of the tail, a croc can capture prey by swatting it from the shore and into the water where it is seized and devoured.

Elephants

We generally think of elephants as friendly, approachable, sometimes cute animals. But don't let that image fool you—each year they crush more than 500 humans. Most elephant attacks occur in Africa and India, but attacks in zoos and circuses around the world are becoming more common. Elephants can be very unpredictable, and even so-called tame elephants have turned on and attacked trainers who have known them for years. The number of elephant attacks continues to rise as humans decimate the habitat of this majestic beast. Although elephants are herbivores, when humans get in the way of their food supply, they will use their six tons of bulk, not to mention their menacing tusks, to trample and gore a person to death in a matter of seconds.

Hippos

Found around rivers and lakes throughout Africa, no animal exudes more raw power than the mighty hippo. They might appear lazy and slow, but a hippo can run faster than a person and can maneuver its bulky head and jaws with deadly efficiency. The hippopotamus is an herbivore, but it won't hesitate to attack a human if it feels threatened. Hippos are responsible for approximately 150 human deaths per year, and, like elephants, they charge, trample, and gore their victims to death.

Box Jellyfish

Nearly a hundred swimmers and sunbathers are fatally stung every year by box jellyfish, which live in the tropical waters of Australia, the Philippines, Papua New Guinea, Malaysia, Indonesia, and Vietnam. A few people have died within a minute of being touched by the cluster of long tentacles, which can number between 40 and 60 in large specimens. When the tentacles come into contact with human skin, they react immediately—clinging to the skin and releasing their venom. If the victim runs or thrashes about, absorption of the venom quickens. And if the victim attempts to remove the tentacles, even more venom is released. Fortunately, the sting from the box jellyfish is usually not fatal, but death by cardiac arrest can occur if antivenom is not given immediately.

Cape Buffalo

Found in Africa south of the Sahara, Cape buffalo are imposing creatures, standing about five feet at the shoulder and weighing nearly a ton. Tip to tip, their horns can measure as much as 58 inches across. Although they are herbivores, Cape buffalo consider humans viable predators, and they won't hesitate to charge and put those horns to work. It's been estimated that each year, Cape buffalo are responsible for about 40 human fatalities.

Leopards

The most adaptable of the big cats, leopards can be found in deserts and forests, on mountains, at sea level, and in lands as diverse as China, India, and Kenya. Leopards have been described as the most physically perfect of the big cats. Weighing 125 pounds or more and averaging two feet tall at the shoulder and seven feet long from nose to tail, they are one of the most powerful animals in the world. Left unchallenged, leopards tend to be shy and retiring, and they will avoid a confrontation with humans. But when challenged, an angry leopard is ferocious, capable of concentrating all its energy into a short-range attack of lightning speed, resulting in about 30 human deaths each year.

I'm No Expert, But...
LITERATURE

✳ ✳ ✳

*For every published author there are dozens of
hopeful writers. The industry doesn't work the
way most laypeople think.*

Q: What are galleys?

A: A galley is a printed version of a work in the process of publication. Publishers print galleys to assist in editing and proofreading, or as advance copies for reviewers. This is the intermediate step between a manuscript and a book. From the publisher's viewpoint, galleys are where editors fix authors' errors, edit boring or outrageous parts, and make the work the best it can be. From the author's vantage, galleys enable editors to insert new errors and cut out all their most brilliant stuff.

Q: How does a writer get "agented"?

A: Getting published is like borrowing money: Just as it's easy to borrow money if you don't need any, it's easier to get published if you've been published. If you haven't been published and want to use an agent, first you get a list of agents who represent the kind of thing you write (there are books listing them). Next, you send a query letter or book proposal that complies with the agent's guidelines. You want to seem enthusiastic but realistic, and don't come off as high maintenance. Agents hate high maintenance, and writers hoping to be published require higher maintenance than old Corvairs.

Q: What *is* a query letter?

A: These days, no one sends or wants a three-inch-thick paper manuscript as the first approach. A query letter is a one-pager introducing the author, describing the work, and attempting to sell it. It needs to be targeted and personal, explaining why you chose that agent or publisher. Even though you know damn well you are mass-producing 30 of them because your last 30 were rejected or ignored, you can't let on. A little sucking up is fine. Yes, the agent will know you're sucking up, but if you can do so with muted artistry, it will imply significant writing talent.

Q: What's a book proposal?

A: Ever seen a business plan? A book proposal is a book's business plan, most commonly used for nonfiction work. It tells about the book, introduces the author, outlines marketing strategies and target audiences, and attempts to convince the agent or publisher that this will make them big money with little effort. It should glow with enthusiasm, but it shouldn't sound like the author's overly enthusiastic. There is no point projecting sales of 20 million copies of a deep study of the ecology of the echidna—publishers know that won't happen.

Q: What are the reasons writers never become published authors?

A: In many cases, they just aren't as good as they imagine they are. Some are taken hard aback by the business end of the literary life; they hold the naive misconception that if they write a great book, they'll succeed. In reality, the right time and place matter as much as quality. Some get sick of rejection; some are so difficult to work with that agents and publishers throw up their hands. Most published authors developed a strategy, implemented it, refined it, adjusted with the buffets and pitfalls, and persevered anyway. They also lucked out a little. They succeeded because they kept marching while others gave up due to the mud, or stepped in dog poop and got disgusted, or got sore feet.

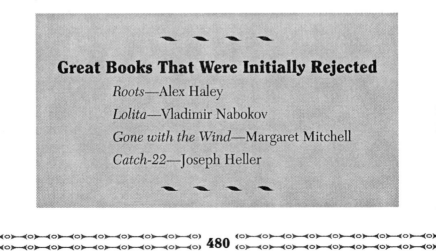

Great Books That Were Initially Rejected

Roots—Alex Haley

Lolita—Vladimir Nabokov

Gone with the Wind—Margaret Mitchell

Catch-22—Joseph Heller

DRAMA, CANADIAN STYLE

✳ ✳ ✳ ✳

Most people know that William Shatner, Michael J. Fox, and Mike Myers are Canadian. In fact, Canada has long been a great source of actors and entertainers, as this list shows.

Dan Aykroyd: born in Ottawa, Ontario. Known for: *Saturday Night Live, The Blues Brothers,* and *Driving Miss Daisy.* A member of the Order of Canada, he's a cop buff and the grandson of a Mountie, and he loves riding his own Ontario Provincial Police bike. Trivia: He has webbed toes and different-color eyes.

Pamela Anderson: born in Ladysmith, British Columbia. Known for: *Baywatch* and a record number of *Playboy* covers (five). Trivia: Pam got her big break at a British Columbia Lions football game, where cameras broadcast her in a Labatt's T-shirt. The beer company quickly signed her to help with promotion.

Raymond Burr: born in New Westminster, British Columbia. Known for: *Ironside* and *Perry Mason.* He probably did more to romanticize the profession of law than any other actor of his era. Trivia: He was badly wounded at Okinawa during World War II.

John Candy: born in Toronto, Ontario. Known for: *Stripes; Planes, Trains, and Automobiles;* and *Uncle Buck.* Loved everywhere as a genuinely nice, principled, and good-spirited man, Candy died of a heart attack at the age of 43. Trivia: Between 1974 and 1991, he made at least one film a year.

Jim Carrey: born in Newmarket, Ontario. Known for: *The Cable Guy, Bruce Almighty,* and *How the Grinch Stole Christmas.* Jim is a two-time Golden Globe winner and has won more MTV movie awards than any other actor. Trivia: Rodney Dangerfield discovered him doing stand-up comedy.

Tommy Chong: born in Edmonton, Alberta. Known for: being half of the comedy duo Cheech and Chong and for the 1978 counter-culture comedy hit *Up in Smoke.* Trivia: Before he hooked up with Cheech Marin, Chong was an accomplished R&B guitarist.

Glenn Ford: born in Portneuf, Quebec. Known for: *Gilda* and *The Blackboard Jungle.* Ford was best at portraying an average Joe in extraordinary situations. Trivia: His real name wasn't Glenn, it was Gwyllyn.

Jill Hennessy: born in Edmonton, Alberta. Known for: *Crossing Jordan* and *Law & Order.* This busy Albertan has a star on the Canadian Walk of Fame. Trivia: Jill's an identical twin. Her sister Jacqueline is a TV host and writer in Canada.

Norman Jewison: born in Toronto, Ontario. Known for: producing *Moonstruck, Fiddler on the Roof,* and *In the Heat of the Night.* Norman has directed three actors to Oscar wins, and nine more to Oscar nominations. Trivia: His three children also work in show business: associate producer Michael, cameraman Kevin, and actress Jennifer.

Rich Little: born in Ottawa, Ontario. Known for: his dead-on impersonations, particularly of U.S. presidents. He got his start in grade school, where he often answered his teachers' questions in their own voices. Trivia: He not only does uncanny impressions; he also draws professional celebrity portraits.

Sandra Oh: born in Nepean, Ontario. Known for: *Sideways, Grey's Anatomy,* and *Dancing at the Blue Iguana.* This Korean-Canadian actor turned down a four-year college journalism scholarship to study drama. Trivia: In high school, she started an environmental group to ban Styrofoam cups.

Shannon Tweed: born in St. Johns, Newfoundland. Known for: her many roles in mainstream erotica and her reign as 1982's *Playboy* Playmate of the Year. Shannon has two children with her longtime partner, Gene Simmons, of the rock band Kiss. Trivia: She was raised on a Newfoundland mink ranch.

WINNING WORDS, THEN AND NOW

✳ ✳ ✳ ✳

*Here is a side-by-side comparison of the Scripps Spelling Bee
winning words from the first 25 years and the past 25 years.*

1925: gladiolus
1926: abrogate
1927: luxuriance
1928: albumen
1929: asceticism
1930: fracas
1931: foulard
1932: knack
1933: torsion
1934: deteriorating
1935: intelligible
1936: interning
1937: promiscuous
1938: sanitarium
1939: canonical
1940: therapy
1941: initials
1942: sacrilegious
1943: not held
1944: not held
1945: not held
1946: semaphore
1947: chlorophyll
1948: psychiatry
1949: dulcimer

1983: Purim
1984: luge
1985: milieu
1986: odontalgia
1987: staphylococci
1988: elegiacal
1989: spoliator
1990: fibranne
1991: antipyretic
1992: lyceum
1993: kamikaze
1994: antediluvian
1995: xanthosis
1996: vivisepulture
1997: euonym
1998: chiaroscurist
1999: logorrhea
2000: demarche
2001: succedaneum
2002: prospicience
2003: pococurante
2004: autochthonous
2005: appoggiatura
2006: Ursprache
2007: serrefine

ALL IN YOUR MIND

✳ ✳ ✳ ✳

- In Australia in the late 1940s, manic depression was the first mental illness to be successfully treated with lithium. In Scandinavia in the 1950s, Dr. Morgens Schou pursued the same course of treatment with beneficial results.

- The disorder known as Alice-in-Wonderland Syndrome causes body-image distortion, making people feel they are extremely tiny or gigantic. People who suffer from the Pinocchio Illusion feel that a particulate body part (such as the nose) has grown disproportionately, and Shrinking Waist Syndrome is self-explanatory. The roots of these conditions are often neurological.

- The first recorded case of dream-induced amnesia occurred in 2004. After a man dreamed that his son had been killed, he woke up screaming and lost all memory of the previous day.

- In the 1600s, mental patients were a tourist attraction in London at Hospital of St. Mary. Anyone who paid a penny could observe and taunt the "lunatics" for their own amusement.

- In 1375, the Bethlem Royal Hospital in London became one of the first mental hospitals to take in "lunatics." The asylum was so chaotic that Bethlem became the origin of the word "bedlam."

- Medical care of the mentally ill became more humane after the publication of Darwin's *Origin of the Species* in 1859, when people realized that insanity was hereditary. Previously, madness had been seen as demonic possession, loss of a soul, weakness of character, or a feminine trait.

- One of the greatest environmental risks for people with schizophrenia is living in an urban area. It is speculated that air and noise pollution, stress, fear, electromagnetic fields, and other factors either cause the condition to develop or make a latent condition active.

RAREST ANIMALS IN THE WORLD

✳ ✳ ✳ ✳

The following are the rarest animals in the world listed in ascending order, with those with the smallest population estimates first.

1. Vancouver Island marmot
2. Seychelles sheath-tailed bat
3. Javan rhino
4. Hispid hare (Assam rabbit)
5. Northern hairy-nosed wombat
6. Tamaraw (dwarf water buffalo)
7. Iberian lynx
8. Red wolf
9. Dwarf blue sheep
10. Yellow-tailed woolly monkey
11. Kouprey (Cambodian forest ox)
12. Riverine rabbit
13. Malabar large spotted civet
14. Saola (Vu Quang ox)
15. Tonkin snub-nosed monkey
16. Sumatran rhino
17. Northern muriqui (woolly spider monkey)
18. Visayan spotted deer
19. Hirola (Hunter's hartebeest)
20. Addax (Sahara antelope)
21. North Atlantic right whale
22. Black-faced lion tamarin
23. Ethiopian wolf
24. Black-footed ferret
25. African wild ass
26. Vaquita (Gulf of California porpoise)
27. Arabian oryx
28. Mediterranean monk seal
29. Bactrian camel
30. Hairy-eared dwarf lemur
31. Southern muriqui (woolly spider monkey)

POTTY TALK

✳ ✳ ✳ ✳

*Our bathrooms are some of the most important rooms
in our homes, and they provide privacy and sanctuary—
in addition to their primary function.*

A Bathroom by Any Other Name
There are quite a few names for this little space—pick your favorite:
restroom, powder room, crapper, loo, little boys room, little girls
room, water closet, WC, porcelain god, lavatory, commode, latrine,
the facilities, the necessary room, the john, washroom.

A Toilet Before Its Time
In 1596, an inventor named John Harrington, godson to Queen
Elizabeth I, tried to create a more advanced chamber pot. The
queen and her godson both used the flush model he came up with,
but Harrington was ridiculed by his peers for fooling around with
such a ridiculous idea, thus ending his career as an inventor.

Toilet Paper Beginnings
In 1857, New Yorker Joseph C. Gayetty produced the first packaged
bathroom tissue in the United States. It was called "The Therapeutic
Paper" and contained aloe for added comfort. The company sold the
paper in packs of 500 sheets at 50 cents apiece, and Gayetty's name
was printed on every sheet.

Germs, Germs, Germs
A lot of people think a public toilet seat is the filthiest place on
Earth, but that may not be true. According to experts, the *floor* of
a public bathroom is much dirtier, with around 2 million bacteria
per square inch—that's 200 times higher than what's considered a
sanitary surface.

Washroom Attendants
Not so long ago, unless you were wealthy and enjoyed eating at
expensive restaurants, washroom attendants were not people you'd
come into much contact with. Now, in both the United States and

United Kingdom, washroom attendants are becoming regular public bathroom "fixtures." An individual stands in the bathroom and hands out towels, dispenses soap, and usually offers gum, candy, mints, and any number of other accoutrements to patrons—for a tip, of course.

Don't Go Left

In places like India and in many parts of Asia, bathrooms provide a little cup of water—but no toilet paper. When you're done doing your business, it's customary to use your left hand to wash your bum of any leftover fecal matter and then wash your hand with the cup of water. This is precisely why it's rude to shake hands with your left hand in most of Asia and the Middle East.

Locate-a-Loo

Thanks to the magic of the Internet, you never again have to search blindly for a bathroom in your hour of need. If you've got a handheld device that connects to the Web, just go to www.thebathroomdiaries .com for info. The Bathroom Diaries site is "the world's largest database of bathroom locations" and lists by state everywhere you can relieve yourself.

Protect Your Seat

What started as a fad for germophobes are now available in bathroom stalls almost everywhere—but do paper toilet seat guards work? Well, sure, but only if the seat is dry to begin with. If the seat guard is placed on a seat that's already wet or dirty, it actually sucks the bacteria and viruses up from the toilet seat onto your bare skin even more quickly.

American Restroom Association

Hey, somebody has to be a watchdog for public restrooms, right? Even though they garner more than a few snickers when they appear in the news (every year the World Toilet Summit is held in a different city), the ARA has a clear mission statement: "The American Restroom Association advocates for the availability of clean, safe, well-designed public restrooms." And no one who's ever had to use a gross public bathroom is going to snicker at that.

IN THE YEAR...1989

✳ ✳ ✳ ✳

- George H. W. Bush succeeds Ronald Reagan as the 41st president of the United States.

- The city council of Los Angeles, California, passes a ban on the sale or possession of semiautomatic weapons.

- France celebrates the 200th anniversary of the French Revolution.

- The oil tanker *Exxon Valdez* runs aground in Alaska, spilling 240,000 barrels (11 million gallons) of oil into Prince William Sound.

- The Ayatollah Khomeini dies.

- The Texas Rangers' Nolan Ryan strikes out the Oakland Athletics' Rickey Henderson to become the first major league baseball pitcher to throw 5,000 strikeouts.

- The television show *Seinfeld* premieres.

- David Dinkins becomes the first African-American mayor of New York City.

- Approximately 2 million people in the Baltic states of Estonia, Latvia, and Lithuania join hands to form a continuous 373-mile human chain, referred to as the Baltic Way, in a symbol of solidarity and desire for independence.

- Baseball great Pete Rose is subjected to a lifetime ban from the sport for illegal gambling, which prevents his induction into the Baseball Hall of Fame.

- A free trade agreement goes into effect between the United States and Canada.

- Chinese pro-democracy demonstrators and students are massacred in Tiananmen Square.

- The Berlin Wall comes down, reuniting East and West Germany.

INDEX

✳ ✳ ✳ ✳

More great titles from West Side Publishing

Yesterday & Today™ is a collection of gift-oriented hardcover books featuring stunning photography that captures the essence and chronicles the history of cherished sports teams, beloved cities, and beyond.

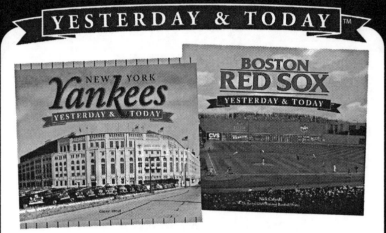

YESTERDAY & TODAY ™

New York Yankees • Boston Red Sox

Coming Attractions

BASEBALL
Chicago Cubs • St. Louis Cardinals

FOOTBALL
Ohio State University Buckeyes
University of Michigan Wolverines
University of Notre Dame Fighting Irish
University of Texas Longhorns

CITIES
San Francisco • Chicago • Seattle • St. Louis

www.armchairreader.com